# Network-Integrated Multimedia
# Middleware, Services, and Applications

# Marco Lohse

# Network-Integrated Multimedia Middleware, Services, and Applications

**VDM Verlag Dr. Müller**

Bibliographic information by the German National Library: The German National Library lists this publication at the German National Bibliography; detailed bibliographic information is available on the Internet at http://dnb.d-nb.de.

Copyright © 2007 VDM Verlag Dr. Müller e. K. and licensors
All rights reserved. Saarbrücken 2007
Contact: info@vdm-verlag.de
Cover image: www.purestockx.com
Publisher: VDM Verlag Dr. Müller e. K., Dudweiler Landstr. 125 a, 66123 Saarbrücken, Germany
Produced by: Lightning Source Inc., La Vergne, Tennessee/USA
        Lightning Source UK Ltd., Milton Keynes, UK

Bibliografische Information der Deutschen Nationalbibliothek: Die Deutsche Nationalbibliothek verzeichnet diese Publikation in der Deutschen Nationalbibliografie; detaillierte bibliografische Daten sind im Internet über http://dnb.d-nb.de abrufbar.

Copyright © 2007 VDM Verlag Dr. Müller e. K. und Lizenzgeber
Alle Rechte vorbehalten. Saarbrücken 2007
Kontakt: info@vdm-verlag.de
Coverbild: www.purestockx.com
Verlag: VDM Verlag Dr. Müller e. K., Dudweiler Landstr. 125 a, 66123 Saarbrücken, Deutschland
Herstellung: Lightning Source Inc., La Vergne, Tennessee/USA
        Lightning Source UK Ltd., Milton Keynes, UK

# ISBN: 978-3-8364-4962-5

# Preface

This book contains a revised version of my dissertation entitled "Network-Integrated Multimedia Middleware, Services, and Applications" accepted as "Dissertation zur Erlangung des Grades des Doktors der Ingenieurwissenschaften der Naturwissenschaftlich-Technischen Fakultäten der Universität des Saarlandes" at Saarland University, Saarbrücken, Germany in 2005.

The thesis includes a description of the software called "Network-Integrated Multimedia Middleware (NMM)". As the NMM software is under continuous development, the version of NMM currently available may differ to the software presented in this document. Please refer to the homepage of the project for more information.

Marco Lohse
November 2007

# Abstract

Today, there is a strong trend towards networked multimedia devices. However, common multimedia software architectures are restricted to perform all processing on a single system. Available software infrastructures for distributed computing – commonly referred to as middleware – only partly provide the facilities needed for supporting multimedia in distributed and dynamic environments. Approaches from the research community only focus on specific aspects and do not achieve the coverage needed for a full-featured multimedia middleware solution.

The Network-Integrated Multimedia Middleware (NMM) presented in this thesis considers the network as an integral part. Despite the inherent heterogeneity of present networking and device technologies, the architecture allows to extend control and co-operation to the network and enables the development of distributed multimedia applications that transparently use local and remote components in combination. The base architecture of this middleware is augmented by several middleware services that especially aim at providing additional support for developing complex applications that involve mobile users and devices. To this end, previously not available services and corresponding abstractions are proposed, realized, and evaluated. The performance and applicability of the developed middleware and its additional services are demonstrated by describing different realized application scenarios.

# Extended Abstract

Despite the fact that there is a strong trend towards networked multimedia devices, today's multimedia software architectures adopt a centralized approach where all processing is restricted to a single system. The network is, at best, used for streaming predefined content deploying a client/server architecture. Network transparent control and cooperation of distributed multimedia devices is not supported.

Available software infrastructures for distributed computing – commonly referred to as middleware – do only partly provide the facilities needed for supporting multimedia in distributed and dynamic environments with users and devices being mobile. Approaches from the research community only focus on specific aspects of distributed multimedia and do not achieve the coverage needed for a full-featured multimedia middleware solution.

Together, one can observe that there is currently a gap between the possibilities provided by the already available physical networking capabilities of the present infrastructures and the realized chances. The overall goal of the work presented in this thesis is to explore this space, to find applicable solutions that cover all important aspects, and to make the realized functionality available in an easy and efficient way.

The Network-Integrated Multimedia Middleware (NMM) presented in this thesis considers the network as an integral part. Despite the inherent heterogeneity of present networking and device technologies, the architecture allows to extend control and cooperation to the network and enables the development of complex distributed multimedia applications that transparently use local and remote components in combination. Within NMM, a specific multimedia functionality is modeled by creating a distributed flow graph of connected processing elements, e.g. multimedia devices or software components. While an application accesses and controls these elements using request-reply interaction, multimedia data and control information needs to be forwarded between connected elements using a streaming approach.

Since many building blocks for such an architecture are already available, we focus on providing an open and integrating framework that combines previously researched techniques in a systematic way. On the one hand, this means that available networking technologies, protocols, and middleware solution suitable for fulfilling the communication aspects needed for distributed multimedia can be used and combined. On the other hand, the framework allows to take advantage of existing multimedia libraries, drivers, and locally operating multimedia software architectures. Correspondingly, the main contribution of this part of the thesis is the identification and realization of a relatively small architectural middleware core that provides the openness and extensibility that allows to take full advantage of existing solutions. This core needs to provide a uniform way of handling the different interaction paradigms needed for multimedia middleware.

Rather than relying on a fixed set of technologies, this approach provides the possibility of integrating and combining available solutions – either for performing communication or handling multimedia – and therefore helps to use previously incompatible technologies in combination. Therefore, the developed framework also offers a higher level of abstraction that allows an application to access resources in a network transparent way *and* a technology transparent way. However, this transparency is scalable meaning that applications can still decide what degree of transparency they require – or if they want to configure lower layers manually.

Because of its openness, the individual building blocks of the NMM architecture can be exchanged and extended. This allows for tailoring the system to available resources – a property that is typically not available for existing middleware solutions.

The base architecture of NMM is augmented by several services that especially aim at providing additional support for developing complex applications that involve mobile users and devices. To this end, previously not available middleware services and corresponding abstractions are proposed, realized, and evaluated.

As a fundamental service, the registry service allows to manage available resources within networks of loosely coupled and heterogeneous systems.

While access to remote resources provides many benefits, the setup of complex distributed multimedia applications needs to be eased by a further service. The resulting graph building and format negotiation service demonstrates new techniques that allow an application to only specify the most relevant parts of an intended functionality; the distribution of the resulting configuration and the connection of originally incompatible components are handled automatically and guided by a user-centric quality measurement.

In order to increase the sense of collaboration among users, a further advanced and previously not available service is derived. This service, called session sharing, allows to automatically map requests sent to the registry service to already running applications. This allows to simultaneously and synchronously access the same (or similar) content on different devices controlled by different users. At the same time, this helps to reduce resource requirements by reusing active configurations and enables shared access to a single hardware device.

To enable mobile users to explore the capabilities of their surrounding environment, a further advanced middleware service is realized that was not presented before. This service allows for the seamless reconfiguration of running applications, for example, to realize adaptation due to a change in the environment. As an application, we demonstrate the handover of audio playback between systems. Being the most timing sensitive part of media handling, such a handover can even be performed lossless and synchronized when using our approach.

Together, the main contribution of this part of the thesis is to explore new ideas and present techniques that have not been researched previously. We demonstrate that once a full-featured and fully implemented multimedia middleware like NMM is available, these approaches can provide high-level abstractions and still be realized efficiently. In particular, we are able to show how advanced services for distributed multimedia can benefit from using the facilities provided by other more fundamental services or by the base architecture of the middleware itself.

The performance evaluations of all parts of NMM, its base architecture and its services, demonstrate that despite the open design approach, the clean, simple and unified design still allows for great efficiency. Especially those performance characteristics that can be directly compared to commercial and highly optimized traditional middleware solutions show competitive or even better results.

The applicability of the developed middleware and its additional services is demonstrated by describing different realized application scenarios. We are especially focusing on the provision of a networked multimedia home entertainment system employing various mobile and stationary devices in combination. Based completely on top of NMM, this shows that even large scale projects can be realized efficiently. To this end, the flexible and extensible architecture of the overall home entertainment system is a further contribution of this thesis.

The result of our work is available as Open Source for the GNU/Linux operating system. NMM is used for current and future research and developments at Saarland University, but also within other organizations and companies, and the Open Source community in general. Last but not least, this was another major goal of our work.

x

# Acknowledgments

First of all, I would like to thank my supervisor Prof. Philipp Slusallek, head of the Computer Graphics Lab at Saarland University. He managed to create an open and inspiring atmosphere, which was invaluable for the success of this project. His continuous encouragement and support were vital for me and this thesis.

Many thanks also to Prof. Thorsten Herfet and Prof. Thomas Ertl who kindly agreed to read and review this thesis.

Special thanks to the Max-Planck-Institut für Informatik, Saarbrücken, Germany, and Motorola Semiconductors, Germany (now Freescale) for financial support. Many thanks to our contact person at Motorola, Martin Raubuch, who provided valuable suggestions.

Many thanks are due to the current and former members of the NMM team, especially the students that work or worked in this project as student research assistants, or as part of their Advanced Practical, Diploma Thesis, Bachelor or Master Thesis (in alphabetical order) : Benjamin Deutsch, Bernhard Fuchshumer, Christian Gerstner, Christoph Wellner, David Maass, David Philippi, Eric Peters, Florian Winter, Marc Klein, Markus Sand, Osama Khan, Pascal Gwosdek, Patrick Becker, Patrick Cernko, Patrick Wambach, Robert Müller, Roger Dostert, Stephan Didas, Wolfgang Enderlein, and Wolfram von Funck. Without your enthusiasm and commitment realizing such a large system would not have been possible. This is especially true for Michael Repplinger, who worked as student research assistant and as part of his Diploma Thesis for the NMM project, and who is by now taking an even more active part in the research and development for NMM as PhD student at Saarland University.

Many thanks to the people who contributed to the Open Source version of NMM, especially to Andrés Otón Urbano and Stéphane Barotin. Thanks to the people that provided feedback on the Open Source version of NMM.

Many thanks to Georg Demme who supervises the VCORE project, designed marketing material for our project, and together with his team administrates all the hardware at our lab.

Many thanks also to Andreas Pomi who always willingly shared his enormous knowledge about audio and video technology with me.

Special thanks go to Hanna Schilt, our secretary, who always helped with all non-technical problems.

Finally, and most importantly, I would like to thank my wife Sandra for her great support and her patience during the final phase of writing this thesis, and my parents for encouraging me.

# Contents

# Chapter 1

# Introduction

The rapid development of the Internet over the last ten years – and as a consequence thereof the evolution of networking technology in general – has led to far reaching paradigm shifts not only in computer science or telecommunications but also in many other areas. To this end, several trends in the area of distributed systems have been predicted. The advent of the network computer has led to marketing driven statements like "the network is the computer". The idea behind this slogan is to move the complexity of computing away from the desktop to the network where it can be managed more easily [Fat02]. Mark Weiser envisioned the ubiquitous computing paradigm, where a large number of sensors and processors, which are invisibly embedded in our environment, perform user-centered tasks [Wei91]. Other trends are commonly referred to as "on-demand computing" technologies, where sufficient computational resources will be available like electricity or water [SJ02].

While the benefits of these ideas are manifold, realizing these visions is still a big challenge. On the one hand, this requires to establish new technological infrastructures like high bandwidth and pervasive networking. On the other hand, it is not enough to simply provide networking capabilities in order to effectively use the possible benefits of these infrastructures. Software architectures need to be developed that are able to use resources within the network in a simple and efficient way.

When looking at the area of multimedia computing or, more specific the area of home entertainment, there is also a strong trend towards networked multimedia devices. For example, the USB standard and particularly the IEEE 1394 standard (also known as FireWire) are commonly used since several years now to connect all kinds of multimedia equipment like video cameras or recorders to the desktop PC. Bluetooth becomes more popular for data exchange between PCs and mobile devices, such as mobile phones, e.g. for transferring audio files. Local area networks are not only basic equipment within companies or universities – where they already start to replace other infrastructure like telephone lines – but are becoming widely available in private households as well. This is even more true since wireless networks like the various IEEE 802.11 standards provide high bandwidth data transfer at an affordable price and can be employed without high costs or installation effort. At the same time, telecommunication companies plan to provide comparable data rates for mobile users with a large coverage all throughout the countries.

Then, of course, there is the Personal Computer that can be found in almost all

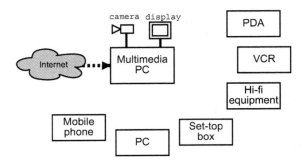

Figure 1.1: Despite the fact that we are surrounded by a constantly growing number of networked multimedia devices – such as mobile phones, PCs, set-top boxes, hi-fi equipment, video recorders, or PDAs – multimedia architectures still adopt a centralized approach where only directly connected devices can be accessed (e.g. a camera or display) and all processing is restricted to a single system. The network is used as sink or source of data only, for example when receiving streamed multimedia content from the Internet. Often, these networked applications need to be set up manually, are restricted to a specific task, and provide no fine-grained control.

households these days – at least within highly developed countries. More often, several PCs are available within a single household. Nowadays, PCs typically provide the capabilities needed for all different kinds of multimedia processing: enough processing power together with sufficient memory capacity and bandwidth, large amounts of hard disk space, high-quality audio and video input/output capabilities, DVD drives, TV boards, and interfaces for FireWire and others. Connected to the local area network and the Internet it seems that the vision of seamlessly networked environments is close. This is even more true, since a growing number of electrical devices already provide networking capabilities together with enough computational power and programmability that would allow them to perform various tasks. As an example, you could take current set-top boxes for receiving and decoding TV that employ modern operating systems, writable memory, and networking interfaces. Such system could also be used for performing other operations, e.g. playing back stored multimedia content. Finally, mobile devices like PDAs or cellular phones became ubiquitous over the last few years. Consequently their capabilities in terms of processing power, networking, display resolution, and programmability also evolved to allow for basic multimedia processing.

However, when looking at the majority of applications that are currently performed within these networks, then you will probably find email, browsing in the web, or downloading files from the Internet. In the area of multimedia computing, besides local playback of multimedia files, you will find transferring data between FireWire devices locally connected to a PC, e.g. for applications like video editing, or file exchange between a PC and a mobile device. Then, there is the area of streaming predefined content from servers in the Internet to clients running within the home networks. Such setups are mostly used for immediate playback of data.

Most often, these application are built on top of platform specific multimedia software architectures. These architectures provide the building blocks for realizing different applications together with support for common multimedia devices and data formats. However, all these application still adopt a centralized approach where processing only takes place within one system; the network is – at best – used for manually transmitting data (see Figure 1.1). The reason for this is that the available multimedia architectures do not provide the capabilities to efficiently use resources available within the network.

## 1.1  Why Distributed Multimedia?

To sum up, despite the fact that the networking and device technology is available and ready for much more advanced applications, the architectures used for building applications do not embrace the potentialities. This is especially unsatisfying due to the fact that for multimedia computing the potential applications for true networked computing are manifold.

Let us consider a simple example scenario with two systems; a set-top box in the living-room that provides television reception and a PC in the study room that has no access to TV. If both systems are connected via some networking technology, an obvious idea would be to allow for watching TV on the PC or to record the TV program to the hard disk installed in the PC. To this end, the PC should be allowed to switch TV channels. Together, one advantage of a software architecture supporting distributed multimedia is the ability to integrate remote processing devices (such as a multimedia device for receiving TV) into local processing.

Consequently, another interesting application scenario would be to allow for receiving the TV program on a mobile device. As such mobile systems often do not provide sufficient processing power to playback the original data stream, other systems within the network could take over the task of converting the original audio and video material to fit the capabilities of the mobile device. To summarize, another advantage of distributed multimedia is the possibility to use processing resources, such as computational power, available within the network to run software components for performing certain tasks.

Together, the two advantages for distributed multimedia pointed out so far allow to provide functionality (such as watching TV) for systems that originally do not provide the required devices, software components, or resources to perform a specific task. Furthermore, such a networked multimedia system allows to be extended to offer more performance (e.g. by adding processing capacity) or additional functionality (e.g. by adding new multimedia devices). In both cases, the system only needs to be extended "somewhere" within the network – at best, the used software architecture will allow all connected hosts to benefit from this extension.

But distributed multimedia provides even more benefits. By combining the capabilities of different distributed resources, totally new "virtual" devices can be realized. As an example, consider a networked camera together with a microphone and loud speakers installed at an entrance that both get activated whenever the doorbell is pressed. By connecting these two devices to a digital video recorder, e.g. a DV recorder connected to the home network via FireWire, a new device similar to an answering machine for telephones can be realized. Video streams of persons ringing the doorbell are captured with the camera and recorded to the video recorder together with an optional voice message. Later, these recordings can be queried from another system, for example a PC at the workplace connected to the home network via the Internet.

Besides these mostly technical advantages, distributed multimedia provides the means to naturally integrate users into application scenarios. On the one hand, this allows for services such as location-aware multimedia access, where users can employ the devices present at their current environment or hand off activities between different devices. On the other hand, distributed multimedia provides the capabilities for different users to be connected in order to perform collaborative activities such as enjoying the same (or similar) content simultaneously using different devices.

## 1.2   Limitations of Client/Server Streaming

Apparently, the first above described application scenario consisting of a networked set-top box and PC could be realized with traditional solutions that allow for streaming multimedia content from a server (the set-top box) to a client (the PC). However, several issues have to be addressed when using this approach. First of all, clients need to know how to locate the system that provides the functionality of the server. If the server process is not running already, clients need to know how to start it. Once this is done, clients need to determine the parameters to establish a network connection with the server. Then, the precise format and characteristics of the data stream the server provides needs to be set for all clients – or this information has to be known in advance. Finally, servers often do not provide options for controlling them. Even if some possibilities for interacting with a server are given, clients still need to determine what functionality is available and how it can be accessed.

Together, streaming client/server solutions often correspond to a "black-box" approach where no – or only coarse grained – control is available. The network is mainly used as source (or sink) of data. Usually, clients and servers are monolithic application developed for a single application scenario and cannot be extended easily. For example, a server for receiving and streaming TV can usually not be used for streaming video provided by a camera. Likewise, a client for playing back multimedia streams does not provide the capabilities needed for storing streams. Consequently, client/server streaming approaches do not provide the facilities for efficiently realizing more complex application scenarios as described above. For example, such approaches do not allow to distribute workload for converting multimedia content within the network.

To summarize, it is not a question of *if* certain application scenarios for distributed multimedia can be realized using a client/server streaming approach; it is a question of *how* easy and efficient it is to do so – and a question of what abstractions provide suitable means for developing more complex distributed applications.

## 1.3   Towards Network-Integrated Multimedia Middleware

Besides the capabilities for handling multimedia, the above described scenarios also have many properties typical for distributed systems in general – a research area that has been studied thoroughly for the last decades. Software architectures that support application development in such environments are often realized as middleware – roughly meaning a software layer running in between the operating systems of distributed systems and the applications running on these systems. In general, middleware is expected to mask out the complexity of the underlying infrastructure and to ease the task of developing distributed applications by providing a programming model that is similar to local execution. This is achieved by providing different dimensions of transparency, e.g. for transparently accessing and controlling distributed entities. An application built on top of middleware is therefore a true distributed application rather than two separate processes running on different systems as in the case of the above described client/server approach. Additionally, the term middleware is closely related with the idea of service provision: a distinct additional functionality that provides a certain service within the programming model.

However, middleware approaches widely available today do not provide the capabilities needed for realizing distributed multimedia applications. First, such solutions mainly cover programming models needed for request-reply interaction, – an interaction paradigm that does not fit the characteristics needed for transmitting high-bandwidth and time-sensitive multimedia data streams. Furthermore, a typical multimedia networking environment can – if at all – best be characterized by its inherent heterogeneity, both in device and networking technology. To put it in other words: "the nice thing about standards is that there are so many to choose from" [Tan96]. Therefore, the extensibility and openness of the overall architecture is of major importance in this area – aspects not addressed by the "black-box" approach taken by many middleware solutions. Finally, in order to realize the above described application scenarios, middleware for distributed multimedia needs different and additional services than traditional middleware.

To summarize, despite the fact that there is a strong trend towards networked multimedia devices, today's multimedia software architectures adopt a centralized approach where all processing is restricted to a single system. Contrariwise, common middleware solutions for distributed computing do only partly provide the facilities needed for supporting multimedia in distributed environments.

Previous approaches from the research community only focus on specific aspects of distributed multimedia and do not achieve the coverage needed for a full-featured multimedia middleware solution. Since implemented architectures are often not made available for future research, this hinders the development of advanced and new middleware services needed for ubiquitous and seamless multimedia computing.

## 1.4 Goals of this Thesis

The overall goal of this thesis is the design and development of a middleware architecture for distributed multimedia that considers the network as an integral part – the Network-Integrated Multimedia Middleware (NMM) [NMMb]. Consisting of a base architecture and additional services, NMM enables the easy and efficient development of the above described applications and allows for realizing even more complex scenarios.

The base architecture provides the means to access, control, and connect compo-

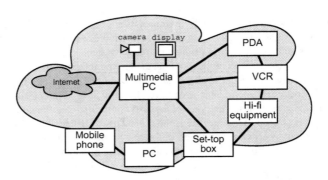

Figure 1.2: The Network-Integrated Multimedia Middleware (NMM) presented in this thesis considers the network as an integral part. The architecture allows to extend control and cooperation to the network. Despite the different underlying technologies, local and remote devices and processing capabilities can be integrated transparently into a single application. The provided framework enables the development of advanced and new middleware services.

nents, such as devices and software modules, available in the network (see Figure 1.2). Such configurations are set up in order to realize a certain application scenario for distributed multimedia. While access and control requires request-reply interaction, a completely different interaction paradigm needs to be provided for supporting streaming data connections between components. However, both types of interaction need to be possible despite the inherent heterogeneity of present networking and device technologies – the middleware should play an integrating role in transparently accessing these different facilities.

Previous approaches for distributed multimedia have mainly concentrated on specific aspects. In contrast, the presented work aims at creating an integrating architecture. Rather than reinventing the wheel, the developed architecture allows for the systematic combination of previously researched techniques where appropriate. On the one hand, this means that available networking technologies, protocols, and middleware solution suitable for fulfilling the communication aspects needed for distributed multimedia can be used and combined. On the other hand, the framework allows to take advantage of existing multimedia libraries, drivers, and locally operating multimedia software architectures.

Together, this results in an open and flexible architecture of the middleware base system, in which a relatively small core only provides the functionality of forwarding information between entities, for example between an application and its controlled multimedia components, but also between connected components. While this functionality is provided in a unified manner, the communication aspects of different interaction paradigms are handled by integrating available lower-level technologies. Based on these facilities is a generic architecture for distributed multimedia that – again – leaves the realization of functionality specific for handling and processing multimedia to already available components or algorithms. The architecture only provides the facilities for integrating arbitrary existing solutions.

Such a strict separation – middleware core, communication, and multimedia – is the key for realizing a flexible and extensible middleware that can be extended in various ways. Due to the possibility of using and combining available technologies, this middleware provides a higher level of abstraction in form of a meta-architecture and helps to use previously incompatible technologies in combination. Identifying the needed core functionality and creating an open and integrating framework for multimedia middleware that covers all aspects involved in a unified manner is the key contribution of this part of the thesis.

Despite the fact that the task of middleware is to mask out the complexity of a distributed system, we also aim at providing scalable transparency by offering different layers of abstraction. This allows for optimizing and tailoring configurations such as used network technologies – either manually or using higher level services.

Although GNU/Linux is rapidly becoming a favored platform not only for PCs but also for embedded systems, multimedia computing is still not well supported on this platform. Besides other mostly technical consideration, this was the main motivation why we chose this operating system as basis for our work. To this end, another challenge for the design of the our architecture was the ability to provide a locally operating multimedia architecture for GNU/Linux. This specialization of our middleware should prove the concept of an integrating and open architecture that is independent of a full-featured middleware solution for distributed computing.

To further ease application development, the architecture should provide the right abstractions to develop not only distributed multimedia applications but should also allow an application – or indirectly an user – to focus on the functional aspects of a given task and not on a possible concrete realization. Therefore, new application scenarios of particular interest should be identified together with the imposed requirements that need to be fulfilled – either by the core architecture of the developed middleware or by additional advanced middleware services. To this end, the main contribution of this part of the thesis is the proposal, realization, and evaluation of new services – services that were simply not possible to realize before due the lack of a fully implemented multimedia middleware. For all developed additional services, appropriate high-level abstractions and suitable programming models have to be established.

To this end, following additional requirements for distributed multimedia in dynamic environments are identified to be handled by middleware services. First of all, available resources throughout the network need to be discovered, administrated, and made available for application development. The resulting registry service is especially designed to operate in networks of only loosely coupled systems and allows for integrating available device technologies.

While distributed multimedia applications provide many benefits as argued above, developers need to be supported in the setup of complex configurations. Therefore, an additional service, called *graph building and format negotiation*, is realized that allows to only focus on the most relevant parts of an application; the distribution of components and the connection of originally incompatible components are handled automatically and guided by a user-centric quality measurement.

Due to the increased number of multimedia devices, applications involving several users are of particular interest. To enhance collaboration among users and to reduce the resource requirements for common tasks, an additional middleware service is developed, which allows to share parts of running applications, possibly across different systems. This service is called *session sharing*.

With users and device being mobile, support for location-aware applications becomes more important. In such scenarios, users are allowed to explore the capabilities of the surrounding infrastructure. To this end, a specific service was developed that provides the possibility to reconfigure a running application in a seamless and synchronized manner, for example when handing over the audio output from a mobile device to a nearby stationary device. However, since this service can be applied in general, it is called *seamless reconfiguration*.

Together, these four services allow for realizing advanced application scenarios easily. Based on a full-featured multimedia middleware, the provided high-level programming models and offer a level of abstraction that was not available before.

Finally, the implementation and the evaluation of the performance of all aspects of the architecture should prove its applicability in various real-world application scenarios using commodity systems offering different resources in terms of computational power or networking bandwidth. Although the NMM architecture can be used to realize all kinds of multimedia applications, the developed applications mainly focus on the area of multimedia home entertainment. This choice was made due to the possible dynamics of such scenarios – especially when multiple users and mobile devices are involved. The main contribution of this part of the thesis is the demonstration of a networked multimedia home entertainment system consisting of various stationary and mobile systems. Since the overall system is built completely on top of the NMM framework and its additional services, several key features not available before can be demonstrated in an integrated manner, for example the sharing of entertainment options, such as watching TV, for multiple users using different devices, or the seamless handover of activities, such as audio playback, between different systems.

To summarize, for the area of distributed multimedia systems, there is currently a gap between the possibilities of the available technological resources – like networking capabilities and device programmability – and the realized chances. The overall goal of this work is to explore this space, to find applicable solutions that cover all important aspects, and to make the realized functionality available for developers and users in an easy and efficient way.

The results of our work are by now available as Open Source. We believe that the implementation of our architecture provides a good foundation for further development and research activities. Last but not least, this was another major goal of our work.

## 1.5   Main Contributions of this Thesis

The main contributions of this thesis are:

- *The design and realization of an open middleware architecture for network-integrated multimedia.* Unlike previous approaches this middleware consists of a relatively small architectural core and strictly separates the handling and forwarding of information from all communication aspects and the multimedia functionality itself. To this end, our approach consists of an integrating communication framework that is independent of a particular application domain and a generic architecture for distributed multimedia developed on top of this framework. Together, this allows for an easy and seamless integration and combination of arbitrary available networking and multimedia technologies and therefore is the key design decision that helps coping with heterogeneous environments [LRS02, LS03, RWLS04, RWLS05].

- *The proposal, realization, and evaluation of new and advanced middleware services.* These services augment the base architecture and especially aim at providing additional support for developing complex applications that involve mobile users and devices. We demonstrate that once a full-featured and fully implemented multimedia middleware like NMM is available, these approaches can provide high-level abstractions and still be realized efficiently. Therefore, the proposed services further help to close the gap between requirements imposed by application scenarios of interest and the facilities provided by the underlying infrastructure. In particular, previously not researched ideas, techniques, and algorithms are presented for the graph building [LS05] and format negotiation service [LSW01], the session sharing service [LRS03b], and the seamless reconfiguration service [LRS03a].

- *Applicability, completeness, and appealing applications – especially for multimedia home-entertainment.* The applicability of the developed middleware and its additional services is demonstrated by implementing various complex real-world applications. We think that especially for multimedia home entertainment, our approach provides the largest coverage within a single architecture presented so far – a result of the clear, simple, and unified design of NMM and its integrating approach. To this end, the flexible and extensible architecture of the overall home entertainment system is a further contribution of this thesis [LS02, LS03, Loh03c, LRS05].

- *Competitive performance, implementation, and free availability.* The performance evaluations of the base architecture of NMM and its services demonstrate that despite the open design approach competitive or even better results can be achieved than available for specialized solutions that do not provide the coverage achieved by our work (see [RWLS04, RWLS05] and Chapter 8). The implementation of NMM is available as Open Source for the GNU/Linux operating system [NMMb]. We believe that NMM provides an ideal test-bed and starting point for future research and development, especially for research institutes, but also for companies and the Open Source community in general.

Together, the presented work consists of a multimedia middleware, its additional services, and applications built on top. Being a software architecture, this thesis also aims at "proving the correctness" of the chosen approach by demonstrating that a middleware can only be as powerful as its design allows to, additional services can only be as powerful as the underlying middleware allows to, and applications can only be as powerful as the underlying services and middleware allow to.

## 1.6   Outline of this Thesis

This thesis consists of five parts. The following gives a brief outline of the structure
and the issues addressed in the specific parts.

### Part I: Foundations of Multimedia Middleware

The main goal of this part of the thesis is to point out the foundations of middleware
supporting distributed multimedia applications. Therefore, we will start with an introduction of the fundamental concepts of multimedia and design approaches of current
multimedia software architectures in Chapter 2. First, we will restrict this review to
commonly available architectures that adopt a centralized approach where all processing is restricted to a single host. This will help to focus on the general requirements
for supporting multimedia, like handling of data streams and synchronization. Within
the review of today's common architectures, we will identify common ideas and dis-
tinguishable features.

Chapter 3 provides insights into the foundations of distributed systems and middleware in general. First, the main requirements for such systems are explained. Special focus will be made on the different dimensions of transparency that should be
supported by a middleware. Again, common abstractions and different architectural
choices are discussed, followed by a review of some of today's most important middleware technologies and standards for distributed object computing.

As an synopsis of the previous two chapters, we then analyze the requirements
for middleware supporting distributed multimedia in Chapter 4. This will include the
review of different research approaches but also the examination of available technologies that could be used as building blocks for a more general integrating architecture.
Especially, we will discuss the main motivation and goals for our work and the requirements that are especially important within this context. Furthermore, we will
point out additional needed capabilities for multimedia middleware that we focussed
on, namely the requested architectural support for masking out the heterogeneity of
the overall system, the assistance for dynamic reconfiguration and as a special case the
support for user and host mobility, the support for collaborative multimedia activities,
and the support for automatic setup of complex applications.

### Part II: Network-Integrated Multimedia Middleware

In this part, the base architecture of the Network-Integrated Multimedia Middleware
(NMM) will be described. In Chapter 5, the fundamental architectural decisions are
pointed out. An overview of the developed architecture is given; in the following chapters, the different aspects of the architecture are presented in more detail. Throughout
the presentation, we will motivate the design decisions by addressing requirement.
First, the developed architecture should be generic in the sense that it allows to realize different specializations, e.g. for handling multimedia in distributed systems, but
also for traditional request-reply interaction. Secondly, the architecture should provide
the openness and extensibility needed in the presence of heterogeneous environments.
Especially the integrating aspects of the presented approach will be discussed. And

finally, the architecture should provide the possibilities to allow for the development of advanced middleware service.

In Chapter 6, the design and implementation of an architecture supporting network-integrated computing in general will be discussed in detail. In particular, a framework for the serialization of arbitrary data types is presented. This framework is the basis for a unified messaging and communication architecture for realizing different types of interaction. An extension that provides type-safe and object-oriented interfaces for these different interaction paradigms is described. Finally, a binding framework that establishes communication between the entities of the architecture and allows to integrate and combine various existing lower level technologies is presented.

While the architecture described in Chapter 6 provides the building blocks for realizing different middleware solutions, an in-depth description of an architecture for distributed multimedia based on these facilities is provided in Chapter 7. The concepts and elements of NMM flow graphs, the underlying processing model, and the facilities provided for realizing distributed synchronization protocols are discussed in the following together with several implementation issues. Again, the design of this part of the overall NMM architecture is especially discussed under the premise of the integrating nature of the approach. To this end, the presented architecture allows for an easy integration of existing multimedia components.

A final summary of the preceding three chapters together with an evaluation of different performance characteristics of the current implementation is provided in Chapter 8.

## Part III: Middleware Services

Besides the base architecture itself, the other important part of middleware are the provided additional services. Part III of this thesis discusses four of these services. Special focus will be paid on the possible benefits that one service gains from using the facilities of another, and the programming model all these services together provide for application development. The presentation of the different services will follow a common structure. After motivating the need for the specific service, related work will be reviewed. Then, the service itself will be described, followed by different exemplary applications. Furthermore, the performance of the service and the achieved results are discussed and conclusions are drawn.

Finding and allocating components within the network – for example an NMM component that represents a certain multimedia device – is a fundamental service multimedia middleware has to provide. The registry service presented in Chapter 9 makes this functionality available. Again, we will discuss what features the registry provides to allow for the integration of third-party components and technologies. Current efforts to integrate support for quality of service (QoS) management into the registry service of NMM are described, mainly to explain the benefits that such facilities provide for the advanced middleware services to be presented in the following chapters.

The setup of complex distributed multimedia applications requires to handle a variety of low-level details, such as the choice of matching data formats or the physical location of components. The need for higher level abstractions led to the development of an additional middleware service that is described in Chapter 10. This service provides automatic setup of distributed multimedia applications from an abstract high-level description. Furthermore, a quality-driven format negotiation tries to meet the user's demand for the best perceived quality of the multimedia presentation. After analyzing the requirements and reviewing related work in this area, the chosen approach is described in detail and the developed service is evaluated.

The session sharing service described in Chapter 11 was developed to accomplish for the demands for collaborative multimedia activities, where a number of users enjoys the same or similar content using different devices. After motivating the need for such a service by describing some application scenarios, related work is reviewed. Then, the required extensions for the middleware architecture described so far are pointed out followed by an in-depth description of the developed algorithms. Finally, different application scenarios and the performance provided by the developed service are evaluated.

The need for being able to dynamically reconfigure a running multimedia application can be seen as the consequence to changes within its underlying infrastructure. Being able to adapt to these changes was also identified as a key feature for multimedia middleware. The service presented in Chapter 12 focuses on seamless reconfiguration of applications. Although such a service can be used in many different scenarios, in this context, we focus on the provision of synchronized hand offs of parts of multimedia applications during run-time. This service builds upon the facilities provided by the distributed synchronization architecture, the session sharing service and the registry in general. Besides showing the relation between our work and other approaches, we demonstrate various results. Finally, we show that a new kind of transparency, namely reconfiguration transparency, should be an essential part of middleware for distributed multimedia. The chapter concludes with an outlook of how such a service could be realized in general.

## Part IV: Applications

Part IV then demonstrates how the facilities of the NMM architecture can be used to easily develop real world applications. Starting from simple applications, which only use some of the possibilities provided by NMM, more complex setups follow that use all or most of the available features in combination.

In Chapter 13 an application that allows to easily set up distributed multimedia application is described: From a textual description of the specific configuration, a distributed flow graph is set up. Additionally, such a description can employ the session sharing service.

The NMM architecture was also used to develop a system that allows for the recording and later playback of all aspects of a talk or lecture. This includes the storage of an audio and video stream of the speaker but also the synchronized recording and later presentation of the used additional material, like electronic slides. The application developed is described in Chapter 14.

A much more complex application is described in detail in Chapter 15, the so called Multimedia-Box: a Linux-PC based multimedia home entertainment center that integrates a variety of different entertainment options (like TV, video recorder, DVD playback, MP3 player, etc.) within a consistent and extensible system that can be controlled with a remote control. The seamless integration of other distributed systems allows for different applications: Remote multimedia devices can be integrated transparently into local processing (e.g. a remote device for receiving TV), or time consuming jobs can be distributed in the network (e.g. transcoding of a DVD to a different format). Within such a network of home entertainment systems, users can join running applications using different devices. Furthermore, mobile systems with restricted resources can be seamlessly integrated and are allowed to hand off media processing to stationary system.

During the time of our work, one main motivation for the development of this application was to have a demanding test-bed for the NMM architecture where all available features can be employed within a complex application framework. To this end, the architecture of the Multimedia-Box itself was thoroughly designed to allow for later extensions.

### Part V: Final Summary, Conclusions, and Future Work

Finally, in Part V, the last part of this thesis, an overall summary is presented, conclusions are drawn, and ideas for future research are discussed.

# Part I

# Foundations of Multimedia Middleware

# Chapter 2

# Foundations of Locally Operating Multimedia Systems

To identify the requirements for an architecture that supports distributed multimedia, an understanding of the subject matter, namely multimedia, is essential. This requires a precise characterization of multimedia systems including multimedia data streams, devices, processing, networking, synchronization, and support for quality of service.

Then, we will identify common abstractions for multimedia systems. This is followed by a review of how available multimedia software architectures have realized fulfilling the imposed requirements. To help focus on the key challenges for supporting multimedia, this evaluation will be restricted to approaches where all processing is restricted to a single host and the network is used as source (or sink) of data only.

## 2.1 Terminology

### 2.1.1 Multimedia

Defining the term multimedia is not straight forward. Although the term multimedia is often used to generally express that information can be represented through audio and video, in addition to text, image, graphics and animation, the following will introduce a more precise definition as presented in [SN95] and a variation that is more generally applicable.

Literally speaking, the word multimedia is composed of the word *multi* (lat.: much) for "many" and *medium* (lat.: middle) as a mean for distribution and presentation of information. Media can be classified according to the following.

- Perception: the way how a human perceives information, e.g. by seeing or hearing.

- Representation: in which format the information is coded within a computer, e.g. a sampled audio signal.

- Presentation: the means through which information is delivered by (e.g. on a screen) or introduced into the computer (e.g. by a camera).

- Storage: the medium on which the information is stored within a computer, e.g. a hard disk.

- Transmission: the carrier over which the information can be transmitted, e.g. cable networks.

- Information exchange: all information carriers to be used for exchanging information between different places, e.g. all storage and transmission media.

According to this classification, multimedia could be defined as the presence of multiple media. From a user's point of view, this would mean the presence of multiple perception media. To further evolve this definition, it is important to notice that different media can also be divided with respect to time.

- Media like text and graphics are considered to be *time-independent* (or *discrete*) if their handling is not subject to a time component. This could for example mean that the processing is not time critical.

- On the other hand, media that periodically change over time are called *time-dependent* (or *continuous*). For example, full-motion video that changes with 25 frames per second. While internally video also consists of discrete video frames, from a user's perspective it is continuous when displayed with 16 frames per second or more [SN95].

Therefore, the term multimedia can also be understood not only in a quantitative but also in a qualitative way [SN95]: Multimedia then requires the presence of at least a discrete *and* a continuous medium.

According to [SN95] a multimedia system can be defined as follows.

> A multimedia system is characterized by computer-controlled, integrated production, manipulation, presentation, storage, and communication of independent information which is encoded at least through a continuous (time-dependent) and a discrete (time-independent) medium.

Besides requiring the presence of a continuous and discrete medium, this definition further demands independent information and computer-controlled integration. The former implies the ability to handle different media independently; the later means that different media could by interconnected in form and content, e.g. by establishing timing relationships between different media. Finally, the communication aspect is also included in this definition – one of the main objective targets of this thesis.

In general, the term *multimedia* and *multimedia system* is also often used as synonym [hypb].

Although this definition is very precise, it is in some sense too restrictive and does not reflect many cases in which the term multimedia or multimedia system is commonly used today. For this reason, we provide a weaker definition of the term multimedia.

> Multimedia is the computer-controlled, integrated handling of a continuous (time-dependent) media and optionally discrete (time-independent) media.

The essence of this definition is the presence of continuous media.

### 2.1.2 Multimedia Architecture

After having defined the term multimedia, it becomes clear that the challenges for developing complex multimedia applications are manifold. An abstraction layer in form of a *software architecture* is needed. In general, a software architecture is the structuring of a system in terms of its basic elements and their interrelationship[1]. According to Shaw [Car], these structural models state that a software architecture is composed of components, connections among these components, plus some other aspect or aspects, like configuration.

A *multimedia software architecture*, or simply *multimedia architecture*, conforms to this definition but can be seen as a special case of a *framework*: a set of architectural elements that embodies an abstract design for solutions to a number of related problems [hypa]. The specific features of a framework that allow to model solutions are commonly referred to as *programming model* [BS98]. Accordingly, Shaw characterizes the primary emphasis for framework models of software architectures to be the coherent structure of the whole system [Car]. Especially, domain-specific architectures should be regarded under this premise.

The term multimedia architecture will be used throughout this thesis to denote such architectures. If the special focus lies on the aspects of the framework, the term framework will be used.

### 2.1.3 Examples for Multimedia Applications

The following gives some examples of what kind of applications a multimedia architecture should support. Together these applications can be divided into *off-line* and *real-time* applications. Off-line applications do only impose weak timing restrictions on handling multimedia data (e.g. "as fast as possible") but require that all multimedia data is processed. Examples for off-line applications are:

- Converting between different media formats, e.g. generating MP3 files from audio CDs.

- Editing multimedia data, e.g. editing personal audio and video recordings. This often includes controlling devices like FireWire DV cameras.

Real-time applications require that the handling of multimedia data follows certain timing constraints, e.g. during playback or recording. Multimedia data that is processed "too late" (like a video frame that is received significantly later than the corresponding audio data) is of no use for these applications. Examples for real-time applications are:

- Handling the playback of files like MP3, MPEG, etc. Sometimes, these files are streamed from servers, e.g. for Internet radio.

- Production of multimedia presentations, e.g. recording of lectures or other presentations including audio, video, and other presented material like slides.

- Live streaming and control, e.g. for controlling surveillance cameras.

---

[1]From this definition follows that every software system has an architecture, which shows the need for documenting an architecture [BCK03].

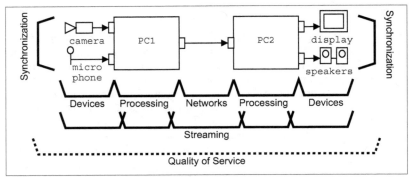

Multimedia architecture

Figure 2.1: A typical multimedia system showing the various aspects a multimedia architecture has to handle: different devices are connected to hosts that process the multimedia data. The network is used as sink or source of data. Streaming data connections are used between these different parts of the system. Synchronization is needed to take the timing constraints of multimedia data streams into account. If possible, all these aspects should provide a certain quality of service to achieve satisfying quality, e.g. as perceived by a user of the system.

## 2.2   Characterization of Multimedia Systems

After having defined the term multimedia, we will analyze the characteristics of multimedia systems as focussed in this work[2]. This is important to understand the requirements for multimedia architectures and the abstractions used within different approaches.

Figure 2.1 shows a typical example for a multimedia system. A camera and microphone are attached to a computer, namely PC1. This host is connected to another computer PC2 that has attached a display and loudspeakers. The motivation for this particular setup is to continuously capture audio and video with the devices attached to PC1, to transfer this data to PC2, and to playback the audio and display the video with the devices attached to PC2.

As can be seen from the figure, there are different aspects involved in this setup. Devices, processing, and networking form the building blocks of a multimedia system. Streaming takes places between these different parts. Synchronization coordinates the overall interaction. Finally, quality of service (QoS) requirements are imposed for all parts.

To focus on the general requirements, we will examine these aspects without looking at the technical details for now. However, despite the fact that networking is also part of these aspects, for the scope of this chapter, the network is only regarded as source (or sink) of data; seen from an application, all processing is restricted to a sin-

---

[2]Aspects of multimedia systems that are not handled within the scope of this thesis include animation, computer-generated images, hardware architectures, storage media, multimedia DBMS, security, or content analysis

gle host. For the application scenario shown in Figure 2.1 this means that there are two separate applications running: a "server" on PC1 that uses the network as sink of data; and a "client" on PC2 that uses the network as source of data. Both applications have no knowledge of the other application apart from the data connection between them.

### 2.2.1 Data Streams

The process of "continuously transferring data" as described above is commonly referred to as *streaming*. According to [hypc], a *data stream*, or simply *stream*, is defined as:

> A stream is an abstraction referring to any flow of data from a source (or sender, producer) to a single sink (or receiver, consumer). A stream usually flows through a channel of some kind. Streams usually require some mechanism for establishing a channel or a "connection" between the sender and receiver.

An additional requirement for multimedia data streams is the time-dependent nature of the information flow.

The concept of streams is fundamental for multimedia systems. In our example, several streams are present: the stream between the camera and PC1, or between the microphone and PC1. Furthermore, depending on the type of processing, data is also "streamed" between different software components running on host PC1. Then, there are one or more streams between the two hosts PC1 and PC2. Again, processing – and therefore streaming – could also take place at host PC2 before video is streamed to the display and audio to the loudspeakers.

For each of these streams, different parts act as "source" or "sink" according to the above definition. Furthermore, a component that acts as a sink can simultaneously be the source for another component. Also, different "channels" are used: data can be streamed between different devices and hosts using some networking technology or streaming can be performed within a single host by moving chunks of data in memory between components.

### Communication Channels

Despite the fact that all these streams could be regarded as "continuous" from a user's point of view, for computer-controlled multimedia, a stream is a sequence of discrete data packets. Therefore, the main characteristics of a communication channel – and therefore also of its corresponding stream – are [CDK01]:

- Bandwidth: the total amount of data that flows from source to sink in a given time.

- Latency: the delay between the start of the flow of a data packet at the source and the beginning of its reception at the sink.

- Jitter: the variation in time taken to deliver a series of packets.

If the traffic between source and sink is not regular, the characteristics of a communication channel are extended by the specification of its burstiness.

- Burstiness: the maximum amount of data that may arrive too early (in respect to a regular arrival rate) in a given time.

### Transmission Modes

Streams can offer different transmission modes [SN95].

- Asynchronous transmission mode provides no time restrictions. It operates at "best-effort" meaning that packets are transmitted as fast as possible from sender to receiver. Therefore this mode is best suited for unsynchronized, discrete media. Handling of synchronized or continuous media requires further effort. Ethernet in local area networks [IEEc] is an example for this transmission mode.

- Synchronous transmission mode specifies a maximum delay for each packet transmitted from sender to receiver. Contrariwise, no minimum delay is specified which could require buffering data at the receiver for ensure proper timing. SDI-Video (ITU-R BT 601) is an example for this transmission mode [WR04].

- Isochronous transmission mode ensures bounded jitter by providing a maximum and minimum delay for each transmitted packet. For example, IEEE 1394 [139] provides such a transmission mode.

Although these characteristics originate from the area of communications systems, they can also be applied to streams of data within a single system. Accordingly, Interprocess communication (IPC) for a standard UNIX operating system without real-time properties could then be classified as asynchronous transmission. Similarly, forwarding references to chunks of multimedia data within a single process can be regarded as the same transmission mode.

### Periodicity, Packet Size, and Continuity

A further important characteristics of continuous data streams is the periodicity of time intervals between consecutive packets. *Periodic* streams provide a fixed interval between different packets – and therefore zero jitter. For *weakly periodic* streams, time intervals follow a periodic function. For *aperiodic streams* no such property holds. Another classification of streams can be done according to variation of packet size. A *regular* stream provides a constant size of packets, whereas this number periodically changes for *weakly regular* streams. *Irregular* streams contain packets of arbitrary sizes. The continuity of a stream is a further discrimination. Consecutive packets can either be transmitted continuously or with gaps in between.

These three characteristics are primarily independent of the used transmission mode; rather they impose different requirements that a certain transmission mode can fulfill or not. On the one hand, streaming a strongly periodic stream in asynchronous mode would destroy its periodic nature and requires additional effort to establish this characteristics again. On the other hand, a non-continuous, irregular, aperiodic stream can be streamed in isochronous mode but will require some preprocessing, e.g. to fit into predefined packet sizes of the isochronous channel.

**Logical Data Units**

The information units of media can be divided or grouped into so called *logical data units (LDU)* [SN95]. What is considered an LDU depends on the particular context. For a video clip, an LDU could be the complete clip, an individual scene, a group of consecutive frames, a single frame, a block within this frame, or a single pixel. The relationship of different LDUs often describes an intended hierarchical structure. LDUs with a predefined duration are called closed, otherwise they are called open.

**Discussion**

For shared resources – like networking bandwidth or computational resources that are used by different processes –, these characteristics pose important implications for resource requirements and utilization. The following sections will further examine what kind of streaming takes place between the different parts of the example setup, namely devices, processing, and networking.

## 2.2.2 Devices

Essential parts of a multimedia system are input devices, like the camera and microphone, and output devices, like the display and loudspeakers in our example (see Figure 2.1).

**Digitization**

As input devices usually capture *true* continuous signals from the real world, these signals have to be *digitized* to be represented in a computer[3]. This includes *sampling* and *quantization* [SN95]. For example, the physical oscillations of a source of sound can be transferred to an analog electrical signals by a microphone. This signal is then measured at some specific points in time, usually at a fixed sampling rate (sampling). The sampled continuous values are then rounded to a discrete level to be represented with a certain number of bits (quantization). Additionally, different channels can be digitized, e.g. two channels for stereo audio, or, for video, different color channels per pixel.

**Rendering**

The inverse of digitization, the process commonly known as *rendering*, takes place for outputting multimedia to the environment: video is displayed by the graphics board on an attached monitor; audio is played out via loudspeakers connected to the sound board. Again, video is usually rendered as single frames, e.g. with 25 frames per second, whereas audio is not played out by an application by individually outputting every sample but by processing bigger chunks of data at one time.

---

[3]A hard disk (or a similar other device) could also be considered as a multimedia I/O device that already works with digital representations.

### Discrete Representation of Continuous Media

Besides many issues involved in these steps, like choosing the "right" sampling rate according to Nyquist's sampling theorem[4], the important observation is that it usually makes sense to represent digitized video as a sequence of individual frames whereas for audio different fractions could be used depending on the requirements of the current application: setups that require low latency should process audio data in chunks of some milliseconds of real time; off-line application could handle several seconds of audio in one step (compare Section 2.1.3).

For both steps, capturing and rendering, this subdivision is not only a natural choice but also analog to the way in which most hardware devices and their corresponding device drivers of the used operating system handle multimedia data. This has implications for the latency of a stream as the design of many systems does not allow to start processing a piece of memory before it is received completely[5]. For video streams, this means that the latency according to the above definition will be increased from the start time to the end time of the reception of the current frame.

### Device Technology

Another important point is that there exists a large variety of different devices and ways to connect these devices to a computer. An analog camera could be connected to a special PC board that performs the digitization step, e.g. a video board for the PCI bus. It could also be connected via USB [AD01] or IEEE 1394 (FireWire) [139]. In theses cases, the digitization is already done within the camera itself.

Controlling a particular device and accessing its data stream strongly depends on the used technology. Fortunately, these differences are mainly covered inside device drivers or higher level standards.

On the one hand, device discovery and control is often handled by the operating system. On the other hand, many different and competing standards for these tasks exist, like UPnP [Uni], or Jini [Jin], to name only the two most popular ones.

Furthermore, different technologies provide features that others do not. For example, most standards allow that devices can be connected or disconnected at any time (hot-plugging). Additionally, standards like IEEE 1394 allow a single device to be connected to several systems at a time, e.g. to two PCs.

Therefore, a multimedia architecture needs to be able to integrate different technologies easily and provide uniform access whenever possible.

### Formats and Requirements

The analysis of the above mentioned multimedia data streams, namely uncompressed audio and video has further implications. First, a audio stream certainly has a different *format* than a video stream. In the context of multimedia systems, a format can

---

[4]The Nyquist sampling theorem states [Nyq28]: "For lossless digitization, the sampling rate should be at least twice the maximum frequency response."

[5]For main stream PC processors several streaming media extensions like ISSE have been introduced over the last years [TH99]. However, these approaches only work on a very low level and are not controllable from high-level programming languages but rather used automatically, e.g. by the used compiler

| Format | Specification | Data rate |
|---|---|---|
| CD-quality stereo audio | 2 channels, 44.1 kHz sampling rate with 16 bits/sample | 1.4 Mbps |
| DVD-quality video (uncompressed) | 720x576 pixel, 12 bits/pixel, 25 frames/second | 124.4 Mbps |
| HDTV video (un-compressed) | up to 1920x1080 pixel, 24 bits/pixel, 24-60 frames/second | 1194.3 Mbps to 2985.9 Mbps |

Table 2.1: Typical data rates for uncompressed multimedia streams in millions of bits per second (Mpbs) for CD-quality stereo audio, DVD-quality video, and High-Definition TV (HDTV). The values indicate the requirements in terms of networking bandwidth, memory throughput, and computational power required for handling multimedia.

generally be seen as the meta-data that specifies a certain stream by precisely defining properties, such as the framerate and resolution of a stream of video frames.

Secondly, these streams are high-bandwidth. This is especially true for video. Table 2.1 gives an overview of some required bandwidths for different data formats. These values show that even with today's computational and networking capabilities, handling these bandwidths efficiently is still a challenging task. This is even more true as the increase of computational power and networking bandwidth leads to more demanding applications – a situation that can be observed in many areas in computer science and that is depicted by the term *window of scarcity* [ATW+90]: for each point on a historical time line, the available resources can be insufficient or abundant to fulfill the requirements of a particular application. In between is the window of scarcity, where application can only be realized when handled properly. For multimedia this means that continuously growing demands in different dimensions (e.g. display size, sample resolution, number of channels) will increase the requirements for handling multimedia. Managing the requirements that lie within the window of scarcity can only be realized when special care is taken.

### 2.2.3 Processing

There is a broad spectrum of different possibilities of processing multimedia data.

#### Input and Output

The operation of capturing and rendering as described above can be seen as "processing" depending of when and how it is performed. Consequently, the reading from or writing to storage media like hard disks or DVDs can also be included. Therefore, the ability to read and write different data formats is essential. As new file formats are emerging continuously, a multimedia architecture should allow to be extended easily.

#### Filtering and Conversion

Besides the input and output of multimedia data, there exit different further possible transformation. On the one hand, the data values of multimedia streams can undergo

| Format | Data rate (uncompressed) | Compression | Data rate (compressed) | Ratio Ratio |
|---|---|---|---|---|
| CD-quality stereo audio | 1.4 Mbps | MPEG2 layer III audio | 128 kBit/s | approx. 10:1 |
| DVD-quality video | 124.4 Mbps | MPEG2 video | 4 Mbps | approx. 30:1 |
| HDTV video | 1194.3 Mbps to 2985.9 Mbps | MPEG2 video | 20 Mbps | up to 150:1 |

Table 2.2: Typical data rates and compression ratios for compressed multimedia streams in kilo bits per second (kBit/s) or millions of bits per second (Mpbs) for CD-quality stereo audio, DVD-quality video, and High-Definition TV (HDTV).

a transformation, also called *filtering*. Examples include: changing of amplitudes of pulse-coded audio; or, for video, the variation of brightness (luminance) of pixels.

The above mentioned transformations keep the original data format but change the content of multimedia data streams. Other transformation are *conversions* that change the data format, e.g. changing the color space of uncompressed video from some YUV representation to an RGB representation [Poy96].

**Compression and Decompression**

Other transformations that are extremely important for multimedia systems are compression and decompression, or more general, encoding and decoding of information. For a specific encoding and decoding technique the term *codec* is used (short for: coder/decoder).

Compression techniques allow to reduce the high data rates of multimedia data streams (see Table 2.2). This is essential to be able to store and transmit these streams. It is important to notice that the space reduction is achieved by increasing the processing requirements for both compression and decompression, respectively.

Compression techniques can be either be lossless or lossy. Lossless means that the original data is obtained when decompressing compressed data. Lossy methods are often domain specific meaning that they were especially designed for a particular medium like audio or video, or even for a specific type thereof, e.g. voice or music. The main concern for lossy methods is to be able to reproduce the original information with comparable "quality", e.g. in terms of the user's audio-visual impression. In general, lossy methods can achieve higher compression ratios.

The methods used for compression is called *asymmetric* if the compression algorithms are more complex – and therefore require more computational resources – than the algorithms for decompression. If this is not the case, the codec is called *symmetric*. Video compression uses either intra-frame compression, where each frame is encoded separately, or inter-frame compression that uses information from other video frames to encode the current frame. These interdependencies are often arranged within distinct structures called group of pictures (GOP).

The bit rate at which a stream is generated by an coder is either constant bit rate (CBR) or variable bit rate (VBR), where *variable* means that for the same incoming data portion, the coder can generate output packets of different size. As a consequence, the resulting streams might require higher peak bandwidth than average bandwidth (compare *burstiness*, defined in Section 2.2.1).

This area has drawn many benefits from various research and standardization activities. Especially the standardization of MPEG-1 [ISO98] and MPEG-2 [ISO04a] has led to the creation of other standards like the digital versatile disc (DVD) [Tay01] or digital video broadcasting (DVB) [Digb].

On the one hand, more efficient codecs are being introduced regularly and new standards like MPEG4 [ISO04b] emerge. A multimedia architecture needs to be able to include these easily. On the other hand, these standards follow a general structure where often a combination of different codecs is used, e.g. lossy and lossless.

### Multiplexing and Demultiplexing

Besides the compression and decompression techniques used, the processes of multiplexing and demultiplexing are also very often part of the various standards. Multiplexing takes two or more streams and mixes them into a single stream. Consequently, demultiplexing extracts different streams out of a single stream. Furthermore, multiplexing often includes the synchronization of the different streams within the resulting new stream, e.g. this also also covered by *Part 1: Systems* of the MPEG-1 and MPEG-2 standards.

### Discussion

Despite the different kinds of processing routines, a multimedia software architecture has to provide the appropriate abstractions that provide uniform access to different routines and allow for combining these within an application. As all these operation are running as processes within the operating system of the host system, the capabilities of this underlying platform are also very important.

### 2.2.4   Networking

Although the introduction of multimedia systems in this chapter is restricted to locally operating architectures, the network is still often used as sink or source of data. This is also the case for the application scenario shown in Figure 2.1.

The term "networking" as focussed within this thesis stands for standards like the Internet protocols and technologies but also for special purpose networks, e.g. in the area of home networking, or emerging technologies like UMTS.

### ISO-OSI Protocol Stack

The ISO Open Systems Interconnection Reference Model (ISO-OSI) consists of seven layers, namely physical (layer 1), link (layer 2), network (layer 3), transport (layer 4), session (layer 5), presentation (layer 6), and application (layer 7) [ISO]. Due to the fact that for most implementations layer 5 to 7 are running within applications, this protocol stack is often restricted to five layers, with layer 1 to 4 as defined in ISO-OSI and a single application layer as layer 5 [KR01]. This approach is also taken by the Internet protocol stack. However, the further refinement of the application layer is especially interesting when considering protocols for transmitting multimedia data or middleware layer protocols.

### Physical and Link Layer

In particular, the term "networking" then includes PCs connected via Ethernet (layer 2), e.g. using commodity PCI Ethernet adapters with 100 Mbps. Furthermore, these hosts are today usually connected by switches with full-duplex mode and dedicated access. Therefore, the bandwidth between each of the networked hosts can be assumed to be typically up to 100 Mbps in both directions, which is sufficient to transmit several compressed audio and video streams but not enough for even a single uncompressed video stream in DVD quality (see Table 2.1 and Table 2.2).

For wireless network access, the different IEEE 802.11 standards [IEEa] are often used. These networks either run in infrastructure mode with dedicated access points or in ad hoc mode as a network with no central control. IEEE 802.11b has a maximum throughput of 11 Mbps but since a significant amount is already used for communication coordination, only up to 5.5 Mbps can be employed [Wikb]. Bandwidth is also shared among different users as the IEEE 802.11 MAC protocol is a carrier-sense multiple access protocol with collision avoidance (CSMA/CA). Adding additional access points that use other non-overlapping channels can increase the total bandwidth [McL03]. The IEEE 802.11g standard is backward compatible to IEEE 802.11b and operates at 54 Mbps which results 24 Mbps maximum throughput.

Notice however that the characteristic values like bandwidth and end-to-end delay are not guaranteed in these networks. This is because link capacity is typically shared between different hosts and applications, and – for wireless networks – may strongly depend on the physical environment.

### Network Layer and Transport Layer

For layer 3, network, the Internet Protocol (IP), is used. While IPv6 [DH98a, Wikd] is supposed to be the upcoming standard, currently IPv4 [Pos81a, Wikc] is still widely used. Mainly two different protocols are used on layer 4, transport: the Transmission Control Protocol (TCP) [Pos81b] and the User Datagram Protocol (UDP) [Pos80].

One main concern for multimedia systems is the service provided by the transport protocols: TCP provides a connection-oriented reliable data transfer; UDP a connection-less unreliable data transfer. Here, unreliable also means that received datagrams are not necessarily ordered.

While the reliability of TCP is important for application layer protocols or for offline multimedia applications, it has several disadvantages for transferring continuous multimedia streams for real-time applications [KLW01] (compare Section 2.1). First, the connection establishment via three-way handshake and the "slow start" of TCP introduce additional delays. Secondly, acknowledgments during transmission take additional time and bandwidth. Thirdly, the reliability of TCP comes at the price of possible retransmission of packets. For a continuous multimedia data stream, timeliness can be more important than reliability. If packets arrive too late they will have to be discarded by the application (compare Section 2.2.5). Retransmission of multimedia data packets therefore wastes bandwidth and processing resources, and – even worse –

usually leads to severe delays for following packets. Finally, the TCP flow control and congestion control may decrease the used sending bandwidth unnecessarily [KR01].

Notice however that TCP/IP and UDP/IP provide *best-effort* delivery service. For both protocol combinations, this means that there are no guarantees for the end-to-end delay of transmission or variation thereof (jitter). This makes it extremely difficult to develop networked real-time multimedia applications.

**Session, Presentation and Application Layer**

In general, the session layer should provide dialog control and synchronization facilities [TvS02]. The presentation layer further looks at the content of data packets, e.g. for the receiver to notify the sender or for notifying the application about the occurrence of a certain event.

On the application layer, a large variety of different protocols is being employed, such as HTTP [FGM+99], FTP [PR85], or SMTP [Pos82] to name only some. As already mentioned above, the session, presentation, and application layer are often regarded as a single layer. Within the scope of Chapter 4, we will further discuss the requirements imposed for a multimedia architecture to handle a constantly growing number of application layer protocols. For now, we will review a protocol already widely employed in the Internet today.

The Real-Time Transport Protocol (RTP) is a standard for the transmission of multimedia data and other time sensitive data [SCFJ96, Sch]. Usually running on top of UDP, RTP can be either seen as an application layer protocol or as a sublayer of the transport layer because it provides services to multimedia applications. RTP defines a header that (among other information) holds a payload type, sequence number, and timestamp. The payload is used to indicate the data format. The list of all payload types includes the most important formats. Depending on the used format, the data stream is split into consecutive RTP packets, for example by using the division given by MPEG packets. Timestamps and sequence numbers can be used to detect lost packets, to reorder received packets, and to synchronize further processing. Together, the creation of RTP packets is called application level framing.

While RTP is used for data transmission, the RTP Control Protocol (RTCP) allows to periodically send statistics like the number of packets sent, the number of lost packets, and jitter [SCFJ96]. This information is computed from the values given in RTP headers. Applications can then use this information to adapt the data stream, e.g. a sender might choose a higher compression ratio or adjust its sending rate.

While the abilities provided by RTP are important for the development of networked multimedia applications, the same restrictions as for UDP apply since this protocol is commonly used to transport RTP messages.

Although not officially specified, RTP can be considered a session layer protocol within the ISO-OSI protocol stack since it provides control and synchronization mechanisms. Correspondingly, RTCP can be regarded as combined session and presentation layer protocol.

**Multi-Party Communication**

A last property important for networked multimedia application is the ability for multi-party communication where one or more senders deliver packets to a number of receivers. In terms of efficient usage of network bandwidth, this can be achieved by using broadcast or multicast networking (when available, see [KR01]). IP multicast is also supported by RTP.

The lack of widely available multicast infrastructures has led to newer approaches for multi-party communication like application-level multicast. These techniques will be further discussed in Chapter 11.

**Other Standards**

Other important standards that partly cover all layers of the above described protocol stack or use a different layers, are Bluetooth [Blu, IEEb] and UMTS [UMT, 3rd]. As both these technologies also provide the possibility to use IP, they can be seen as augmentations or replacements for other IP networks – although with lower bandwidths, e.g. 723.1 kBit/s for Bluetooth [Wika] and depending on the provider even less with UMTS. Especially interesting for home-networking is the possibility to create ad-hoc networks using Bluetooth.

### 2.2.5   Synchronization

In the scope of this thesis, the term *synchronization* is used to describe temporal relations between media objects or LDUs (see Section 2.2.1). This notion can be further classified.

- *Intra-stream synchronization* refers to the temporal relations between LDUs of the same media stream. An example is the relation between consecutive frames of a video stream with a specified rate of 25 frames per second. In this example, the goal of the intra-stream synchronization would be to reduce jittering as much as possible by trying to present each frame for exactly 40 msec.

- *Inter-stream synchronization* maintains the temporal relations of LDUs of different streams. Here, the goal is to minimize the *skew* (or offset) between corresponding LDUs. A special case thereof is lip synchronization of audio and video from a human speaker.

The actual requirements for synchronization strongly depend on the used media and their combination. Furthermore, the requirements can only be specified by human observers, which makes it necessary to determine bounds by perceptual experiments. Such experiments have shown that for lip-synchronization (and similar audio/video combinations) skews of up to a maximum of +/- 80 msec are tolerable [SN95]. In particular, humans accept larger delays for audio signals since such situations are known from everyday experiences due the difference between the speed of sound and the speed of light.

In general, there are two phases of synchronization. First, temporal relations have to be established. This can be done automatically during capturing of multimedia data or by explicitly specifying timing constraints later on, e.g. by adding an audio track to

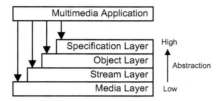

Figure 2.2: Four-layer reference model for synchronization according to [SN95]. The media, stream, object, and specification layer offer different degrees of abstraction. The services provided by each layer are either used in higher-level layers or directly accessed by an application.

a video. Secondly, these relations are used during the presentation of the multimedia data. The term *live synchronization* refers to the goal of exactly reproducing captured temporal relations during the presentation. On the other hand, *synthetic synchroniza-tion* uses explicitly specified timing constraints, e.g. set by a human with a special editing tool.

**Mechanisms for Synchronization**

For performing synchronization for both discrete and continuous media, some tim-ing information needs to be added to the discrete chunks of data. Therefore, in gen-eral *timestamps* are added to LDUs. The generation, modification, and interpretation of timestamps is then performed by the different layers of a synchronization architec-ture.

For both intra-stream synchronization and inter-stream synchronization, these time-stamps are then used to trigger the processing of LDUs at the "correct" time according to some time-line: processing is then delayed until the value of the timestamp corre-sponds to the current value on the time-line. For example for a video stream of 25 frames per second, the presentation is started at a particular time given by the time-stamp of the first frame. Consecutive frames are then displayed for 40 msec each.

As multimedia data streams are delay sensitive, data packets that arrive too late to be processed in time should be discarded in order to be able to process following packets in time. Special care must be taken for late packets of inter-stream encoded multimedia data. For example for an MPEG video stream, if an I-Frames of a group of pictures (GOP) is dropped and discarded, all following P-Frames and B-Frames of this particular GOP cannot be decoded correctly.

**Four-Layer Reference Model**

So far, we have defined synchronization to operate on LDUs. These units can also refer to different abstractions (see Section 2.2.1). In order to further specify the requirements for synchronization, a four-layer reference model was introduced [SN95].

As can be seen in Figure 2.2, the different layers are called *media, stream, object*, and *specification*. The services provided by each layer are either used in higher-level layers or directly within an application. The media layer operates on the sequence of LDUs of a single continuous stream and only offers intra-stream synchronization. The stream layer then extends this model for inter-stream synchronization. Following is the object layer that handles complete, synchronized presentations given in specification languages like SMIL [W3Cc, W3Cb]. Such descriptions were generated within the specification layer that needs to offer corresponding tools like authoring systems.

**Source, Sink, and Stream Synchronization**

Our example setup as shown in Figure 2.1 uses both intra and inter-stream synchronization in live mode. For achieving lip-synchronization, it is important to notice that synchronization is not only performed during playback of multimedia data at PC2, but also during capturing at PC1. This is due to the fact, that in many cases different hardware devices (e.g. the camera plus connected PCI board and the microphone plus connected sound adapter) use different clocks within their hardware design. In general, different clocks are not synchronized and therefore also impose a *drift* that needs to be taken into account. For this reason, the timing relationship between video LDUs and audio LDUs needs to be established explicitly, e.g. by setting corresponding timestamp for both audio and video data chunks.

A drift can also be found between different clocks of devices for outputting multimedia data. To synchronize different streams, LDUs can either be delayed, discarded, or adapted to match the intended presentation time, e.g. chunks of audio data can be "stretched" to compensate for the drift between a clock of a sound adapter, which controls the playback of the audio data, and an other clock.

Furthermore, if both audio and video data are to be transmitted to PC2 as a multiplexed data stream, it is often useful to further synchronize data streams, e.g. by placing corresponding LDUs of the two streams in consecutive transmitted packets. This eases synchronization during presentation. A corresponding operation is for example specified in *Part 1: Systems* of the MPEG standards [ISO98, ISO04a, ISO04b].

**Discussion**

Synchronization is an important aspect of multimedia systems. Correspondingly, a multimedia architecture needs to support source, sink, and stream synchronization. Furthermore, the realization of different synchronization protocols specific for a particular application scenario should be supported.

### 2.2.6   Quality of Service

Besides the pure functionality provided by a certain aspect of a system, the *quality* with which this functionality is provided is also important. This is especially true for multimedia systems that handle delay-sensitive audio and video streams to be consumed by humans. The term *quality of service (QoS)* in general denotes the non-functional properties of a service [BS98]. The most important properties that effect the quality of service are reliability, security, and performance [CDK01]. Within the scope of this work, QoS will mainly be considered as the reliability and performance of a service. Furthermore, the way a service can adapt to changing system configurations is also an important part of service quality [Bir97].

According to [BS98], quality of service management consists of static aspects like QoS specification, negotiation, admission control, and resource reservation, and more dynamic aspects like QoS monitoring, maintenance, and renegotiation.

- QoS specification: provides appropriate means for specifying QoS requirements in form of a QoS contract.

- QoS negotiation: in this step, the precise values of all QoS parameters are negotiated. As a result of this process, the contract can either be fulfilled or is rejected.

- Admission control: determines, whether the system can deliver the requested resources at that particular time.

- Resource reservation: follows the admission control; reservations for resources are performed during this step.

- QoS monitoring: checks the resources needed for achieving a certain QoS; monitors if the negotiated QoS can be achieved and reports discrepancies.

- QoS maintenance: tries to keep a certain QoS level by performing specific operations.

- QoS renegotiation: if QoS monitoring reports that the QoS contract is broken, renegotiation can be performed in order to adapt to the new situation.

In order to achieve a certain quality of service, required devices plus necessary processing and networking resources need to be available at the appropriate times. We will further examine, how – or, if at all – this can be realized considering the underlying infrastructure as described in the previous sections.

### Hard and Soft Real-Time Constraints

The QoS aspect of performance refers to the fact that multimedia systems handle high-bandwidth and computational expensive streams of data with *real-time* constraints (compare the notion of a real-time application in Section 2.1.3). In this context, real-time describes the fact that a process delivers the result in a given time-span [SN95].

Real-time constraints are either classified *hard* or *soft*. Hard deadlines need to be kept in order for a system to work properly, e.g. for controlling an air-bag. For multimedia system, soft real-time constraints apply. In the best case, an unmet deadlines is not even noticeable to humans, e.g. like a single video frame that arrived 20 msec too late and is therefore not presented. In other cases, these violations can lead to a decreased quality of the presentation as perceived by a user, e.g. dropped audio samples are easily noticeable for human listeners.

### Layered Reference Model

In [Ste00], a layered reference model for QoS management is described. As can be seen in Figure 2.3, QoS management operates on different levels: user, application,

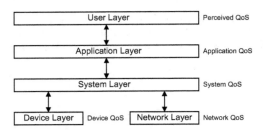

Figure 2.3: Quality of Service (QoS) reference model according to [Ste00]. Specifications of perceived QoS at the user layer are mapped to the lower layers application, system, device, or network. These mappings can also be performed from bottom to top.

system, device, and network. Furthermore, appropriate mappings between the different layers exist. While users will specify QoS in terms of "best possible quality for this device", the application handles such a specification as a certain multimedia data format, e.g. 25 fps, resolution of 720 by 576 pixel in YV12 color space. This format is then mapped to the system layer where it requires a certain utilization of resources. Furthermore, networking bandwidth might be needed for receiving or sending multimedia data. Finally, resources of devices need to be allocated, e.g. a certain memory area of a display adapter needs to be reserved in order to be able to render the video frames with the specified resolution and color space.

All these mappings can be done from higher to lower layers or the other way round. In this sense, a certain device capability could restrict the quality of service as perceived by a user to "poor quality".

**Operating System Support for QoS**

Although a lot of research been done in the area of real-time operating systems and multimedia support for operating systems, today's commodity operating systems for PCs and also for many mobile devices like PDAs do not provide features needed for handling multimedia with strict QoS guarantees. One can say, that these systems still only offer best-effort services: resources like memory and computational power are shared by all competing processes. In general, main memory can be swapped to secondary memory, which increases access times by several magnitudes. Processes can – if at all – be divided into different priority classes that get assigned processing time differently.

Although many devices specifically made for multimedia home-entertainment use real-time operating systems like RT-Linux [Yod], these approaches still suffer from limitations. For example, the main memory that can be used within real-time processes is restricted to the kernel memory. Copying between real-time memory and general purpose memory is not subject to real-time scheduling.

### QoS for Multimedia Devices

In contrast to commodity operating systems running on PCs, specified QoS parameters can often be *guaranteed* to be met for specific multimedia devices. For example, a camera connected to a PC via IEEE 1394 can use an isochronous transmission mode that will guarantee a certain bandwidth, e.g. for receiving full-motion and high-resolution video.

However, if these devices are connected to a PC that does not offer a real-time operating system (see above), the QoS settings still often cannot be achieved. For example, the high bandwidth of the stream between the memory of the device driver and the main memory of the operating system can be too resource intensive. If this is the case, frames that are not processed fast enough will simply be discarded by the device driver.

Another example is a video adapter that could in principle render video frames without any jittering. This adapter is still triggered by its corresponding device driver within the host's operating system. Therefore, no strict frame rate can be guaranteed – the main reason why commodity PC technology is up to today not used in production-quality video studios [Khr01b]. Upcoming standards like OpenML, especially the OpenMLdc subsystem, try to overcome these limitations [Opeb, How01]. OpenML will be discussed in more detail in Section 2.5.

### Network QoS

Different approaches for QoS in networks have been proposed so far. IntServ [BCS94] and its corresponding signalling protocol for reservation, RSVP [BZB$^+$97, Wro97], can provide hard, mathematical provable guarantees on the delay of data packets. As this comes at the price of maintaining per-flow state in routers, the DiffServ [BBC$^+$98] architectures was proposed that operates at the "edges" of the network and therefore can only offer different traffic classes. Another approach is Multiprotocol Label Switching (MPLS) [RVC01] that is especially used by Internet Service Providers (ISP) in order to divert and route network traffic based on labels that identify different data-stream types.

However, today's commonly available networking infrastructure mainly still operates at best-effort. This is especially true for commodity networks used in the area of multimedia home networking like Ethernet LANs or 802.11 WLANs. Bandwidth can not be reserved and throughput cannot be guaranteed. Similarly, there are no guarantees for end-to-end delays. Observed jittering is also not bounded. Finally, packets can not be assumed to arrive ordered at the receiver; they might even get lost (compare Section 2.2.4).

## 2.3   From Best-Effort to Predictable QoS

On the one hand, the discussion in Section 2.2.6 shows that *guaranteed* QoS can by far not be realized with the technological infrastructure available today. On the other hand, multimedia systems certainly need QoS since they handle high bandwidth continuous data streams that impose real-time requirements.

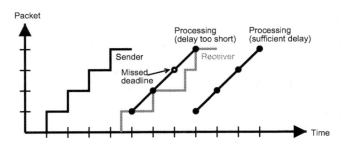

Figure 2.4: Removing jitter: By buffering packets at the receiving side, the varying delay of a communication channel can be hidden and all deadlines for the processing of data can be fulfilled. This comes at the price of additional buffer space and delay [KR01].

Together, two different extremes to overcome this problem have been discussed over the last years. One can argue that end-to-end QoS needs to be realized by making fundamental changes in the underlying infrastructure. The other extreme follows the concept of over-provisioning. By simply adding abundant resources, QoS can be made available.

Both these approaches are followed today. However, instead of providing *guaranteed* or *over-provisioned best-effort* QoS, the realization of *predictable* QoS with the underlying best-effort mechanisms seems to be worthwhile. Predictable QoS can be achieved by different approaches. First, the drawbacks of best-effort services can partly be hidden by additional concepts. Secondly, adaptation to the currently available resources can further help to provide acceptable behavior of applications – even when only weak QoS guarantees are provided by the infrastructure.

### 2.3.1   Hiding Best-Effort

Different techniques such as buffering, prefetching, forward error correction, or interleaving can be used to hide the drawbacks of best-effort services. Furthermore, traffic shaping allows to control and restrict bandwidth requirements.

**Buffering**

As described in Section 2.2, with today's technological infrastructures, communication channels used for streaming data can in general suffer from jittering and loss of data.

To establish timing relations, timestamps and sequence numbers are used within logical data units (LDUs) like multimedia data buffers (see Section 2.4.3) or packet header fields of protocols like RTP (see Section 2.2.4).

While the sending side of a communication channel emits data packets with a certain rate these packets arrive at the receiver with varying delay. To hide the jitter imposed by the communication channel, *buffering* at the receiver side can be used. By delaying the further processing of packets by a certain interval, the constant rate of the sender can be reproduced. Figure 2.4 shows this process.

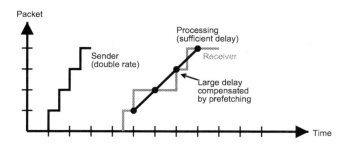

Figure 2.5: Removing jitter by prefetching: By artificially increasing the sending (and therefore the receiving) rate, the varying delay of a communication channel can be hidden and all deadlines for processing data can be fulfilled. This technique requires the ability to artificially increase the sending rate (e.g. for stored media), temporary higher bandwidth, and additional buffer space [KR01].

Buffering needs additional resources like main memory at the receiver sides. Furthermore, for choosing a fixed delay, the maximum jitter of the communication channel must be known or estimated. However, there is certainly a trade-off between the delay and the number of packets that arrive too late and are therefore discarded: a large delay will allow a large number of packets to arrive in time but could destroy the interactive nature of the application. Therefore, more sophisticated approaches adaptively vary the delay [RKTS94].

### Prefetching

Another technique that can be used to hide the effects of jitter is *prefetching*. Here, the sending side of a communication channel temporarily increases its outgoing rate when extra bandwidth and additional buffer storage at the receiving side is available (compare Figure 2.5). The ability to artificially increase the sending rate is only available for certain kinds of interaction, e.g. for streaming stored media. It also requires additional coordination between the receiving side and the sending side.

### Hiding Unreliability

Unreliable communication channels may either lose data packets or change the order of data packets received. Due to timing constraints of multimedia data, retransmission or reordering can destroy the real-time requirements imposed. Therefore, loss recovery schemes can be used. *Forward Error Correction (FEC)* adds redundant information to the original stream in order to increase the chance of reconstruction lost packets. Different media-dependent or media-independent FEC mechanisms have been proposed so far [KR01, PHH98].

FEC mechanisms increase the needed bandwidth. Alternatively, different *interleaving* schemes can be used. These approaches resequence adjacent chunks of data before transmitting several reordered chunks within one packet. The receiver then needs to reorder the data. Therefore, interleaving techniques increase the delay of a communication channel. Correspondingly, additional buffer storage and processing time is needed. A lost packet of an interleaved stream results in several small gaps in the reconstructed data stream – whereas a lost packet in a non-interleaved stream would result in a single large gap. Depending on the used data format, several small gaps are more tolerable or can be reconstructed from adjacent data.

**Traffic Shaping**

As described in Section 2.2.1, multimedia data streams are often bursty. This is especially true for inter-stream encoded formats like MPEG video [ISO98, ISO04a, ISO04b]. If the bandwidth requirements for a stream vary over time, traffic shaping techniques can be used to smooth the data flow [CDK01]. This has two advantages. First, the varying (and unknown) bandwidth requirements of the original stream become controllable. Secondly, by using additional scaling techniques described in Section 2.3.2, a predefined maximum bandwidth can be specified.

In general traffic shaping is realized by using a buffer at the sending side of the communication channel and an algorithm that defines which data elements leave the buffer at which time.

The *leaky bucket* method for traffic shaping uses a first-in-first-out buffer of size B. This buffer can be filled arbitrarily until it is full. Data leaves the buffer with rate R. This guarantees that the data flow will never flow with a rate higher than R. Furthermore, bursts of a maximum size B can be handled by this method.

While the leaky bucket method completely eliminates bursts, the *token bucket* method provides an upper bound of the bandwidth: tokens are generated at rate R and collected in a bucket of size B. Data of size S can be sent by taking S tokens out of the bucket. The peak bandwidth is therefore limited by B.

Similar to prefetching described above, traffic shaping requires additional buffer storage and is only partly applicable for interactive applications or streaming of captured live sources.

**Discussion**

The described methods for hiding best-effort services are certainly useful and mostly straight forward to realize. However, the diversity of different approaches, e.g. for media-dependent FEC, demands architectural support for the easy control and integration of new algorithms.

## 2.3.2   Adaptation

As discussed in Section 2.2.6, quality of service (QoS) cannot be guaranteed for the infrastructures we are focusing on in the scope of this work. Therefore, besides trying to achieve predictable QoS by using the above described methods, adaptation is another fundamental approach for handling varying QoS levels. These variations can either by explicit or implicit: a user of the system can explicitly request for a different QoS; or the resources needed to achieve a certain QoS can vary implicitly, either because handling the multimedia data requires varying resources (and this effect cannot be hidden by the above mentioned techniques), or the load of the overall system changed –

a common situation for multi-user multi-tasking environments. Together, multimedia applications need to be able to adapt to these variations.

In general, it is more useful to adapt multimedia data streams at the sources of data: adapting data streams before they enter the system has much more influence on resource requirements. Different *scaling* techniques can be used [CDK01, Ste00]. All these techniques are media-dependent. For video streams, following techniques can be used.

- Temporal scaling reduces the number of samples in the time domain, e.g. by dropping frames of a video stream.

- Spatial scaling subsamples in the spatial domain, e.g. by reducing the x and y-resolution of a video frame.

- Frequency scaling increases the compression ratio by using less frequencies of an image transformed to frequency domain, e.g. by using fewer coefficients of the transformation used.

- Amplitudinal scaling reduces the depths of different color channels of an image, e.g. by requantization of coefficients.

- Color space scaling reduces the number of entries in the color space, e.g. by removing chrominance channels from an image.

Similar techniques can be applied to compressed or uncompressed audio streams, respectively.

Further adaptation techniques include *splitting* and *conversion* [PSG00]. Splitting separates different media from the original stream and allows to process each medium individually. For example, an audio/video stream can be split into audio and video. Then, only audio could be presented; video could be discarded in order to reduce resource consumption. Media conversion such as text-to-speech or speech-to-text can be used to adapt content to the capabilities of available devices.

Finally, hierarchical coding schemes for video frames process the original data using different resolutions. While such approaches require additional computational resources during encoding and more bandwidth for the transmission of encoded data, they allow to adaptively reduce the requirements during decoding by only accessing low-resolution versions of encoded frames [Ste00].

**Discussion**

On the one hand, scaling can be seen as a special QoS maintenance operation (compare 2.2.6). This is certainly true for simple techniques like dropping single video frames. On the other hand, scaling could also require a complete QoS renegotiation. For example, scaling can require to decode a data stream and encode it again. This step requires additionally components to be set up.

## 2.4   Common Abstractions

After examining the characteristics of multimedia systems, we will now identify the abstractions commonly used within multimedia architectures. These abstractions al-

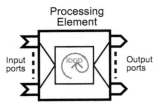

Figure 2.6: A generic processing element with several input and output ports. The main loop either generates data or pulls data from input ports. After data is processed, it will be forwarded to output ports or consumed.

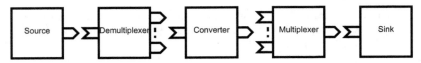

Figure 2.7: Different types of processing elements can be distinguished according to the number of input and output ports: source, demultiplexer, converter, multiplexer, and sink element

low applications to access multimedia devices or to create configurations for processing components.

### 2.4.1 Processing Elements

As can be seen from the description of the characteristics of multimedia systems, there exits a large variety of different multimedia devices and media operations. Therefore, this specific functionality is encapsulated in basic processing elements. The main idea behind this concept is to provide generic access to all these different operations and to allow different elements to be connected.

Each elements offers a certain number of input and outputs ports (see Figure 2.6). The main loop of a processing element then either generates data itself or pulls data from its input ports. Operations like transformation, multiplexing, or demultiplexing of data can be performed within a processing element. Finally, data is either forwarded to output ports or consumed by the element itself.

Processing elements can be distinguished according to the number of inputs and outputs (see Figure 2.7). Source elements only offer outgoing ports, sinks only incoming ports. Arbitrary transformations require one or more input and one or more output ports. Typical conversion elements have a single input and output, respectively. Multiplexing operations require several inputs and only a single output. Correspondingly, demultiplexing elements provide a single input and several outputs.

The names for the basic processing elements differ between different architectures as we will see in proceeding sections. Furthermore, different granularities are used. A single multimedia devices can either be represented by several independent processing elements or by only a single element that provides different functionalities.

Figure 2.8: A simple flow graph for the playback of MPEG encoded audio: compressed audio data is read from a file by the FileReader element, then forwarded to the MPEGAudioDecoder element where it is decoded, then forwarded to and played out by the AudioOutput element.

## 2.4.2 Flow Graphs

In order to realize a certain functionality, several processing elements are connected to a directed graph, a so called *flow graph*. The edges within this graph then specify the streaming data connections. Correspondingly, the overall setup of such a flow graph represents a certain multimedia operation.

Multimedia data is then generated at source elements. By forwarding data from output ports to connected input ports, streaming data connections between connected elements are created. Multimedia streams are then transformed, multiplexed, or demultiplexed, and finally consumed at sink elements. The data flow from output ports to input ports of elements is referred to as *downstream*. Notice, that a flow graph can also be cyclic. Additionally, *upstream* data flow could also be possible. Conceptually this results in two edges between elements: one is directed downstream; the other directed upstream. Input and output ports can then be used to receive or send data.

Obviously, connecting two elements should only be allowed for *matching* input and output ports. In this case, matching refers to the fact that the format of the outgoing stream is compatible to a format that is supported by the input port.

A flow graph based design approach offers a number of benefits [SG96]. First of all, the elements within a flow graph act independently. As a consequence, this approach naturally supports parallel and distributed processing. Furthermore, its modularity allows to reuse the functionality provided by a certain processing element within different setups. Therefore, it is important that elements represent very fine-grained processing units. In addition, new capabilities can be provided by developing new elements and inserting them into flow graphs. Finally, flow graphs provide a very simple and intuitive model, which allows to set up even complex configurations easily.

Notice that the concept of a flow graph is not restricted to handling multimedia data. Other "pipelined" tasks can also be realized with this approach, e.g. modular router architectures [KMC+00].

Figure 2.8 gives an example of a simple flow graph. Three elements are connected: a source that reads data from a file, e.g. MPEG2 Layer 3 audio (*FileReader*). Data is forwarded to a decoder (*MPEGAudioDecoder*). Within this element, data is decompressed and then forwarded to a sink node that outputs the data, e.g. by using a sound board (*AudioOutput*).

### 2.4.3   Data Encapsulation

Although multimedia systems handle continuous streams, data is transported within discrete chunks of data (compare Section 2.2.1). Furthermore, timestamps are needed for synchronization (see Section 2.2.5). Therefore, *multimedia data buffers*, or simply *buffers*, are commonly used. Such a buffer typically references a chunk of memory that contains the multimedia data. An additional header includes information like a corresponding timestamp or meta-information like the specific data format.

Although the largest part of a data stream consists of buffers, often additional control information needs to be forwarded between processing elements. This is for example the case, if a data streams ends. Then, the sending side is informed about this fact (since this side stopped streaming), but the receiving side needs to be notified as well – otherwise it cannot distinguish between a delay of data buffers or the final end of a stream. Therefore, streaming data connection should be able to transmit control information as well. This makes is possible to send control information like an "end-of-stream" messages downstream to receiving processing elements.

## 2.5   Examples for Multimedia Architectures

This section will review today's commonly used multimedia architectures. As already mentioned, all these approaches adopt a centralized approach. All multimedia processing is restricted to a single host. The network is only used as source or sink of data.

### 2.5.1   Industry Approaches

DirectShow [Mica] from Microsoft is the most widely available architecture and therefore reviewed first. Then, the Java Media Framework [Sun99] is presented. As the general design approaches of all locally operating multimedia architectures are very similar, only their main concepts and their differences will be high-lighted. In addition, the emerging industry standard OpenML [Opeb] will be briefly introduced.

#### DirectShow

DirectShow is a multimedia architecture developed by Microsoft [Mica]. It was first introduced in 1995 under the name ActiveMovie [CH98]. Being part of the DirectX architecture [Micc], DirectShow is by now part of all recent operating systems from Microsoft. It is used as underlying framework for the applications MediaPlayer and MovieMaker.

DirectX is a collection of low-level libraries (DirectX Foundation) and high-level architectures like DirectShow (DirectX Media Layer). The Component Object Model (COM) is used as underlying object model for DirectX [Mice]. COM mainly provides encapsulation for reusable code objects. Interfaces are specified independently of their realization with a concrete implementation language. Consequently, DirectShow can be seen as a specification of a standard set of COM interfaces together with an implementation for Windows operating systems.

DirectShow uses the design approach described in Section 2.4. *Filters* can be connected by their specific input and output *pins* to form a *filter graph*. Filters are divided into source, transform, or renderer filters. The implementation of filters is closely tied to other technologies like the Windows Driver Model (WDM) and other DirectX architectures like DirectDraw or DirectSound [Micc].

Upon connecting an output with an input pin, a negotiation process is executed that determines a connection format and a transport mechanism; finally an allocator is created for one of the pins. Formats are described with *majortype* and *subtype*. More specific information about the data format is stored as an unique identifier called *formattype*. A dynamically allocated block of memory then contains information specific to the given type [Pes03]. DirectShow also offers a procedure called *Intelligent Connect* that allows to setup incomplete filter graphs, e.g. by adding additional converters [Micb]. This algorithm will be described in Section 10.

The transport mechanism to be established during connection setup is either *local memory transport* or *hardware transport*. Hardware transport refers to the usage of dedicated memory in hardware like a video board. Local memory transport uses the main memory of the system. Transport is done in *push* or *pull* mode meaning that data is either forwarded from an output pin to an input pin, or explicitly requested from by an input pin, respectively. Finally, the allocator provides a pool of buffers and manages streaming by copying data from one pool to another (see [Pes03], page 192).

The basic operations to be performed on a filter graph object are run, pause, and stop. While pause only halts the current streaming, the stop command additionally flushes the buffer space within the filter graph. For synchronization, a software based clock is used. Often this clock internally uses the hardware clock of a sound adapter because the timing of audio processing is very sensitive. Furthermore, sound adapters usually provide the most accurate internal clock.

**Java Media Framework**

The Java Media Framework (JMF) is a specification and reference implementation originally developed by Sun Microsystems, Silicon Graphics, and Intel Corporation. Starting with version 2.0, JMF was developed by Sun Microsystems and IBM.

The Java Media Framework is a multimedia architecture that allows to incorporate time-based media into Java applications and applets [Sun99]. The framework provides support for capturing, storing, playback, and custom processing of multimedia data. JMF can be extended by developing additional plug-ins. Although the core architecture of JMF is developed in Java, separate platform packages are available that natively implement resource intensive parts.

JMF also uses a flow graph based approach. However, the architecture provides several distinct entities [Kur01]. A *Data Source* is the origin of multimedia data like a file or incoming stream from the Internet. Such a source is either a *push* or *pull* source (compare push/pull operations within DirectShow described above). When connected to a Data Source, a *Player* renders the stream of media data. While this possibly includes demultiplexing and decoding, a Player does not provide control over any processing it performs. A *Processor* is a specialized Player that allows to control the actual processing. This is split into several optional stages: demultiplexing, preprocessing, transcoding, postprocessing, multiplexing, and rendering. For each stage, different *Plug-ins* can be chosen for the different media tracks, e.g. in form of a *codec chain*. The output of a Processor can then be used as source of data again. Finally, a *Data Sink* can be connected to a Data Source and is then used to to "consume" data. Notice, that an element for rendering audio or video is modeled as a Plug-in not a Data Sink.

Multimedia data formats are modeled by several subclasses of the type Format. When a Player is created for a certain Data Source, a negotiation process is used to find suitable demultiplexer and decoders. This algorithm will be described in Section 10.

The JMF already provides support for RTP/RTCP [SCFJ96], and RTSP [SRL98] for streaming data connections. Furthermore, with the JMF RTP API, this part of the architecture can be extended (e.g. with custom packetizers or depacketizers) similar to the way in which new multimedia devices or codecs can be integrated. While Direct-Show does not provide such an architecture originally, a similar research prototype is described in [CDK+98].

### OpenML

The Open Media Library, or OpenML, provides a specification and implementations for a cross-platform standard programming environment that can be used to capture, process, render and synchronize digital media like 2D and 3D graphics, audio, and video [Opeb, How01]. Developed by the Khronos Group, a group that represents several companies, OpenML especially aims at providing a portable, reliable and well-documented, royalty and licensing free standard.

OpenML is a low-level standard. For example, memory management is not part of the standard. While the specification of a cross-platform standard for multimedia is certainly desirable, OpenML needs additional services to provide an architecture similar to DirectShow or JMF. The main objectives of the OpenML API are as follows [Khr01a].

- Support for streaming communication between an application and different devices. This includes buffering mechanisms.

- Provision of processing capabilities for media streams.

- Device control and querying of device capabilities.

- Provision of synchronization mechanisms.

OpenML makes use of other specifications and technologies. SGI's dmSDK 2.0 [CM96] lays the foundations of the input/output component of OpenML. For controlling display devices, SGI's Xdc extension was chosen as basis for MLdc. Furthermore, extensions to the OpenGL graphics standard [Opea] are used to further integrate graphics and video. Finally, synchronization primitives are included into the OpenML standard.

### Discussion

Other relevant multimedia architectures comparable to DirectShow or JMF are Quick-Time SDK [App] and RealMedia SDK [Reab]. The RealMedia SDK is by now called

Helix SDK. Some parts of it were made available under a restricted Open Source license in October 2002 [Hei02]; the Helix Player was first made available under the GPL in August 2004 [Hei04]. The QuickTime SDK comes together with the QuickTime container format that was chosen as basis for MPEG-4. Similar to DirectShow and JMF, both architectures also employ an approach were multimedia applications are composed out of a set of connected components. Together, all these architecture adopt a centralized approach, where – seen from an application – all processing is restricted to a single host. Networking is only performed using a client/server approach.

While the described standard OpenML is by now available for different platforms, it only provides a relatively low level of abstraction and can therefore only be used as building block for a full featured multimedia architecture; networking is not addressed.

### 2.5.2 Open Source Approaches

**Multimedia Applications**

For Open Source operating systems like GNU/Linux, there exists a large variety of different application for handling multimedia, in particular for playing back multimedia. Many of the media player applications available as Open Source have reached a maturity equivalent to commercial applications. According to freshmeat.net [frec], the three most popular Open Source media players are Mplayer [Mpl], xine [Xina], and xmms [xmm].

In general, these applications are able to playback a large number of different media formats. A plug-in concept is used to allow for adding new functionality, e.g. to support a new codec or output device. Often, such a functionality is realized by using an external library.

While the architecture of such a media player application needs to provide features like synchronization, the overall architectural design is often restricted to the special case of media playback and can not be used for creating arbitrary flow graphs. As an example, the architecture of the xine application consists of a stream layer, which includes input layer, demuxer layer, stream FIFOs, decoder layer, and an output layer [Xinb]. Specific plug-ins like a video decoder then run within a video decoder loop as part of the decoder layer.

Other application available as Open Source that are widely used support operations like audio processing and filtering. Yet other applications provide audio and video streaming clients and servers for multiparty multimedia conferencing in the Internet using the overlay network provided by the Multicast backbone, or Mbone [Nat96, Elk96].

To summarize: Due to the lack of a common multimedia framework for Open Source operating system, available applications mostly employ a monolithic design that is not based on a full-featured multimedia architecture.

**Multimedia Architectures**

During the last years, the need for a unified multimedia architecture for Open Source operating systems has been identified. Until today, there are several competing projects that aim at developing a locally running architecture. Some approaches, such as ALSA [Adv], aRts and artsd [aRt], EsounD [Eso], or jack [jac], focus on providing a sound server that provides uniform access to various audio devices together with mixing operations for concurrently running applications. Other architectures, such as the Simple DirectMedia Layer (SDL) [Sim], are designed to offer access to different hardware, such as audio devices and 2D or 3D video devices.

While these approaches only address certain requirements that need to be fulfilled by a locally operating full-featured multimedia architecture, VideoLAN [Vidb] and GStreamer [GSt] aim at developing generic multimedia frameworks. Since both architectures employ similar concepts and have reached similar levels of maturity, only one of them, namely GStreamer, will be described in more detail in the following.

**GStreamer**

GStreamer is an Open Source project that aims at creating a framework for creating locally operating streaming media applications [GSt]. The basic architectural design originates from the video pipeline at Oregon Graduate Institute and Direct-Show [TBW04, BWB$^+$04]. The GLib object model is used, which allows to employ inheritance using the mechanisms provided by GObject [GLi].

Again, a flow graph based approach is taken: *elements* that provide *source pads* and *sink pads* can be linked together to form a *pipeline*. Pads provide capabilities that provide a name, a MIME type, and a set of properties that hold further information. These capabilities can be queried during run-time. Signals can be used to control objects, e.g. to set a filename of a source element by calling a function for a particular element that takes the string "location" and another string that carries the filename.

Setting up pipelines is eased by a mechanism comparable to DirectShow's Intelligent Connect that is called *Autoplugging*, respectively a specific element called *Spider*. The algorithms used will be further explained in Chapter 10.

For hierarchically structuring flow graphs, so called *bins* are used. Specialized bins are *threads* and *pipelines*. A pipeline is the top-level structure that needs to be present at least once. Threads are bins that run in a separate thread of execution, e.g. in a separate thread within the operating system. In order to connect two flow graphs encapsulated within a thread bin, a queueing element that supports concurrent access needs to be inserted manually. These queueing elements are also needed – and have to be placed carefully within the flow graph – in order to allow for synchronized processing of multimedia data. Further information on synchronization methods are not available from the documentation of GStreamer.

Receiving data from or sending data to the network is intended to be realized with specific elements. An architecture comparable to JMF's RTP framework is not available for GStreamer. Furthermore, a mature implementation of these networking elements was only made available recently in late 2004 – for example, single compressed video frames could not be transmitted before [GSt04].

## 2.6   Summary

Multimedia systems need to handle high-bandwidth data streams. Furthermore, multimedia systems can be best characterized by a constantly growing variety and heterogeneity in all design dimensions.

Different multimedia devices with diverse and incompatible underlying technology and interfaces need to be integrated. Various processing options, like different codecs, require large amounts of computational and networking resources. The characteristics of different networking technologies need to be taken into account.

Often the processing of these streams imposes soft real-time constraints. As the processing of multimedia data is very delay sensitive, quality of service mechanisms need to be provided. However, as today's infrastructures often operate at best-effort, different alternative approaches are needed to be able to provide at least a predictable quality of service.

As new techniques and approaches emerge continuously in these different areas, a multimedia software architecture needs to be easily extensible and – at the same time – provide uniform access to the different components. Therefore, often the concept of a flow graph of simple processing elements with streaming data connections between these elements is used.

Today, media player applications – also the ones provided as Open Source – are able to playback nearly all available media formats. While commercially available media players are often built on top of a general purpose multimedia architecture (like in the case of the Windows MediaPlayer built on top of DirectShow), most Open Source approaches still adopt a monolithic application design. These applications offer a plug-in concept that allows to integrate new codecs or output devices but the restricted architectural design cannot be applied to other tasks. Sometimes even the provided plug-ins are so tightly coupled to the application design that they cannot be used in other setups.

Then, there are a lot of different locally operating multimedia architectures available. They provide a number of benefits. At the best, following features are available.

- Flow graph based architecture: These approaches provide general-purpose multimedia architectures that support the creation of locally running streaming multimedia applications.

- Unified access: Different multimedia devices and software routines are encapsulated in basic processing elements.

- Extensibility: New elements can be developed easily by implementing specific functionality within the plug-in concept provided by the architecture.

- Synchronization: Synchronized processing is supported for capturing and playback of multimedia data.

- Connection setup: Setup of flow graphs is eased by providing automatic connection procedures.

- Networking: Often, the network can be used as source or sink of data by using specific processing elements.

- Support: Finally, these architectures often provide support for a large number of multimedia devices, file formats, codecs, and processing routines.

While all these points were certainly already true for the commercially available architectures when we started our work in the beginning of 2001, Linux was still lacking a decent multimedia architecture at that time.

However, none of the above mentioned architectures provides the specific networking functionality as identified as goal for our work. At best, existing architectures allow to realize typical client/server application scenarios – a design approach that does not provide the capabilities needed to realize complex distributed setups as discussed in Section 1.2.

At most, such a locally operating architecture could be used as basis for our approach, but would require far reaching modifications and extensions. Unfortunately, at the beginning of our project, the solutions that provided the maturity needed were not available as Open Source. A special case is the Java Media Framework (JMF) that is released under the Sun Community Source Licensing (SCSL). However, this license is very restrictive. For example, modified source code cannot be distributed without the written permission of Sun and new public methods or classes may not be added [Sunc]. Furthermore, the Linux version of the JMF was not considered to provide the needed performance at the beginning of our project. Other promising approaches were simply not available at that time. For example, the first alpha version of an implementation of the OpenML specification was released in July 2003 [Opeb].

Some Open Source multimedia architectures allow for controlling and combining distributed processing elements, in particular, aRts [aRt] as underlying framework for artsd used for KDE [KDE], and the recently emerged MediaApplicationServer (MAS) [Shi]. The architectural elements of these approaches allowing for distributed multimedia will be further described in the scope of Chapter 4. However, both approaches only provide limited functionality, mostly for handling audio only. Furthermore, the first version of MAS was made available in late 2001.

Because of these reasons, we decided to start a completely independent approach. The developed multimedia architecture should not only provide the architecture for network-integrated multimedia but also serve as a locally running solution that allows for other existing architectures to be integrated.

# Chapter 3

# Foundations of Distributed Systems

The field of distributed systems and middleware is introduced in this chapter by first defining the important terms in this area. In particular, the role of a middleware in this context will be described. Then, the goals and the imposed requirements for a middleware supporting distributed computing are pointed out. This is followed by the introduction of common abstractions and design approaches to fulfill the identified requirements. The chapter ends with a review of different technologies and standards for distributed object computing.

To help focus on the key requirements for distributed computing, we will restrict this introduction to approaches that do not cover the handling of multimedia.

## 3.1 Terminology

### 3.1.1 Distributed System

According to [CDK01], a *distributed system* can be defined as:

> A distributed system is one in which components at networked computers communicate and coordinate their actions only by passing messages.

A more precise definition is given by [BS98]:

> A distributed system is a system designed to support the development of applications and services which can exploit a physical architecture consisting of multiple, autonomous processing elements that do not share primary memory but cooperate by sending asynchronous messages over a communications network.

Here, the term *autonomous* is important. It distinguishes a distributed system from tightly coupled specialized approaches like parallel hardware architectures or distributed multicomputer operating systems. Despite the fact that these specialized architectures might provide several benefits, as a matter of fact, today's infrastructure consists of independent hosts that run commodity operating systems.

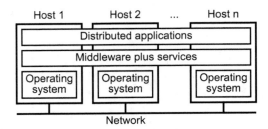

Figure 3.1: A distributed system realized as middleware that resides between the operating system and the applications. Applications can use the core functionality and the additional services provided by the middleware layer to implement distributed applications. The middleware masks out the heterogeneity in terms of network and machine technologies, operating systems, and programming languages [TvS02].

Another important generalization is the fact that a distributed system not necessarily consists of networked computers. Even independent processes that run on a single system and do not share the same address space can be regarded as a distributed system. In the following, the terms *distributed* or *remote* will be also used for this case.

The second definition also includes the notion of *asynchronous* communication, which in this context means that no assumptions about the time intervals involved in any execution (like processing or networking delays) are allowed (compare [BS98], page 4, or [CDK01], page 51).

Another definition of a distributed system stresses the fact that the compound of networked computers should be accessible transparently [TvS02]:

> A distributed system is a collection of independent computers that appears
> to its users as a single coherent system.

In the following, these three possible definitions together will be used to characterize a distributed system.

### 3.1.2　Middleware

Today, many distributed systems are realized using *middleware* that is defined as follows [BCP03].

> The role of middleware is to ease the task of designing, programming and
> managing distributed applications by providing a simple, consistent and
> integrated distributed programming environment. Essentially, middleware
> is a distributed software layer, which abstracts over the complexity and
> heterogeneity of the underlying distributed environment with its multitude
> of network technologies, machine architectures, operating systems and
> programming languages.

For autonomous systems, this definition positions middleware in between applications and the operating systems (see Figure 3.1).

Additionally, the term middleware is closely related with the idea of *services*. In this context, a service is a distinct additional functionality that fulfills a certain requirement within the programming model of the middleware [HV99].

As a middleware resides between the operating system and the applications, it can be regarded as the session and presentation layer (layer 5 and 6) of the ISO-OSI architecture as described in Section 2.2.4.

The following sections will further identify the challenges for middleware, the programming models derived from these requirements, and the services needed to fulfill the goals of distributed systems as stated in the above definitions.

## 3.2 Challenges for Distributed Systems

### 3.2.1 Goals

According to [CDK01, BS98, TvS02], a number of goals for distributed systems can be identified and will be reviewed in the following in regard to their relevance for this thesis. The most important goal is to allow *sharing of resources* by enabling access to possibly remote entities. Consequently, this capability also supports *connecting users* to perform collaborative activities.

Due to possibly redundant resources within a distributed system, a higher level of *availability* can be achieved. Despite the fact that networking communication introduces additional delay, *performance* for each individual application can still be improved by using remote resources.

A further benefit is the capability to extend a distributed system in various ways. On the one hand, the overall system performance can be *scaled* by adding additional resources. To realize this, both the distributed system and the applications running on top of it has to be designed in a scalable way. On the other hand, even the *integration of additional new functionalities* should be possible to realize.

### 3.2.2 General Requirements

While the benefits of distributed systems are manifold, they also impose a number of challenges. In order to explore the possibilities given, resources and processes in a distributed environment need to be *located* and *accessed*. This is particular demanding, if entities are allowed to *migrate* between different hosts. Furthermore, for accessing remote entities, an understanding of the means and possibilities for controlling them is needed, e.g. by sending a specific message of a particular protocol to a remote component using a supported networking technology.

In addition to this, resources in a distributed environment are typically accessed *concurrently*. Other challenges for distributed systems are the provision of *secure, fault-tolerant* services.

### 3.2.3 Transparency

To achieve these goals, a distributed system – or a middleware that realizes such a system – needs to fulfill several requirements. First of all, the fact that the resources and processes are physically distributed across multiple hosts in the network and all implications of this fact should be hidden from applications and users. This is in general referred to as *transparency*. While the concept of transparency is needed in order to ease the task of developing distributed applications, different aspects can be distinguished.

- *Access transparency* hides the differences in how a local or remote resource is accessed.

- *Location transparency* hides the physical location of a resource.

- *Migration transparency* hides the fact that a resource may move to another location.

- *Relocation transparency* hides the fact that a resource may move to another location while in use. This is also called mobility transparency.

- *Concurrency transparency* hides that a resource is used by several competitive tasks.

- *Performance transparency* hides the reconfigurations of the system to improve performance when load varies.

- *Failure transparency* hides the failure and recovery of a resource.

- *Replication transparency* hides the fact that multiple instances of a resource are used to increase performance or reliability.

- *Scaling transparency* hides that the system can be expanded in scale without the need to change the system structure or the application algorithms.

Section 3.3 will describe how these different aspects of transparency can be supported by a software architecture.

The presence of access and location transparency is referred to as *network transparency*. To this end, the provision of network transparency is regarded as one of the main goals for middleware.

The key point in realizing location transparency is the provision of a *name service* that abstracts over the physical location of possibly distributed resources. More precisely, such a service allows to map a name to a network-wide reference of a specific entity.

### 3.2.4  Masking out Heterogeneity

The realization of the different aspects of transparency is very demanding due to the inherent *heterogeneity* of a distributed system in terms of networks, computer hardware, operating systems and programming languages. Therefore, a middleware has to provide a certain level of independence from the heterogeneous infrastructure [BS98].

Network and hardware independence is today well understood, for example by providing standard network protocols and interchange formats. Platform independence is more complicated to realize but can be achieved by using common abstractions on the operating system level, e.g. by providing standard means like processes.

The key for independence from programming languages is the definition of agreed abstractions over the interfaces offered by different languages together with mappings to specific implementation languages. That is where middleware solutions become important. The common type systems and interface definition languages of current middleware technologies will be reviewed within the scope of Section 3.4.

### 3.2.5  Openness

The *openness* of a distributed system is a key point to achieve its goals. First of all, openness characterizes whether the services provided by a system operate according to standard rules [TvS02]. These services therefore need to conform to well-defined interfaces that describe syntax and semantics. Such a specification needs to be complete and neutral. Together with conformance testing, this allows to ensure interoperability and portability [BS98].

Secondly, the architecture of the system itself should be open in the sense that it can be extended, configured and reimplemented in various ways [CDK01]. The key to this feature is that not only the highest level interfaces are exposed but that the complete architecture with its individual components is open. This is several benefits [BS98].

- The advantages of interoperability and portability extend to all components of the architecture.

- The architecture is flexible in the sense that it is easy to configure or replace components. This allows to specialize or evolve the overall system.

- The architecture can be extended in various ways by providing new components that conform to specific interface definitions.

However, currently available middleware solutions often do not offer such a high degree of openness but are rather restricted to provide interoperability.

### 3.2.6  Reflection

Another important property for distributed systems is *reflection* that can be defined as follows [Cou03]:

> Reflection is the capability of a system to reason about and act upon itself. A reflective system contains a representation of its own behavior, amenable to examination and change, and which is causally connected to the behavior it describes which means that changes made to the system's self-representation are immediately reflected in its actual state and behavior, and vice-versa.

The important point for middleware is that reflection enables both *inspection* and *adaptation* [BCCD00]. While inspection provides the facilities to observe the current state of the system (or specific components thereof), adaptation allows for changing the behavior of the system including severe reconfigurations.

Inspection is an essential property for distributed systems in heterogeneous environments, where new and unknown entities can become available at any time. In

addition, it allows for quality of service monitoring (compare Section 2.2.6). As discussed in Section 2.3, adaptation is especially interesting for multimedia systems in
the absence of guaranteed quality of service.

## 3.3   Common Abstractions

### 3.3.1   Programming Models for Middleware

There exist different programming models for middleware. The most important ones
are *object-based*, *event-based*, or *message-oriented* [BCP03].

**Object-Based Middleware**

Object-based middleware offers network transparent access to distributed objects. An
interface definition language (IDL) is used to abstract over the interfaces offered by
a particular programming language that is used for implementing objects. From an
interface definition, an IDL compiler generates an interface class and an implementation class – possibly in different programming languages and for different hardware
architectures. Implementation classes are then to be implemented in a particular programming language; instances of interface classes are used by the application. The
middleware transparently realizes method invocations on remote objects.

In order to provide the same interaction paradigm as for locally running object-
based approaches, the communication with remote objects is performed *synchronous*:
method calls block until a response is received. Therefore, object-based middleware
is often closely related to the concept of client/server architecture: the client provides
the local representation of the interfaces of the remote object; the remote object itself
acts as server and processes the request of the client triggered by a method invocation.
However, this concept is very different to client/server approaches for streaming multimedia as described in Section 1.2. On the one hand, middleware provides transparent
access to objects, e.g. to the individual objects a client *and* server are composed of. On
the other hand, middleware for distributed multimedia allows for realizing an application for streaming multimedia between different hosts with more sophisticated design
approaches as discussed in Section 4.2.

In order to locate possibly remote objects, they are identified by globally unique
references. The naming and location of objects is typically realized by a service, var-
iously called Name Service, Object Directory, Interface Trader, Yellow Pages, etc.
Method invocations including parameters are serialized (or marshalled), transmitted,
and deserialized (unmarshalled). Correspondingly, return values are handled. This
will be discussed in more detail in Section 3.3.3.

OMG's CORBA [Objb] and Microsoft's DCOM [Micd] are examples for object
based middleware. Section 3.4 will provide further details on CORBA.

**Event-Based Middleware**

Event-based middleware allows a distributed collection of heterogeneous entities to
communicate. In contrast to client/server approaches, where a request-reply interaction paradigm is used, event-based architectures rely on the concept of publish-

subscribe. A number of sources "publishes" events, which are received by a number of interested sinks that have previously "subscribed" to receive particular types of events. Correspondingly, interaction is performed *asynchronous* (non-blocking).

As a major difference to object-based approaches, distributed entities do only need to provide a very simple interface, e.g. for receiving notifications on new events and to subscribe to events.

The Jini distributed event specification is an example for an event-based architecture that allows subscribers running in one Java Virtual Machine (JVM) to register for receiving events for an object running on another JVM on a remote host [Jin, AOS+99].

**Message-Oriented Middleware**

Similar to event based middleware, message-oriented middleware (MOM) offers an asynchronous form of communication. However, the focus for this approach lies in the provision of extensive support for persistent communication [TvS02]. This is achieved by using intermediate-term storage, which allows both sender and receiver to be inactive during the actual transmission.

In general, these message-queuing systems only guarantee that a message is inserted into the incoming queue of the receiver; no timing guarantees are given. Furthermore, the processing of the message and handling of its content is up to the receiver. Similar to event-based approaches, only a very simple interface needs to be provided to applications to realize this interaction paradigm.

The MQSeries from IBM is an example for message-oriented middleware [GS96].

**Discussion**

The synchronous request-response interaction offered by object-based middleware extends the model of object-oriented programming languages to distributed systems. However, the asynchronous one-way interaction offered by event-based or message-oriented middleware is claimed to allow better scaling for loosely coupled systems with a large number of hosts. This is mainly because in large real-world scenarios, mobile systems like laptop computers or PDAs are only occasionally connected to the networking infrastructure. In such cases, the tightly coupled client/server approaches of object-based middleware introduce a large number of possible failure conditions.

Furthermore, object-based middleware only offers one-to-one communication instead of the one-to-many or many-to-many interaction offered by the publish-subscribe paradigm. Therefore, many object-based middleware technologies also allow for event-based interaction, for example by providing additional services.

As all these different middleware paradigms hide the details of the communication with distributed entities – for example by locating objects and allowing for remote method invocations –, they can be said to provide network transparency. Notice however, that different middleware implementations still distinguish between local and remote entities. These difference in the programming model are mainly due to the fact that distributed systems introduce additional possibilities to fail. However, these differences are mostly negligible. For instance, different exceptions or error values might occur when communicating with remote entities.

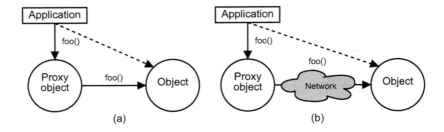

Figure 3.2: An application controls an object via a proxy object: a method foo() is called on the proxy object but indirectly executed by the object the proxy refers to (a). If a remote object is accessed, the method call has to be forwarded over a network (b). For simplicity, no parameters or return values are shown in either case.

### 3.3.2   Proxy Design Pattern

As described in Section 3.2, achieving a certain degree of transparency can be identified as a key requirement for middleware. This is true for all three middleware approaches presented in the preceding section. For example, network transparent communication is similarly useful for both method invocations on remote objects and the forwarding of events or messages between distributed brokers. In all cases, functionality of a remote entity should be transparently accessed. Only the interfaces used are different. Therefore, we will restrict the terminology used for the following sections to object-based systems.

To realize access to remote entities a common design pattern called *Proxy* can be used [GHJV94]. A proxy acts as a surrogate for another entity. Accordingly, a proxy can control access to the entity itself.

Figure 3.2(a) shows the usage of the Proxy pattern for object-based approaches. The application controls an object by calling a method on the corresponding proxy object. The proxy object forwards the request including all given additional parameters to the object it refers to. Therefore, the proxy object needs to provide the same interfaces as the object itself. This can be realized in two ways. Either the same interfaces are inherited by both proxy and object, or, the proxy exports additional interface objects to the application that represent the interfaces inherited by the object the proxy refers to. In this case, method calls are forwarded from the interface objects to the proxy and then from the proxy to the object. For request-reply interaction, return values or exceptions will be forwarded the same way back to the application.

#### Realizing Transparency

The separation of interfaces that are used by an application and the objects that implement these interfaces is important for developing distributed applications. This property of the Proxy pattern provides several benefits. First of all, it allows to separate method invocation and execution. This allows for transparently redirecting an invocation to a remote object. Therefore, the proxy pattern can be used to realize access and location transparency (see Section 3.2.3). In this case, the method call plus additional parameters needs to be forwarded over a network (see Figure 3.2(b)). Likewise, return values or exceptions need to be transmitted back. The following section will give more details on these steps.

If the physical location of an object changes, only the way in which this communication is performed needs to be updated. The application will continue to use the same proxy object. This allows to realize migration transparency or even relocation transparency.

Similarly, a simple form of failure transparency can be accomplished. If the proxy detects that the connection to the object broke down, it can try to establish a new connection. If this also fails, a new object can be requested, possibly on a different host.

In the same way, the proxy pattern can be employed to increase replication transparency. A proxy can connect to more than one objects at a time. In the simplest way, method calls are then forwarded round-robin to the different objects.

**The Adapter Design Pattern**

Additionally, all communication between application and the object can be "filtered" by the proxy, e.g. parameter values can be checked prior to forwarding them to the object. A proxy can even be used to adapt the interfaces provided by the object to other interfaces. In this case, the Proxy pattern is extended to an *Adapter* or *Wrapper* pattern [GHJV94].

**Discussion**

Besides providing the means to realize different dimensions of transparency, the Proxy and Adapter design patterns can be used to allow for interoperability and portability (see Section 3.2.5). Furthermore, these design patterns support an open design of the overall architecture. While the application uses uniform interfaces, the communication between proxy and target object can be realized in different ways. Section 3.4.2 will describe the concept of a *channel* as an abstraction that provides a compound of exchangeable and configurable objects, which realize the communication between two entities.

Although the Proxy pattern is closely related to request-reply interaction with the proxy being the client and the target object being the server, in general, the design pattern can be used for different kinds of interaction.

### 3.3.3 Distributed Objects

In order to implement the Proxy pattern for realizing the different types of transparency addressed above, several issues have to be resolved. Again, we will restrict these observations to the case of object-based middleware. Typically, distributed objects are realized as core service by a middleware (see Figure 3.3).

**Bindings**

To access a remote object, a network-wide remote object reference is needed [CDK01]. Typically, such a reference is obtained from a name service or passed via another

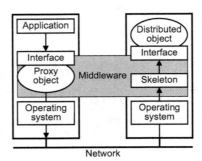

Figure 3.3: A distributed object is accessed via a client-side interface provided by the corresponding proxy object [TvS02]. Request are serialized by the proxy, transmitted, and then deserialized by the skeleton that performs the method invocation. Such distributed objects are typically realized as core service of middleware.

interface. A remote object reference carries information of how to establish the means for communicating with the object, generally called *binding* [TvS02].

Depending on the physical location of the application and the target object, three different types of bindings can be distinguished. The easiest way is a *local binding*, where both application and target object reside within the same address space. If this is not the case, but the two entities run on the same system, a *system binding* can be established. In contrast, a *network binding* is needed for application and target object running on two different systems. Depending on the underlying platform, a system binding can be realized more efficiently than a network binding where all communication needs to go through the complete network protocol stack.

**Serialization and Deserialization**

After a binding is established, method invocations can be performed on the client-side interfaces. In order to be able to call the corresponding method at the target object with all corresponding parameters, such an invocation needs to be forwarded to the target object. If a network binding is used, this information needs to be transformed into a sequence suitable for network transmission. This step is called *serialization* (or *marshalling*) and is usually provided by the proxy object (or a special component within the middleware architecture).

During this step, complex data structures are decomposed into simpler data types. Notice, that also the information needed for establishing a binding can be serialized. As the target object might reside on a different hardware architecture, serialized data needs to additionally carry precise type information.

As can be seen in Figure 3.3, a *skeleton* at the server side then performs the *deserialization* (or *unmarshalling*). Then, the method is called at the target object. Return values (or exceptions) are then transmitted from the server back to the client. Both, skeletons and proxies are typically generated automatically by an IDL compiler (see Section 3.3.1).

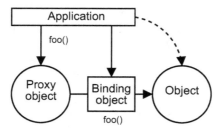

Figure 3.4: Explicit binding with binding object. Explicit binding allows the application to choose the type of binding and configure specific parameters. The binding object is realized as a first class data type that can be used and manipulated like any other object.

**Discussion**

Notice, that method invocations can be optimized when a system or local binding is used. For system bindings, data could simply be copied between different processes; for a local binding, references to already allocated memory areas could be used. We will see in Part II of this thesis, how such optimizations can be integrated into a middleware.

### 3.3.4   Implicit and Explicit Binding

For establishing bindings, two different approaches can be distinguished. With *implicit binding*, the middleware automatically creates and configures a binding, e.g. when a method is called the first time on a client-side interface of a proxy that refers to a remote object. As the application has no influence on this process, this approach is also called *black-box* design.

Explicit binding approaches allow to manually choose the type of binding to be established and configure specific parameters thereof. This corresponds to a *white-box* design, where the application can access internal properties of the core functionality of the middleware.

For explicit bindings, the concept of a *binding object* as shown in Figure 3.4 can be used [BS98]. Binding objects are modeled as *first class data type* meaning that they can be used and manipulated like any other object.

As a binding object needs to allow to configure both client and server-side, depending on the actual implementation, a binding object can also be realized as a distributed object.

## 3.4   Standards for Distributed Object Computing

Within this section, two middleware standards will be reviewed, namely the Common Object Request Broker Architecture (CORBA) [Objb] and the Reference Model for Open Distributed Processing (RM-ODP) [ISO98]. As CORBA acts as an representa-

tive for other architectures, such as DCOM [Micd] or Java Remote Method Invocation
(RMI) [Sunb], these approaches will not be reviewed in detail since the main concepts are identical; major differences can be found in the way communication is performed [Raj98]: DCOM relies on COM together with a protocol called the Object Remote Procedure Call (ORPC). Since the COM specifies interaction at the binary level,
several programming languages, such as C++ and Java, are supported. Java relies on a
protocol called the Java Remote Method Protocol (JRMP). In contrast, RMI is based on
Java Object Serialization and therefore only available for Java virtual machines (VM).
Also, advanced technologies, such as Java 2 Enterprise Edition (J2EE) [Suna] or the
CORBA Component Model (CCM) [Vin98], are not considered, since they address
a different problem domain, namely the development, deployment, and management
of scalable, transactional, multi-user, and secure multi-tier and server-centric applications.

In contrast, the Reference Model for Open Distributed Processing (RM-ODP) is
described because it represents a meta-architecture from which different implementations were derived. Furthermore, within the scope of Chapter 4, different extensions
of CORBA and RM-ODP to handle multimedia will be discussed.

As many foundations of these approaches were already described in the preceding
sections, only the key points important for the following discussion will be highlighted.

### 3.4.1   Common Object Request Broker Architecture

The Common Object Request Broker Architecture (CORBA) specifications [Obj04]
have been developed by the Object Management Group (OMG) [Obja]. CORBA can
be seen as a concrete object-oriented middleware specification that provides interoperability in heterogeneous environments [BS98]. Furthermore, CORBA specifies a
number of services.

#### Overall Architecture

The overall architecture of CORBA consist of four main components: the Object Request Broker (ORB), the Object Services, the Domain Interfaces, and the Application
Interfaces [HV99]. The ORB is the mediating core component and provides the facilities for object interaction. The domain-independent Object Services provide the
functionality for many distributed object applications, e.g. to obtain references to objects. The Naming Service and the Trading Service are also part of the Object Services. Domain Interfaces provide services needed for a particular application domain.
Finally, Application Interfaces are developed for a specific application domain and are
not standardized.

CORBA provides a number of different services. The Naming Service provides
a mapping from human-readable names to object references. More advanced is the
Trading Service that provides facilities to publish and retrieve the services an object
offers.

#### Interface Definition and Mappings

CORBA adopts the client/server approach described in Section 3.3.1. Objects and
services are described in CORBA IDL. Exact rules for mapping IDL descriptions

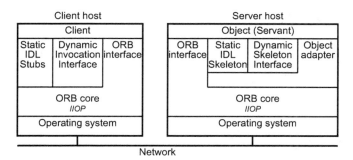

Figure 3.5: CORBA adopts a client/server approach for realizing an object-based middleware [TvS02]. Applications perform method invocations on distributed objects by either calling methods statically (stubs) or dynamically (Dynamic Invocation Interface). The object adapter dispatches requests either statically (skeletons) are dynamically (Dynamic Invocation Interface). The ORB core provides communication means via standard protocols like the Internet Inter-ORB Protocol (IIOP).

to client-side and server-side entities for programming languages like C, C++, Java, Smalltalk, Ada, and COBOL are provided. During runtime, an Interface Repository provides access to the interface objects. An implementation repository allows to access and instantiate server-side objects.

Among other things, CORBA IDL allows to specify inheritance for interfaces. To realize optimized communication, an additional qualifier (namely in, out, or inout) has to be defined for each parameter of a method in order to define the "direction" of the associated parameter. Correspondingly, in parameters are only transmitted from client to server, out parameters only from server to client, and inout parameters in both directions.

**Request Invocations and Data Flow**

Figure 3.5 gives on overview of the general architecture of a CORBA system. Object references in Interoperable Object Reference (IOR) format are used to identify, locate, and address CORBA objects. In the simplest way, an IOR is passed manually from the server to the client. Alternatively, facilities like the CORBA Naming Service can be used. In general, CORBA uses an implicit binding mechanism.

Using a reference, a client can make requests either via static stubs that were generated from IDL descriptions or via the Dynamic Invocation Interface (DII). The DII allows clients to construct requests dynamically at runtime by calling a generic invoke operation. These entities also perform the marshalling of requests and the unmarshalling of results.

The ORB at the client side than forwards (e.g. transmits) the request to the ORB at the server, which again forwards the request to the object adapter that created the server-side object. The request is dispatched to the servant. Similarly to the client-side, this is done statically via skeletons, which were generated by the IDL compiler, or dynamically via the Dynamic Skeleton Interface (DSI). Finally, the server processes the request and a reply is returned in the same manner.

The role of the object adapter is to act as an interposed object that uses delegation and allows the calling ORB to access the upper layer facilities like skeletons without knowing their particular interface. The object adapter is designed according to the Adapter design pattern [GHJV94].

In order to allow interoperability between different ORBs, the General Inter-ORB Protocol (GIOP) provides an specification of transfer syntax and a standard set of message formats. The Internet Inter-ORB Protocol (IIOP) specifies how to implement GIOP over TCP/IP [HV99].

**Interaction Models**

Different types of interaction are supported by CORBA. Most commonly, requests are performed *synchronous*. In this mode, the caller blocks until a response is returned – or an exception is raised. *Deferred synchronous* requests are forwarded to the server; the client can immediately continue to work and block later until a response is delivered. The delivery semantics for these two modes is "at-most-once", which means that the requests are processed by the server if no error occurs. As an alternative, when using one-way request, the server will not send any response. Furthermore, the semantics for this mode is "best-effort delivery", which means that the request will not necessarily be processed by the server at all.

Although CORBA adopts an object-oriented design, it also offers event-based and message-oriented communication as described in Section 3.3. The CORBA Event Service works as follows. An event can be produced by one or more suppliers and is then delivered through an event channel to subscribed consumers. This can be done either in push or pull mode. In push mode, suppliers forward events to event channels that push the event to all registered consumers. In pull mode, consumers try to poll events from an event channel, which in turn tries to poll events from suppliers. A Notification Service enhances the Event Service by allowing filtering operations [Obj02b].

Events are generally not stored within the underlying communication system. This functionality can be realized with the CORBA Messaging Service that provides a callback model and a polling model (see [Obj04], Chapter 22). Using the callback model, the client provides a callback object with its invocation that is used to deliver the response back to the client. Contrariwise, when using polling model, an invocation returns a handle that can be used to poll and wait for a response [Vin98]. In contrast to the deferred synchronous interaction described above, such *asynchronous* requests are using the IDL and static stubs and therefore provide type safety.

### 3.4.2   Reference Model for Open Distributed Processing

ISO/ITU-T's Reference Model for Open Distributed Processing (RM-ODP) is a meta-standard that defines a generic framework from which specific standards can be derived [BS98].

**Overall Architecture**

RM-ODP adopts an object-oriented approach. In order to manage the complexity, the standard is structured into five different viewpoints that target towards a particular audience.

- The *Enterprise Viewpoint* describes distributed systems in the operation of an enterprise.

- The *Information Viewpoint* considers the different information units, the flow of information, and the processes that manipulate information.

- The *Computational Viewpoint* describes the logical structure of the distributed system in terms of interacting entities.

- The *Engineering Viewpoint* is concerned with provision of the infrastructure that is required for realizing distributed systems.

- The *Technology Viewpoint* considers the development of distributed systems in terms of installing particular hardware and software technologies.

RM-ODP defines a number of *functions* for fulfilling a number of different additional requirements. These functions can therefore be seen as services as defined in Section 3.1.

**Interaction Models**

With regard to the scope of this thesis, the more important concepts are described within the Computational and Engineering Viewpoints. In particular, the Computational Viewpoint describes the object-oriented approach of RM-ODP, where each object provides a number of interfaces. In order to interact with objects via interfaces, a binding to the target object is needed. Three different types of bindings are supported:

- *Operational bindings* support the invocation of methods.

- *Signal bindings support* the processing of simple signals in real-time according to available quality of service capabilities.

- *Stream bindings* support continuous media interaction.

**Selective Transparency**

While transparency is in general useful for reducing the complexity of distributed systems, the Computational Viewpoint allows applications to provide an *environmental contract* that specifies the required level of transparency.

The Engineering Viewpoint is responsible for providing this *selective* transparency. Therefore, *transparency functions* are defined that allow to achieve a desired level of transparency. Furthermore, the Engineering Viewpoint provides abstract concepts needed to model communication. The concept of a *channel* is used. A channel consists of several interaction entities, namely *stubs*, *binders*, *protocol objects*, and *interceptors*.

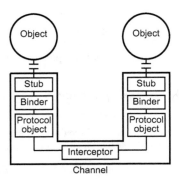

Figure 3.6: RM-ODP describes the concept of a channel as an abstraction that provides a compound of exchangeable and configurable objects that realize the communication between two objects [BS98].

Stubs are a generalization of the stubs and skeletons described in the context of the introduction to CORBA in the previous section. They provide an interface between the object (e.g. the proxy or the target object) and the underlying communication infrastructure. Stubs are the only parts of a channel that have information about the type of data to transfer.

The binders are responsible for setting up and maintaining the communication means of a channel. They handle possible failures or relocation of objects, e.g. by interacting with the services provided by the architecture. Together, they provide the different dimensions of transparency.

The protocol objects provide the functionality of different underlying communication protocols. Thus, these objects may also rely on other services specific to the used protocol. Protocol objects are also responsible to realize possible optimizations, e.g. when communicating with a colocated object.

In order to establish communication between objects that do not share a common interaction protocol, interceptors can be used. These entities perform necessary transformations, e.g. for translating between different protocol formats.

### 3.4.3   Discussion

While RM-ODP defines an open meta-standard, other middleware solutions, such as CORBA, traditionally use a black-box approach. However, over the last years, especially CORBA was extended to follow more the design guidelines provided by RM-ODP. Especially the introduction of new services for event-based and message-oriented interaction make CORBA an interesting choice for developing distributed application – or for developing middleware for distributed multimedia. The following chapter will further discuss this topic.

## 3.5  Summary

Today, distributed systems typically consist of independent hosts running commodity operating systems. The task of middleware is to mask out the complexity and heterogeneity of the underlying infrastructure and to provide transparent access to distributed resources.

The various standardization efforts in the area of networking, operating systems, and programming languages have facilitated the creation of middleware for distributed systems. Consequently, various standards for middleware technologies provide the functionality needed for efficiently developing large-scale distributed applications.

However, at higher levels, there still exist a lot of incompatible technologies. Despite the fact that middleware technologies try to hide the heterogeneity of the underlying infrastructure, the presence of multiple competing standards for all areas of multimedia computing and networking – and the continuous emergence of new standards – introduces a new degree of heterogeneity. This is even more true since various design approaches for middleware exist, like object-based, event-based, or message-oriented architectures.

Therefore, bridging technologies that connect originally incompatible solutions emerged recently [Sta04]. Furthermore, the introduction of another software layer called "upperware" on top of current technologies was proposed [TvS02]. Such a software layer could then be used as meta-architecture to provide *technology transparent* access to different middleware. Obviously, such a layer must provide the ability to integrate different architectures easily and to translate between alternative approaches.

Despite the fact that many distributed systems are successfully employed today, often their architectures are not fully *open* as described above. However, the openness of a middleware architecture is a key point in realizing extensible and customizable solutions in the presence of today's heterogeneous environments. This is especially true when considering the requirements for distributed multimedia systems as discussed in the following chapter. To this end, the *channels* introduced by RM-ODP provide an interesting architectural design that allows to realize explicit binding with parameterizable and customizable communication strategies. Combined with the concept of selective transparency, this results in an white-box approach that still provides transparency when needed.

# Chapter 4

# Challenges for Distributed Multimedia Systems

In this chapter, we will answer the question why middleware support for distributed multimedia is especially demanding. Therefore, as an synopsis of the previous two chapters, the challenges and requirements for multimedia middleware will be pointed out.

More precisely, we will answer the question: "Middleware + multimedia = multimedia middleware?" [Pla02] . Is it enough to add the capabilities of a middleware to a locally operating multimedia architecture to realize multimedia middleware? If not, what else needs to be done? What are the major challenges when considering today's heterogeneous infrastructures and the pace in which new standards for distributed multimedia emerge? What additional services are needed to satisfy the needs of users – especially for multimedia home entertainment? What are the corresponding services a middleware should provide to allow for efficient application development?

To answer these questions, we will first give an overview of the relevant aspects and the relationships between them. Then, each of these aspects is described in detail. In this context, related work concerning the core architecture for multimedia middleware will be reviewed. In addition, the need for additional and advanced middleware services will be motivated; corresponding related work will be discussed in detail within the specific chapters of Part III of this thesis. Together, the presentation in this chapter includes a definition of the term "network-integrated multimedia middleware" as focussed in this thesis.

## 4.1   Overview

Figure 4.1 gives an overview of the most important concepts for network-integrated multimedia middleware as focussed on in this thesis. As we will see, the openness required for such middleware is apparently contradictory to the transparency generally needed for developing distributed applications efficiently [Pla02]. Therefore, there is a trade-off between openness and transparency. Consequently, one major goal for this thesis is to develop the "right" abstractions, or – if different degrees of openness are required – a solution that provides *scalable* transparency.

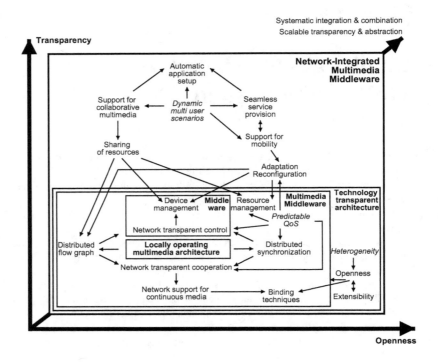

Figure 4.1: Challenges for network-integrated multimedia middleware. Starting from a locally operating multimedia architecture, multimedia middleware can be developed by providing the facilities of a general-purpose middleware solution for distributed object computing and the additional properties for distributed multimedia. The inherent heterogeneity of today's infrastructures further requires openness and extensibility in order to realize a technology transparent architecture. Additional challenges imposed by the dynamics and complexity of the overall system require additional services. Together, the systematic integration and combination of all these aspects defines a *network-integrated multimedia middleware*.

The positions of the different concepts as indicated in Figure 4.1 roughly correspond to the taken approach. Concepts that impose external requirements or challenges are shown in *italics*. The relationships between different concepts are indicated through directed edges. These edges provide a rather loose semantics like "influences", "is important for", or "requires" for the direction they are pointing to. Notice however, that these indications are not exhaustive. Finally, the major steps in the development of the notion of a network-integrated multimedia middleware are indicated by boxes.

To give an overview of the concept of a network-integrated multimedia middleware, we start with a locally operating multimedia architecture as described in Chapter 2. By providing the facilities of middleware for distributed object computing (see Chapter 3) and by extending this approach with properties needed for distributed multimedia, a multimedia middleware can be realized. Section 4.2 will further describe this step.

Due to the inherent heterogeneity of today's infrastructures, such a solution further requires openness and extensibility. This allows to realize a technology transparent architecture. Different additional dimensions of heterogeneity that need to be considered will be identified in Section 4.3.

For the efficient development of appealing multi-user application scenarios, additional services are needed. These service are needed to handle the complexity and dynamics of the overall system by providing suitable abstractions and programming models. Section 4.4 will provide more details on these aspects.

## 4.2 Requirements for Multimedia Middleware

### 4.2.1 Distributed Flow Graphs

Locally operating multimedia architectures as described in Chapter 2 often allow for using the network as source or sink of data – for example for streaming data between two separate applications running on different hosts. These architectures do not provide network transparency. More precisely, the concept of a *distributed flow graph* is not provided: A flow graph of processing elements as described in Section 2.4, where the individual elements are allowed to reside on remote hosts. While such a flow graph spans across different systems, the application needs to be able to transparently control and connect the distributed processing elements.

Figure 4.2 shows a simple distributed flow graph with two processing elements (source and sink). These two elements and the application are located on different hosts. The two fundamental concepts for realizing distributed flow graphs, namely network transparent control and cooperation, are discussed next.

### 4.2.2 Network Transparent Control

In order to realize such a distributed flow graph, several requirements have to be fulfilled. First of all, a multimedia middleware needs to enable applications to transparently control the distributed processing elements that form the flow graph.

As this requirement is well-known from the object-based middleware, many approaches directly extend existing solutions in order to develop multimedia middleware. For example, the Multimedia System Services (MSS) [Hew93] offer an architecture for

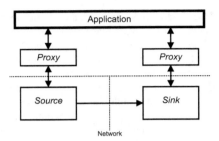

Figure 4.2: A distributed flow graph with two distributed processing elements (source and sink). The application controls these remote elements via object-based client/server interaction using proxies. The one-way streaming data connection between source and sink includes data transmission over a network.

building distributed multimedia application using CORBA. MSS has been adopted as the underlying platform for the ISO Presentation Environment for Multimedia Objects (PREMO) [DH98b]. While PREMO is restricted to a high-level conceptual description rather than an approach for implementation, MSS provides a detailed specification for a specialization of CORBA. In particular, a class hierarchy defined in IDL for multimedia devices and data formats is provided.

Multimedia middleware approaches like [EB02] are based on implementations of the Open Services Gateway initiative (OSGi) architecture [Opec]. The specifications developed by the OSGi Alliance define an open service platform for the delivery and management of multiple applications and services to all types of networked devices in home, vehicle, mobile, and other environments [MK01]. While OSGi provides a standard way to connect devices such as home appliances, it does not provide facilities especially needed for handling multimedia, e.g. synchronization. Correspondingly, the system described in [EB02] uses external components like commodity media players for realizing multimedia functionality, fine-grained distributed flow graphs are not supported.

### 4.2.3 Network Transparent Cooperation

Besides being able to control distributed processing elements, the streaming data connections between these elements are the other important part to consider when realizing a distributed flow graph. The establishment of stream bindings should be supported by a middleware for distributed multimedia in the same way as for a locally operating architecture: a third-party binding between two processing elements created by the application should allow for network transparent cooperation of distributed processing elements.

While the development of multimedia middleware can greatly benefit from the programming model provided by object-based middleware, in general these solutions lack the support for handling continuous media. In particular, streaming high-bandwidth multimedia data with timing constraints is not supported efficiently [MSS99].

This is mainly due to the fact that the interaction paradigms of most middleware solutions were originally not designed to operate efficiently in this case. While reliability is certainly required for synchronous request-reply interaction, the timeliness of data transmission is more important for real-time multimedia application. This includes the possible dropping of data in order to keep up with the imposed timing constraints. As discussed in detail in Section 2.2.4, specialized protocols are often used to provide such features.

Unfortunately, traditional middleware design uses a black-box approach, were binding mechanisms are not exposed to applications and correspondingly cannot be queried, configured, or extended by providing additional implementations, e.g. for streaming data connections. However, especially transferring multimedia data often requires to optimize network parameters like sending or receiving buffer sizes. Furthermore, the implicit binding mechanisms also forbids to monitor QoS parameters, like bandwidth or delay, for streaming data connections – a property that is of great importance to identify situation in which a dynamic reconfiguration or adaptation is needed.

**Middleware Service Enhancements**

To overcome this problem, several different approaches have been proposed. First, to overcome the limitations of traditional middleware architectures, existing services are extended. Especially enhancements of the CORBA event service seem to be promising. The approach described in [CLD01] extends the standard CORBA event service to support multimedia and includes data types for multimedia data flows. In [OB00] an extension for the CORBA event service is described that offers different levels of reliability, congestion control mechanisms, and jitter suppression strategies.

However, such approaches do not offer the openness needed for distributed multimedia. Furthermore, throughput and delay of these kinds of transmissions are severely affected by the underlying event service. For example in [CLD01], even when using relatively large data packets of 4096 bytes, throughput with acceptable loss rates is limited to 1.3 Mbps.

**Middleware Extensions**

While the approaches described so far enhance an existing middleware service, others try to overcome the limitations of traditional middleware architectures by providing additional services for establishing streaming data connections.

Specializations of middleware, like the Multimedia System Services [Hew93] specified for CORBA, provide additional interfaces for establishing and configuring multimedia connections. In particular, MSS also defines an additional middleware layer protocol, the Media Stream Protocol (MSP), for such connections. A restriction of this approach is that the representation of the connection does not provide a high degree of openness once it is established [Fit99]. Further important protocols, such as RTP, are not supported.

A similar approach is followed by the specification of the CORBA audio/video streaming service [ION97]. This extension provides well-defined modules, interfaces, and semantics for stream establishment together with efficient transport-level mechanisms for data transmission [MSS99]. Although the specification defines an explicit binding mechanisms that allows to specify QoS parameters, again, the connection is not realized as first-class object and therefore does not provide direct access to its internal parts [WH98].

### Recursive, Hierarchical, and Open Bindings

The approaches described so far no not provide binding objects as described in Section 3.3. In [BS98], an engineering model for multimedia based on RM-ODP is introduced. This model describes an explicit binding approach for the channels described in Section 3.4.2. Furthermore, as an generalization, *recursive binding* allows binding objects to be constructed of configurations that include other bindings. The only constraint for such a binding object is that is provides stubs as interfaces for the binding itself.

Factories for instantiating bindings can then be used to realize a particular binding protocol. Binding factories and protocols are extensively used within the CORBA based Sumo-ORB [BS98]. The possibility to extend these factories introduces a new degree of openness into middleware architectures.

Another hierarchical binding model is described in [WC97]. This approach uses delegation – for example, a service binding is delegated to a client and server binding, and a network service binding.

An approach similar to recursive binding is described in [FBC$^+$98] as *open binding*. Such a binding is represented by an object graph. An object graph consists of processing elements and other bindings that create a specific binding. Interfaces of internal parts are exposed by the wrapping binding object. External interfaces then act as proxies for internal interfaces. An important distinction of the open binding approach is that the processing objects of an object graph inside a binding can contain elements like encoders or decoders – processing elements that are usually not considered to lie on the "edges" of a flow graph. However, since an open binding exposes its internal configuration, this concept allows for fine-grained adaptation within the binding itself, e.g. by changing the compression ratio of an encoder object. A similar approach is followed for the QoS aware binding objects in MULTE-ORB [EKPR00].

### Transparency versus Abstraction

While the above described approaches provide explicit binding and partly binding as first-class objects within the middleware, other approaches try to provide new abstractions that explicitly represent communication means within flow graphs. The Infopipes architecture is an example for this direction [KBH$^+$01, BHK$^+$02]. Instead of "hiding" the communication details in binding objects that might automatically been created by binding factories, the Infopipes approach uses pictorial abstractions like sources, buffers, pumps, filters, tees, or sinks to model multimedia streaming. The input and output ports of these elements operate either in push or pull mode, respectively. For example, pumps pull data from their predecessor and push it to their successors.

To this end, a so called remote pipe transports information from one address space to another. The input and output port of such a pipe therefore exist in different address spaces. A netpipe furthermore provides buffering of the information flow. While the Infopipes architecture uses the Squeak Smalltalk environment for remote method invocations on distributed components, netpipes are implemented within the architecture itself. Notice however that the approach deliberately only provides access transparency. Since netpipes have to be inserted manually, location transparency for the creation of flow graphs is not provided (compare Section 3.2.3).

While the abstractions are certainly useful for modeling explicit binding, only little support for configuring netpipes is provided. Furthermore, the manual insertion of netpipes and pumps complicates application development. In addition, realizing migration transparency seems to be complicated with this approach because moving parts of a flow graph from one address space to another might require the manual insertion of additional netpipes. In Section 4.4, this topic will be further discussed.

A similar approach is followed by the MediaApplicationServer (MAS) [Shi] that aims at providing a network-transparent audio server [NSO04]. Within this architecture, networking connection between processing elements are established by automatically inserting a "net device" as an additional element.

### Static versus Dynamic Specification of Streaming Connections

RM-ODP and derived architectures, such as TOAST [FGB+01], follow the approach of statically defining input and output ports of processing elements that can be used for streaming data connections by using an extended interface definition language (IDL) that provides additional keywords. This idea is also followed by the aRts architecture [aRt] (compare Section 2.5.2). However, since the precise content of a multimedia data stream is not always known a priori – e.g. for a multiplexed MPEG stream as described in Section 2.2.3 – and the content of a stream can also vary over time, we argue that inputs and outputs of processing elements should not be specified statically within an IDL. Instead, an arbitrary number of ports and the corresponding properties need to be accessible via a generic interface. The multimedia middleware architecture presented in Part II of this thesis employs this approach.

### Discussion

Explicit binding and the provision of binding objects representing communication between two objects provide great benefits for distributed multimedia. Applications can setup and configure communication means according to their needs. Even more promising is a semi-automatic approach where applications only specify higher level goals and binding factories perform the binding process autonomously.

However, explicit binding should not be restricted to streaming communication between the processing elements of a flow graph, but rather be used for all bindings – including operational bindings between proxy and target object. This is especially important when considering heterogeneous environments as discussed in Section 4.3, where only certain technologies for establishing communication are available. Therefore, we aim at providing an unified yet extensible approach for establishing different kinds of interaction, such as between proxy and target object or between connected processing elements of a distributed flow graph.

### 4.2.4   Distributed Synchronization

As a distributed flow graph potentially spans across different hosts, an application for distributed playback of multimedia might therefore chose to render different media on different systems or to capture data from distributed sources. In both cases, the underlying middleware needs to provide facilities for synchronizing media streams on distributed systems [BS98].

Different synchronization protocols where developed so far. The most prominent ones are the Concord algorithm [SSNA95] and the Adaptive Synchronization Protocol (ASP) [RH97]. As an example, the ASP aims at the synchronized playback of buffers at different distributed data sinks. Therefore, corresponding data units are marked with the same timestamp. In the beginning, a maximum delay for all units to reach their corresponding sink node is assumed and all data is played out at the time of the corresponding timestamp plus this additional delay. Since this offset introduces an artificial extra delay for the play back of buffers, the protocol aims at minimizing the value used.

While intra-stream synchronization can be accomplished by local operations, e.g. by delaying or dropping buffers, distributed inter-stream synchronization requires further effort. Therefore, common protocols often adopt a master-slave approach, where one processing element within the flow graph acts as a master and all other processing elements that perform some sort of synchronization are adapted to the master.

The basis for performing distributed synchronization is a common source for timing information. Commonly, the Network Time Protocol (NTP) is used to synchronize the system time of distributed hosts [LMS85, Mil91]. The accuracy of this process strongly depends on the networking conditions and the accuracy of the system clock. However, clock offsets in the range of some milliseconds can be achieved using NTP [NTP]. As we have seen in Section 2.2.5, such values are sufficient for lip-synchronizing audio and video. For application setups that require higher precision, alternative approaches can be used [LKW03].

#### Discussion

While several sophisticated synchronization protocols exist, the focus for developing a multimedia middleware – and therefore the focus for our work – should be to realize a framework that allows various protocols to be implemented and used for supporting different application scenarios, for example capturing or presentation of multimedia, but also more advanced services like hand off of media processing from one device to another as discussed in Section 4.4.3.

### 4.2.5   Device Discovery and Management

So far we have not considered how remote processing elements like multimedia devices or software components are located within the network. This is in general referred to as *service discovery*. Service discovery itself is a service according to our definition in Section 3.1.2 that allows to deploy, discover, and interact with the capabilities of "services" within the network. These services can then be used by other services. For multimedia middleware the discovery of processing elements is particularly interesting. Therefore, the terms *device discovery and management* or *registry* are also often used for such a service.

In any case, such a service needs to provide different facilities. First, devices and software components need to be registered with a detailed description of supported capabilities. Second, facilities for applications to query the service need to be provided. Finally, such queries result in reservation and instantiation of corresponding entities.

One possibility for realizing a registry service is to use the capabilities of existing middleware solutions. In the case of using CORBA, the naming and trading services provide the required functionality (compare Section 3.4.1). However, especially for the area of home networking, a variety of different standards for service discovery exists like Universal Plug and Play (UPnP) [Uni], Jini [Jin, AOS+99], the Bluetooth Service Discovery Protocol (Bluetooth SDP) [Blu01], the Home Audio Video Interoperability (HAVi) standard [Hom], and many others. Then, there are also protocols like the Service Location Protocol (SLP) [GPVD99] initially developed to operate in larger networks. While the different approaches share a number of attributes, it is important to notice that they also provide a number of distinguishing features [SSJH03]. This topic will be further discussed in Section 4.3.2.

### 4.2.6 Predictable Quality of Service

The provision of quality of service (QoS) for distributed systems has seen tremendous efforts both in research and standardization activities. To this end, specifications for extending commodity middleware solutions have emerged. As an example, the Real-Time CORBA extension provides defined behavior for parameters like computational load, network bandwidth, or latency by managing processor, communication, and memory resources [SK00].

However, this end-to-end behavior is only predictable for systems that support real-time scheduling within operating systems, networks, and protocols. As can be seen from the discussion in Section 2.3, the underlying infrastructure we are considering does only provide best effort QoS. Predictable QoS can only partly be achieved by mechanisms like buffering, prefetching, traffic shaping, or forward error correction. Therefore, we argue that adaptation offers a more promising and widely employable approach.

As adaptation is not necessarily a fixed part of multimedia middleware but more often realized as additional service or within the application, related work in this area will be reviewed in the scope of Section 4.4.1.

However, for adaptation techniques to operate effectively, multimedia middleware needs to provide the appropriate facilities. Correspondingly, we focus on architectural support for QoS specification, QoS monitoring, and QoS maintenance (compare Section 2.2.6). Admission control and resource reservation is only performed on the middleware layer since no platform support is available. Ongoing work in this area will be briefly presented in Section 9.5.

## 4.3    Additional Dimensions of Heterogeneity

As discussed in Chapter 3, the task of traditional middleware is to mask out the complexity and heterogeneity of the underlying infrastructure in terms of networks, computer hardware, operating systems and programming languages. However, especially
for distributed multimedia systems additional dimensions of heterogeneity exist. These
dimensions will be further discussed in the following.

### 4.3.1    Multimedia Devices, Processing, and Architectures

Multimedia middleware must allow to integrate different multimedia devices and processing routines, such as newly available codecs. Obviously, this is also a requirement
for a locally operating multimedia architecture. In general, the concept of a flow graph
consisting of processing elements together with their specific multimedia formats provide the abstractions to fulfill this requirement.

However, since middleware for distributed multimedia possibly operates on different systems, it needs to provide a generic architectural processing model that allows
to integrate existing software components specific for a particular platform, such as
device drivers, multimedia libraries, and even locally running software architectures.
This processing model must provide high level abstractions and is not allowed assume
a certain behavior of components to be integrated.

### 4.3.2    Device Discovery and Management

As described in Section 4.2.5, there exists a variety of different standards for device
discovery and management. The different approaches share a number of attributes –
but they also provide a number of distinguishing features. As a multimedia device will
typically only support some of these standards, this heterogeneity adds another level
of complexity.

The distinguishing features are key properties like initial device discovery, device
description, or interaction. For example, some architectures employ a peer-to-peer
approach for advertising services. Peer-to-peer (P2P) architectures do not rely on
centralized services but rather consist of individual peers voluntary participating in
a dynamic and ad-hoc infrastructure [SGG02]. Others use registration of services in a
central service repository.

While standards like SLP or Bluetooth SDP do not provide mechanisms for accessing remote services or devices, others, e.g. Jini, UPnP, and HAVi, also provide
ways to access these entities once they were discovered – even if varying widely in the
way how this is achieved.

Although Jini and HAVi are both based on Java, both define their own discovery
protocol to register and access services. Another main difference between the two is
that HAVi defines a fixed set of interfaces for different devices, were Jini only specifies
how to define an interface [RBZ01].

UPnP provides an infrastructure that uses existing Internet standards like HTTP
and XML to integrate, access, and describe devices. For controlling devices, UPnP
uses the Simple Object Access Protocol (SOAP) [W3Ca]. Unlike other approaches,

UPnP is therefore independent of the used physical networking medium, the used programming language, and operating system. While these features make UPnP a good choice for heterogeneous environments, one can observe that the area of home networking has always seen and will always see technological changes – existing standards will become less important; new standards will emerge.

Therefore, we aim at providing a registry service that allows for the integration of different technologies. This service will be described in detail in Chapter 9. In the scope of this context, in particular in Section 9.2, current research that addresses the problem of heterogeneity for device management will be discussed.

### 4.3.3 Networking and Middleware Technologies

As discussed in Section 4.5, at higher layers within the ISO-OSI protocol stack (e.g. layers 4 to 7), there exist a lot of different approaches:

- Different transport layer protocols, like TCP and UDP discussed in Section 2.2.4 but also many other proposals for multimedia streaming that operate on the same IP infrastructure [KLW01].

- Different protocols for the transmission of multimedia data that operate on top of transport layer protocols, like RTP/RTCP discussed in Section 2.2.4.

- Different middleware protocols like CORBA's IIOP discussed in Section 3.4.1 but also Open Source alternatives like the Desktop Communication Protocol (DCOP) [Bro] and the Multimedia Communication Protocol (MCOP) [Wes] originated from the KDE project [KDE] and the aRts project [aRt], respectively.

- Different application layer protocols specific for multimedia. To this end, forward error correction (FEC) mechanisms or protocols for digital rights management (DRM) play an important role (see Section 2.3.1).

Consequently, multimedia middleware needs to support the integration of these different protocols and mechanisms. To this end, even existing middleware solutions for distributed multimedia should be allowed to be integrated.

Two Open Source approaches for distributed multimedia, namely aRts [aRt] and MAS [Shi] were already briefly discussed in Section 2.6. Besides the fact that these frameworks only allow to handle audio streams, they are both also tightly coupled to a specific lower level networking technology. While aRts relies on the above mentioned MCOP, MAS employs RTP on top of TCP for realizing communication – further extensions of the architecture are not explicitly supported.

For traditional middleware, pluggable protocol frameworks were proposed. An example for this approach for CORBA is described in [OKS+00] for The ACE Orb (TAO), which allows for the development and usage of custom inter-ORB messaging and transport protocols. While such protocols are not compliant to GIOP/IIOP, they provide better performance in terms of message footprint size, latency, and jitter. The support of application specific protocols together with CORBA compatibility is also one of the main goals for the development of the middleware platform GOPI [CBM02]. However, the tight coupling with CORBA certainly limits the general applicability of these approaches and requires all components that are to be integrated into the multi-media architecture to be adapted to the CORBA object model with its restricted set of data types. Contrariwise, NMM especially aims at providing an framework that does allow for the easy integration of existing components. Since external components, such as libraries or device drivers, internally and externally already use a fixed set of data structures, a seamless integration of existing types is important.

Other systems, such as Da CaPo++ [SCW+99], provide general protocol frameworks that automatically configure stacks of protocol modules from a given specification that includes parameters like the required level of security. While this framework provides the benefits of modularity and extensibility for multimedia communication, network transparent control of components is not addressed.

Furthermore, current research activities aim at the development of micro-broker-based middleware that builds a communication infrastructure around a relatively small middleware core. Examples for this approach are BASE [BSGR03] or Universally Interoperable Core (UIC) [RKC01]. Especially BASE provides a plug-in concept for all communication means through proxies and interoperability protocols. This allows different communication patterns such as request-response or event-based interaction to be handled by the middleware. The solution is especially suited for systems with scarce resources. For such systems, a minimum configuration of the middleware can be used. However, while being still restricted to a prototypical implementation without full anticipated functionality, this approach does not consider the functionality needed for distributed multimedia [RKC01]. A similar approach that allows to plug-in different communication mechanisms such as HTTP within the Virtual Networked Applicances (VNA) architecture is presented in [NT02]. While the architecture is also suitable for distributed multimedia application, it is restricted to communication between different high-level services – fine-grained configuration of applications using distributed flow graphs is not supported.

NMM also follows the approach of providing a micro-core middleware together with pluggable components for realizing communication. However, its architecture is intentionally designed to support different interaction paradigms, such as request-reply or one-way interaction for multimedia data.

### 4.3.4    System Characteristics

As discussed in Section 2.2, distributed multimedia applications might require a lot of networking and processing resources. However, in heterogenous environments, the various mobile and stationary systems provide different resources in terms of computational power, memory capacity, and networking performance.

While stationary systems like multimedia PCs or set-top boxes nowadays provide sufficient resources to allow multimedia middleware or middleware in general to operate efficiently, for resource-poor devices, like PDAs, specifications like Minimum CORBA were developed [Obj02a]. Contrariwise, recent results also showed that commodity mobile devices are able to operate commercial CORBA implementation specialized for embedded environments efficiently [KAVP03]. However, the performance strongly depends on the optimizations provided for a particular platform. While these performance results are quite promising, the memory requirements for standard middleware might still be too high. Furthermore, as discussed before, support for streaming multimedia is not included in middleware for distributed object computing and requires additional resources. In contrast, NMM aims at providing a unified approach for object-based interaction and multimedia streaming.

### 4.3.5 Existing Applications

While the availability of some open middleware technology on all platforms is certainly a desirable goal, many end-systems are closed in the sense that they do not even allow to install additionally software. For example, many mobile phones only offer a fixed set of installed applications such as web browsers and media players. Together, these two applications allow mobile phones to act as a "traditional" streaming clients that access multimedia streams via links embedded in web pages. Other systems might allow to install additional software components for receiving streaming data but are still restricted to use the preinstalled media player for multimedia data processing.

In order to integrate these systems into distributed multimedia computing environments, proxy architectures can be used. While the Proxy design pattern is also used within distributed object computing middleware (compare Section 3.3), in this context, the term proxy refers to an intermediate system between a data source (e.g. a streaming server) and a data sink (e.g. a streaming client). The proxy can then be used to process the data received from the source before forwarding it to the sink. The system that represents the data sink, often runs special software components that handle the receiving of streaming multimedia before forwarding data to the preinstalled media player.

Different approaches were proposed that employ this concept, e.g. [SDEF98] or the system described in [MSK01]. Often, a multimedia middleware then runs on servers and proxies. While such scenarios are not addressed in more detail in the scope of this thesis, the communication framework of NMM can also be used to realize traditional client/server setups. Since web browsers can be used as control point, the generation of web interfaces can be achieved by using the reflective capabilities of NMM.

### 4.3.6 QoS Management

Heterogeneous environments offer different means to specify and maintain QoS requirements. Consequently, a large variety of different standards exists in this area (compare Section 2.2.6). Therefore, recent research concentrates on the provision of integrated generic solutions for QoS management for such heterogeneous environments [EGPJ02]. While these approaches certainly share similar goals with other integrating architectures, we concentrate on the case where the underlying infrastructure does only provide best-effort QoS and the middleware needs to provide reflection to guide the adaptation process (see Section 2.3).

## 4.4 Coping with Dynamics and Complexity

The middleware facilities discussed so far already provide suitable abstractions for developing distributed multimedia applications. However, due to the dynamics and complexity of distributed systems in general, multimedia middleware needs to provide additional services such as adaptation and reconfiguration, support for user and host mobility, seamless service provision, support for collaborative activities, and high-level abstractions together with services that help setting up complex distributed flow graphs.

Together, the described application scenarios and requirements motivate the development of advanced middleware services to be described in Part III of this thesis. Correspondingly, related work is reviewed within the scope of the different chapters of that part.

### 4.4.1   Adaptation and Reconfiguration

Within a distributed systems, applications – or more generally, *tasks* – run concurrently and therefore compete for all kinds of resources. In the context of a multimedia system, "resources" can be anything from computational power or networking bandwidth to specialized multimedia input/output devices.

The resource requirements for a single task can vary dynamically. Correspondingly, the resource availability for all tasks in the distributed system change over time. The variation of resource requirements can be the result of internal or external changes. On the one hand, as explained in Section 2.2, the different characteristics of even a single multimedia stream impose varying internal resource requirements. For infrastructures without strict quality of service guarantees, a single concurrently running task might therefore violate the resource requirements for all other tasks. On the other hand, the variation of resource requirements can be the result of external changes. For example, a user might choose to alter her preferences, e.g. by selecting a higher quality in terms of video resolution.

As no strict quality of service (QoS) guarantees are provided by the underlying platforms, multimedia middleware needs to be able to detect these changes. Then, different adaptation techniques like the scaling techniques described in Section 2.3.2 can be applied. Such fine-grained techniques have been used by several approaches, e.g. for controlling the behavior of components running on intermediate host that act as proxy [SDEF98, NXWL01], for maintenance operations performed on arbitrary components along a data path [MSK01], or for adaptations within object graphs of open bindings [FBC+98].

If these fine-grained adaptation techniques are insufficient, dynamic reconfigurations of complete flow graphs or application setups can be used. This is used for example to instantiate additional components running on hosts that act as proxies [SDEF98] or by providing alternative application specific configurations for flow graphs together with rules describing when to use a certain configuration [LXN02].

### Discussion

While the provision of adaptation techniques is certainly an important task for multimedia middleware, we focus on the more complex case of reconfigurations of active distributed flow graphs. Especially, we aim at providing suitable abstractions for such reconfigurations within the middleware layer to be used by applications or other middleware service. In this context, we focus on the special case for dynamic reconfigurations due to user and device mobility as discussed in the following. However, as will be described in Chapter 12, the taken approach can be applied in general.

## 4.4.2 User and Device Mobility

A special case for a dynamic reconfiguration of a flow graph occurs due to the mobility of either users, devices, or both together. For example, a user might initiate a multimedia application such as the playback of audio/video data on a nearby stationary system. Upon moving to another location, the user might want to continue this application using another nearby system. For the example of media playback, this would result in performing the output of audio and video data on the system closest to the user.

This is a typical example of location-aware multimedia access. Similarly, an application running on a mobile device can be reconfigured depending on the location of the device itself.

Another variation of user mobility is referred to as "follow-you-and-me" [NT02]. In such scenarios, the devices that act as sources of data are chosen according to the location of one person, and the devices that act as sinks of data according to the location of another person. An example for a "follow-you-and-me video" would record a video with a camera chosen according to the location of one person and display this video stream on a device according to the location of another person.

### Multimedia Access for Mobile Users

A special case of user and device mobility works as follows. Let us consider an application for watching TV running on a stationary system. Such an application is represented by a flow graph of possibly distributed processing elements (compare Section 4.2.1). Typically, the processing elements that perform the output of audio/video are located on a system nearby the user. Notice, that the distributed synchronization provided by a multimedia middleware allows the sink elements for audio and video to be located on different systems. Furthermore, the source of data – such as a TV board for DVB reception – can be used from a remote system.

A distributed flow graph further allows such an application to run on one system, e.g. a mobile device, while all processing elements of the flow graph itself run on other systems. To this end, a mobile device acts as a "remote control" for the distributed flow graph since network transparent control is provided by the underlying middleware.

Again, if the user moves to another location, the distributed flow graph can be reconfigured to perform media output on systems nearby. In particular, the processing elements that act as sinks need to be migrated to a new system. In the best case, middleware should therefore provide mobility transparency as described in Section 3.2.3.

This requires to relocate processing elements but also to perform a *handoff* of the connection between proxy and target object, and the streaming data connections between processing elements of the flow graph. Figure 4.3 shows a simple example for such a migration process. Most commonly, the term *handoff* is used to describe the change of an existing network connection. While *vertical handoff* describes the functionality of changing connections between heterogeneous networks, the term *horizontal handoff* is used when such a change occurs between networks of the same type. Often, these two cases can be handled similarly.

The integration of resource-poor mobile devices into this scenario is particular interesting. For example, while moving from one location to another, the user might want to continue media playback on a mobile device. Due to the limitations in terms

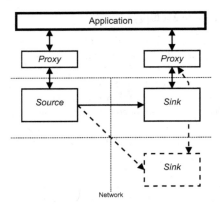

Figure 4.3: Reconfiguration of flow graph for location-aware media output (compare Figure 4.2). The sink element is migrated to another host during runtime. This requires to handoff the connection between proxy and target object, and the streaming connection between source and sink elements.

of networking bandwidth and processing power of such a device, this might require to adapt the media streams received by the processing elements running on the mobile device. Such a dynamic adaptation therefore might require to insert additional processing elements into the used flow graph and to distribute the additional workload of these elements to different powerful systems within the network.

**Realizing Location-Awareness**

The above described application scenarios are typical examples for ubiquitous computing. A major research topic in this area focuses on the development of infrastructures where computers are fulfilling user-centered task while acting invisible in the background [Wei91].

For realizing the above described scenarios, some environmental factors such as the locations of the user and devices, the identity of the user, or the preferences of the user – together, generally referred to as *context* – need to be acquired and considered. Especially the location of users and devices is important.

There exist many different approaches for acquiring location information, like radio-frequency (RF) based systems [BP00], infrared-based systems [BBK00], systems using the Global Positioning Systems (GPS), or combinations thereof [BKW02]. Furthermore, different middleware solutions study architectural support for context-aware applications, e.g. [CNM01] and [Dey00].

Although the user's experience will benefit when context information is acquired and integrated automatically, applications still need to be reconfigured due to changes in context. However, while this task is often not addressed by solutions for context-aware computing, the various challenges that need to be solved for this step are specifically addressed in Chapter 12 of this thesis.

Correspondingly, we are not discussing topics related to context-aware computing – such as acquiring context information – in the scope of this thesis but rather assume that this information is given. In the simplest case, this is realized by user interaction, e.g. by manually selecting the current position.

### 4.4.3   Seamless Service Provision

Several solutions for dynamic reconfigurations and handoff for distributed multimedia systems were proposed so far. These approaches are described in detail in Chapter 12, more precisely in Section 12.2. However, the main disadvantage of these approaches is the lack of synchronized playback during reconfiguration.

Let us again consider a playback application running on a mobile device, e.g. a PDA, playing audio data through its internal speakers or earphones. When the user moves around and enters an environment with richer I/O capabilities (e.g. a hi-fi system in a living room, a car, or an office) the output could be handed off to these more capable devices. If the user later leaves this environment the output should be handed back to the mobile device.

To realize this scenario, the application must be able to dynamically adapt an active multimedia flow graph to changing environments. In addition, the reconfiguration and handoff should be seamless and continuous. This means that no data is lost or duplicated and media playback is fully synchronized at all times, which is especially important when listening to music. To this end, even the final change of the used output devices should be absolutely "seamless" in the sense that no interruption is noticeable for humans.

#### Discussion

Such seamless service provision by using horizontal handoffs is already known from network technologies for mobile phones like the Global System for Mobile Communications (GSM). However, the scenario described above additionally requires to reconfigure and migrate parts of an active flow graph while keeping multimedia processing continuous and synchronized at all times. Furthermore, we aim at establishing such seamless handoff as a general service that is independent of a particular transmission protocol.

In general, such a seamless service allows to adapt and reconfigure active distributed flow graphs. To realize this, middleware needs to provide distributed coordination and synchronization mechanisms that can be extended easily to implement a particular handoff protocol. Furthermore, appropriate abstractions need to be provided that allow to specify what parts of an active flow graph need to reconfigured. In Chapter 12, the developed service will be presented in detail and related work will be reviewed.

### 4.4.4   Collaborative Multimedia Applications

Besides seamless service provision, the increased number of mobile and stationary devices with multimedia capabilities enables further new application scenarios.

Particularly interesting is collaborative multimedia access, where a number of users simultaneously enjoys the same (or similar) content – possibly at different locations using different devices.

## Application Scenarios

For collaborative multimedia entertainment, different application scenarios can be envisioned. For example, different users within a household can enjoy the same content: a sports event being watched at a TV set in the living-room can then at the same time also be followed with a mobile device, e.g. while being in the garden, or with another stationary device, e.g. in the kitchen. While such a scenario could be realized by using a TV receiver in each devices (e.g. for receiving digital TV via DVB-T), such abundant resources are not necessarily needed. On the contrary, a multimedia middleware solution that operates on top of commodity networking technology such as IP-based LANs or WLANs could provide shared access to a single device for receiving TV. Using such a solution, the described application scenario would also not be restricted to TV but work for other media as well.

A particularly interesting option arises for shared access to media like DVD that usually provide different audio tracks, e.g. for different languages. Here, different users could jointly watch the video material on the same large screen but use individual mobile devices (like PDAs) together with earphones to listen to different audio tracks.

Another example that includes wide-area networking could provide an opportunity for video conferencing together with collaborative access to additional media. A setup particularly interesting for multimedia home entertainment could allow a user to playback personal media files including audio and video (e.g. from the last vacation) on the local system and to present the same content simultaneously on a remote system to another user. By using an additional channel for video conferencing, both users could interactively comment on the media being presented. This scenario stresses the importance of synchronized playback on distributed systems.

Yet another scenario provides a similar setup: two users at the same location spontaneously "connect" their personal mobile devices in order to simultaneously enjoy the same content. For example, one user could playback media on a laptop computer, while a second user accesses the content on a mobile system, e.g. a PDA or mobile phone.

## Middleware Support for Shared Applications

These application scenarios motivate a general requirement for multimedia middleware: parts of an application (in form of a flow graph) need to be *shared* to be used by another application.

This feature provides different benefits. First, this possibility is necessary in cases where only one distinct device exists to perform a certain operation and a number of different users want to access it simultaneously (e.g. a device for receiving TV). Secondly, sharing of flow graphs allows to share the computational resources consumed by a certain task (e.g. the decoding of digital TV). Consequently, this also helps to integrate devices with scarce resources by reusing parts of the multimedia processing performed on systems with sufficient resources.

In order to allow rich multimedia access (such as watching TV) for users with mobile devices, media adaptation needs to be performed to cope with the limited resources of these devices. This adaptation is a dynamic process and has to be performed on demand and possibly includes the extension of a shared flow graph.

Another important fact for collaborative multimedia is the possibility to jointly control media processing. All users participating in such a shared application should be provided the possibility to control all parts of the flow part if not restricted otherwise.

### Discussion

Different solutions for group communication such as IP multicast or application level multicast were proposed so far and will be discussed in Section 11.2. While these approaches consider a different problem domain, the benefits of sharing of multimedia flow graphs were not considered previously. A middleware service especially developed for such application scenarios will be described in detail in Chapter 11 of this thesis.

### 4.4.5 Automatic Application Setup

While the middleware facilities described so far already provide a lot of support for developing distributed multimedia applications, a key issue remains: the creation of flow graphs.

Multimedia middleware must allow an application – or even a user – to create and configure complex flow graphs without having to deal with low level details such as data formats and how certain processing elements must be connected to be compatible with each other. Especially in a distributed environment, new multimedia devices or software codecs and associated new data formats may become available at any time and should be seamlessly supported by the multimedia middleware and thus all of its applications.

At best, multimedia middleware could provide interaction mechanisms where a user simply needs to specify what tasks should be performed (e.g. playback of media) using what content (e.g. some audio/video file) employing what devices (e.g. a TV set). Such a representation is then automatically converted to a valid and fully configured flow graph meaning that only "matching" elements are connected with fully specified connection formats. Finally, such a representation needs to be mapped to physical instances of processing elements and connections. In this last step, resource such as devices, processing capacity of hosts, and networking bandwidth need to be reserved. In addition, adaptation and dynamic reconfiguration steps might be needed in order to maintain the initial setup of a flow graph.

### Discussion

From the above described requirements, one can conclude that many different aspects are involved in true automatic application setup. Therefore, this task can be considered to be an open problem for distributed multimedia systems. For the scope of this thesis we will concentrate on the problem of finding and configuring valid distributed flow graphs starting from a given high-level description. The optimization criteria we use is oriented to the quality of service perceived by users of the system. The quality-driven format negotiation and graph building service will be described in detail in Chapter 10.

## 4.5  Summary

Together, middleware that allows to set up distributed flow graphs masks out the complexity of developing distributed multimedia applications by providing the same programming model as locally operating multimedia architectures.

Therefore, a service for device discovery is needed that allows to locate and access distributed multimedia devices and software components in order to integrate them into a distributed flow graph. Such a flow graph provides network transparent control of distributed processing elements.

While these requirements can partly be fulfilled by traditional middleware solutions, multimedia middleware needs to provide additional features and services. Network transparent cooperation allows to connect distributed and local elements. Streaming data connections between elements need to provide appropriate bindings. Distributed synchronization is a further requirement for multimedia middleware. In addition, QoS management for predictable QoS in best-effort environments concentrates on QoS specification, monitoring, and maintenance within the middleware layer.

As we have seen in Chapter 2, multimedia data streams have very different properties. Furthermore, even two streams with the same characteristics (e.g. the same format) need to be handled differently if used in real-time or off-line applications. For example, real-time applications generally need timely delivery of multimedia data and thus prefer protocols like RTP whereas off-line application choose TCP because of the provided reliability.

Therefore, explicit binding approaches allow to manually choose the binding to be established and configure specific parameters thereof. This corresponds to a white-box design, where the application can access internal properties of the core functionality of the middleware. Often explicit binding is realized by providing first-class binding objects to applications. Such abstractions provide an elegant way to to express the imposed requirements for a binding in terms of channel characteristics. Furthermore, they allow to monitor and to inspect the binding. Finally, binding objects can be used to reconfigure or adapt a communication channel.

Different dimensions of heterogeneity in distributed multimedia systems require additional architectural choices to be made. To summarize, one cannot assume the availability of a certain technology on all platforms. To this end, even the existence of different middleware solutions increases this heterogeneity problem. Therefore, it seems more promising to develop an open meta-architecture that consists of a very small middleware core. Rather than relying on a particular technology, such a solution allow for integrating different existing solutions. Also, different communication models can be realized uniformly. In addition, reflection needs to be provided – a property especially important for multimedia middleware because it allows to inspect heterogeneous components, to register for notifications in distributed environments, and to apply different adaptation and reconfiguration strategies.

Based on such a framework, a very generic processing model for multimedia data flow graphs can be realized that allows to integrate different other locally operating components such as devices, software routines, or other multimedia architectures. Finally, the openness of the architecture should be applied to all aspects of the middleware, like distributed synchronization, or additional services such as device discovery.

While the challenges due to heterogeneity are considered in areas like Enterprise Application Integration [Gei01], system research for ubiquitous or multimedia computing only started to consider this area [BSGR03, NT02]. The key challenge for such integrating architectures lies in the challenge to not just simply add another middleware solution, but provide a meta-level on top of other solutions.

Despite the fact that multimedia middleware needs to provide a certain degree of openness, it should provide transparency and appropriate abstractions to mask out the complexity of developing distributed multimedia applications. The concept of distributed flow graphs greatly helps to ease application development. In addition, the separation of middleware into an open architectural core and additional higher level services further helps to provide scalable transparency. Services are allowed to access all internal properties of the middleware core but provide a higher level of transparency to applications.

The dynamics and complexity of application scenarios for distributed multimedia require additional services to be provided by multimedia middleware. A service particularly interesting is the seamless adaptation or reconfiguration due to user and device mobility. More precisely, middleware should support the migration of users' activities to different locations and devices without interrupting the tasks.

Rather then requiring to manually integrate processing elements for networking connections within flow graphs [BHK+02], it seems more promising to "hide" this fact within the edges connecting distributed elements. We argue that such an approach provides the appropriate abstractions for supporting transparent relocation of processing elements. In such cases, the overall structure of the flow graph stays the same. No networking elements need to be inserted (or removed); only the connecting edges need to be reconfigured. However, such stream bindings need to provide the openness needed to realize scalable transparency.

Furthermore, middleware for true network-integrated multimedia enables new and exciting application scenarios where a number of users simultaneously enjoys the same content using different devices. To enhance the sense of collaboration among users, such activities need strict synchronization.

Finally, the setup of complex distributed multimedia data flow graphs needs to be facilitated by additional middleware services. Due to the complexity of this task, an overall solution for this problem is still actively researched. However, basic support for setting up applications in distributed environments can already be provided when focusing on the important aspect of the quality of service as perceived by users of the system.

To summarize, a lot of challenges and requirements have to be addressed by a multimedia middleware solution for true distributed multimedia. To this end, The formation of the Digital Living Network Alliance (DLNA) [Diga] clearly shows the need for defining frameworks for interoperable multimedia systems and advanced services, and their commercial relevance. In June 2004, DLNA published a white paper addressing several use case scenarios that focus on seamless home entertainment [Dig04b]. While the DLNA Home Networked Device Interoperability Guidelines v1.0 is not available freely, from a white paper published in June 2004, its general design principles can be derived [Dig04a]. Instead of defining an open framework, DLNA tries to achieve interoperability by strictly specifying the building blocks for network, device, codec, and software technologies. The guidelines name JPEG, LPCM audio, MPEG2, HTTP, UPnP, IPv4, Ethernet, and 802.11a/b/g as these building blocks. For integrating new and emerging technologies, the DLNA standards need to be evolved. Furthermore, the architecture mostly adopts a client/server approach with streaming data transmissions mainly taking place between Digital Media Servers (DMS) and Digital Media Players (DMP); required media adaptations needed for serving devices with restricted capabilities are to be performed by servers, a distribution of workload does not seem to be possible.

In contrast, the work presented in the following aims at providing a more open framework that adopts the concept of a distributed flow graph. However, it will be interesting to evaluate if DLNA products can be integrated into our approach – once they are available.

# Part II

# Network-Integrated Multimedia Middleware

# Chapter 5

# An Open Middleware Architecture for Network-Integrated Multimedia

In this chapter, the design of an open middleware architecture for network-integrated multimedia is presented [LRS02, LS03, Loh04d]. The major design goals and the derived architectural decisions are discussed first. While the presented base architecture is not restricted to multimedia computing, we will continue by giving an overview of a concrete realization of a flow graph based multimedia middleware. The following chapters of this part of the thesis will provide more details on the developed middleware – the Network-Integrated Multimedia Middleware (NMM).

## 5.1 Architectural Decisions

From the discussion in the preceding chapters, it can be derived that the different dimensions of heterogeneity of today's infrastructures impose new challenges for multimedia middleware and for middleware in general [Gei01]. Furthermore, the dynamics and complexity of distributed multimedia applications requires suitable abstractions to allow for the development of advanced middleware services. The following discussion will introduce the core concepts as provided by the Network-Integrated Multimedia Middleware (NMM) to address these challenges.

### 5.1.1 Open and Integrating Micro-Core Architecture

First of all, one can observe that the benefits of object-oriented programming naturally fit into the task of developing middleware for distributed multimedia:

> *An object-oriented approach provides a suitable programming model for multimedia middleware.*

In particular, we choose the programming language C++. This choice was mainly made because many low-level multimedia libraries (e.g. for encoding or decoding data) for GNU/Linux are available as C libraries. While offering the benefits of an object-oriented programming language, C++ allows to integrate these libraries easily. The following sections will extensively use terminology typically for object-oriented programming such as inheritance or exceptions [Str97].

The key design challenge is to provide a high degree of openness and at the same time allow for scalable transparency in order to ease the development of distributed multimedia applications. It is important to notice that *openness* implies that the architectures allows the composition of the overall system out of individual components and at the same time provides access to these components. These properties should be fulfilled not only for the main externally visible components but also for all internal components. Such a degree of openness then allows for configurability and extensibility. To summarize:

> *An open middleware allows to be extended, configured, and tailored.*

Our approach aims at providing an integrating meta-architecture that does not rely on a particular technology or middleware. Instead, it allows the flexible usage of different technologies:

> *An integrating meta-architecture is chosen over of a close coupling to a specific technology.*

Consequently, the architecture consists of a very small middleware core – a property important for resource-poor devices – and additional components for realizing different aspects. Together:

> *A micro-core architecture is suited for heterogeneous environments with varying resource availability.*

Distributed multimedia systems imply a high degree of dynamics – for example, due to the possible mobility of users and devices. Therefore, such systems can be regarded as loosely coupled organizations of distributed resources. The characteristics of such environments are better supported by peer-to-peer (P2P) architectures that do not rely on centralized components but rather consist of individual peers voluntary participating in a dynamic and ad-hoc infrastructure:

> *The architecture prefers a peer-to-peer approach over a centralized client/-server approach.*

Finally, the approach of providing a pluggable and generic peer-to-peer architecture that offers openness is also applied to facilities like synchronization and all additional services to be developed:

> *The above defined design principles are applied to all aspects of the middleware.*

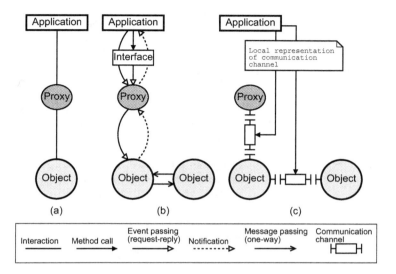

Figure 5.1: Different aspects of the NMM architecture. The architecture is based on the Proxy design pattern shown in (a). By providing a unified messaging system, different kinds of interaction can be realized as depicted in (b). Events can be passed either manually or by method invocations on interfaces. In addition, listener notification and one-way message passing between different objects are available. In (c), the communication channels are shown that provide an abstraction for all kinds of bindings. Different transport and serialization strategies can be chosen and configured for each communication channel.

### 5.1.2 Mediating Proxy Objects

The architecture is based on the Proxy design pattern (see Figure 5.1(a)). As described in Section 3.3.2, proxy objects allow to separate method invocation and execution. Therefore, they can be used to realize various degrees of transparency. Furthermore, a proxy object can act as mediator or adapter that controls access to its target object. Together:

*The architecture allows to take full advantage of the benefits of the Proxy design pattern.*

### 5.1.3 Unified Messaging System

As discussed in Section 4.2.1, the concept of a distributed flow graph is a central architectural element for multimedia middleware. Streaming one-way interaction between processing elements of such a flow graph is mainly used for forwarding multimedia data encapsulated in messages of type buffer. However, the possibility of forwarding additional arbitrary control information in between the multimedia data stream is an essential requirement for realizing advanced functionality within flow graphs (see Section 2.4.3). Therefore, this interaction needs both buffers *and* control information encapsulated in messages of type event to be transmitted over a network. Consequently, it is necessary to realize serialization, transmission, and deserialization for these different message types (see Section 3.3.3). The concrete realization of this functionality can then be employed for all other interaction as well.

The resulting unified messaging system allows for realizing different interaction paradigms like synchronous request-reply interaction, event-based asynchronous interaction, or message-oriented store-and-forward interaction (see Section 3.3.1). Consequently, the messaging system can be used to implement object-based interaction via interfaces (see Figure 5.1(b)). For each method call performed on an interface, a message of type event – or simply an event – is generated, forwarded to the object, and dispatched for executing the corresponding method. Then, return values or exceptions are sent back to the caller using the same event.

Stream interaction is realized via one-way asynchronous calls – possibly in different directions as can be seen in Figure 5.1(b). A serialized message can even be stored on intermediate-term storage in order to realize decoupled message-oriented interaction as described in Section 3.3.1. To summarize:

*A unified messaging system allows for realizing different interaction paradigms.*

In general, messages of arbitrary type and content are allowed. However, in order to optimize for the requirements for distributed multimedia computing, two different types of messages can be distinguished. Multimedia data is placed into messages of type *buffer*; messages of type *event* contain arbitrary control information. This distinction allows to handle high-bandwidth multimedia streams in an optimized way. Furthermore, for control events within a multimedia stream, different quality of service properties such as reliability can be provided. To summarize:

*The unified messaging system allows for realizing possible optimizations*
*for high-bandwidth communication and quality of service improvements*
*for control events.*

### 5.1.4   Object-Oriented Interfaces

While method invocations on interfaces exported by components have the same semantics as event passing, interacting with interfaces provides a more type-safe and comfortable way than manual creation of events. Furthermore, interfaces provide the possibility to group related functionality and to use inheritance. In addition, interfaces provide the well-known interaction and handling as known from object-oriented programming environments. Therefore, we chose to provide a complete interface definition and code generation system on top of the unified messaging system:

*An object-oriented interface system provides a suitable programming model.*

### 5.1.5   Reflective Middleware

By providing a unified messaging system for all interaction, components can dynamically add and remove supported functionality. More precisely, this is done by adding or removing the handling of certain events. Furthermore, components can be queried for their supported features – either by querying supported events or interfaces, respectively. In addition, applications can register to be notified by components when a certain event occurs. Since method invocations on interfaces exported by components have the same semantics as event passing, notification is performed for both kinds of interaction. Together, this allows to develop a reflective middleware as described in Section 3.2.6. To summarize:

> *A reflective middleware is provided that allows for realizing inspection, notification, and adaptation.*

### 5.1.6 Communication Channels

All communication is based on the same abstraction: communication channels (see Figure 5.1(c)). These channels represent a first class data type and provide a bidirectional binding between two entities. Network transparent control and cooperation is realized with communication channels (see Section 4.2.1):

> *Communication channels provide a unified abstraction for communication.*

Notice that for network transparent cooperation, communication channels "hide" the specific configuration of connections between different processing elements of a flow graph within the connecting edges. This is according to the way in which network transparent control for object-based request-reply interaction is realized by using communication channels. While this design decision is in contrast to approaches that require additional processing elements for networking connections within flow graphs, it provides better abstraction for realizing migration transparency as the overall structure of the flow graph stays the same even if communication channels have to be reconfigured. However, communication channels provide the openness needed for setting up streaming multimedia connections. Applications or middleware services can decide what degree of transparency they require – or, if they want to manually set up communication channels. Together:

> *Communication channels "hide" communication means for all kinds of interaction but provide scalable transparency.*

Messages sent across a communication channel are serialized, transmitted, and then deserialized. The way in which these steps are performed can be configured during the explicit binding process. Explicit binding allows to choose the serialization and the transport strategies independently for the transmission of multimedia data and the transmission of control events. Appropriate parameters can be set for every connection. This is an important property for multimedia middleware. Not only streaming data connections require specific configuration, but also request-reply interaction with objects such as multimedia devices require appropriate communication setup. To summarize:

> *Explicit binding with parameterizable serialization and transport strategies is provided.*

Together, the serialization and transport strategies allow to realize a uniform way of communication by providing generic interfaces to different underlying technologies or protocols. In contrast to other middleware approaches, transport strategies represent individual entities and do not rely on a centralized component such as an object request broker. However, they allow to act as wrappers for such solutions. To this end, even technologies like CORBA can be integrated into our architecture.

Different extensions to existing middleware technologies as well as new technologies in general will emerge in the future (see Section 4.3). Our architecture can take advantage of this progression by using these new technologies as additional communication strategies (e.g. for serialization or transport), or by integrating new multimedia middleware functionality with suitable proxy objects:

> *Extensibility is provided through easy integration of new communication strategies and mediating proxy objects.*

Resource-poor devices can be integrated by providing specialized and light-weight strategies. Furthermore, the tight coupling of a multimedia middleware to an existing technology might incur significant overhead, which is often permanent even for locally operating applications. This overhead can be removed by using simple and efficient strategies within communication channels. To summarize:

> *Efficiency can be improved through the usage of specialized and light-weight communication strategies.*

### 5.1.7  Generic Multimedia Middleware Architecture

Based on the provided facilities, a generic multimedia middleware architecture for distributed flow graphs is provided. The architecture is generic in the sense that it allows to integrate all kinds of multimedia devices, algorithms, synchronization protocols, or other multimedia architectures. The streaming data connection between processing elements are realized with communication channels and therefore allow bidirectional communication using all message types:

> *A generic multimedia middleware architecture and processing model for distributed flow graphs with full-featured bidirectional communication is provided.*

This architecture is described in detail in Chapter 7 of this thesis.

### 5.1.8  Local Specialization

Finally, the taken approach allows to prove the feasibility of the concept of an integrating open architecture by providing a specialization for a purely locally operating multimedia architecture that is independent of a full-featured middleware solution.

> *A purely locally operating multimedia architecture as specialization of the developed multimedia middleware solution proves the configurability of the chosen approach.*

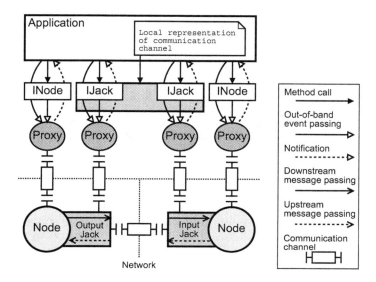

Figure 5.2: A distributed flow graph using the facilities provided by the NMM architecture. Objects, such as nodes and connecting input or output jacks, are controlled via mediating proxy objects. Method calls on object-oriented interfaces (with prefix "I") and out-of-band event passing provide the same semantics. Instream communication for data buffers or events via streaming one-way interaction can be performed upstream and downstream. Proxies can notify registered listeners within applications for a certain instream or out-of-band event to occur. All communication is based on the unified messaging system and the abstraction of communication channels that provide an explicit binding mechanism. As an example, the application accesses the instream binding via a local representation of the communication channel.

To this end, the architecture can also be used to develop locally operating desktop applications or "traditional" client/server streaming solutions. In this case, the networking functionality is integrated into the processing elements of a flow graph rather than into the edges.

## 5.2 Overview

Figure 5.2 provides an overview of the developed architecture by showing a concrete distributed flow graph that uses the facilities provided by our middleware. Two distributed processing elements – called *nodes* in NMM terminology – are connected via their input and output ports. These ports are represented by so called *jacks*; in particular *input jacks* and *output jacks*. In general, all distributed objects are controlled via mediating proxy objects. These proxy objects provide object-oriented *interfaces* to applications.

By using the *unified messaging system* and *communication channels*, different types of interaction can be realized. Request-reply interaction between proxies and corresponding target objects is performed by sending *out-of-band* events and blocking until results of the operation invoked are received. In this case, events are generated automatically by interface objects according to the specific method called. Using interfaces provides a type safe and more convenient way of interacting with objects. Interfaces and corresponding implementation classes are generated from interface definitions written in NMM IDL. However, this mechanism can be bypassed by creating events manually and sending them to proxy objects directly. Together, this type of interaction allows to transparently *control* any kind of distributed object, e.g. nodes and jacks, but also arbitrary other objects.

*Instream* streaming data connections between connected input and output jacks are also realized by using communication channels. When handling multimedia, this kind of interaction mostly consists of sending buffers *downstream* meaning from nodes that represent sources of data to nodes that process or consume data. In this case, non-blocking one-way interaction is used in order to fulfill the requirements for streaming data connections. As discussed above, the ability to insert events into this data stream is essential for realizing advanced functionality. Furthermore, especially the possibility to send messages *upstream* is also of great importance to enhance interaction between the nodes of a flow graph. Therefore, bidirectional streaming data connections are provided for all connected jacks of NMM flow graphs.

For both instream and out-of-band communication, the architecture offers explicit access to all aspects of the binding by providing local representations of communication channels. For the case of instream communication, this is shown in Figure 5.2. Notice that the internal parts of a communication channel can themselves be distributed objects.

In addition, the messaging system offers the ability for registering an application as *listener*. Then, *notifications* are sent from proxy objects to registered components within the application. Such notifications are then performed whenever an event occurs at a particular object; either for all events or for some specific events only. Notice that the unified messaging system allows to register for instream and out-of-band events in the same way.

## 5.3   Summary

In this chapter, the architectural decisions for the design of the Network-Integrated Multimedia Middleware (NMM) were presented and an overview was given. Our approach provides an open micro-core architecture. As its basic functionality, a messaging system allows for forwarding information in form of multimedia buffers and control events, which is essential for realizing different interaction paradigms in a uniform way. The key for the openness and extensibility of the NMM is that this messaging system is strictly separated from the multimedia processing aspects and the communication aspects of the architecture: Available multimedia functionality is encapsulated within NMM nodes; communication channels handle all communication aspects. We argue that this simple yet effective design is the key for regarding NMM as an network-integrated architecture – one of the main contributions of the presented work. Instead of relying on specific solutions, this approach allows for the flexible integration, usage, and combination of available technologies and therefore achieves a degree of openness not presented before.

The following chapters demonstrate how the discussed design choices were applied by presenting the NMM architecture in more detail. In Chapter 6, the integrating communication framework of NMM is described. Based on the provided facilities, a generic multimedia middleware was developed that is presented in Chapter 7. Finally, Chapter 8 provides an evaluation of the performance of different aspects of the current implementation.

## Note

The following chapters will provide structural class diagrams using the notation of the Unified Modeling Language (UML) according to [SSR00]. However, these diagrams do not necessarily represent the concrete implementation of NMM. Rather, they are used to further clarify and formalize the concepts and design issues discussed in the corresponding text. Therefore, often only subsets of the concrete interfaces of classes are shown or the signatures of methods are simplified.

# Chapter 6

# An Integrating Communication Framework

In this chapter, the concrete design and implementation of communication framework for distributed computing is presented that follows the architectural decisions discussed in the preceding chapter [LRS02, LS03, Loh03g, Rep03a, Rep03b, Loh04d, RWLS04, RWLS05]. This framework provides a unified approach for realizing different interaction paradigms, such as out-of-band and instream interaction, needed for multimedia middleware. Furthermore, it allows to integrate arbitrary data types, serialization protocols, and networking technologies.

In the following, the different parts of the communication framework are described in detail, namely the serialization framework, the unified messaging system, the communication and proxy architecture, and the object-oriented interface system. Finally, the connecting parts of the architecture, so called communication channels, and the corresponding binding framework is presented.

## 6.1 Serialization Framework

As we have seen in Section 5.1, the serialization and deserialization of objects such as buffers and events is an important building block for multimedia middleware. On the one hand, serialization and deserialization is required to transmit objects over networks. On the other hand, this functionality is also needed for realizing message-oriented communication with intermediate storage. Within NMM, serialization and deserialization is supported by a dedicated framework [LRS02, LS03, Rep03a, Rep03b]. As the concepts of the developed framework are essential for the other parts of the architecture, serialization is described first. For the scope of this thesis, the term "serialization" stands for both serialization and deserialization, unless otherwise indicated.

### 6.1.1 Requirements

Several requirements have to be fulfilled by a serialization framework.

- Requirement 1: *Support for basic data types.* First, since the chosen programming language C++ does not provide facilities for serializing objects, the framework needs to support the serialization of the basic data types of C++.

- Requirement 2: *Support for new complex data structures.* Furthermore, a mechanism is needed that allows to easily realize serialization for newly developed complex data structures.

- Requirement 3: *Integration of existing data structures.* In addition, the framework should offer support for integrating existing data structures – even when no direct modifications are possible. However, such data structures then need to provide access to all internal members that are needed for reconstructing them.

- Requirement 4: *Integration of additional serialization strategies.* As described above, besides providing different transport strategies, the provision of different serialization strategies is an important aspect for realizing technology transparent middleware. Therefore, the serialization framework should provide the appropriate means and abstractions for implementing additional strategies.

- Requirement 5: *Stacking of several serialization strategies.* Furthermore, to enhance configurability, different strategies can be combined to form a stack of serialization (and corresponding deserialization) operators. For example, one operator can be used to transform an object into a certain representation and another operator can add a header to the data.

- Requirement 6: *Efficiency of serialization process.* Finally, the efficiency of the serialization process is of great importance. Therefore, one major goal for our framework is to reduce the amount of data that has to be copied *implicitly* (i.e. without the influence of the framework) during serialization and deserialization. Especially when serializing high-bandwidth data streams for network transmission this is a crucial factor [GS98]. To this end, the framework itself should add no copy operation at all. However, there is a trade-off between the amount of copied data during serialization and the number of lower level function calls needed for network transmission. Therefore, copy operations performed for buffering data are allowed to be used as part of a specific serialization strategy.

Notice that the serialization framework developed to fulfill the above described requirements is not restricted to certain data types. While this is in contrast to other middleware solutions that are typically only support a restricted set of data types, this choice was made in order to be able to integrate and serialize arbitrary data structures as given by a certain technology to be integrated. Of course, when mapping between different technologies, this might require conversions. However such operations can also be performed within the serialization framework. Furthermore, by fulfilling the above described requirements, our framework allows different ways to integrate data types. To this end, one can choose a technique that best suits the requirements for integrated an existing approach.

## 6.1.2   Architecture

The serialization framework makes use of the concept of streams as known from the *iostream library*, a component of the C++ standard library [Str97], where output operators, `operator<<`, allow to recursively decompose complex data structures; input operators, `operator>>`, operate the other way round.

The general approach for the serialization framework is as follows. The serialization of basic data types is realized by specifying specific stream operators for each type. As data arrays are important when handling multimedia, additional methods are defined for such types. For all these operators, implementations have to be provided for different serialization strategies. These implementations also need to handle type information.

Complex data types are composed out of basic data types. For complex data types, a mapping to (or from) other data types has to be provided for serialization (or deserialization). For serialization, such a mapping recursively uses lower level operators until the complex data type is decomposed into the basic data types that are provided by a specific serialization strategies. Therefore, such mappings only have to be provided once for each complex data type.

For integrating complex data types different possibilities exist. First, for newly developed data types – or existing data types that can be modified for integrating them into the framework – parameterizable types provided by the serialization framework can be used, which act as wrappers for the attributes of the complex data type to be integrated. These wrappers provide full access to the internal data types but already provide the interfaces and functionality needed for serialization. The complex data structure to be integrated needs to inherit from a super class that implements serialization for all its registered internal data types. Secondly, for data types where this option can not be realized, corresponding serialization and deserialization operators can be implemented. As described above, such operators need to be provided only once for the decomposition and composition of complex types and can then be used together with another specific serialization strategy for basic data types. To this end, even closed source data types that allow to access all attributes needed for reconstruction them after deserialization can be integrated into the framework transparently. For both approaches, unique type information has to be provided and the data type itself has to be registered with a factory that allows to create objects during deserialization.

### 6.1.3 Implementation

Figure 6.1 shows the base classes for all specific serialization strategies, namely classes IStream and OStream. These classes define operators for serializing and deserializing C++ basic types, respectively. Since arrays of basic types are additionally defined by their size, the corresponding operations are realized by methods that allow to specify this value as a parameter (e.g. writeBuffer(char*&, size_t) for arrays of type char).

For combining different streams, a *partner stream* can be set. This allows a concrete implementation of an operator to forward information (e.g. a serialized object) to its partner. By configuring a specific stack of operators, the complete serialization process can be composed out of different steps. However, a serialization strategy might also need to buffer data before forwarding it to its partner. Therefore, the method writeData() can be used to trigger the flushing of such an internal buffer and forward data to the partner stream. With readData(), an analog operation exists for deserialization.

For all data to be serialized the exact type information needs to be added. This is needed to perform type-safe reconstruction of data structures during deserializa-

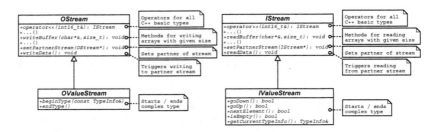

Figure 6.1: The classes `IStream` and `OStream` define operators for serializing and deserializing basic types of C++, respectively, and for interacting with partner streams. The classes `OValueStream` and `IValueStream` add interface methods for handling type information. Concrete serialization and deserialization strategies are derived from these classes.

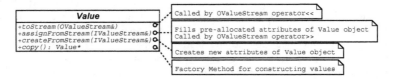

Figure 6.2: The abstract super class `Value` provides the interface for serialization, object creation, and deserialization.

tion. Therefore, the input and output streams are extended to so called *value streams*, namely `IValueStream` and `OValueStream` (see Figure 6.1). As C++ does not provide type information[1], a class `TypeInfo` is provided that holds type information in form of strings. For basic types of C++, corresponding type information is already provided. In order to create unique type information, other types need to provide this information according to their class name and namespace.

Specific serialization strategies inherited from `OValueStream` need to implement the methods `beginType(const TypeInfo&)` and `endType()` to begin respectively end the serialization of a complex type. During deserialization with subclasses of `IValueStream`, read type information obtained via the method `get-CurrentTypeInfo()` is compared with the expected type information of the performed operator. For navigating within complex data structures the methods `goDown` is called to start processing the stream of values, `isEmpty` to test for the end of the stream (as marked by `OValueStream::endType()`, and `goUp()` to finish processing a complex data type.

As described above, parameterizable wrappers are needed. In addition, a base class that handles all aspects of serialization and deserialization of all registered internal data types needs to be provided as base class for newly developed data types. The

---

[1]C++ Runtime-Type-Information (RTTI) depend on the used compiler [Str97] and can even change between consecutive executions of the same binary [And01].

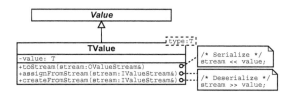

Figure 6.3: The parameterizable class `TValue<T>` acts as wrapper for basic data types. Serialization and deserialization are implemented by calling the corresponding operator.

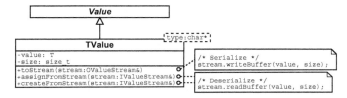

Figure 6.4: The template specialization for arrays (e.g. `TValue<char*>`) implements serialization and deserialization by calling `writeBuffer()` and `readBuffer`, respectively.

base class for these different classes is `Value` (see Figure 6.2). This class provides an abstract `copy` method that allows to delegate object creation to sub classes according to the Factory Method design pattern [GHJV94].

The different subclasses of `Value` need to be able to provide their own implementation for serialization and deserialization. Therefore, two abstract methods `to-Stream(OValueStream&` and `assignFromStream(IValueStream&)` are to be called by the corresponding operators (see Figure 6.2). While `assignFrom-Stream(IValueStream&)` sets internal preallocated attributes of the object, the method `createFromStream(IValueStream&)` is used when internal attributes have to be constructed during deserialization. This mode is needed for creating dynamic and polymorphic objects and for handling unknown data types during deserialization as discussed below.

As can be seen in Figure 6.3, a parameterizable subclass `TValue<T>` exists that acts as wrapper as described above. Furthermore, wrapper classes for arrays of basic data types exist (e.g. for `char*`) that allow to handle data buffers efficiently by calling the specialized methods of the serialization strategy (see Figure 6.4).

The class `SerializedValue` can be used as base class for integrating newly developed data types into the framework. In addition, existing data types that can be modified can be handled that way. This class allows to register attributes of type `Value`, e.g. basic data types of C++ wrapped in objects of type `TValue<T>` (see Figure 6.5). The serialization and deserialization is then handled by recursively triggering the corresponding operations of all internal registered values. In this step, the processing of the specified type information is also performed.

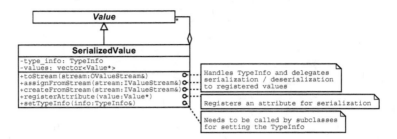

Figure 6.5: The class `SerializedValue` can be used as base class for data types to be integrated into the framework. Registered attributes of type `Value` are serialized and deserialized using the provided type information.

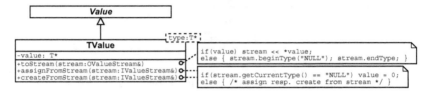

Figure 6.6: The class `TValue<T*>` handles pointers to dynamically and polymorphic objects. The type information *NULL* is used to identify NULL pointers.

For handling C++ pointers to dynamically allocated and polymorphic objects, a specialized class `TValue<T*>` is provided (see Figure 6.6). The type name *NULL* is used for arbitrary NULL pointer. The serialization framework also provides common abstractions, e.g. the class `SequenceValue<Value*>` as a subclass of `vector` of the STL and `Value`. Such abstractions can be used when developing new complex data types to be integrated into the serialization framework.

For creating objects of type `Value`, a `ValueFactory` is used that allows to instantiate new `Value` objects during deserialization. A value factory is provided as Singleton [GHJV94]. The registration of value objects is performed by providing a static global instance of a parameterizable `ValueConstructor`. More precisely, two different subclasses are available: `TValueConstructor` are used for types that are not subtypes of `Value` and therefore need a `TValue` wrapper; `TConstructor` constructs objects of type `Value`.

### Handling Unknown Data Types

Especially for distributed systems, one cannot assume that an object that is forwarded between different hosts can be reconstructed and handled on all systems. For example, an object forwarded between connected processing elements of a distributed flow graph might only be available on some systems involved. However, the serialization framework allows to handle such situations. If a concrete data type cannot be con-

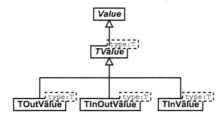

Figure 6.7: As an example, the subclasses of `TValue<T>`, namely `TInValue<T>`, `TOutValue<T>`, and `TInOutValue<T>`, are shown that provide different memory management and allow for efficiently realizing different interaction paradigms by only forwarding values in the specified direction.

structed by the `ValueFactory` (because it is unknown and therefore not registered), an object of type `SerializedValue` is created using the current type information. This object then recursively holds all values obtained by the deserialization process. In such situations, these values have to be created by the `SerializedValue` object. Therefore, in this mode, the method `createFromStream(OValueStream&)` of `Value` is used.

**in, out, and inout Values**

As described in Section 3.4.1, technologies like CORBA require to specify the "direction" of parameters of method signatures by the keywords in, out, or inout. In accordance with this approach, the value classes of NMM allow to set such a property. On the one hand, this is important for different kinds of memory management. On the other hand, this distinction allows to optimize serialization and network transmission. For example, for request-reply interaction, in-values only have to be transmitted within a request; out-values only within a reply. Only inout-values have to be included within the request and the reply. Figure 6.7 shows the different subclasses of `TValue<T>` that provide the implementation for in, out, or inout-values.

## 6.1.4 Realized Serialization Strategies

Several serialization strategies have been implemented in the scope of our work. Figure 6.8 gives an overview of the developed classes. The *XML value streams* and the *magic number value streams* are subtypes of the corresponding value stream classes that handle type information. Therefore, they can be used at the top layer of a stack of serialization strategies. The *standard streams* and *net streams* are only meant to handle to lower layers of the serialized stack, e.g. the forwarding respectively receiving of byte streams using a certain communication technology. Therefore, they do not need to process type information and are only subtypes of the corresponding stream superclasses.

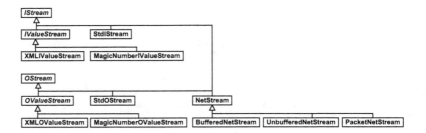

Figure 6.8: The concrete serialization strategies. Strategies that are to be used at the top layer of a stack of serialization strategies need to handle type information and are therefore subclasses of the corresponding value stream. The lower-layer strategies are subclasses of the simpler stream classes. For realizing bidirectional network communication, the networking streams inherit from both input and output streams.

### XML Value Streams

Using the XML value stream for serialization, XML representations of objects can be generated. Correspondingly, the value stream for deserialization allows to reconstruct an object from such an XML representation.

While the generated byte streams are not very efficient in terms of memory consumption for storage or bandwidth consumption for network transmission, they offer a convenient way for generating information for long term storage using a data format convenient for humans [BSL00]. Furthermore, these streams were mainly developed as proof-of-concept. Since technologies like UPnP use the XML based protocol SOAP for all communication (compare Section 4.3.2), this shows that such technologies can easily be integrated into and accessed within NMM.

### Magic Number Value Streams

For realizing efficient communication within NMM, the magic number value streams were developed. These streams map type information to a 32 bit number, the *magic number*. For the basic types of C++ these numbers are predefined. The serialization operator of these streams then prepends the magic number of a type before serializing its value; the operator for deserialization compares the magic number with the expected value.

For registering magic numbers of complex data types, the *magic number manager* can be accessed (singleton of class `MagicNumberManager`). Figure 6.9 shows an example of a serialized `vector<int32_t>` with five elements. However, if no magic number is registered for a certain data type, objects of this type can still be handled. This happens when the corresponding type is simply not available on a certain but needs to be forwarded from that system to another system – a situation that needs to be handled to support instream interaction between connected processing elements of a distributed flow graph running on heterogeneous systems. In such cases, a special number is used and the complete type information as provided by `TypeInfo` is written.

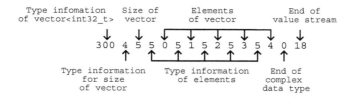

Figure 6.9: A complex data type `vector<int32_t>` with five elements serialized with the magic number value stream; for vectors of basic data types, the current implementation can be optimized to only serialize the type information once [Rep03a]

### Standard Streams

The standard streams were developed to use the existing iostreams of C++ within NMM, e.g. for writing serialized objects to files. The implementations of the operators of these classes invoke the operator of the corresponding C++ stream.

### Unbuffered Networking Streams

For writing data to and reading data from the network, GNU/Linux and other operating systems use the concept of sockets that allows to call functions like `send` and `recv` with a file descriptor [Ric98]. As discussed above, for efficiently serializing and transmitting objects, it is necessary that the serialization framework of NMM itself adds no implicit copy operation. The unbuffered networking streams provided with NMM demonstrate this feature (class `UnbufferedNetStream`). Within these classes, the methods `writeValue` and `readValue` implement the sending and receiving of data, respectively. These methods are called by the corresponding operators, e.g. from the operators for type `int32_t` implemented in class `NetStream`.

### Buffered Networking Streams

As mentioned above, there is a trade-off between the amount of buffered data during serialization and the number of lower level function calls needed for network transmission. Especially when serializing data types with many attributes that only contain a small number of bytes, the relatively large number of functions calls imposes a certain overhead. This is even more true since these function calls are typically directly executed within the kernel of the operating system.

Therefore, we also provide buffered networking streams (class `BufferedNet-Stream`). These streams internally use a preallocated buffer with a certain size. Data to be processed (e.g. to be written to a socket) is tried to be buffered within this memory area if sufficient space is available. Otherwise, the buffer is emptied (e.g. by writing buffered data to a socket) and the data to be processed is either handled directly (if the amount of data still does not fit into the buffer) or buffered within the freed memory area.

An analog strategy is followed for reading data from sockets. Performance evaluations of the different networking streams are presented in Section 8.1. Within this context, we will also discuss the "optimal" size of the internal buffer for these networking streams.

**Packet Networking Streams**

Another networking stream was developed in order to offer enhanced quality of service for unreliable low-level networking technologies [Win06], e.g. for transport protocols like UDP (compare Section 2.2.4). This stream provides in-order delivery and the guarantee that serialized objects, which were split into several data packets during network transmission, are either received completely or discarded. This latter property is especially important for being able to properly deserialize objects such as messages or events.

Together, these capabilities are implemented as follows within class `Packet-NetStream`. The complete byte stream of each serialized object gets a unique sequence number $s$ assigned to be used internally. In general, such a serialized objects is split into $n$ lower-level data packets, e.g. according to the UDP packet size. Each packet gets another sequence number $p$ assigned, which corresponds to the order of packets of the serialized object. Within the header of each packet, following additional information is stored: the sequence number $s$ of the object, the packet sequence number $p$, and the total number of packets $n$. On the receiving side of the stream, packets are ordered lexicographically according to $(s, p)$. Whenever all packets of an object are received, these packets are combined and forwarded and all preceding packets are discarded.

### 6.1.5  Discussion

The described framework allows to easily develop new or modify existing data types for integrating them into the serialization process (Requirement 1 and Requirement 2 discussed in Section 6.1.1). As the serialization and deserialization operators can be defined external to the definition of the data type itself, Requirement 3 can be fulfilled by implementing corresponding operators. No additional changes are needed for the framework. Notice that such an operator only needs to be implemented once for `OValueStream` and for `IValueStream`, respectively.

The framework allows to integrate new serialization strategies (Requirement 4). Such strategies only have to provide the specific functionality for handling basic data types (and arrays). Furthermore, the stacking of serialization strategies provides suitable abstractions for decomposing complex protocols and integrating new data formats (Requirement 5). To this end, even the interaction with low-level networking interfaces can be realized by developing a suitable strategy.

Since the signature of the C++ operators are to be defined with a typed reference, no additional copy operation is performed by the framework itself; Requirement 6 can be fulfilled. However, the interfaces provided also allow to buffer data within serialization strategies; a property important for optimizing the relationship between the number of low-level function calls needed for network communication and the buffered data.

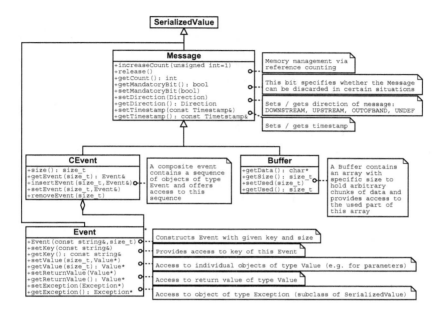

Figure 6.10: The messaging system of NMM provides a base class Message that provides functionality like reference counting and time stamping. The subclass Buffer allows to store multimedia data; the subclass CEvent (composite event) allows to store a sequence of objects of type Event. All classes are derived from SerializedValue and therefore can be used within the serialization framework described in Section 6.1.

## 6.2  Unified Messaging System

The unified messaging system of NMM consists of different parts [LRS02, LS03].

- Message types for control information and multimedia data buffers.

- Abstract interfaces for realizing different kinds of interaction, e.g. out-of-band request-reply or instream one-way communication.

- Dispatchers that trigger registered methods upon receiving a message and listeners that can be additionally be notified.

These different entities will be described in more detail in the following together with the most important aspects of their implementation.

### 6.2.1  Message Base Type

The base class for all messages called Message provides the interface for realizing memory management via reference counting (see Figure 6.10). Furthermore, a message can be specified to be *mandatory*. In this case, the message is not allowed to be discarded. In general, this functionality is needed to distinguish between messages that need different quality of service requirements. While control information often needs reliable transmission or intermediate storage, messages containing multimedia data may be dropped in different situations, e.g. when dropping a message that violates synchronization requirements or when flushing the data currently buffered within a flow graph.

For messages sent via undirected interfaces – for example, the messages generated within the processing elements of a flow graph – , the message base class allows to set an direction; in particular DOWNSTREAM for messages that flow from sources to sinks, and UPSTREAM for messages that are to be forwarded in the opposite direction. In addition, messages sent out-of-band can be marked with the corresponding value OUTOFBAND. However, as described below, this option is not used within the NMM architecture but rather provided for completeness.

An essential feature for multimedia middleware is the ability to synchronize different streams of data. Therefore, the base type for all messages allows to set and query a Timestamp. The synchronization architecture of NMM will be discussed in detail within the scope of Chapter 7.

Derived from the message base type are the two different major types, CEvent (for composite event) and Buffer, to be described next. Notice that Serialized-Value is used as base class, which allows all messages to be handled by the serialization framework as described in Section 6.1.

### 6.2.2   Events and Composite Events

Events are the basic elements that can carry all kinds of control information. An event is identified by a name and can hold arbitrary parameters of type Value (e.g. basic data types wrapped in TValue<T> as described in Section 6.1) that can be queried and modified. In order to realize request-reply interaction via events, an event must also allow to store a return value and an exception. The most important interface methods of the class Event are shown in Figure 6.10.

While an event corresponds to single execution step – e.g. a single method call – , it is often useful to group several events. This is especially important, when a certain functionality can only be achieved by a sequence of several events and this sequence needs to be handled in a single and atomic step of execution. This kind of service is needed when realizing advanced features within a flow graph by forwarding a compound of events instream between different processing elements. Different examples for this approach will be discussed in the scope of Section 7.7.3. Therefore, the class CEvent (for *composite event*) is introduced as subclass of Message, which allows to carry an arbitrary number of events[2]. In addition, within a composite event, events can be inserted, replaced, or removed.

---

[2]For the scope of this thesis, the term *event* will be used for instances of CEvent or instances of Event. However, from the context of the text it should always be clear, which type is meant. Only if the differences between these two cases are important, we will explicitly speak of the two types.

Figure 6.11: Different interface classes are provided to explicitly identify different types of interaction. IEventSender and IEventReceiver are used for blocking request-reply interaction; IMessageSender and IMessageReceiver for non-blocking one-way interaction.

### 6.2.3  Buffers

Messages of type Buffer provide the functionality to store larger amounts of arbitrary data, for example the discrete memory chunks of a multimedia stream (compare Section 2.2.1). Handling multimedia typically requires high memory bandwidths. While allocating and deallocating memory are expensive operations, reference counting is a common technique that allows to reuse preallocated data buffers. Within the NMM architecture, this functionality is provided by specialized *buffer managers* to be described in more detail in Section 7.6. In general, buffer managers administer a pool of preallocated buffer objects. Upon request, a buffer with a reference count of one is provided. If the buffer is no longer needed within this address space, the reference count is decreased to zero and the buffer is returned to its buffer manager for later reuse.

A lot of multimedia processing routines have no a priori knowledge of how much data they will produce. For example, the compression ratio for a certain amount of memory typically depends on its content (compare Section 2.2.3). However, if an upper bound of the needed size of output memory is known, a buffer can still be requested from a buffer manager. To be able to handle such situations, the interface of Buffer provides methods for setting and requesting the amount of data that is actually used of the overall available memory of this buffer (see Figure 6.10).

### 6.2.4  Interfaces for Different Interaction Paradigms

One major goal of the messaging system is to provide a unified architecture that allows to realize different interaction paradigms. To explicitly identify which kind of interaction is intended, different interface classes are provided as shown in Figure 6.11. However, the architecture is apparently not restricted to these specific interfaces; they rather offer one possibility to use the provided facilities.

For realizing request-reply interaction using events, the abstract interface classes IEventSender and IEventReceiver are provided[3]. An event sender forwards a single event and its own reference to an event receiver. The sender blocks until the event is processed and returned. The return value of the method receiveEvent() indicates the success of this process. If successful, the event contains updated out or inout values and a return value – or an exception, if the method that processed the

---

[3]In general, the prefix 'I' denotes interface classes, e.g. virtual classes, as in this case, or interfaces defined in NMM IDL as discussed in Section 6.4

event threw an exception. This option is extensively used for realizing communication for NMM interface classes to be described in Section 6.4.

One-way interaction can be realized by implementing the abstract interface classes `IMessageSender` and `IMessageReceiver`. In this case, the implementation of `receiveMessage()` is required to operate non-blocking. This kind of interaction is extensively used between connected processing elements of a flow graph. More precisely, the output jack of a processing element and the input jack of a connected second processing element both use these interfaces to forward messages upstream or downstream as described in Section 5.2. Notice that this kind of communication is restricted to objects of type `Message`; a single object of type `Event` is not supported. This choice was made to allow for an uniform handling of all instream interaction.

### 6.2.5  Dispatching

For realizing different communication patterns such as instream and out-of-band interaction, the mapping of messages to triggering certain actions is required. This is commonly referred to as *dispatching*. For instream communication, the messaging system needs to distinguish between objects of type `Buffer` and `CEvent`. As the realization of this step is straightforward, the implementation for this process is up to the specific architecture that employs the messaging system. Furthermore, this allows for an easy extension of the messaging system by introducing new subclasses of type `Message` specific for a certain domain. Chapter 7 will provide more details on the usage and extension of the messaging system for realizing the generic multimedia architecture of NMM.

While the handling of objects of type `Message` has to be provided by a specific architecture, the messaging system provides facilities to process all events of a composite event and to dispatch a single event. This functionality is realized by the *event dispatcher* `EventDispatcher` together with parameterizable *event dispatcher objects*, in particular the subclasses of `EDObject` as shown in Figure 6.12. These *template event dispatcher objects*, or *TED objects*, have knowledge about the complete information for dispatching a method of a particular object, namely:

- The type of the object they refer to and the address of that object.

- The type of the method they should dispatch and the address for the method of the object they refer to.

- The type of the return value.

- All types of parameters[4].

An event dispatcher object is registered with the event dispatcher by defining a *key*. A key is a unique name represented as `string`. The event dispatcher allows to dynamically register event dispatcher objects – or to remove the capability to handle a certain key. This allows to dispatch single NMM events identified by a key (compare Figure 6.10). Furthermore, the class `EventDispatcher` provides methods for handling composite events. Then, each event of the composite event will be dispatched.

---

[4]The current implementation allows methods with up to seven parameters to be dispatched by TED objects.

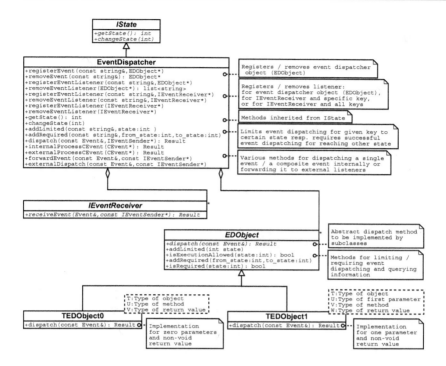

Figure 6.12: The class EventDispatcher allows to register event dispatcher objects. The subclasses of EDObject provide parameterized function wrappers, e.g. TEDObject0 and TEDObject1. Additional listeners can be registered in the form of event dispatcher objects or objects of type IEventReceiver. The event dispatching system is state driven: dispatching can be *limited* to certain states or *required* to reach other states.

As composite events are used for instream communication, this process also allows to insert, replace, or remove events of the composite event during this process.

**Reflection and Listener Notification**

As discussed in Section 5.1.5, multimedia middleware needs to provide reflection. Several aspects of reflection are supported by the event dispatcher. First, all registered keys can be queried. For each registered key the corresponding event dispatcher object can be accessed. This allows to determine the precise signature of the method that handles the key.

Second, the event dispatcher allows to register additional *listeners*. This can be done in several ways. First, an additional event dispatcher object can be registered for a particular key. In this case, the method specific to the event dispatcher object will be triggered whenever such a key is handled by the dispatcher. Then, an object implementing the IEventReceiver interface can be added; either for a specific key, or for all keys. In the latter case, the events have to be further processed by the listener.

**State-Driven Dispatching**

Finally, the event dispatching system is state-driven. This means that the state of an event dispatcher can be changed and queried (through the implemented abstract interface IState). Furthermore, the event dispatching itself is state driven. This means that for each key, two properties can be specified.

- The dispatching of an event with the specific key can be *limited* to certain states. For all other states, dispatching is not performed; instead, an exception is thrown.

- The successful dispatching of an event with a specific key can be *required* for reaching another state. In this context, *successful* means that the event could be dispatched and no exception was thrown by the method that handled the event.

While these two extensions are optional and could also be realized for individual implementations of methods that handle events, we argue that they are fundamental concepts for multimedia middleware. More precisely, these extension were motivated by the observation that many multimedia devices or software components operate according to the above described properties. For example, to use a specific multimedia device, it first has to be configured, e.g. by setting corresponding parameters such as the particular hardware device. Then, operations like changing parameters such as a particular property of a hardware device can only be performed when the device is already configured. The same observations can be made for software components, e.g. a file name can only be specified when the component is not processing another file, but needs to be provided in order to use the component.

## 6.2.6   Discussion

The messaging system provides different entities for carrying information. On the one hand, events act as basic elements for holding arbitrary control information. On the other hand, different message types are provided: Buffers for holding multimedia data and composite events for grouping a sequence of events. While the base class of all message types offers functionality especially needed for instream communication such as reference counting and time stamping, a single event used for out-of-band request-reply interaction does not need these features and is therefore deliberately not a subtype of message.

For distinguishing different types of interaction, specific interfaces are provided. However, further specialization are also possible. Message dispatching is realized in two steps. While the distinct handling of the different message types, namely buffers and composite events, needs to be provided by architectural components built on top of the messaging system, the dispatching of composite events and single events is performed by an event dispatcher. This component of the architecture provides the functionality for realizing a reflective middleware: the dispatcher can be queried for its

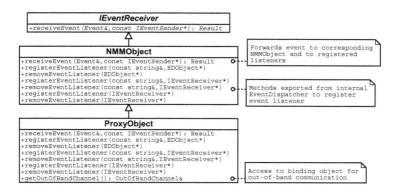

Figure 6.13: The Proxy design pattern is realized by server-side objects of type NMMObject and client-side objects of type ProxyObject. NMM objects act as event receivers and allow to register additional listeners; proxy objects act as a surrogate for NMM objects and therefore provide the same interface. Furthermore, a proxy object provides access to the communication channel OutOfBandChannel that provides access to the binding between proxy and NMM object.

supported functionality in terms of registered event keys; the interface system of NMM to be described in Section 6.4 extends this capability to allow for querying supported interfaces from an object. Furthermore, the capability of handling specific events can be added and removed dynamically. Finally, the dispatcher allows to register additional listeners.

As a further feature, the messaging system operates state driven. As discussed above, this extension was observed to be important for multimedia middleware. Therefore, this capability is also offered by the interface definition language and code generation tools built on top of the messaging system.

## 6.3 Communication Architecture

As discussed in Section 5.1, the NMM architecture uses the Proxy design pattern to access objects [LRS02, LS03]. The two base classes that realize this pattern are presented in the following, namely NMMObject and ProxyObject.

While the interaction between proxy object and target object follows the request-reply paradigm, the other important aspect of communication is one-way interaction between connected processing elements of a flow graph. As described in Section 5.2, these connections are realized with so called jacks. The corresponding base classes will be presented briefly in the following.

### 6.3.1 NMM Object

For the Proxy design pattern as used within NMM, the server side objects are of type NMMObject. As can be seen in Figure 6.13, an NMM object acts as event

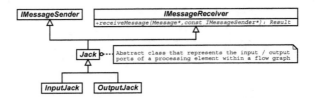

Figure 6.14: The classes that represent the input and output ports of a processing element are called `InputJack` and `OutputJack`, respectively. Their superclass `Jack` inherits the two interfaces `IMessageSender` and `IMessageReceiver` for providing bidirectional instream communication.

receiver. Furthermore, it uses an event dispatcher as described in Section 6.2 to realize event handling. The interface of class `EventDispatcher` is partly publicly exported by the class `NMMObject`. In particular, the methods for registering additional listeners are provided. Section 6.4 will demonstrate the usage of NMM objects in combination with the NMM interface definition language (IDL) and the corresponding code generation tools.

### 6.3.2  Proxy Object

The class `ProxyObject` represents the client side of the Proxy design pattern. In order to act as a surrogate for an NMM object this class inherits from `NMMObject` (see Figure 6.13). Received events are first forwarded to the NMM object, where they are dispatched. Then they are handled by the dispatcher of the proxy object to notify registered listeners. Notice that several proxy objects can refer to a single NMM object. Since a proxy object provides the interface for receiving arbitrary events, it represents a concept similar to the Dynamic Invocation Interface (DII) of CORBA (compare Section 3.4.1).

As described in Section 5.1, the binding between proxy object and NMM object is realized by a *communication channel*. In the case of request-reply interaction between proxy object and NMM object, an `OutOfBandChannel` is used. Further details on communication channels will be provided in the scope of Section 6.5.

### 6.3.3  Instream Connections with Jacks

For instream interaction, the class `Jack` respectively the two subclasses `InputJack` and `OutputJack` are provided (see Figure 6.14). An input jack represent an input of a processing element within a flow graph; an output jack its output. These classes are described in detail in Chapter 7. For the scope of this chapter, it is only important to notice that for realizing bidirectional one-way communication, the class `Jack` inherits the two interfaces for sending and receiving messages as described in Section 6.2.

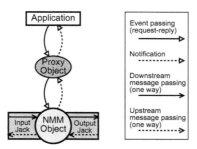

Figure 6.15: Request-reply interaction is realized by sending events to the proxy object where they are forwarded to the NMM object, dispatched, and then returned. Registered listeners are dispatched by the proxy object. Events received as part of one-way instream communication in upstream or downstream direction are dispatched within the NMM object and then forwarded to the proxy object if listeners are registered.

### 6.3.4 Out-of-band and Instream Communication

As already discussed in Section 5.1 and Section 5.2, the unified messaging system should provide the functionality for handling both out-of-band communication between application and objects (via proxy objects) and instream communication between connected jacks of processing elements within a flow graph.

Figure 6.15 shows these concepts for the architectural components of NMM described so far (compare Figure 5.2 in Section 5.2). Events sent from the application to the proxy object are forwarded to the NMM object, where they are dispatched, processed, and returned to the proxy object. Then, registered listeners are triggered by the proxy object. Finally, the processed events are returned to the application.

However, this mechanism transparently works for instream communication as well. Messages passed upstream and downstream via jacks are first handled according to their type, e.g. `Buffer` or `CEvent`. While this process and the handling of messages of type `Buffer` will be discussed in detail in Chapter 7, it is important to notice that for messages of type `CEvent`, all internal events are dispatched the same way as for out-of-band communication.

If additional listeners are registered, events received instream are also forwarded from the NMM object to its proxy object (or its proxy objects, if more than one client side object exists). To optimize this step, this is only performed when needed, e.g. when a listener is really registered at the proxy object for that particular event key, or a listener is registered for all event keys. This is especially important to avoid unnecessary network traffic for the case when NMM object and proxy object reside in different address spaces. The facilities provided by the connecting communication channel are used when forwarding events from an NMM object to the corresponding proxy object.

### 6.3.5   Discussion

While this section only provided the basic details on the proxy architecture of NMM, following sections will describe the approach in more detail. In particular, the usage of the NMM interface definition language (IDL) and the generated client side and server side classes will be described next. Furthermore, as a major component of the NMM architecture, communication channels for realizing the binding between proxy object and NMM object will be presented in Section 6.5.

## 6.4   Interfaces

The proxy architecture as described in the preceding sections allows for realizing request-reply interaction between proxy objects and NMM objects by sending events. However, in order to provide the benefits of object-oriented programming within the NMM environment, an object-oriented interface system is provided that is built on top of the facilities described so far [LRS02, LS03, Loh03g]. According to other approaches, such as CORBA described in Section 3.4.1, interfaces are defined with an interface definition language (IDL). By convention, interfaces described in NMM IDL should use the prefix "I" [Loh03e].

From an IDL definition, code generation tools produce a client-side *interface class* and a server-side *implementation class* (with suffix "Impl"). While the interface class internally employs events, the server-side implementation class registers abstract methods to be called when dispatching the corresponding methods (compare Section 6.2). An implementation for the abstract interface of the implementation class need to be provided by a server-side object, e.g. a subclass of the implementation class. Together, this approach offers following benefits.

- The grouping of methods within an IDL definition provides suitable abstractions as known from object-oriented programming. This point is especially important for multimedia middleware, where interfaces offer an ideal way to describe the features of a processing element, e.g. a multimedia device or a software component providing a multimedia processing routine. This option is supported by the registry service described in Chapter 9 when specifying queries.

- The possibility to use inheritance for interfaces as known from object-oriented programming allows to further refine this process. For example, a generic interface for a certain multimedia device such as a camera can be specialized for different device types that offer unique features.

- Rather than creating events with their corresponding parameters manually within applications, they are generated automatically within interface classes. Therefore, the usage of these classes within applications provides type-safety. Furthermore, the programming model known from object-oriented programming is offered.

- By using the facilities of the unified messaging system as underlying technology, the interface system offers the same semantics and advantages, namely reflection, listener notification for method invocations, and the extensions for limiting or requiring method execution to certain states.

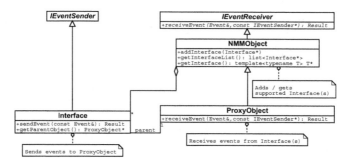

Figure 6.16: The client-side interface classes inherit from `Interface` that acts as event sender for a proxy object. The base class for server-side objects is `NMMObject` that allows to add and request supported interfaces.

- Finally, the registered methods of server-side objects will not only be dispatched when handling out-of-band events, but also when processing events received instream. This allows to unify the specification of events to be handled out-of-band and instream.

### 6.4.1 Base Class

The base class for all client-side interface classes is `Interface` shown in Figure 6.16. It acts as an event sender forwarding events to a proxy object that provides the interface for an event receiver (compare Section 6.3).

The class `NMMObject` is used as a base class for all server-side implementation classes. It allows to add a supported interface and to request all or a specific interface. This latter option is realized by providing a parameterized method that can be used as follows.

```
NMMObject* object = // create some NMM object ...

// request interface called IExample from object
IExample* my_interface = object->getInterface<IExample>();
```

The same method is available for `ProxyObject`.

### 6.4.2 Interface Definition Language

As discussed above, IDL descriptions within NMM are used to specify all kinds of interaction, namely the interfaces for out-of-band and instream interaction. The syntax of NMM IDL is very similar to CORBA IDL [HV99]. As this choice was made to ease the usage of NMM IDL, some extensions were made [Loh03g].

Within an NMM IDL file, an interface is defined with the keyword `interface` as part of a `module`. Each interface may inherit from other interfaces. An interface typically contains one or more methods specified by return type, a name, and zero or more parameters. Additionally, according to other middleware solutions, for each parameter, a qualifier has to be specified, namely in, out, or inout. In-parameters are only sent to from sender to receiver, out-parameters are only from receiver to sender, and inout-parameters are sent in both directions (compare Section 3.4.1). Furthermore, a method can be declared to throw exceptions.

**Supported Data Types**

For return types and parameter types, NMM IDL allows arbitrary types, only reference-types are currently not supported. This is in contrast to other interface definition languages that only support a limited number of types, e.g. the basic types available for all supported platforms and programming languages, and some common abstractions like sequences. However, the choice for supporting arbitrary types was made in accordance with the general approach of NMM to provide an *integrating* solution. This approach originates from the observation that most of the existing multimedia software libraries that are of interest to be integrated into NMM offer interfaces that *do* use arbitrary data types. Allowing for the seamless integration of these components is one of the strengths of NMM.

If the IDL would only allow for a restricted number of data types, two possibilities exit for integrating complex *existing* data types. First, the interface of the software library to be integrated could be modified to only use this restricted set of data types. Complex existing data types need to be changed to be composed out of the available data types of the used IDL, e.g. by using types such as struct [HV99]. However, this solution has several drawbacks. Such modifications might be too time consuming and need to be incorporated in all upcoming versions of the library. For closed source software, this approach is simply not possible at all.

Secondly, data types of external libraries could be integrated by providing mappings between these existing types and newly developed types that are to be composed out of the restricted set of basic types available. Again, this approach has a major drawback. In particular, it requires to provide new data types and implementations for the mappings.

While this second solution might be an option that also works for closed source software libraries, the serialization framework of NMM described in Section 6.1 provides all facilities to integrate existing complex *and* closed-source data types without modifications, e.g. by implementing corresponding serialization and deserialization operators.

### 6.4.3   IDL Extensions

Compared to other interface definition languages, NMM IDL provides several extensions. Each method may be further specified by several modifiers. The limited modifier can be used to limit the possible execution of a method to a certain state. If the object is not in this state, an exception is thrown (IllegalStateException). The required modifier can be used to specify that a certain method has to be called and processed successfully before the current state can be left and another state can be reached. In this context, *successful* means that no exception was thrown by the method that was called. If a required method was not called with success, and the state of the object is changed via the IState interface, an exception is thrown (UnsuccessfulRequiredCallException). Both, the limited and the required modifier can be given several times for each method.

To realize the semantics of the two modifiers, the facilities of the state driven messaging systems are used. As already discussed in Section 6.2, these extensions are especially useful for multimedia middleware and are therefore extensively used to specify the intended behavior of NMM processing elements.

While all defined methods of an interface are dispatched for out-of-band and instream interaction, methods that are triggered by instream interaction are subject to certain restrictions. This is due to the fact that instream interaction has a *one-way* semantics. In general, return values, exceptions, and out-parameters should not be used; inout-parameters can be specified if the modification of parameter values is allowed. Therefore, the instream modifier has to be used for marking methods that can be triggered by instream interaction. While the return value of such methods should be void in general, the NMM architecture also allows the enum of type Result to be used. This provides the possibility to realize special mechanisms by returning different Result-values. For example, the value DELETE can be used to remove the corresponding event from a composite event after handling it with the specific method.

The instream modifier also forces the generation of a utility method, a so called create_ method. This method is generated for the client-side interface class and is named create_<method name>. It takes the same parameters as the method itself but returns a newly created object of type Event with all given parameters set. A create-method is used to provide a type-safe way to generate events within the main loop of processing elements of a flow graph. Such an event can then be forwarded instream within a composite event. Section 7.7 will provide some examples for this mechanism.

IDL files can also be included in other IDL files. This is needed if an interface inherits an interface defined in another IDL file. While this feature is provided in accordance to other middleware solutions such as CORBA, NMM IDL also offers the possibility to include arbitrary other files into the header and source code files generated from an IDL file. Again, this feature is available in order to provide an integrating solution. For example, this allows to include external type definitions to be used within IDL method signatures. More details on NMM IDL can be found in [Loh03g].

### 6.4.4 Code Generation

As a summary for the concepts discussed so far, an example for an interface definition is provided together with the corresponding generated classes. Figure 6.17 shows the IDL file for *IExample* with the two methods *foo* and *bar*. From this IDL description, two classes are generated by using the NMM IDL tools[5]. The interface class IExample is a subclass of Interface and wraps event creation and sending within method calls. Notice the usage of the different TValue objects for the return value and the different types of parameters. Notice that for complex data type source code is generated correspondingly, e.g. for subtypes of SerializedValue or ex-

---

[5]The NMM IDL tools are implemented using lex/yacc [LMB92].

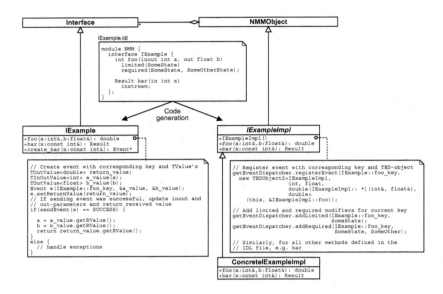

Figure 6.17: Code generation for NMM IDL. From an IDL description, the interface class `IExample` and the implementation class `IExampleImpl` are generated. Defined methods have to be implemented by subclasses of `IExampleImpl`, e.g. `ConcreteIExampleImpl`.

ternal closed-source subtypes that are integrated by providing specific operators. For instream methods, a create-method is generated.

The implementation class `IExampleImpl` is a subclass of `NMMObject` and registers pure virtual methods to be called by the event dispatcher of the NMM object. Notice how the required and limited modifiers are handled during this step. A concrete implementation of these method is provided by class `ConcreteIExampleImpl`.

Event creation is wrapped within the interface class. The registration of pure virtual methods for handling events is realized within the constructor of the implementation class.

### 6.4.5   Discussion

The presented unified messaging system of NMM allows for realizing different interaction paradigms such as out-of-band request-reply communication or one-way instream communication (see Figure 6.18). For both types of interaction, the NMM IDL offers appropriate means for specifying interfaces. Furthermore, the generated interface classes provide the type-safety and programming model known from object-oriented programming. Together, for the design and development of the NMM base system, more than 45 interface definitions were created. For accessing the specific functionality of the various processing elements, more than 100 interfaces were defined. Especially for querying the NMM registry for a processing element that supports a certain

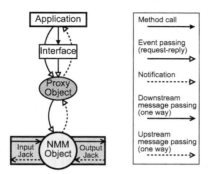

Figure 6.18: The interface system is built on top of the unified messaging system (compare Figure 6.15). All interfaces are defined in NMM IDL. Client-side interface classes allow for type-safe and convenient generation of events for out-of-band interaction and provide the programming model as known from object-oriented programming. One-way instream interaction is supported by the same mechanisms.

feature, these interface definitions have proven to offer suitable abstractions.

While the syntax of NMM IDL is very similar to CORBA IDL, several extensions where made to take the special requirements for multimedia middleware into account. However, some features available in CORBA IDL are currently not supported, e.g. the definition of structures. On the one hand, this option can be implemented easily by using TValue objects as wrappers for the members of generated struct types. On the other hand, from our experience, for an open and integrating solution it is less important to allow to create *new* data types. Instead, the NMM architecture offers the possibility to include *existing* data types easily by using the facilities of the serialization framework together with the NMM IDL.

## 6.5 Binding Framework

So far, we have only considered the components of the NMM architecture without the connecting elements that establish communication between these components. In the following, a framework is described that allows to establish explicit bindings by integrating and combining the capabilities of available technologies [LRS02, LS03, Rep03a, RWLS04, RWLS05, Win06].

### 6.5.1 Requirements and Overview

As discussed above, different kinds of interaction – and therefore different kinds of bindings – need to be provided for multimedia middleware. For out-of-band request-reply interaction and listener notification between proxy object and target object, NMM events are used. One-way instream interaction in upstream and downstream direction, e.g. between two connected processing elements of a flow graph, consists of an ordered stream of NMM messages, either of type buffer or composite event.

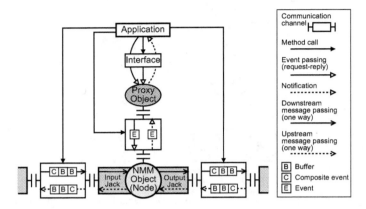

Figure 6.19: Communication channels realize bidirectional explicit bindings between two entities. For out-of-band request-reply interaction and listener notification between proxy objects and NMM objects, such as nodes or jacks, NMM events are used. One-way instream interaction between connected jacks forwards messages of type composite event or buffer (compare Figure 6.18).

### Communication Channels and Transport Strategies

Within NMM, all communication is based on *communication channels*. A communication channel provides an abstraction for a bidirectional binding between two entities and acts as first class data type that allows to access and configure all aspects of the binding it represents (see Figure 6.19).

For realizing a binding, a communication channel internally uses one or more pairs of *transport strategies* with each of these transport strategies possibly employing a stack of serialization strategies. While the serialization strategies described in Section 6.1 offer different ways to transform entities to other representations, a transport strategy allows to transmit or receive such representations using a particular *transport mechanism*. In this context, a *mechanism* can be understood as the facilities provided by a particular middleware, networking library, or lower-level protocol, or the process of forwarding references to allocated memory between two objects.

Figure 6.20 shows an example for the setup of a binding. In this case, the binding only allows for transmitting an object from one address space to another via the transport strategy on the sending side and the corresponding strategy on the receiving side. Both sides internally employ a number of serialization strategies that are configured as a stack. Notice that seen from an application, a binding consists of at least a single pair of transport strategies, which can both run in different address spaces then the application itself. Therefore, a transport strategy itself is a distributed object and accessed via NMM interfaces.

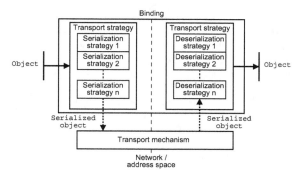

Figure 6.20: Example for a unidirectional binding using a sending transport strategy and a corresponding receiving transport strategy. Both strategies internally use a stack of serialization operators.

**Chosen Approach**

Efficient implementations for a large variety of transport mechanisms already exist. Therefore, NMM as a middleware solution does not aim at providing new mechanisms. Instead, we focus on providing a framework that allows to integrate and combine the capabilities of different existing and emerging technologies. However, as the properties of present technologies differ widely, the following aspects have to be considered.

- The addresses needed for locating and connecting two entities within the network (or within different address spaces of a single system) are dependent on the underlying technology.

- The connection setup differs. While some technologies already offer such functionality as distinct service, others inherently cannot provide such a feature. For example, connectionless transport layer protocols like UDP need higher level services for establishing communication.

- The transport mechanisms themselves are of very different nature. In particular, the interfaces offered and the service guarantees and properties provided vary widely between different protocols or middleware solutions.

Especially this last aspect is of great importance. On the one hand, some transport mechanisms are especially suited for realizing a certain kind of interaction and should therefore be supported by a multimedia middleware solution. For example, out-of-band interaction typically needs reliable transmission of events containing arbitrary data structures. While this can be achieved by using protocols like TCP, reliable data transport requires acknowledgments and possible retransmission. This is in contrast to the properties needed for the instream transmission of multimedia data, where it is acceptable to sacrifice reliability in favor of meeting the timing requirements of media processing, e.g. by dropping buffers instead of handling them too late. Compared with this, composite events sent instream are not allowed to be discarded since they are used to represent critical points in the data stream, e.g. when the multimedia format of following buffers changes or a new media track is started. These messages should only be allowed to be discarded if explicitly indicated, e.g. by setting an unreliable transport strategy for the transmission of NMM composite events.

On the other hand, technologies – and implementations thereof – that especially support one type of interaction often cannot be used for other types of operation. In particular, protocols handling multimedia data streams are typically required to process the content of a stream in order to operate properly. Therefore, such approaches can only handle a certain number of well-known multimedia formats – the transmission of arbitrary data, such as NMM events or composite events, is not supported a priori. While buffers holding multimedia data typically have a much higher density, composite events sent instream only occur at a few points in the stream. However, since these events contain critical control information, their positions within the data stream need to be maintained during transmission.

As typical examples, let us briefly compare RTP/UDP and TCP (also see Section 2.2.4). RTP running on top of the unreliable protocol UDP is especially designed for handling time critical data streams. RTP provides support for different payload types, mainly for handling multimedia formats. Typical implementations of RTP only provide a restricted set of payload types. While general support for RTP for realizing streaming multimedia data connections is certainly a key requirement for multimedia middleware, the instream transmission of control information stored within NMM composite events is not supported by RTP. Even when using the possibility to send user data within the RTP stream [Sch], this data might get lost since UDP is used as underlying protocol. However, TCP provides reliable transmission for arbitrary data. Therefore, TCP can be used for realizing out-of-band interaction using events and instream interaction using composite events. Furthermore, formats not supported by an available implementation of RTP can be handled that way – even though with a different service model.

The binding framework of NMM is especially designed to allow for the integration and combination of available transport technologies. This provides the following advantages. First, such an approach also allows to cope with the inherent heterogeneity of today's environments where a certain transport mechanism cannot be assumed to be available on all platforms. Emerging technologies or technologies needed for communicating with proprietary devices can be included later on or specialized transport strategies can be used for efficiency reasons. Second, for every binding, appropriate combinations of transport strategies can be selected and configured manually – or, an automatic setup procedure can be used. Third, in order to meet the quality of service requirements for the different messages types used for instream interaction, multiple transport mechanisms can be used in parallel, in form of a *parallel binding*. Since the ordering of messages within such a stream needs to be maintained, the developed framework allows to resynchronize received messages.

### 6.5.2  Transport Strategies

As described above, for realizing a binding, pairs of transport strategies are used that transmit and receive serialized objects. A transport strategy offers the functionality provided by a particular transport mechanism. Since this functionality is very specific

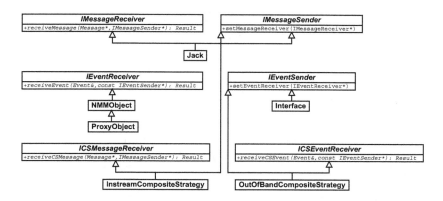

Figure 6.21: Composite strategies for out-of-band and instream interaction. These strategies implement mid-level interfaces for receiving objects and high-level interfaces of senders for forwarding objects to higher-level receivers such as jacks or NMM objects, respectively.

for the underlying technology used, a transport strategy is characterized by the *communication roles* it can fulfill and by the additional *service capabilities* it provides.

### Composite Strategies

For establishing a particular type of binding, such as a out-of-band or instream binding, different communication roles have to be provided by the used pairs of transport strategies. For representing such a top-level binding, *composite strategies* are made available that internally employ a number of sub-bindings, again realized using transport strategies. In particular, NMM offers an *out-of-band composite strategy* and an *instream composite strategy*. The corresponding classes `OutOfBandCompositeStrategy` and `InstreamCompositeStrategy` are shown in Figure 6.21.

During the process of transmitting and receiving NMM buffers, composite events, or events, a stack of interfaces is traversed; from *high-level interfaces*, to *mid-level interfaces*, to *low-level interfaces* on the sending side and vice versa on the receiving side[6]. The high-level interfaces were first presented in Section 6.2.4 and use the prefix 'I'; mid-level interfaces the prefix 'ICS' for *interface composite strategy*, and low-level interfaces the prefix 'ITS' for *interface transport strategy*. According to the naming convention for high-level interfaces, the term "receive" corresponds to the process of receiving an object from another object.

For instream interaction, an NMM jack that provides the high-level interface named `IMessageSender` forwards messages to the mid-level interface `ICSMessage-Receiver` implemented by `InstreamCompositeStrategy`. On the receiving side, the instream composite strategy then acts as `IMessageSender` and forwards

---

[6]Notice that all these interfaces are internally used within NMM and are defined in C++ and not in NMM IDL. Since a transport strategy is a distributed object, for accessing the capabilities of a transport strategy from an application, additional interfaces defined in NMM IDL are provided.

messages to a jack providing the high-level interface `IMessageReceiver`. For the class `OutOfBandCompositeStrategy`, the corresponding relations and interactions exit for `IEventSender` and `ICSEventReceiver`, and `IEventSender` and `IEventReceiver`, respectively.

**Communication Roles**

Communication roles are described on a lower level but are again represented by a set of abstract interfaces. Inside a composite strategy, the interaction paradigm offered by a mid-level interface is then mapped to these low-level interfaces and vice versa. Together, the different available interfaces help to provide a clean design and precisely define the required functionality of subclasses implementing this functionality.

Following two pairs of interfaces are provided for instream interaction.

- `ITSOneWayBufferReceiver` and `ITSOneWayBufferSender`: The receiver interface is to be implemented by a transport strategy that allows to receive NMM buffers from a mid-level component, such as a composite strategy. This strategy then transmits buffers (or their serialized byte stream) as part of a one-way interaction by using a particular transport mechanism. We found that the integration of arbitrary implementations of transport mechanisms needs to be supported, e.g. for easily integrating available libraries that provide RTP support. However, since a transport mechanism might not be able to handle the complete information of an NMM buffer, only the transmission of the multimedia data of NMM buffers is required for this interface; all additional members of the NMM message are optional. This is further defined by an additional capability of the transport strategy to be described below. The sender interface is to be implemented by the part of the transport strategy that receives (and deserializes) the transmitted NMM buffer and sends it to the mid-level transport strategy, i.e. the instream composite strategy.

- `ITSOneWayCEventReceiver` and `ITSOneWayCEventSender`: The receiver interface is to be implemented by a transport strategy that allows to transmit NMM composite events together with the arbitrary data types of internal events as part of a one-way interaction. Again, the sender interface forwards the received NMM composite event to the mid-level transport strategy.

Since instream interaction operates non-blocking, additional abstract low-level interfaces `ISignalReceiver` and `ISignalSender` are provided that allow a receiving component to signal its current state to a sending component. These interfaces are especially needed to control message forwarding in cases were transport strategies and processing elements within a flow graph operate concurrently.

For out-of-band interaction, following two pairs of interfaces are provided.

- `ITSRequestReplyEventReceiver` and `ITSRequestReplyEvent - Sender`: The receiver interface is to be implemented by a transport strategy that allows to perform request-reply interaction. An NMM event together with the internal arbitrary data types is first transmitted as "request" and then received again as "reply". The sender interface forwards the received NMM event as "request" to the mid-level transport strategy, i.e. the out-of-band composite strategy, where it is further processed. Then, the "reply" is sent back.

- `ITSOneWayEventReceiver` and `ITSOneWayEventSender` The receiver interface is to be implemented by a transport strategy that allows to transmit NMM events together with the internal arbitrary data types as part of a one-way interaction. Again, the sender interface forwards to received NMM composite event to the top-level transport strategy. However, for realizing request-reply interaction, two pairs of such a transport strategies are needed, one for transmitting and receiving the request and one for performing the same operations for the reply.

A particular transport strategy is allowed to implement as many interfaces as wanted. This allows a single strategy to be used in different contexts, e.g. for out-of-band or instream interaction. Furthermore, a specific implementation can also provide the functionality of the receiving and sending parts of the strategy within a single class.

When setting up a communication channel using a composite strategy, a specific set of communication roles needs to be fulfilled. An application can influence which transport strategy is to be used for which role. All other roles are automatically negotiated. In this step, already determined transport strategies can be used to fulfill the remaining functions.

**Service Capabilities**

To further characterize the service model provided by a particular transport strategy, a set of capabilities can be specified. This set can be extended to take the requirements of future developments into account. In order to be able to integrate a specific transport mechanisms as "black-box", i.e. by integrating it without further modification, the service capabilities help to identify the features of the available implementation. This information is needed in order to determine *if* and *how* the corresponding transport strategy can fulfill the requirements that were specified for a certain binding. These requirements are either given by an application or an automatic binding mechanism as described below.

Currently, the service capabilities include following entries. First, the reliability of the strategy is defined. This allows to choose reliable transport strategies for out-of-band interaction or for instream interaction for applications, such as off-line media transcoding, that cannot accept dropped buffers.

Second, the real-time properties of the transport strategy are set. This entry can be used to request protocols, such as RTP, for the multimedia data flow of connecting edges of a distributed flow graph. Third, the possibility to specify a stack of serialization operators is defined. This capability needs to be specified since the technology used within a transport strategy – or the implementation providing access to that technology – might already include serialization mechanisms.

Then, the possibility to handle arbitrary data types is specified. This option can be queried if the transmission of the complete data structure of NMM buffers is needed for instream communication. Otherwise only the multimedia data will be forwarded and additional information, such as NMM timestamps, are discarded. In this case, an

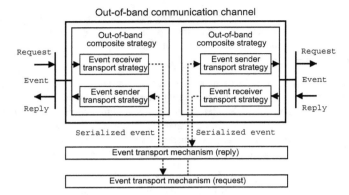

Figure 6.22: Communication channel of out-of-band interaction. In general, eight communication roles need to be fulfilled by the internal low-level transport strategies of the used pair of composite strategies. Four communication roles for handling request-reply interaction and four communication roles for realizing listener notification that operates in the opposite direction. For simplicity, only the components for request-reply are shown: two communication roles for transmitting and receiving the request, two for handling the reply correspondingly.

additional attribute specifies if the transport strategy internally modifies the sequence number of NMM messages, e.g. by splitting the data contained within an NMM buffer into different packets used for transmission.

Furthermore, the multimedia formats supported by a transport strategy are specified and therefore stored as a set of NMM formats (see Section 7.4). This allows to determine the set of strategies that are suited for handling a certain format used for the connection between two processing elements of a distributed flow graph.

As a final capability, the supported types of binding according to Section 3.3.3 are specified, namely local, system, or network. On the one hand, this allows to determine which strategy allows to set up a binding to a remote entity. On the other hand, strategies that only support local bindings typically operate more efficiently than strategies that support network, system, and local bindings.

### 6.5.3    Out-Of-Band Communication Channels

In general, a communication channel for out-of-band request-reply interaction and listener notification has to fulfill eight different communication roles, more precisely four matching pairs of roles. A pair of transport strategies is needed as event receiver and sender for the request; a pair of transport strategies is needed as event receiver and sender for the reply. The same roles need to be provided in the opposite direction for listener notification. Figure 6.22 shows the setup of such a communication channel; for simplicity only the components needed for request-reply interaction are shown.

A request is generated as an NMM event within an NMM interface and forwarded by the corresponding proxy object. Then, the event is handled by one part of the composite strategy by forwarding it to the receiving lower-level transport strategy. This strategy serializes and transmits the event using a particular transport mechanism. The serialized event is received and deserialized by the other part of the lower-level transport strategies. This strategy acts as sender for the corresponding composite strategy. The request is handled (e.g. by the event dispatcher of the NMM object), a reply is generated, (e.g. by setting the return value of the NMM object), and the event is send back. Listener notification is performed correspondingly.

In general, different pairs of transport strategies can be used – one for handling the request, one for the reply. This is especially useful for heterogeneous environments where only certain combinations of strategies are available for establishing communication between connected systems. Furthermore, this allows to reconfigure the used communication channel, e.g. in cases where an target object was migrated during the processing of a request and the previously set transport strategies for handling the reply are no longer available.

Since events can be sent concurrently to a single proxy object of an NMM object, the usage of two pairs of transport strategies requires to include an identifier into every event. This identifier needs to be unique for a particular communication channel in order to determine the reply that corresponds to a particular request. This service can be provided by the composite strategy for out-of-band interaction.

As discussed above, a pair of transport strategies can provide more than two roles. For example, a single transport strategy object can fulfill the role of the receiver and sender of one side of the binding. Thus, a single pair of transport strategies suffices to fulfill all eight communication roles. In this case, only a single transport mechanism is employed for request-reply interaction and listener notification.

### 6.5.4   Instream Communication Channels

In contrast to out-of-band interaction, one-way interaction is used for instream communication. As can be seen in Figure 6.23, the composite strategy for instream communication defines eight different communication roles. Two pairs of transport strategies for handling buffers in upstream and downstream direction, and another two pairs for composite events in both directions. Therefore, in general four different transport mechanisms can be employed.

### 6.5.5   Parallel Bindings

As discussed above, a single pair of transport strategies on top of a single transport mechanism can potentially be used to fulfill these eight communication roles. However, in order to provide different quality of service for different types of messages, the binding framework of NMM supports *parallel bindings* that allow for combining different transport strategies especially suited for a particular type of message [RWLS04, RWLS05].

If different strategies are used for handling buffers and composite events sent in one direction, the instream composite strategies also needs to provide a demultiplexing and multiplexing operation. Sent messages are forwarded to the transport strategy that fulfills the role specific for the type of message. On the receiving side, the stream of buffers and composite events is again multiplexed to a stream of messages. While

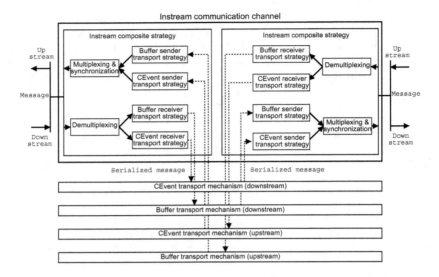

Figure 6.23: Communication channel for instream interaction. In general, eight communication roles need to be fulfilled by the internal low-level transport strategies of the used pair of composite strategies: two pairs of transport strategies for handling buffers in upstream and downstream direction, and another two pairs for composite events in both directions.

such a parallel binding allows to specify different quality of service properties for the transmission of buffers and composite events, the ordering of message needs to maintained. This is especially demanding in the common case where an unreliable transport strategy, such as RTP, is used for buffers and a reliable strategy, such as TCP, is used for composite events.

In general, different types of sub-bindings to be used within a parallel binding can be distinguished.

- *Reliable sub-bindings* use reliable transport mechanisms for transmitting arbitrary information.

- *Unreliable sub-bindings* use unreliable transport mechanisms for transmitting arbitrary information.

- *Multimedia sub-bindings* use unreliable transport mechanisms suited the transmission of time-sensitive multimedia data but only support specific formats and cannot transmit arbitrary information.

In order to maintain the order of messages we use sequence numbers as ordering constraints. These numbers are assigned during the demultiplexing step. We use the notation $m_i$ for "the message with sequence number $i$". Since different transport mechanisms that incur different delays can be used for realizing a single parallel binding, the resynchronization of the message stream can only be performed during the multiplexing step at the receiving side.

While transport mechanisms are in general treated as "black-box" within a transport strategy, several requirements have to be fulfilled by a sub-binding of a parallel binding.

1. The used transport mechanism must be able to transport unique and continuous sequence numbers.

2. If the used transport mechanism changes the sequence numbers of given messages, feedback must be provide about the sequence numbers actually used.

3. Messages are transmitted in-order through a transport mechanism, i.e. when sending message $m_j$ after message $m_i$, $m_j$ is not allowed to be forwarded from the receiving side of the sub-binding before $m_i$.

Protocols for handling multimedia data streams typically already fulfill the first requirement. For example, RTP makes use of a sequence number as part of its protocol header [SCFJ96]. Also, the second property can be fulfilled by protocols such as RTP that require splitting or merging of media buffers into packets that get new sequence numbers assigned. The third requirement greatly simplifies the multiplexing step. However, it might not be available for a certain transport strategy. While implementations of RTP already provide a reordering service, other unreliable transport strategies require to add an additional layer for message ordering, e.g. by discarding messages that are received out of order after some timeout expires [RWLS04, RWLS05].

Notice that for a multimedia sub-binding, we cannot specify which sequence numbers are to be used. In particular, sequence numbers are only unique and continuous for the sub-binding itself, but not for all parallel sub-bindings. Therefore, when using such a multimedia sub-binding in parallel with a binding that allows for arbitrary data to be transmitted, the above defined requirements need to be modified. In particular, the sequence numbers of the sub-binding that allows for arbitrary data to be transmitted only need to provide monotonic increasing sequence numbers, i.e. a single sequence number can be used for transmitting several message. However, since a multimedia sub-binding uses *strictly* monotonic increasing sequence numbers that cannot be influenced, the lastly used sequence number of the multimedia sub-binding is being applied for all following messages sent via the other sub-binding. Since this sub-binding allows to transmit arbitrary information, an additional internal sequence number can be used for realizing in-order transmission for the sub-binding itself. On the receiving side of the binding, a message $m_i$ received from the multimedia sub-binding then needs to be forwarded before all other messages $m_j$ with $j \geq i$ received from the other sub-binding.

### Handling two Reliable Sub-Bindings

If a parallel binding internally uses two reliable sub-bindings, i.e. one for the transmission of composite events and another for the transmission of buffers, the maintenance of message ordering during the multiplexing step can be achieved by a simple algorithm. Since all sub-bindings provide reliable in-order transmission of messages, the forwarding of a received message $m_j$ is delayed until all messages $m_i$, with $i < j$ have been forwarded.

### Handling a Reliable Sub-Binding and an Unreliable Sub-Bindings

For reestablishing the correct order of messages when using a reliable sub-binding in parallel with an unreliable sub-binding, this algorithm has to be extended. Let $i$ be the sequence number of the latest message that has been forwarded from the composite binding to the receiving high-level interface. If the next message $m_j$ to be handled by the multiplexing unit has a sequence number $j > i + 1$, it cannot be forwarded immediately. Instead, one has to "wait" for all *missing messages* $m_k$ with $i < k < j$. More precisely, for each missing message $m_k$, we need to determine if it will arrive – and therefore we need to wait for it – or, if it was lost and we can ignore it. The derived algorithm works as follows.

1. If $m_j$ was received from the reliable sub-binding, all missing messages $m_k$ with $i < k < j$ can only be received from the unreliable sub-binding because in-order reception is provided by all sub-bindings. Since missing messages are transmitted using the unreliable sub-binding, some $m_k$ might get lost. Therefore, the forwarding of $m_j$ is delayed until a message $m_l$ with $l \geq j - 1$ was received from the unreliable sub-binding. If this happens, we can conclude that none of the missing messages $m_k$ with $i < k < j$ will be received and forwarded anymore.

2. If $m_j$ was received from the unreliable sub-binding, one of the following two statements is true for each of the missing messages $m_k$ with $i < k < j$.

   (a) The missing message $m_k$ was sent via the unreliable sub-binding and was lost. This is because $m_j$ with $j > k$ was received from the same unreliable sub-binding and in-order reception is provided by all sub-bindings.

   (b) The missing message $m_k$ was sent via the reliable sub-binding, will be received, and needs to be forwarded before $m_j$.

   To determine, which of the two cases is true, we extend the information transmitted for each message sent via the unreliable sub-binding to include the sequence number $r$ of the latest reliably sent message. This is possible since an unreliable sub-binding allows to include arbitrary additional information. For the message $m_j$ received from the unreliable sub-binding, the multiplexing unit is able to determine if one or more reliably sent messages are still to arrive. This is the case if $r > i$. Then, the forwarding of $m_j$ is delayed until message $m_r$ was handled.

Notice that for case 1, the worst case occurs if the last unreliably sent message before a large number of reliably sent messages gets lost. In this case, the forwarding of all reliably received messages is delayed until the next message is successfully received from the unreliable sub-binding. However, composite events that are typically sent using a reliable sub-binding only occur very rarely within the stream of multimedia buffers sent over an unreliable sub-binding. Therefore, also for case 2, an additional delay is only introduced if we have to wait for a reliably sent message $m_r$.

**Handling a Reliable Sub-Binding and a Multimedia Sub-Bindings**

When using a reliable sub-binding and a multimedia sub-binding in parallel, the algorithm described above cannot be applied since no additional information can be added to the stream of multimedia buffers. However, for every message $m_j$ received from the unreliable multimedia sub-binding, the multiplexing unit of the binding needs to determine whether it needs to wait for a reliably sent message $m_r$ (compare case 2 above). The most convenient way to achieve this, is to avoid situations in which messages are sent via the unreliable and the reliable sub-binding in parallel: Whenever a message $m_r$ is sent using the reliable sub-binding, the unreliable sub-binding stops sending further messages until the reception of $m_r$ was acknowledged. For example, for messages sent in downstream direction, this can be achieved by sending an additional message via the already established reliable sub-binding in upstream direction.

An obvious drawback of this approach is that it introduces an additional delay needed for sending and processing acknowledgments and therefore violates the one-way semantics of instream interaction. However, again we argue that this situation only occurs for the relatively small number of composite events to be sent. Furthermore, we identified our approach to be the only possible solution that allows to consider multimedia sub-bindings as "black-box" as described above. The only facility that needs to be provided is a feedback mechanism that allows to determine the lastly used sequence number for sending messages via the multimedia sub-binding – the position at which the message $m_r$ needs to be inserted into the stream of messages at the receiving side of the binding.

**Handling the End of a Message Stream**

The above described strategies for handling an unreliable or multimedia sub-binding in parallel with a reliable binding require to explicitly handle the overall end of a stream. This is due to the fact that both approaches compensate for missing messages by waiting for following messages to arrive. For example, if the lastly streamed message was sent using the reliable sub-binding and its preceding message was lost, the reliably received message needs to be forwarded anyway.

This situation can be resolved in different ways. First, the final end of a stream can be marked using a specific instream event, e.g. an "end-of-stream" event. When handling this event during the multiplexing step, the corresponding composite event is forwarded after a timeout has expired. Second, before a binding is destroyed, all pending messages stored within the multiplexing unit can be forwarded to the receiving component.

### 6.5.6 Establishment of Bindings

Since the NMM architecture is designed to be independent of a particular lower level networking or middleware technology, the addressing of objects and the binding process cannot rely on a single mechanism. Instead, for each transport mechanism to be integrated, specific components can be provided. In addition, hierarchical connection addresses and corresponding connection setup mechanisms are made available for establishing connections using composite transport strategies as described in Section 6.5.2.

**Addressing and Connection Setup**

When an NMM object is created, it registers itself with a reference manager (class `ReferenceManager`). The reference manager assigns an NMM reference of type `NMMReference` to the object, which uniquely identifies the object within a single address space. In addition, a `UserInfo` object is made available that holds information specific to the system and process in which the object is running, e.g. the names of the corresponding host and domain and process ID. An NMM object can also be registered as an *NMM service* identified with a name given as `string`. In this case, the reference manager acts as simple naming service that allows to request an object by specifying the corresponding NMM service name. Together, this information allows to identify an object within the network; it does not specify how a binding can be established.

For establishing a binding using a particular transport strategy, different subclasses of `TSAddress` are provided for representing addresses. While the base class offers the interface to access the intended NMM reference, subclasses extend this class with interfaces and attributes needed for supporting a particular technology.

For addressing top-level bindings, i.e. using a pair composite strategies, the class `CompositeAddress` and its subclasses for out-of-band bindings respectively instream bindings are used. Within these classes the different roles needed for the particular type of binding have to be set by specifying different low-level addresses. Since we aim at providing scalable transparency, this is either done manually or fully automatic as described below.

The provision of different address classes for low-level transport mechanisms allows for using the most efficient or suitable way for establishing connections between a pair or corresponding transport strategies. If the used underlying transport mechanism provides a distinct service for setting up connections, these facilities can be used. For example when using TCP as transport mechanism, connections can be established by using the internal connection setup procedure of TCP sockets.

In order to support the setup of bindings for technologies that do not provide an internal mechanism for connection setup, *connection managers* are used. A singleton object of type `ConnectionManager` runs within each address and enables access to connection managers running in different address spaces. It also administrates all available transport strategies, e.g. by providing a factory for transport strategies, and corresponding acceptor objects, e.g. for enabling specific setup mechanisms. All communication is performed via NMM interfaces, in particular the interface named `IConnectionManager` provided by a connection manager.

Obviously, for using a locally running connection manager to communicate to a remote connection manager, these two objects need to be connected first. Therefore, at least one technology that offers an internal connection setup mechanism has to be provided. Since TCP can be assumed to be available widely, our current implementation uses a TCP acceptor bound to a well-known port for realizing this functionality. However, as described below, an NMM interface holds all possible addresses that can be used for setting up connections to a remote object. Once such an interface is received, a suitable and available transport strategy can be chosen.

Two connection managers establish a reliable request-reply connection to initiate and configure new connections for technologies that do not provide this possibility, e.g. UDP or RTP operating on top of UDP. For such technologies, corresponding address classes are subclasses of `ConnectorAddress`. Such an address holds the interface `IConnectionManager` of the connection manager object that is local to the corresponding object. Upon receiving such an interface, the initial link between different address spaces can be established as described in the following.

**Out-Of-Band Connections**

A binding is locally represented by a communication channel, i.e. an object of type `CommunicationChannel`. Thus, the main task of a communication channel is to provide a local interface to possibly distributed parts of transport strategies. Furthermore, the communication channel realizes the negotiation of connection parameters, e.g. by determining a composite address to be used for the binding.

For out-of-band bindings, a specific subclass `OutOfBandChannel` exists. When establishing an out-of-band binding to an NMM object, the supported low-level transport strategies that can be used for configuring the corresponding top-level binding have to be known. More precisely, for each low-level transport strategy available within the address space of the NMM object, all available attributes need to be determined, namely the supported communication roles – i.e. the implemented low-level interfaces for out-of-band interaction – and the provided service capabilities. Furthermore, the addresses that allow to establish a connection have to be provided for each supported transport strategy. For transport strategies that offer such a service, the corresponding address is provided by an object of a type specific for the transport strategy, e.g. a `TCPAddress` representing a TCP acceptor listening to a well-known port. Otherwise, an address of type `ConnectorAddress`, e.g. a `UDPAddress` or `RTPAddress`, contains the NMM interface of the locally running connection manager object. Such an object can then be accessed from a different address space as described above and bridges the gap to remote objects.

Therefore, possible connection addresses are stored within each NMM interface object. Since such an interface object can be serialized and then transmitted between different address spaces, all information for setting up a binding is provided. Notice that a serialized NMM interface can be compared to a CORBA IOR (see Section 3.4.1). However, in contrast to CORBA and other middleware solutions, a serialized NMM interface provides access to different lower level transport mechanisms supported by the binding framework.

Since a top-level binding consists of at least of a single pair of *matching* low-level transport strategies and not all strategies can be assumed to be available for all distributed system, a communication channel needs to determine all possible transport mechanisms. For determining what kind of binding can be used – i.e. a local, system, or network binding –, the classes `Interface` and `NMMObject` provide a `UserInfo` that holds information specific to the system and process in which the object is running. Also, the sets of available strategies of both sides of the binding are compared. For example, when establishing a connection to a remote object, the address objects of the corresponding NMM interface are compared with the set of available strategies provided by the connection manager.

The only thing required is to provide an initial reliable channel for transmitting NMM interfaces of instantiated remote objects. In Chapter 9, the registry service of

NMM is described that allows to request and instantiate processing elements on remote hosts. Again, a well-known port is used together with a reliable transport strategy based on TCP to establish the initial communication between different address spaces and to exchange NMM interfaces of instantiated processing elements.

**Instream Connections**

Instream top-level bindings establish communication between an output jack and an input jack of two connected processing elements of a flow graph. A subclass `Instream-Channel` is provided that implements the specific aspects of such a binding.

Notice that the setup of instream connections establishes a binding between two jacks, possibly running on different remote systems. The jacks themselves are also NMM objects and are therefore accessed using NMM interfaces. In contrast to out-of-band bindings, the multimedia format used for connecting the two corresponding processing elements needs to be taken into account. This is because especially transport strategies suited for the transmission of multimedia data often only support a restricted set of formats. Therefore, the chosen connection format limits the set of available low-level transport strategies for realizing instream interaction. As all transport strategies are registered with the connection manager, this component allows to map a given connection format to a list of possible strategies to be used.

**Scalable Transparency during the Binding Process**

As discussed in Section 5.1, we aim at providing scalable transparency. In this particular context, this goal is realized as follows. On the one hand, top-level bindings can be set up automatically. Then, all transport strategies for all communication roles are chosen according to the particular type of binding and predefined preferences. For example, for out-of-band communication, reliable transport strategies are preferred.

On the other hand, all aspects of such a top-level binding can be configured manually – settings that are not specified directly are then, again, negotiated automatically. During the establishment of the binding, all available strategies can be requested first together with their service capability. Then, a strategy can explicitly be requested to fulfill a particular role. To further ease this step, the developed API supports to set the receiving and sending part of a transport strategy – i.e. the two roles required – with one command. For example, this allows for specifying an RTP strategy for instream transmission of buffers in downstream direction.

If, however, only a subset of available communication roles was specified, the already set transport strategies are tried to be reused to fill the remaining roles. For all roles that are not fulfilled by already available strategies, additional transport strategies are chosen according to predefined preferences.

Once a top-level binding is set up, interfaces specific for the chosen lower level transport strategies can be queried. This allows for manually configuring capabilities, such as sending or receiving buffer sizes of a TCP sub-binding. Especially when integrating mobile devices with scarce resources using wireless networking technology, such configurations allow for realizing various optimizations.

**Local Optimization**

As a further optimization, the automatic setup of bindings also tries to establish the most "efficient" kind of binding. The most obvious optimization criterion is given by the physical locations of the objects to be bound. In particular, for a local binding, a transport strategy that simply forwards references to allocated memory is to be used. Since the main components of the NMM architecture, such as NMM object and proxy object, and input jack and output jack, also directly offer the corresponding high-level interface of establishing communication, a purely locally operating transport strategy can be completely left out; instead, components are connected directly. This option is currently already implemented for instream communication; the NMM architecture can also be extended to use this optimization for out-of-band bindings.

To this end, the NMM architecture allows to be tailored to a purely locally operating system that does not incur the constant overhead of a middleware solution for distributed computing. The chosen approach even allows to configure and compile NMM without including the parts of the architecture that provide some kind of "networking".

### 6.5.7   Realized Transport Strategies

Different low-level transport strategies were implemented, in general as pairs of sending and receiving components. In this section, these strategies will be described briefly. In particular, we will focus on the provided communication roles and service capabilities, the supported multimedia formats, and the additionally provided control interfaces. More details can be found in [Rep03a] and [Win06].

**Local Transport Strategy**

As described in Section 6.5.6, a local transport strategy simply forwards references between connected components. Therefore, it allows to handle arbitrary data types and correspondingly also implements all available low-level interfaces presented in Section 6.5.2 within a single class. The local transport strategy is the most efficient strategy for establishing communication for colocated entities – other types of bindings, i.e. system and network bindings, are obviously not supported.

**TCP Transport Strategy**

The implemented transport strategy based on TCP provides the corresponding service capabilities, namely reliable transmission of arbitrary data types and multimedia formats. According to the properties of TCP, our implementation offers the interfaces for one-way interaction using buffers or composite events, and the interfaces for out-of-band request-reply interaction within a single class. Furthermore, this class realizes the sending and the receiving parts of the transport strategy. Therefore, a single pair of instances of this strategy can be used to fulfill all communication roles for bidirectional instream interaction or out-of-band interaction. Another approach for an implementation based on TCP might split these different functionalities into different classes.

Internally, a stack of serialization operators is used, in particular operators for serializing NMM objects, such as messages or events, on top of a networking stream operator (see Section 6.1.4). While this stack of operators can be configured manually, a magic number value stream on top of a buffered networking stream is chosen as default.

For manually configuring various parameters specific for TCP, an additional NMM interface is provided that allows to set properties, such as sending and receiving buffers of the protocol, or to enable flags such as the "no delay" setting.

Since TCP inherently provides a connection setup mechanism, the TCP strategy uses a distinct acceptor for establishing connections via a well-known port specific for all TCP connections. Internally, the common design patterns for a Reactor [SSR00] and a pool of "worker" threads [NBPF96] are used to efficiently realize communication in a multi-threaded environment.

### UDP Transport Strategy

Another transport strategy is based on UDP and provides unreliable transmission of arbitrary data types and multimedia formats and offers the same interfaces for interaction as the above described TCP strategy. Internally, the magic number value stream is configured as default. However, as described in Section 2.2.4, data packets sent using UDP can get lost or arrive out-of-order at the receiving side. Therefore, the packet networking stream described in Section 6.1.4 is used instead of the buffered networking stream. This stream provides in-order delivery together with the guarantee that serialized objects that were split into several data packets during network transmission are either received completely or discarded.

Since UDP as connection-less protocol does not provide a service for connection setup, a UDP address stores a reference to the NMM interface of the corresponding connection manager. During runtime, UDP transport strategies are handled by the multi-threading facilities that are also used for TCP. Finally, multicast networking can be realized using this strategy.

### RTP Transport Strategy

For integrating support for RTP into NMM, we use the external library libliveMedia provided by [Liv]. According to the properties of this library, the developed RTP transport strategy provides unreliable transmission of multimedia data streams on top of UDP – in particular, the strategy only supports the formats available from the library, e.g. MPEG1/2 audio or video. Since a single RTP connection operates unidirectional, we implemented a class that acts as one-way buffer receiver and another class that acts as one-way buffer sender (compare Section 6.5.2). Other communication roles are not provided. Multicast networking is available for this strategy.

As RTP is especially suited for multimedia communication, the real-time flag of the service capabilities of the transport strategy is set. Furthermore, this strategy internally modifies the NMM sequence numbers but provides a feedback mechanism needed for realizing a parallel binding. The specification of additional serialization operators is not allowed for this strategy. Similar to UDP, an RTP address stores a reference to the NMM interface of the corresponding connection manager. The used RTP library internally uses an own approach for scheduling and multi-threading. Together, this transport strategy is therefore a good example for a transport mechanism that is integrated into NMM as "black-box".

### 6.5.8 Discussion

The binding framework of NMM allows for the integration and combination of various existing transport mechanisms. Furthermore, explicit binding and scalable transparency provide a suitable programming model for multimedia middleware. This openness is in contrast to monolithic traditional middleware solutions.

Similar to other approaches for explicit binding, e.g. hierarchical [WC97] and open bindings [FBC+98] described in Section 4.2.3, our architecture considers top-level bindings to be composed of lower-level binding objects. In addition, the developed framework uses the concept of communication roles and therefore strictly distinguishes between the sending and receiving parts of a bidirectional binding. This allows to use different underlying transport mechanisms for different communication roles. While this feature is also provided by the system described in [BSGR03] for request-reply interaction, NMM extends this concept to instream interaction in upstream and downstream direction. This capability is especially important for heterogenous environments, where only certain combinations of transport mechanisms might be available. Furthermore, due to the mobility of users and devices, possible configurations are constantly changing and need to be adapted to the technologies present.

Within NMM, a communication channel is composed of several interacting components. While this general concept is similar to the setup of channels in RM-ODP as described in Section 3.4.2, our architecture provides a more flexible approach that allows a single component to perform different tasks. This choice was made in order to be able to integrate various existing implementations of transport mechanisms that all provide different capabilities. Furthermore, NMM offers the possibility to use a stack of serialization operators.

Finally, we extended previous approaches for open and explicit bindings by introducing the concept of parallel bindings that allows to transmit a stream of ordered messages with different QoS requirements using different transport mechanisms. Since parallel bindings are handled within the middleware layer, additional emerging transport layer protocols can be included seamlessly, e.g. the Stream Control Transmission Protocol (SCTP) [SXM+00, JRST01] or the transport protocol for heterogenous packet flows (HPF) [LHB99].

While parallel bindings are still being researched within the scope of the NMM project, first evaluations of their performance presented in Section 8.1.3 are quite promising. Future extension focus on supporting a third type of message stream within a parallel binding, a stream of only partially ordered and unreliable composite events that are sent with a higher density than reliably sent composite events. Such frequent events carry arbitrary non-critical information, like the progress of a task. In addition, further transport mechanisms are investigated, e.g using the dynamic any-types provided by CORBA.

While the provision of communication channels for instream interaction allows for providing network-transparent cooperation as described in Section 4.2.3, the developed networking components can also be used within different contexts, e.g. within processing elements of a flow graph instead of within the connecting edges of the graph. If wanted, this allows for realizing traditional client/server approaches with sources and sinks of data being at the edges of the network.

## 6.6   Summary

In this chapter, the design and implementation of an integrating communication framework was presented. Based on an extensible system for the serialization of arbitrary data types and a unified messaging system, an architecture for realizing different interaction paradigms was developed. On top of this architecture, an object-oriented interface system provides suitable abstractions and a convenient programming model for multimedia middleware or middleware in general. The binding framework offers the connecting elements of the architecture. In particular, communication channels realize interaction between entities and can be composed out of different lower-level components. Finally, the concept of parallel binding allows for transmitting an ordered stream of messages with different quality of service properties using different and appropriate technologies. Together, the design of this part of the NMM architecture offers an open and integrating approach and provides scalable transparency.

In the following chapter, a concrete realization of a flow graph based multimedia middleware solutions that employs the facilities of the architecture presented here will be presented. Together, these two chapters describe the base architecture of the Network-Integrated Multimedia Middleware (NMM). As a summary, Chapter 8 provides performance evaluations of different aspects of the current implementation.

# Chapter 7

# A Generic Multimedia Middleware Architecture

The architecture presented in the previous chapter provides the building blocks for realizing different middleware solutions. In this chapter, we will describe a concrete multimedia middleware based on this architecture [LSW01, Wam01, LRS02, Did02, DL03, LS03, Loh03a, Loh03d, Loh03f, Loh04d, Loh04a, LRS03b]. We will first give an overview of the general design of the middleware. Since many concepts of our approach are direct applications or combinations of the components presented in the previous chapter, this overview can also be seen as another viewpoint of the NMM architecture as presented so far.

The different basic elements of the developed multimedia middleware will then be presented in more detail. In particular, the processing elements and the connecting parts between these elements that allow to create distributed flow graphs will be explained. Facilities for describing and interacting with multimedia formats are another important part for every multimedia architecture and are described next. The setup and represenation of distributed flow graphs is discussed next. Then, the memory management of NMM is presented. The generic processing model of the NMM architecture is discussed in detail. This is the most concrete part of the description and shows that the concepts provided by NMM allow for an easy integration of existing multimedia software libraries and other multimedia architectures – one of the main goals for the development of NMM. Finally, a generic architecture that allows to realize different synchronization protocols for distributed multimedia is presented. As a summary, the development of plug-ins for NMM is described.

Together with the architectural elements introduced in the previous chapter, the following description covers the complete base system of the Network-Integrated Multimedia Middleware (NMM).

## 7.1 Overview

Figure 7.1 gives an overview of how the architectural components as described so far are used to develop a concrete multimedia middleware [Loh04d]. The general design approach for this part of the architecture is according to the abstractions for multimedia architectures in general as discussed in Section 2.4. Within NMM, processing

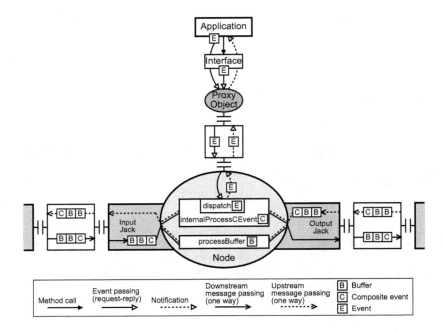

Figure 7.1: The facilities of the NMM architecture as described so far are used for realizing a concrete multimedia middleware. Distributed objects such as nodes and jacks
are controlled via the proxy architecture of NMM. Jacks represent the input and output
ports of a node. Internally, jacks buffer received upstream and downstream messages.
Within a node, events, composite events and buffers are handled. All communication
is realized with communication channels.

elements, such as hardware devices and software components, are represented by so
called *nodes* (see Section 7.2). An important aspect of a particular node is the number
of input and output ports, called *input jacks* and *output jacks* (see Section 7.3), and
the *formats* supported by the different jacks (see Section 7.4). We define format as
the meta data that describes a multimedia data stream (compare Section 2.2.2). Nodes
and jacks are distributed objects that implement one or more implementation classes
that were generated from definitions in NMM IDL. Correspondingly, these objects are
controlled by an application using request-reply out-of-band interaction via interface
objects or direct event forwarding via the proxy object. Event dispatching is performed
automatically by the corresponding implementation classes.

Nodes can be connected via their jacks to create a flow graph. In order to connect
an input jack to an output jack, both need to support the same format. Due to the large
number of different formats, this aspect is especially important for multimedia middleware and will be extensively discussed in Section 7.4, Section 7.5, and in the scope
of Chapter 10, where a format negotiation algorithm is presented. With data flowing
instream between connected nodes, the structure of this graph then specifies the op-

eration to be performed. For one-way upstream and downstream interaction, buffers and composite events are used to forward information. Both, instream and out-of-band interaction use the concept of communication channels for realizing communication.

As discussed in Section 2.2.5 and Section 4.2.4, synchronization is an important part of handling multimedia. An generic architecture that allows to provide different synchronization protocols for distributed flow graphs is presented in Section 7.8.

While the processing of single events received via out-of-band interaction is already provided by the event dispatcher that is part of every implementation class (compare Section 6.4), the messages received instream are to be handled manually by a node. During this step, received composite events are forwarded to the event dispatcher where the individual events are dispatched. As the definitions of methods for instream interaction are also defined in NMM IDL, a node only has to provide the particular implementations. To enable advanced interaction using instream events, the parameters of events can be modified. Furthermore, individual events within a composite event can be deleted or replaced, and additional events can be inserted into the composite event.

Messages of type buffer are handled differently. The method *processBuffer* is called with a single buffer as argument. This method is the place where the main work in terms of multimedia processing is done. As this work is specific for a particular processing element, it is implemented individually for different elements. Such a specific implementation is also called *plug-in node* or simply *plug-in*. Similar to the processing of composite events received instream, various possibilities exist for handling buffers. The contents of the memory area of the buffer or its header information, such as its timestamp, can be modified. Incoming buffers can be released and new buffers can be requested, e.g. for implementing a specific multimedia processing routine. The buffer managers presented in Section 7.6 allow for efficiently realizing these operations. Finally, new composite events to be sent instream can be generated by calling the corresponding method for event creation (see Section 6.4.2).

As can be seen from the above exemplification, the processing of a single message received instream can have different results. For example, the message can be modified, deleted from the stream, or new messages can be inserted into the stream – either upstream or downstream. In order to allow for an integration of different existing multimedia processing components within NMM plug-ins, no assumptions about a particular interaction pattern are made. Instead, the generic processing model presented in Section 7.7 allows for realizing arbitrary interaction schemes.

This generalization also needs to be applied for the realization of input and output jacks. In particular, a jack acts as a first-in-first-out buffer of messages. Messages received instream are buffered and need to be requested explicitly by the node. This behavior is needed to allow for a connection of the different components, namely jacks and transport strategies – or a direct connection between two jacks within the same address space as described in Section 6.5.6. For all these components, no assumptions about a particular interaction pattern can be made. Therefore, buffering elements between these components are needed. However, the size of these buffers and their particular behavior can be influenced by the application. The buffering within jacks also allows to partly hide best-effort service provision as discussed in Section 2.3.1. This will be further described in Section 7.3.

Finally, the registration and notification of listeners is realized by employing the

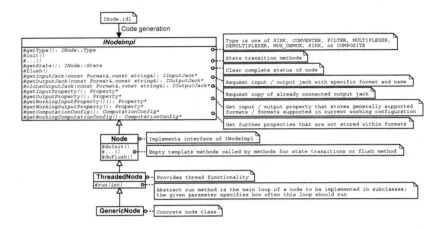

Figure 7.2: The interface `INode` provides access to the aspects common to all processing elements within NMM. Properties store the supported formats. The computation configuration holds additional settings relevant for the resource requirements of a node. Methods for changing the state of a node allow to control its life-cycle. For connecting nodes, methods for requesting jacks are provided that take a format and the name of the jack as parameters. The class `Node` implements the interface as provided by the implementation class `INodeImpl`. The class `ThreadedNode` adds multi-threading functionality. The class `GenericNode` provides an implementation of the generic processing model described in Section 7.7.

facilities discussed in the previous chapter. In particular, applications can register to be notified for events received instream or out-of-band, respectively. Especially the possibility to register for instream events is of great importance for multimedia middleware because this feature is essential for realizing advanced middleware services such as the service for seamless reconfiguration of flow graphs as discussed in Chapter 12.

## 7.2 Nodes as Processing Elements

Within NMM, nodes represent the processing elements. While all functionality specific for a certain plug-in node (e.g. a plug-in node that accesses a camera) is accessed via specific interfaces (e.g. the interface `ICamera`), the main purpose of the interface `INode` shown in Figure 7.2 is to provide access to the aspects common to all processing elements. In particular, this includes:

- The *properties* of a node. In general, a property stores a set of formats. The *input property* and *output property* of a node provide access to the *generally* supported input and output formats, respectively. These properties are also called *static* and are stored within the registry (see Section 9). In contrast, the *working input property* and *working output property* reflect the supported formats of the *current* configuration of the node. This is an important distinction needed for modeling multimedia processing elements. For example, the currently supported output formats often strongly depend on the chosen configuration. As an example, consider a plug-in for reading media files from secondary storage. While such a plug-in might support various output formats, the format stored in the working output property strongly depends on the currently read file. Correspondingly, the working input property reflects the currently used input formats as specified when requesting an input jack (see below). In general, the working properties typically only contain subsets of the formats stored in the static properties.

As the supported multimedia formats are specific for a particular plug-in node, these values are set by the plug-in itself. Section 7.2.2 will describe when the different properties are to be specified. Formats are essential for setting up flow graphs and will be discussed in detail in Section 7.4.

- The *computation configuration* is a set of key-value pairs that allows to store all other configurations that are not part of input or output formats but also influence the resource requirements of a processing element[1]. For example, when encoding multimedia streams, the chosen algorithm or parameters thereof strongly influence the needed computational resources. However, such configurations are typically not part of a format. Again, a distinction is made between the *static computation configuration* and the *working computation configuration*.

- The methods for accessing and changing the *state* of a processing element. The state machine to be described in detail in Section 7.2.2 is an essential aspect for providing a framework that allows for the efficient development and integration of new plug-ins by defining strict guidelines for the life-cycle of a node; from being constructed to the point where data is flowing through it. In addition, a method for clearing the internal status of a node is provided – the *flush* operation.

- For creating a streaming data connection between two processing elements, the output jack of one element has to be connected to the input jacks of another node. Therefore, every node allows to request jacks by specifying the format specific for the connection. Furthermore, as a node is allowed to provide several inputs and outputs, a *jack tag* can be given. If this value is not specified, the *default jack* is requested, e.g. the only input or output jack available, respectively. While jacks are described in more detail in Section 7.3, the connection setup will be discussed in Section 7.2.2 and Section 7.5.

Within NMM, a node represents the smallest entity of multimedia processing. In order to be able to extensively reuse specific nodes in different application scenarios, nodes should represent fine-grained processing units. The innermost loop of a node handles instream interaction. Within this loop, the node produces messages, performs a certain operation on received messages, or finally consumes messages. The class `ThreadedNode` extends `Node` to provide a separate thread of execution for this loop. The class `GenericNode` provides a generic processing model that handles the different message types like composite events and buffers. Both classes are discussed in Section 7.7.

---

[1]The current implementation of NMM uses the same class for format and computation configuration objects (see Section 7.4).

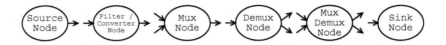

Figure 7.3: The graphical representations for the different types of NMM nodes, namely for source nodes, filter or converter nodes, multiplexer nodes, demultiplexer nodes, multiplexer-demultiplexer nodes, and sink nodes. These representations only indicate the direction of the downstream message flow.

### 7.2.1   Node Types

Depending on the number of input and output jacks *and* the provided functionality, different types of nodes can be distinguished (compare Section 2.4.1).

- A *source node* provides a single output. Within its internal processing loop, it produces messages to be forwarded by its output jack.

- A *sink node* provides a single input. It processes and consumes messages received by its input jack.

- A *processor node* provides a single input and a single output. It processes received messages and generates messages to be sent. Depending on the type of media processing, two different types can be distinguished.

  - A *filter node* does not change the format of the multimedia data received, i.e. its input format and output format are identical. The received data is only filtered or manipulated.

  - A *converter node* transforms data received from one format to another, i.e. its input format is different from its output format.

  This distinction will be of great importance for the development of the format negotiation service presented in Chapter 10. While filters can be characterized as elements that transform the contents of multimedia streams, converters offer the possibility to transform incompatible formats.

- A *multiplexer node* provides two or more inputs and a single output. Such a node requests messages from its input jacks and generates messages to be forwarded to its output jack.

- A *demultiplexer node* provides a single input and two or more outputs. This type of node receives messages from its single input jack and forwards messages to its output jacks.

- A *multiplexer-demultiplexer node* provides an arbitrary number of inputs and outputs. It is a generalization of the different node types presented so far.

Figure 7.3 shows the graphical representations for the different types of nodes as used in the following. As these representations are mostly used to present the structure of a flow graph, they do not explicitly depict input or output jacks; only connections

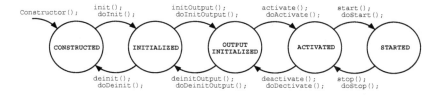

Figure 7.4: The state machine for NMM nodes defines a framework for their life-cycle and offers template methods that allow to integrate plug-in specific functionality via so called do-methods. These methods are executed when the corresponding state transition is performed.

between nodes are shown and the direction of the downstream flow is indicated. In addition, some graphical representations of NMM flow graphs will include the jack tags for connected jacks.

### 7.2.2 State Machine

One major goal for the development of the NMM architecture is to allow for an easy development of plug-in nodes. These plug-ins nodes can be used to implement new multimedia processing routines. However, since a lot of multimedia software libraries or locally operating multimedia architectures already exists, an important aspect of NMM is the integration of these existing components.

The state machine of NMM defines strict guidelines for the life-cycle of a node; from being constructed to the point where data is flowing through the processing element [Loh03f]. In order to allow for an integration of various different multimedia processing routines, the state machine needs to be generic enough to cover all different cases that might occur.

Figure 7.4 shows the states and methods for performing state transitions. For each of these state transition methods, a *do-method* is called internally, e.g. for init() the method doInit(). This design is according to the Template Method pattern, which delegates specific parts of an algorithm to subclasses that implement a template method that is called by the superclass [GHJV94]. Applied to the state machine of NMM, this allows to implement code specific for a particular plug-in to be executed during state transitions. The state transitions themselves are already provided by the node base class and internally use the facilities of the state driven event dispatcher (see Section 6.2). To this end, the state machine is defined in NMM IDL by using the keyword limited as additional modifier for state transition methods, e.g. the method init() is limited to the state CONSTRUCTED (compare Section 6.4). For a state transition to complete successfully, the invocation of corresponding state transition method has to be allowed for the current state, all plug-in specific *required* methods have to be completed, *and* the corresponding do-method has to be processed with success, e.g. without throwing an exception. Otherwise, an exception is thrown indicating that the state transition failed and the state is not changed.

The different states that specify the life-cycle of a plug-in node are defined as follows.

- CONSTRUCTED This state is reached after the creation of a node. The internal status of the node should be initialized within the constructor, which acts as do-method for this state. Within this state, all resources that have influence on the supported formats or features of the node have to be specified but are not allocated. For example, the handle to a particular multimedia device has to be given.

- INITIALIZED When reaching this state by calling the method init(), resources have to be requested and allocated. Furthermore, the static input and output formats of a node have to be fully specified within its static input and output property, respectively. Often, these formats depend on the allocated resources, e.g. the formats supported by a particularly chosen multimedia device. In addition, if the number of inputs of the node also depends on configurations to be made in constructed state, input jacks have to be created; otherwise, this can be done during the construction of the node. Finally, the static computation configuration has to be set. As all these steps are specific for a particular plug-in, they are to be implemented within the doInit()-method.

  Within this state, input jacks can be requested from the node by specifying a format and optionally the name of the jack if more than one input is available. Only if the name and format is supported, an input jack is provided and the corresponding format is stored internally. A requested input jack can be connected to an output jack to be provided by another node that is within the state OUTPUT_INITIALIZED.

- OUTPUT_INITIALIZED Upon calling the method initOutput, the working properties of the node have to be specified for reaching the next state. In particular, the working input property has to be filled in respect to the chosen input formats as specified when input jacks were requested in state INITIALIZED. Correspondingly, the working output property has to be filled with all output formats that are available for the currently configured input formats. Furthermore, the correct number of output jacks with corresponding names have to be created. Again, this is done by providing a custom implementation within the method doInitOutput(). Output jacks can then be requested by providing a format and optionally the name of the jack. This specification seems to be similar to the requirements for state INITIALIZED. However, an additional property of multimedia streams has to be taken into account. Depending on the chosen input formats, the supported output formats and the number of outputs of a processing element can only be determined by considering the actual content of the input streams. For example for multiplexed MPEG streams, the number and formats of elementary streams is not known a priori and can only be determined by analyzing the stream of data. A similar property can be observed for streams of compressed data, where the precise output format of the decoding routine is first known after some decompressed buffers were generated.

  However, fully specified output formats are needed in order to be able to connect output jacks and input jacks. Furthermore, the process of analyzing incoming data in order to determine the correct output formats is also needed for handling different multimedia streams with the same flow graph. A simple example for this case would be the playback of several files of the same file format by using a single flow graph. Therefore, the generic processing model of NMM presented in Section 7.7 allows to handle both cases transparently. Correspondingly, the development of plug-in nodes is greatly simplified. Together, for a node to analyze data, its predecessors within the flow graph – also called *upstream nodes* – need to provide enough buffers for determining the format. Therefore, all upstream nodes need to be in the state ACTIVATED to be discussed next.

Since the computation configuration stores additional settings relevant for the resource requirements of the node that are independent of the chosen connection formats, the specification of the working computation configuration is not restricted to a certain state. However, within doInitOutput(), an initial working computation configuration has to be specified.

- ACTIVATED When calling the method activate() the input and output formats of all requested jacks are determined and the jacks are connected. Within the method doActivate() resources that depend on the chosen formats have to be reserved. From this point on, the node can be started to perform the actual multimedia processing. Since this is also the first time during the life-cycle of a node that all required resources have been requested, the state ACTIVATED needs to be reached for all upstream nodes before a call of initOutput() for a specific downstream node can be performed.

- STARTED Finally, by calling the method start() the internal loop of the node is triggered and the node starts to perform the intended processing by handling messages. A concrete implementation of such a main loop is described in detail in Section 7.7. If needed, plug-in nodes can provide custom functionality to be performed prior to being started within the method doStart().

As can be seen in Figure 7.4, state transition methods also exist for reaching preceding states, namely stop(), deactivate(), deinitOutput(), and deinit(), together with corresponding template methods. In general, all operations and reservations performed should be reverted during these transitions. Figure 7.5 shows an example for the manual connection setup between two nodes [Loh04a]; Section 7.5.1 will discuss an automatic approach.

### Discussion

The state machine for NMM nodes shows the applicability of the state driven event dispatching as described in Section 6.2 and the corresponding extensions of the interface definition language (IDL) of NMM discussed in Section 6.4. On the one hand, the state machine itself is described in NMM IDL. On the other hand, the IDL extensions for limiting and requiring method executions have proven to be convenient for defining plug-in specific functionality. For example, setting a specific multimedia device is often limited to the constructed state and required for reaching the initialized state. Correspondingly, many features specific for a certain device can only be accessed in the initialized state or all following states.

Other locally operating multimedia architectures also provide a state machine for their processing elements. While these approaches often include less states and are

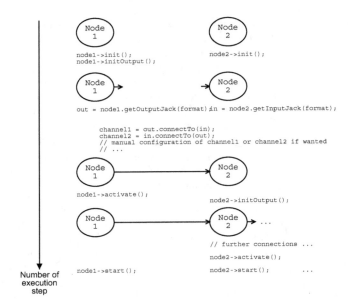

Figure 7.5: The state transitions methods of NMM nodes as called during the manual connection setup between several nodes. Starting from a source node (Node 1), a converter/filter node is connected (Node 2). These steps are repeated for all other connections within the flow graph. Both calls of `connectTo()` return a communication channel that refers to the same connection and can be configured manually or automatically (compare Section 6.5.6).

simpler, the NMM state machine uses a more fine-grained approach. However, this is needed to allow for an integration of different multimedia components and architectures. We especially found the strict definitions of the different states to be essential for developing plug-in nodes that can be seamlessly combined within a flow graph – despite the fact that different underlying technologies with varying processing models are used.

Finally, the state machine of NMM allows to realize advanced features – like the update of connection formats within a running flow graph – to operate transparently for plug-in nodes when compared to the initial setup of the flow graph. This operation will be described in the scope of Section 7.7.

Notice that input and outputs of NMM nodes are not defined via an interface definition language. This is in contrast to other approaches that offer the possibility to specify the concrete number and type of input and output ports within an IDL description [FGB+01]. However, as discussed above, such an approach does not take the dynamic nature of processing elements into account. More precisely, the number of inputs and outputs often strongly depends on specific configurations *and* the format of the processed multimedia streams – a property that can only by determined by the particular processing element itself during runtime. Therefore, we chose to generically

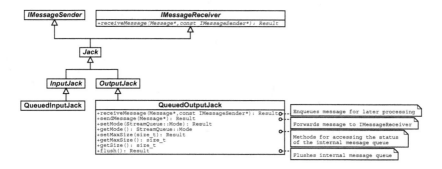

Figure 7.6: The classes `QueuedInputJack` and `QueuedOutputJack` internally use an object of type `StreamQueue` to buffer incoming messages in a first-in-first-out manner. All parameters of the queueing model can be queried and set to take application specific requirements into account.

provide access to input and output jacks via the base interface of NMM nodes. Furthermore, this functionality is embedded into the state machine for NMM nodes, e.g. by limiting possible access jacks to well-defined states within the life-cycle of nodes.

## 7.3   Jacks as Connecting Elements

As already discussed before, jacks represent the input and output ports of NMM nodes. While the connection setup between distributed jacks in general – and two jacks within the same address space in particular – is described in Section 6.5.6, this section presents the concrete jack classes that are used within the generic processing model of NMM.

### 7.3.1   Queueing Model

The class `QueuedInputJack` and the class `QueuedOutputJack` are shown in Figure 7.6. These classes internally use an object of type `StreamQueue`, which offers the functionality of first-in-first-out queue (FIFO), to buffer messages received via the interface `IMessageReceiver`. For two locally operating jacks, message passing is directly performed between a message sender (interface `IMessageSender`) and a message receiver (interface `IMessageReceiver`); for distributed jacks, the two composite transport strategies involved provide the corresponding interfaces for each jack (see Section 6.5).

The queued jack classes provide access to all parameters of the internal message stream queue. In particular, this allows to set the maximum size of the queue and the queueing mode. Three different modes are available.

- MODE_SUSPEND When using this mode, the queue can be filled until its maximum size is reached. Then, the queue blocks. A message sender is not allowed to insert another message into the queue as long as the actual size of the queue is not smaller than its maximum size. As soon as the size of the queue is again smaller than its maximum size, the queue notifies suspended message senders via a signalling interface. Within this mode, a stream queue can be used to automatically regulate the message flow. However, certain soft real-time characteristics of the message flow are destroyed if they are not handled by other mechanisms such as connecting transport strategies or synchronization facilities.

- MODE_KEEP_OLDEST In this mode, whenever the queue is completely filled, the queue discards the "newest" message to arrive and keeps the "older" messages already enqueued. However, in order to maintain the quality of service settings of messages, this step is also performed with respect to the mandatory flag. If this flag is not set for the message to be inserted into the filled queue, it is discarded. Otherwise, the newest non-mandatory message within the queue is discarded. If no such message exists, the newly received message is inserted as well, but the queue is suspended as described above. Notice that for composite events the mandatory flag is set per default; for buffers it is not. Also, we assume that mandatory composite events are only inserted very rarely into a stream of buffers. Therefore, this mode allows to maintain the characteristics of the stream – with the restriction of discarding newly arrived messages.

- MODE_KEEP_NEWEST In contrast, this mode discards the "oldest" message within the queue whenever the queue is filled completely and a new message is to be inserted. Again, the mandatory flag is taken into account as described above. Therefore, this mode also allows to maintain the characteristics of the stream – in this case, with the restriction of discarding "old" messages within the queue.

The default mode for stream queues is MODE_SUSPEND and the default size is 16. However, this size is usually changed to other values by plug-in nodes with respect to their performed operation.

### Discussion

Together, the setting of queue modes and sizes allows to control the behavior of flow graphs. Furthermore, the suspending queueing mode automatically regulates the in-stream message traffic within flow graphs – for both, local and distributed cases. While the default values of the queueing model have proven to be applicable for nearly all flow graphs as described within the scope of this thesis, special requirements like lower latencies still require application specific manual settings.

For future work, it would be interesting to realize automatic adaptation of the queueing parameters. Since the interfaces for querying and modifying queueing behavior are already available, the NMM architecture provides the reflection needed for realizing such an approach.

### 7.3.2   Jack Groups

As discussed in Section 2.2.4 and Section 4.4.4, multi-party communication and collaborative applications are important aspects for distributed multimedia systems. As

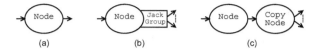

Figure 7.7: The node shown in (a) is extended to use a jack group instead of a single output jack (b). In general, all downstream messages received by a jack group are forwarded to all jacks within this group. In (c), an alternative realization of this functionality is shown that uses an additional node (more precisely a demultiplexer called CopyNode), which forwards all downstream messages to all its output jacks.

a basic service, NMM provides the abstraction of *jack groups*. In order to forward downstream traffic to multiple receiving nodes, such a group allows to hold several identical output jacks. Conceptually, downstream messages are then forwarded to all jacks within such a group (see Figure 7.7 (a) and (b)).

NMM allows to dynamically add jacks to a jack group by invoking the method cloneOutputJack() provided by the node interface (compare Section 7.2). Since a jack group is used to forward a *single* stream to multiple receiving nodes, the format given as parameter for this method has to be identical to the already set format.

**Discussion**

An alternative realization of the functionality of a jack group employs an additional node – the CopyNode in Figure 7.7 (c) – that acts as demultiplexer and forwards all incoming messages to all its single output jacks. However, we did not chose this possibility due to several reasons. First, within the NMM architecture, nodes generally represent the smallest entity of *processing*; jacks represent the *connecting* elements. The approach of providing jack groups is coherent with this abstraction. Secondly, such an additional node would have to be inserted in advance – and might not be needed during runtime –, or it has to be inserted during runtime, which requires to tear down existing connections. Finally, the introduction of an additional node would unnecessarily complicate operations like dynamic migration of nodes. In this case, the node *and* the corresponding copy node would need to be migrated. However, this would require to explicitly establish and maintain this relationship.

Together, the additional overhead of using jack groups for downstream traffic is negligible. Therefore, jack groups are always employed instead of output jacks. However, jack groups are only depicted if more than a single output jack is connected.

Notice that the abstraction of a jack group intuitively only makes sense for downstream traffic. This is due to the fact that downstream interaction is the dominating traffic within flow graphs; upstream interaction is mainly used for forwarding control events. Downstream traffic is characterized by the flow of message from a source of data to a sink of data – or to multiple sinks of data, as in the case of using a jack group. However, for other middleware solutions, the notion of a jack group for upstream traffic might also be feasible.

Together, a jack group offers an abstraction of multi-party communication within distributed flow graphs. Internally, it can rely on different underlying mechanisms. This is especially interesting for multimedia networking. On the one hand, a jack group can employ several unicast connections. This allows to manually control the parameters of each connection but comes at the cost of additional network traffic per receiver. On the other hand, a jack group also allows to "hide" multicast networking within a common abstraction.

## 7.4   Multimedia Data Formats

In general, multimedia formats provide the meta data that precisely describes a data stream. While these dynamic aspects are stored within the working properties, formats are also needed to characterize the capabilities of processing elements, e.g. via the static properties stored within the registry to be described in Chapter 9. Formats are also important for the creation and setup of flow graphs. When connecting an input and an output jack, their supported formats have to "match". Furthermore, advanced middleware services like the format negotiation discussed in Chapter 10 need appropriate interaction mechanisms for formats.

For realizing all these functionalities, a well-defined and unique scheme for defining formats needs to be provided that offers an intuitive way to precisely specify a format. However, with regard to the available components that are of interest to be integrated into NMM, one cannot find a common standard for format definition. More precisely, a large variety of different solutions exists. Some of these approaches lack the flexibility and extensibility needed for an integrating architecture. For example OpenML defines a fixed set of media parameters [How01]. Other approaches, e.g. DirectShow [Pes03], provide a relatively flat hierarchy of formats that was extended many times over the years and therefore does not provide an intuitive way to specify or group formats.

Therefore, we chose to use an own approach, which provides extensibility together with an intuitive scheme for defining formats [LSW01, Wam01, Loh03d]. This decision requires to map existing format definitions to our scheme. However, due to the heterogeneity of available approaches, this work has to be done regardless to the chosen solution.

### 7.4.1   Format Definition

The format definition of NMM is divided into two parts; the *format classification*, which defines a hierarchy of formats, and the *format specification*, which provides precise information for individual formats.

#### Format Classification

The goal of the format classification is to divide all possible multimedia formats into possible main categories. In our approach, formats are classified by *type* and *subtype*. This terminology is similar to other architectures such as DirectShow, which uses major type and minor type [Mica].

However, while the major type and minor type within DirectShow are used to represent different concepts, NMM introduces a stricter definition. The type is closely related to the perception medium; the subtype roughly characterizes the representation medium (see definitions in Section 2.1.1). In particular, the type is one of "audio",

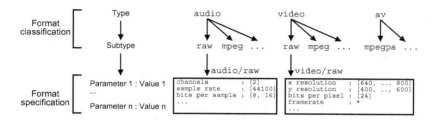

Figure 7.8: Format definition is divided into format classification and format specification. The hierarchy of the format classification is created according to type and subtype of media. The two examples for format specifications show the different values available for parameters, namely sets of values, sets of ranges, or wildcards.

"video", "av" for "audio and video", or "text". Furthermore, the chosen subtype for defining the representation medium is tried to be easy to understand for users. Therefore, the subtype for all uncompressed media is chosen as "raw". The precise structure of representation is then given by the format specification to be discussed below. However, for compressed media, the general type of compression forms a new subtype since this information might be of great importance for users. Again, the precise parameters of the used compression scheme are included in the format specification. Together, we believe that this allows for an intuitive navigation within the hierarchy of formats. Figure 7.8 gives an overview of some the currently used types and subtypes.

**Format Specification**

The format specification precisely defines all properties of a particular format. These properties are specified as *format parameters*, or *parameters* for short. A parameter consists of a key, which is a unique name for a particular parameter within a format, and a value.

The values of parameters are stored as a *set of values*, or as a *set of non-intersecting ranges*. For sets of values, data types representing integers, floating-point numbers, or strings are allowed; for ranges, integer or float-point numbers can be used. If no constraints are given on a certain parameter, a *wildcard*-attribute can be used. Furthermore, a set a values can include other formats. This allows for representing arbitrary complex formats in a hierarchy. Figure 7.8 shows two examples of format specifications.

**7.4.2   Modeling Dependencies**

There are different types of dependencies for multimedia formats to be modeled. First, for a single format, only certain combinations of parameters might be feasible. For example, consider a camera, which supports a higher framerate together with a lower resolution, or a lower framerate with a higher resolution. In order to define which combinations are allowed, two separate formats have to be provided by the plug-in.

Secondly, a processing element can only operate for certain combinations of in-

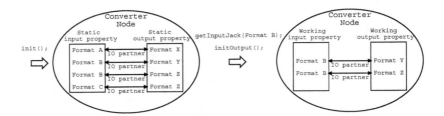

Figure 7.9: The concept of I/O-partners is used to model dependencies between input and output formats. A converter node is shown that allows to process four different combinations of input and output formats that are defined within the static properties during the initialization of the node (method `init()`). The chosen input format (method `getInputJack(Format B)`) and all remaining I/O-partners are updated and stored within the working properties during the execution of `initOutput()`.

put and output formats. For specifying this relationship, the concept of *I/O-partners* (input/output-partners) is provided. Each input format is associated with one or more output formats and vice versa. This association has to be made according to the number of inputs and outputs of the node. For a multiplexer, several input formats (i.e. one format per input) map to a single output format; for a demultiplexer, a single input format maps to several output formats (i.e. one format per output). For filter or converter, each input format is associated with an output format. Formats of sources and sinks do not specify I/O-partners. If more than one combination of input and output formats is allowed, all possible associations have to be modeled explicitly. An example for this case is shown in Figure 7.9. A single converter allows four different combinations of input and output formats. These combinations are stored within the static properties to be constructed during the initialization of the node. However, after this step, the input jack of the node can be requested by specifying a format. During the initialization of the output, the chosen input format and all remaining I/O-partners are reflected within the working properties of the node (see also Section 7.2.2).

While the entries within the static properties generally are allowed to include formats with sets of ranges or wildcards, the formats for connecting jacks need to be *completely specified*. This means that for all parameters only a single value is given; no ranges or wildcards are allowed. This restriction is needed to allow a plug-in node to operate with meaningful parameter values during runtime.

This brings up another dependency that is modeled *implicitly* during the initialization of the working properties. Consider following relationship within the static properties: an input format with a wildcard parameter that maps to an output format with the same wildcard parameter, e.g. a node that is able to handle arbitrary framerates. In this case, the specification of the working output property allows to define different dependencies in correspondence with the chosen input format. For example, if the same parameter value must be used within the output format, the value as chosen when requesting the input jack of the node has to be specified within the format of the working output property. If such a dependency does not exist, a wildcard parameter value can still be used.

For the static properties, such dependencies are not modeled. For the above described example, a wildcard would be used within the output format for both cases. The reason for this is that in general, a node cannot conclude its fully specified output format from a given input format without examining the content of the incoming multimedia data stream (compare Section 7.2.2). Therefore, the dependency between input and output formats is first fully specified during the initialization of the working properties.

### 7.4.3 Quality Model

As a node might support different formats, it is important to provide the possibility to assign a certain *quality* to a format. In this context, the term "quality" defines the quality as perceived by a user of the system. While this kind of quality is very complicated to define, one can observe that the users of a multimedia system in general prefer "higher" values: higher x and y video resolutions, higher values for color depths, higher framerates, higher audio sampling rates, larger numbers of audio outputs, etc. Therefore, NMM provides two approaches that can be used in combination to guide the process of finding the format that provides the "best quality" out of the set of supported formats.

First, for each input or output, a *default format* can be specified as part of the corresponding property. This format reflects the default mode of a node and is very useful when an application (or an user) does not have any knowledge about the supported formats of a particular node.

Secondly, a *weighting model* is provided. Each entry in a set of possible parameter values is assigned a weight reflecting its respective quality, e.g. a framerate of 30 frames per second (fps) receives a higher weight than a framerate of 15 fps. This weight is specified as floating-point number in the range of 0 to 1, where a weight of 1 stands for "best quality". For values which are specified as a range, the weights of the lower and upper bounds have to be given. Wildcards are assigned maximum weight. The total weight of a format is computed as the average of the weights of its parameters. For ranges, the weight of the upper bound is used. An additional factor for each parameter can be used to stress the importance of a particular parameter.

Both approaches require to define the "quality" of supported formats during the development of a plug-in node – or to apply the decisions that were already made for other plug-ins that use similar formats. Correspondingly, the default formats of a node should be chosen according to the weighting value. Notice that the definition of quality is not fixed and might be needed to be updated from time to time, e.g. when new plug-in nodes are introduced into the system. However, the notion of "quality" of formats is not to be meant too strict. It rather should provide the possibility to compare the quality of different formats.

### 7.4.4 Interacting with Formats

The quality model of NMM will be extensively used for the setup of flow graphs. While the process of connecting two single nodes is described in Section 7.5, a more advanced format negotiation algorithm is presented in Chapter 10. In order to realize such services, formats within NMM provide different possibilities for interaction.

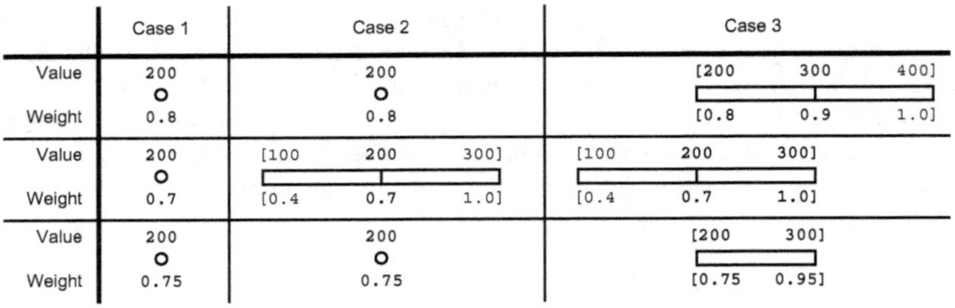

| | Case 1 | Case 2 | Case 3 | | |
|---|---|---|---|---|---|
| Value | 200 | 200 | [200 | 300 | 400] |
| | ○ | ○ | | | |
| Weight | 0.8 | 0.8 | [0.8 | 0.9 | 1.0] |
| Value | 200 | [100    200    300] | [100 | 200 | 300] |
| | ○ | | | | |
| Weight | 0.7 | [0.4    0.7    1.0] | [0.4 | 0.7 | 1.0] |
| Value | 200 | 200 | [200 | 300] | |
| | ○ | ○ | | | |
| Weight | 0.75 | 0.75 | [0.75 | 0.95] | |

Figure 7.10: When creating an intersection format, the weight of a parameter value is computed as average of the weights of the parameter values of the two interacting formats. Case 1 shows the intersection of two single values; case 2 the intersection of a single value and a range; case 3 the intersection of two ranges.

### Intersection Formats

When trying to connect an output jack to an input jack, a test for compatible formats has to be performed. This test tries to create an *intersection format*. An intersection format of two formats exists if their types and subtypes are equal, all parameter keys in one format exist in the other format and vice versa, and all intersections of the values of corresponding parameter keys are a non-empty set. The existence of an intersection format is called a *match*.

A special case occurs, if a plug-in supports all kinds of formats. For example, NMM provides a source node that allows to read files with arbitrary content, the GenericReadNode. In such cases, the plug-in specifies a single format called *wildcard format* with type and subtype set to "*/*" within its static output property. However, when initializing the output of the node, the working output property contains a format with specified type and subtype (if possible). Per definition, the intersection of a given format with a wildcard format results in the given format.

During the creation of an intersection format, its weights are computed according to the weights of the two interacting formats. Three different possibilities have to be taken into account during this step (see Figure 7.10).

- *Case 1.* When intersecting two single values, the intersection contains a single value if the two values are identical. The new weight of this value is computed as average of the weights of the two values involved.

- *Case 2.* When intersecting a single value with a range, the intersection only contains the single value if it is included within the range. The weight of this value is computed as average of the weight of the single value and the weight of the single value within the range. This latter weight is computed as linear combination of the weights of the lower and upper bounds of the range.

- *Case 3.* When intersecting two ranges, the intersection contains the range of their intersecting values. The weights of the new lower and upper bounds are computed according to case 2.

**Format Inclusion**

Instead of testing two formats for a matching, they can also be checked for inclusion. A format is *included* in another format, if their types and subtypes are equal, all parameter keys in the first format exist in the other format, and all intersections of the values of corresponding parameter keys are a non-empty set. This relation between two formats is useful because it allows to only specify some wanted parameters of a format. For example, an application might want to specify the framerate between two connected jacks but leave all other parameters up to the automatic connection mechanism.

### 7.4.5 Discussion

The format definition within NMM provides an extensible scheme that allows to integrate various other approaches. Since the format hierarchy is defined according to the presentation and representation medium, it offers intuitive access for users. However, the required parameters for a particular format still need to be defined and documented to allow different processing elements to cooperate. The weighting model for NMM formats together with the possibility to create intersection formats allows to ease the setup of flow graphs.

## 7.5 Distributed Flow Graphs

Creating a distributed flow graph of NMM nodes consists of two steps. First, nodes need to be requested. Then, nodes can be linked together by connecting input jacks to output jacks, where every two connected jacks need to support the same format. While the registry service, which allows to request and instantiate nodes within the network, is described in detail in Chapter 9, we will provide some details on the connection setup between two nodes in the following. In Chapter 10, this approach will then be extended to a quality-driven format negotiation that automatically creates flow graphs from a high level description.

### 7.5.1 Connection Setup

For connecting two nodes, the `connect` method or the `c_connect` method can be used [Loh04a]. These two methods are identical up to the point where the communication channel connecting the two nodes via their jacks is configured. While the first method chooses the first transport strategy out of the list of available strategies, the second method returns a handle to the corresponding communication channel. This allows an application to explicitly chose the transport strategy during the setup of the connection (compare Section 6.5).

For calling one of the two connect-methods, at least two nodes have to be specified. The output jack tag of the upstream node (the "left" node) and the input jack tag of the downstream node (the "right" node) can be given as further parameters. Finally, a connection format can optionally be provided. However, even if such a format is given, it does not need to be fully specified, i.e. it is sufficient to use a subset of the actual intended connection format (see Section 7.4.4). This allows for an easy specification of only the relevant parameters of the connection format. As all other concepts of the connection setup between two nodes have already been described before, the only important decision for this process is, which connection format to choose – either if no format or only a subset is given. Notice that within the scope of this section, we only consider this problem to be a local decision, which might lead to unresolvable conflicts within other parts of the flow graph.

The process of finding a "suitable" connection format is implemented within the connect-methods and is guided by the quality model as defined in Section 7.4.3. As the upstream node is in state OUTPUT_INITIALIZED and the downstream node is in state INITIALIZED (see Figure 7.5), the formats of the working output property respectively the static input property are considered during this step.

In general, an output format of the upstream node is intersected with an input format of the downstream node. If a match exists, the optionally given connection format further needs to be included within this intersection format. Remember, that the given connection format might not be fully specified. However, a fully specified format is needed for requesting jacks. Therefore, the given format can only be used in combination with the intersection format.

This general test is performed in following order to determine a fully specified connection format.

- The default output format of the upstream node and the default input format of the downstream node are tested for a match. If successful, the generated intersection format is used for requesting the two jacks.

- The default output format of the upstream node is intersected with all available input formats of the downstream node (except the default input format, which was already checked in the preceding step). The resulting list of intersection formats is then sorted according to their weight, i.e. their "quality". The same procedure is performed for the default input jack of the downstream node and all available output formats of the upstream node (except the default output format). However, intersections with the default output format are preferred. This choice is made since multimedia streams generally flow from sources (i.e. outputs) to sinks (i.e. inputs).

- If no solution was found so far, all combinations of all non-default input respectively output formats are tested.

Together, we found this algorithm sufficient to setup a large variety of flow graphs. However, all nodes have to be inserted manually. Furthermore, the algorithm only makes local decisions. This can lead to conflicts in other parts of the flow graph. A more advanced approach is presented in Chapter 10.

### 7.5.2   Composite Nodes

An abstraction for representing a flow graph is a *composite node*. This abstraction is an application of the Composite design pattern [GHJV94]. A composite node provides the same base interface as a node, namely INode. However, it only acts as wrapper for other nodes (or composite nodes) connected to a flow graph and does not provide a multimedia processing routine itself. Composite nodes provide suitable abstractions

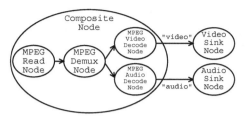

Figure 7.11: A composite node acts as wrapper for nodes (and other composite nodes) connected to a flow graph. Composite node offer the same generic interface as simple nodes. They provide uniform access to different internal flow graphs and allow to "hide" complex flow graphs. In this example, a composite node, which holds a flow graph for reading, demultiplexing, and decoding MPEG files, is connected to sink nodes for rendering audio and video, respectively.

for handling different flow graphs uniformly. Furthermore, complex flow graphs can be "hidden" inside a composite node, which can then be used as single processing element within other flow graphs.

In order to realize such a behavior, a composite node provides access to all aspects of its internal elements. To allow for recursively adding nodes, a composite node offers an additional interface ICompositeNode. By default, all capabilities of internal nodes are also provided externally. In particular, the interfaces specific for a plug-in node are exported by the composite node. When dispatching an out-of-band event, e.g. an event generated by an interface, the plug-in specific functionality is triggered for all internal nodes that support the handling of that particular event. While this interaction mechanism is feasible for events that only carry in parameters, it is not suitable for handling out or inout parameters, return values, or exceptions. Therefore, during the construction of a composite node, internal processing elements can be added with a restricted set of interfaces. This allows to specify a single internal node that should provide a certain functionality.

The input and output jacks of internal nodes are accessible via the composite node. However, only the jacks that are not already connected are provided externally. To avoid name clashes, jacks are renamed according to their node. On the one hand, this allows to hide the internal structure of the composite node. On the other hand, such a composite node can then be connected to other nodes (or composite nodes) via the common interface.

Composite nodes are extensively used to realize the functionality of playing back different file formats. In this scenario, a composite nodes holds the corresponding flow graph for decoding the contents of the specified file to uncompressed audio and/or video streams. This allows for a uniform handling of the specific flow graphs. Figure 7.11 shows as an example a composite node that holds a flow graph for reading, demultiplexing, and decoding MPEG files. This composite node is connected to sink nodes for rendering audio and video, respectively.

Figure 7.12: When locally streaming a buffer to multiple receivers (e.g. from node `Source` via a jack group to nodes `Node1` and `Node2`), only a reference to a single object is forwarded; no copy operation is performed. Read-only access can operate concurrently on such a buffer; write-access requires to call `getWriteableInstance()`, which creates a copy of the buffer if its reference count is greater than one, i.e. if it is referenced by more than a single node.

## 7.6 Memory Management

Handling multimedia requires to process high-bandwidth streams. Since allocating, deallocating, and copying of memory are expensive operations, NMM provides an advanced memory management architecture and an efficient implementation [Deu02]. In general, we use the common approach of providing a set of preallocated buffers that can be requested by plug-in nodes. Reference counting allows to reuse buffers that are no longer in use and controls concurrent access to buffers.

### 7.6.1  Buffers

As described in Section 6.2.1, NMM messages provide an interface for realizing reference counting. In particular, the methods `increaseCount()` and `release()` shown in Figure 6.10 provide the basic operations for this mechanism. Furthermore, NMM provides *buffer managers* that administrate a certain amount of memory and offer the interface for requesting a buffer with a particular size. Such a buffer then initially has a reference count of one. Whenever this counter reaches a value of zero, the buffer is returned to its corresponding buffer manager.

When streaming buffers between connected colocated processing elements of a flow graph, only the corresponding reference are forwarded; no copy operation is performed (see Figure 7.12). However, since a single buffer might be forwarded to multiple receivers (e.g. when using a jack group), special care must be taken. First of all, the reference count needs to be increased according to the number of receivers. Then, additional checks must be provided for accessing the memory area of such a buffer. While concurrent read-only access imposes no limitations, writing access needs to be restricted. In order to efficiently realize this functionality, we chose to use the *same* instance of a buffer *as long as possible*, and only to create of copy of a buffer if *explicitly* requested. This feature is realized via the method `Buffer* Buffer::getWriteableInstance()`. This method requests a new buffer and creates a copy of the current buffer, if the reference count of the buffer is greater than one, i.e. the buffer is concurrently used within at least two different branches of the flow graph. If not, the buffer itself is returned.

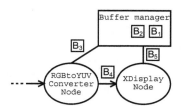

Figure 7.13: Buffer manager administrate a pool of preallocated buffers. Specific implementations of buffer managers offer access to memory areas provided by software libraries or devices drivers. As an example, the buffer manager of `XDisplayNode` administrates shared memory pages of the X window system. The shared usage of buffer managers allows to avoid time-consuming memory operations. In this example, the `RGBtoYUVConverterNode` requests a buffer from the buffer pool of shared memory pages of the sink node. The data conversion is then directly performed within this memory area. The buffer is forwarded to the display, rendered, and returned to the pool of available buffers.

This allows all parts of the flow graph that only require read-only access to the buffer to operate on the same instance; a copy is only generated for nodes that explicitly need to modify the contents of the buffer. Notice that this also includes modifications of the header information, e.g. timestamps. Since converters, such as encoders or decoders, typically do request a new buffer for transforming incoming data to outgoing, copy operations are mainly performed for concurrently operating filter nodes that operate in-place, i.e. using the memory area of the incoming buffer.

### 7.6.2 Buffer Managers

In order to reduce the number of allocation and deallocation operations, a number of preallocated buffers is administrated by a buffer manager. If all buffers were already requested, new buffers are allocated upon request. However, a buffer manager then tries to limit the total amount of allocated memory by deallocating returned buffers when this amount is exceeded. Since packet sizes of multimedia streams can be irregular, the sizes of requested buffers vary. To avoid unnecessary allocations of memory, a buffer out of the pool of available buffers is also returned if its size is larger than the requested size. Therefore, NMM buffers also allow to set and query the used amount of memory of buffer objects (compare Figure 6.10).

In addition, plug-in nodes can provide specific implementations of buffer managers. This allows to provide access to memory areas administrated by software libraries or device drivers used as a basis within plug-in nodes. For example, the X window system offers shared memory pages [BCE+02, Kle03]. Access to such specific buffer managers then further reduces the number of time-consuming operations.

As a further optimization, NMM allows to share buffer managers between different colocated nodes. For example, the buffer manager provided by a node for rendering video via the X window system can be used by its predecessor. Figure 7.13 shows this scenario with a color space converter as predecessor of the sink node. In this case, the sharing of buffer managers allows to directly use the memory provided by the X window system within the converter node. Therefore, no copy operation at all is performed when streaming data between these two nodes.

Buffer managers are also automatically shared between nodes and components that perform the deserialization of buffers, in particular transport strategies configured within a communication channel (compare Section 6.2 and Section 6.5).

### 7.6.3   Events and Composite Events

For composite events, no such services are provided by NMM. These objects are created manually and are copied when being forwarded to multiple receivers. This choice was made due to following observations. First, composite events store very specific data, namely different events; reuse of memory needed for events is not applicable in this case. Secondly, composite events allow to insert, modify, and remove internal events. This functionality will be described in detail in Section 7.7.3. Providing such features in the presence of concurrent access would require to copy composite events upon certain conditions, e.g. the deletion of an event within another branch of the flow graph. Implementing this feature is complicated and would require coarse-grained locking mechanisms.

Together, this effort would not be worthwhile the possible improvements of the performance – this is especially true when considering the comparatively small amounts of memory needed for composite events and events. However, if larger amount of memory are to handled by events, our current implementation would need to be extended.

## 7.7   Generic Processing Model

An NMM node represents the smallest entity of processing. Its innermost loop handles instream interaction. Within this loop, a node produces messages, performs a certain operation on received messages, or consumes messages.

Although many aspects are already provided by the NMM framework as presented so far – for example the handling of out-of-band events is provided by the event dispatcher and interface system of NMM –, several issues still have to be addressed in order to provide a processing model suitable for multimedia. This section will describe the realization of instream interaction for the concrete multimedia architecture developed within the NMM framework. We chose to realize a model that is *generic* in the sense that no assumptions about the internal processing of plug-ins or their external interaction patterns are made. More precisely, this refers to the fact, that on the one hand a single received message might result in arbitrary patterns of sent messages, and on the other hand, for sending a single message, also an arbitrary pattern of received messages might be required. For example, a single received message can result in no, a single, or multiple messages to be sent; or, in order to sent a message no, a single, or multiple message need to be received first. For both cases, this includes all possible combinations of sent and received messages in upstream and downstream direction. In addition, arbitrary patterns have to be supported for sending and receiving messages for nodes with more than a single input or output.

Fulfilling these requirements in a generic way is essential for providing a suitable programming model for developing plug-ins. Since plug-ins are developed independently from each other, situations for complex interaction patterns are present all the time. For example, a plug-in that reads data from a file will typically try to optimize its I/O performance. When being connected to a further plug-in, buffer sizes typically do not match the intended operation and need to be adapted.

Together, a generic processing model is needed to allow for an easy integration of various existing technologies in form of device drivers, multimedia libraries, or full-featured locally operating multimedia architectures. Furthermore, we chose to realize this model by providing a single component that offers all the functionality needed. This allows developers of plug-in nodes to access the same functionality when implementing different types of nodes.

### 7.7.1   Concurrent Processing

An essential property for the elements of flow graphs is the ability to operate concurrently. This is needed in order to be able to handle the varying interaction patterns that might occur in different parts of the graph. In addition, this allows for efficiently handling the various processing elements within a single flow graph that are bound to a certain resource, such as network I/O, secondary storage I/O, or CPU. The concurrent processing of nodes is also required for synchronizing media processing as discussed in Section 7.8. Finally, this also allows to take full advantage of multi-processor systems.

The class `ThreadedNode` extends `Node` to provide a separate thread of execution for the main loop of processing elements (compare Figure 7.2). More precisely, the method `run()` is called, which is to be implemented by subclasses. This method provides the functionality for state `STARTED` (compare Section 7.2.2). While threading is realized using generic classes, our current implementation employs a specialization for the pthreads standard [RL02, NBPF96]. This allows for a simple yet efficient provision of multi-threading by using the facilities of the underlying operating system.

Notice that this is in contrast to approaches (e.g. GStreamer, see Section 2.5.2) that aim at developing custom schedulers for multimedia pipelines that operate in user-space. We deliberately did not choose such an approach because of following reasons. First, developing a custom scheduler that supports synchronized processing for arbitrary multimedia flow graphs is complicated, in particular since each processing elements consumes and generates messages with its own specific rate. A custom scheduler needs to offer better performance than the highly-optimized scheduler of the operating system – even when used on multi-processor systems. It also needs to operate effectively in the presence of distributed flow graphs with messages and control events arriving from the network at any time. Finally, since the main processing time for multimedia flow graphs is spent *within* the actual processing routines, even large flow graphs only require a relatively small number of context switches per second. Correspondingly, only a relatively small performance benefit can be achieved – even when using an "optimal" scheduler.

However, if wanted, custom scheduling systems can also be integrated into NMM, e.g. [KMC+00, Jas97]. The run-method offers the possibility to specify the number of iterations of the main loop. The default value of "0" stands for an unlimited number of

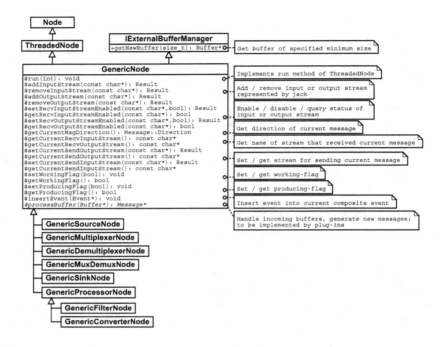

Figure 7.14: The class GenericNode realizes a generic processing model for nodes with an arbitrary number of inputs and outputs. Input and Output jacks can be added and removed dynamically. Single inputs and outputs can be enabled for receiving and sending messages. The working-flag and the producing-flag allow to further control the behavior of the main loop of a plug-in. The processBuffer-method to be implemented by all plug-ins is the central point of this class. The interface IExternalBufferManager provides access to the buffer manager of the node. Subclasses of the generic node set properties specific for the different types of nodes.

iterations, i.e. until the processing of the node is stopped. By calling the run-method with a parameter of "one", a custom scheduler could trigger a node manually, e.g. to process exactly one message. The different conditions upon which a scheduling algorithm can trigger the run-method are discussed in Section 7.7.3.

### 7.7.2 Generic Base Classes

The class GenericNode offers a generic processing model by implementing the run-method of class ThreadedNode (see Figure 7.14). In particular, this class provides all facilities for handling bidirectional instream interaction for an arbitrary number of inputs and outputs.

Subclasses of the generic node provide a specialization for realizing a particular type of node as presented in Section 7.2.1. However, since all functionality is provided by class `GenericNode`, subclasses only set the corresponding number of fixed inputs and outputs. Together, these nodes are called *generic nodes*.

**Specifying the Number of Inputs and Outputs**

For node types with a fixed number of inputs or outputs, the corresponding jacks are already created during the construction of the specific node by calling `addInput-Stream()` and `addOutputStream()`, respectively. For cases, where the number or the jack tags of input or outputs are not fixed, the base class for all generic nodes allows to dynamically add and remove input and output jacks by calling these methods within different states of the life-cycle of a node. Corresponding to the state machine for NMM nodes described in Section 7.2.2, input jacks need to be available in state `INITIALIZED`, e.g. by specifying the corresponding jacks within the method `doInit()`. Since output jacks can only be requested in state `OUTPUT_-INITIALIZED`, they can be added within the method `doInitOutput()`.

As previously discussed, not only the supported output formats but also the number and names of output jacks might depend on set input formats or even on the content of received incoming messages. Therefore, the generic nodes also provide the possibility to access multimedia data during the initialization of output jacks. This step is transparently provided for all plug-ins by the concepts described in detail in Section 7.7.5.

### 7.7.3 Instream Interaction

As can be seen in Figure 7.15, a processing element needs to handle different aspects of instream interaction. In particular, these aspects include:

- Dispatching a single message according to its type.

- Controlling the flow of messages for both upstream and downstream traffic.

- Handling the flow of messages in the presence of multiple inputs and outputs.

- Providing support for arbitrary patterns of instream interaction for both buffers and composite events.

In general, the following approach is used. The central part of the processing model is the method *processBuffer()*, which is to be implemented for each plug-in node. Within this method, messages – in particular composite events or buffers – are generated. Messages are then forwarded upstream or downstream to be processed by other nodes within the flow graph. When processing a composite event, the individual events are dispatched to registered methods of implemented interfaces (compare Section 6.2 and Section 6.4). Events can be modified, replaced, or deleted, and additional events can be inserted. Buffers are handled by the processBuffer-method. Again, the content of buffers can be accessed and modified, buffers can be deleted, and new messages can be generated – either composite events or buffers.

**Controlling Message Flow**

The message flow is automatically controlled by using the facilities provided by the queueing model of jacks presented in Section 7.3.1: Whenever all queues are empty

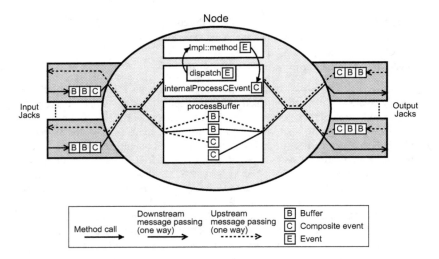

Figure 7.15: The generic processing model of NMM. Messages buffered within input and output jacks are requested and then dispatched according to their specific type. Individual events of composite events are handled by the event dispatcher. Implementations of interface methods are allowed to modify, delete, replace or insert events. Buffers are forwarded to the processBuffer-method. Within this method, buffers can be processed or deleted, and new buffers can be requested. Furthermore, additional composite events can be created. All messages returned by the processBuffer-method are then forwarded upstream or downstream.

and the node has finished its processing, it is suspended until a new message arrives. Whenever the queue within a jack becomes full and is suspended, the connected predecessor is suspended. Other queueing modes allow to discard the oldest respectively newest message enqueued in such situations.

Notice that these mechanisms also work for connections between distributed jacks. However, in such cases, also the used transport mechanism needs to be considered. In particular, the provided reliability either supports the suspending mode of queues or not. For example, while TCP will "propagate" the status of a suspended queue, other protocols, such as UDP, will start dropping messages in such cases. By choosing a particular queueing mode and transport strategy, applications can control the behavior for each instream connection.

The overall control of the message flow and the corresponding processing model works as follows: Upon certain conditions, the main loop of the processing model is triggered. According to the specific condition, an action is performed. In the simplest case, this means that a message is dequeued, handled, and then, a message is forwarded. In the following, we will further define the conditions that need to be fulfilled for the main loop to be triggered, and what differences exists between the different node types.

Let us first consider the downstream traffic of a filter/converter node. Such a node has a single input and a single output. It is only allowed to try to get a message from its input if a message can be passed to its output. A message can only be dequeued from an input if the predecessor of the node already provided one. A node can only pass a message to its output if its successor does allow to. This is the case if the input of the successor is not congested. And this is true, when using a queueing mode that allows to discard messages, or a free slot is available within a queue using the suspending mode.

An important implication of this observation is that *only a single message* is allowed to be generated for each iteration of the main loop. Otherwise, too many messages could be inserted into queues and application specific settings, such as the maximum queue size, would be violated. However, for supporting arbitrary interaction patterns a suitable programming model is needed, which will be further defined in the following.

A further positive property of this implication is that the development of plug-in nodes is guided to provide the lowest latency possible. For example, when receiving a buffer with a relatively large amount of data, which results in a number of outgoing messages, the programming model supports the processing of the buffer using a step-by-step mode: For each iteration of the main loop, an outgoing message is generated.

Correspondingly, the processBuffer-method is only allowed to generate a single message for each time it is called. This message is then returned; no additional method for explicitly sending additional messages is provided. However, if this programming model is inherently not supported by the internal processing part of a node, an additional queueing operation has to be realized within the processBuffer-method.

### Handling Upstream and Downstream Traffic

While the processing model presented so far is restricted to downstream traffic, upstream traffic is handled by applying the above described test also for messages enqueued within output jacks and the predecessors of a node. Since multimedia is mostly streaming from sources to sinks, we assume that messages sent upstream only occur rarely but are of greater importance then. Therefore, upstream traffic is prioritized by first checking for this kind of messages.

As described above, the generic processing model of NMM does not make any assumption about traffic patterns. Therefore, a further extension is required. Since single message received in downstream direction can result in one (or more) upstream messages and vice versa, when dequeuing a message, *all* connected nodes in upstream *and* downstream direction must allow to insert a resulting message.

For specifying the direction of a newly generated message, the method `set-Direction(Direction)` is to be called with either UPSTREAM or DOWNSTREAM as parameter; per default all message are created with the direction set to downstream. Furthermore, if a message is received, processed and forwarded, its direction is not changed, i.e. downstream messages are streamed downstream, upstream messages in upstream direction.

**Handling Multiple Inputs and Outputs**

While the general direction of a message is to be set for each message to upstream or downstream, for handling multiple inputs and outputs, two questions have to be addressed (see Figure 7.15). First, since only one message can be dequeued for each iteration of the main loop, a strategy for determining from which jack a message is pulled has to be defined. We chose to use a hybrid approach, where on the one hand, the generic node provides a general strategy, and on the other hand plug-in nodes can further guide this process. For realizing this concept, the method `setRecvInputStreamEnabled()` and the method `setRecvOutputStream-Enabled()` can be used in order to enable or disable the dequeuing of message from input and output jacks, respectively (compare Figure 7.14). Per default, all jacks are enabled. The overall algorithm for dequeuing the next message is as follows:

- The preconditions as described above have to be fulfilled, namely all connected predecessors and successors within the flow graph have to allow to receive messages.

- As described above, upstream messages are preferred over downstream messages. Therefore, a message is tried to be dequeued from all output jacks that are enabled. If no such message is found, the same test is performed for all enabled input jacks.

- If a message was successfully dequeued, the next iteration will start to query for messages by starting from the next jack in the sequence of available jacks. This corresponds to a round-robin strategy.

- If no message at all could be dequeued, the node is suspended until a new message is enqueued again.

The direction of the currently processed message can be queried via the method `get-CurrentMsgDirection()`; the corresponding jack, from which the message was dequeued, is available via the method `getCurrentRecvInputStream()` respectively `getCurrentRecvOutputStream()`.

Notice that the round-robin strategy avoids the risk of potentially dequeuing only messages from a single jack. For example, if all jacks are enabled and receive messages in regular intervals, this guarantees a continuous flow without the manual specification of enabled and disabled jacks. If, however, a different interaction pattern is required, plug-ins are able to control the dequeuing process. For example, if a multiplexer with two input jacks requires to dequeue two messages from its first input for each message dequeued from its second input, jacks can be enabled and disabled correspondingly.

The second topic to be addressed is to which jacks a message should be sent. Again, we use a hybrid approach. First of all, the direction of received messages is not changed and can only be altered explicitly. As described above, a message generated within the processBuffer-method can be sent upstream or downstream by setting its direction. Then, for each iteration of the main loop, generated messages are per default sent to all corresponding jacks, i.e. downstream messages are sent to all output jacks; upstream messages to all input jacks. A specific plug-in can influence this behavior by calling the method `setCurrentSendOutputStream()`

and `setCurrentSendInputStream()`, respectively (compare Figure 7.14). If a specific stream is set, a message will only be sent to the corresponding jack.

The idea behind this strategy is as follows. Composite events that are handled automatically by the event dispatcher should in general be sent to all jacks in the corresponding direction. For messages generated within the processBuffer-method, the specification of the current sending stream is typically to be implemented together with the specific processing routine for a stream. For example, when demultiplexing an MPEG stream, this choice is done according to well-defined bytes within the stream of data. In order to avoid the risk for developers of plug-in nodes to not reset the current sending stream for each iteration, this is done automatically.

### The processBuffer-Method

The processBuffer-method is the central part of a plug-in node that needs to provide all functionality related to handling multimedia data buffers. Also, composite events are generated within this method. The processBuffer-method takes a single buffer as argument and is allowed to return a message – either a buffer or a composite event. Following is a typical implementation for a filter node.

```
Message* FilterNode::processBuffer(Buffer *in_buffer)
{
  // get writeable instance of current buffer
  in_buffer = in_buffer->getWriteableInstance();

  // get data of buffer
  char* p = in_buffer->getData();

  // modify data ...

  // forward current buffer
  return in_buffer;
}
```

Buffer objects are requested via the method `getNewBuffer()` provided by the interface `IExternalBufferManager` (see Figure 7.14). Since a filter node typically converts data in-place, the method `getWriteableInstance()` is called. This part of the architecture is described in detail in Section 7.6.

For a converter, a typical implementation will be similar to following code.

```
Message* ConverterNode::processBuffer(Buffer *in_buffer)
{
  // get new buffer with defined size
  Buffer* out_buffer = getNewBuffer( out_buffer_size );

  // get data of buffer
  char* p = in_buffer->getData();

  // some code ...

  // release in_buffer since it is no longer needed
  in_buffer->release();
```

```
// forward current buffer
return out_buffer;
}
```

For a sink node that generates an upstream composite event for each received buffer,
following lines of code are needed (for the specification of the interface IExample,
compare Section 6.4.4).

```
Message* SinkNode::processBuffer(Buffer *in_buffer)
{
  // release in_buffer since it is no longer needed
  in_buffer->release();

  // create composite event that includes a single event
  CEvent* cevent = new CEvent( IExample::create_bar(4711) );
  // set direction to UPSTREAM
  cevent->setDirection(Message::UPSTREAM);

  // forward created composite event
  return cevent;
}
```

### Working-Flag and Producing-Flag

If a plug-in node needs to receive more than a single buffer to produce a new message,
the processBuffer-method can simply return a null pointer for each iteration that does
not produce a message. Contrariwise, for generating more than a single message from
a received buffer, a special flag needs to be set, the *working-flag* (see Figure 7.14. As
long as this flag is set, no buffer is tried to be dequeued and processBuffer is called
with a null pointer. This allows to disable dequeuing new messages as long as the
current message is not processed completely.

    This flag could also be used for permanently triggering the processBuffer-method
of source nodes for generating downstream messages. However, if the working-flag
is set, received upstream messages will never be dequeued. Therefore, another flag is
provided, the *producing-flag*. If the value of this flag is true, processBuffer is called
with a null-pointer *unless* there is a message that can be dequeued. This flag should
mainly be set to true in one case. The node is a source and wants to produce messages
all the time while still being able to process new messages received. Per default, only
the GenericSourceNode has set this flag to true. The producing-flag can also be
set to true or false depending on a timer, e.g. to achieve a certain output rate, or to trigger the processBuffer-method of a node on the completion of a certain asynchronous
task.

### Handling of Instream Events

As already described above, when processing a composite event, the individual events
are dispatched to registered methods of implemented interfaces (see Figure 7.15). A
composite event is guaranteed to be handled in one iteration of the main loop of the
generic node. In addition, registered listeners are automatically notified.

During the handling of a composite event, additional events can be inserted into, or deleted from the composite event. Correspondingly, replacing an event is also possible. The parameters of the currently processed event can be modified if specified as inout parameter (see Section 6.4). Furthermore, the handling of an event can also set the working-flag or the producing-flag. Following code fragments show these different cases.

```
Result MyNode::handleEventAndInsertNewEvent()
{
  // create a new event.
  Event* new_event = IExample::create_bar(4711):

  //insert the event at current position in composite event
  insertEvent(new_event);

  return SUCCESS;
}

Result MyNode::handleEventAndDelete()
{
  // return DELETE to delete current instream event
  return DELETE;
}

Result MyNode::handleEventAndReplace()
{
  Event* new_event = IExample::create_bar(4711):
  insertEvent(new_event);
  return DELETE;
}

Result MyNode::handleEventAndManipulateParameters(int &i)
{
  ++i;
  return SUCCESS;
}

Result MyNode::handleEventAndSetWorkingFlag()
{
  setWorkingFlag(true);
  return SUCCESS;
}
```

### 7.7.4 Examples for Instream Interaction

Together with the ability to define instream events within an interface definition given in NMM IDL, the developed programming model for instream interaction has proven its applicability during the development of various plug-in nodes for NMM. Instream events were extensively used to transport various types of information, such as markers for the start and end of a media track, corresponding meta-data (e.g. title, album, artist, year, and genre for music tracks), progress information (e.g. for accessing the progress of media playback within different parts of the flow graph), or information needed for complex tasks like rendering the menus or subtitles of DVDs.

Due to the possibility to register listeners for events received instream, complex interaction patterns can be realized. For example, a component within an application can be registered to be notified for the start and end markers to be handled by sink nodes. This allows for triggering actions such as updating elements of a graphical user interface [Loh04a].

Furthermore, the "flushing" of streams is also realized using instream events. In order to reset all downstream nodes including their internal data structures, a flush-event can be sent downstream. While this operation can be implemented specifically for each plug-in node within the method doFlush(), the generic node handles such a flush-event by discarding all enqueued messages that have the mandatory flag set to false (compare Section 6.2.1). In general, this will drop all buffers. For example, this event can be used to decrease the delay of a seeking operation performed on the source node of a running flow graph: The source than stops to generate data, seeks to the specified position, and then insert a flush-event before continuing to stream data starting from the new position. This will force all "old" buffers that are enqueued to be discarded. However, enqueued composite events will still be handled to guarantee proper operation.

### 7.7.5   Format Analysis and Instream Format Change

As discussed above, output jacks and supported output formats need to be determined for reaching the state OUTPUT_INITIALIZED. Consequently, the method doInit-Output() needs to be implemented. However, some nodes need to access and analyze data received from predecessors within the flow graph in order to specify these properties. From our experience, a possible implementation for this step often requires to provide the same functionality as during normal operation of the node. Furthermore, when the data formats of a fully connected and running flow graph change (e.g. due to a different file that is processed), the same functionality has to be performed again.

Therefore, we chose to transparently provide this feature by allowing to trigger the processBuffer-method during the initialization of the outputs of a node (i.e. during initOutput()) and when handling a format change event sent instream (i.e. during setFormat() defined in interface IFormatChange as implemented by GenericNode). While the method setFormat() is automatically triggered when handling the corresponding instream event, within an implementation of doInit-Output(), the method analyzeData() can be called to use this feature. In general, this step is called *analyze phase*.

Let us consider this phase for the initial setup of the output of a node during the execution of initOutput(). As can be seen in Figure 7.5, the node itself is in state INITIALIZED and all its predecessors are in state ACTIVATED. Therefore, messages are not generated and forwarded automatically but are iteratively requested from upstream nodes. Using these messages, the common code for handling messages is then performed, e.g. by calling the processBuffer-method. This process is performed until the node has successfully specified its output jacks and supported formats by analyzing incoming data (or a maximum number of iterations is exceeded). Since the node is not yet connected in downstream direction, all generated messages for that direction are stored for later processing. In particular, these cached messages are the first messages to be sent to downstream nodes to be connected to the outputs of the current node.

When performing the analyze phase due to a setFormat-event received instream, a similar operation is performed. First, the node "pretends" to change its state from state `STARTED` to state `INITIALIZED` by calling all corresponding do-methods. Then, the method `doInitOutput()` is called. This might result in `analyzeData` being called, which is handled as described above. However, output jacks that were already available are not created again. Instead, the implementation of the method `setFormat()` tests if the newly determined supported output formats and jacks are still compatible with the values given by the current configuration, i.e. the connection formats of output jacks. If this is the case, the node is started again by calling all corresponding do-methods for reaching the state `STARTED`, and the setFormat-event is forwarded to all successor nodes, where the process is continued. Only if the new configuration of the node proves to be incompatible, the process is stopped. In such case, the application needs to reconfigure the flow graph manually, e.g. by connecting different successor nodes.

## 7.8 Distributed Synchronization

As discussed in Section 2.2.5 and Section 4.2.4, synchronization is an important part of handling multimedia. As described in in the previous sections, our middleware allows an application to transparently control remote nodes the same way as local nodes and to integrate them into a common flow graph. Such a distributed flow graph might therefore be used to capture, process, or render media on different systems. For these operations to be performed synchronously, different facilities need to be provided.

For distributed scenarios, it is especially important to minimize network communication needed for synchronization. Therefore, the developed approach strictly distinguishes between intra-stream and inter-stream synchronization. As described in Section 2.2.5, intra-stream synchronization refers to the temporal relations between several presentation units of the same media stream (e.g. subsequent frames of a video stream), whereas inter-stream synchronization maintains the temporal relations of different streams (e.g. for lip-synchronizing of audio and video).

The goal for the generic synchronization architecture is to offer only a few general elements that can be used to realize different synchronization protocols [Did02, DL03, LRS03b, LRS03b, San03]. These architectural elements will be presented first. Then, two different protocols and their implementations are discussed in the following: A protocol for synchronizing the rendering of a number of media streams and a protocol for synchronized media capture. While these approaches fulfill only the basic requirements for distributed synchronization, they have been successfully used within different application scenarios (compare Part IV of this thesis). However, we we especially designed the interfaces and underlying facilities of the synchronization architecture generic enough to support even advanced protocols such as [SSNA95] or [RH97]. To this end, even a protocol that allows to seamlessly hand over parts of a running flow graph can be implemented within the framework (see Chapter 12).

As our solution for distributed synchronization resides within the middleware layer, only the media and stream layer of the four-layer reference model for synchronization are handled (see Section 2.2.5); upper layers such as the object or specification layers need to be provided by additional middleware services or applications built on top of NMM. To this end, the application described in Chapter 14 shows how a subset of SMIL [W3Cc, W3Cb] can be handled using the facilities provided by our solution.

### 7.8.1  Architectural Elements

The generic synchronization architecture of NMM consists of basic data types (for representing points in time, intervals, and timestamps), clocks, stream timers for setting timestamps, generic synchronized nodes that use a controller object for handling timestamps, and synchronizers that implement a specific synchronization protocol.

**Basic Data Types**

For representing a point in time, the type Time is provided. A time consists of seconds and nanoseconds, and therefore provides much higher accuracy than usually provided by clocking elements, such as the clock of the underlying operating system. However, this choice was made to provide compatibility with the OpenML standard [How01]. Time durations are represented with the same precision using the type Interval. The distinction between time and intervals allows to provide more type safe and meaningful interfaces for various computations. For representing frame rates, rational numbers can be specified by using the type Rational.

Each message holds a *timestamp* (struct Timestamp). The two most important entries of a timestamp are a *time* and a *stream counter*. Usually the time value indicates the intended beginning of the processing of a message in respect to some arbitrary time base. When rendering a buffer, this corresponds to the time a buffer should be presented. The stream counter is used to count the messages of a stream and allows for detecting dropped messages.

Furthermore, a timestamp holds an additional flag *is_valid* that indicates if the timestamp has been set correctly. For example, this flag is needed to indicate that a simple plug-in node for reading various media data from a file is not able to set timestamps.

Although all messages – namely composite events and buffers – hold a timestamp, our current implementation does only evaluate this entry for messages of type buffer; composite events are handled as soon as they are dequeued. However, this limitation can be removed if needed by some slight modifications of our architecture. Nevertheless, the following discussion will use the term *buffer* instead of *message*.

**Clocks**

The basis for performing distributed synchronization is a common source for timing information. We are using a static *clock* object (class Clock) within each address space. This clock represents the system clock. We assume that it is globally synchronized by the Network Time Protocol (NTP) [NTP] and therefore represents the same time basis throughout the network. For this reason, we will refer to this clock as *global clock*. Section 7.8.4 will further discuss this topic and provide some results we have obtained when synchronizing the clocks of different systems.

### Stream Timer

As described above, timestamps correspond to a time base. The time base and the values of generated timestamps are specific for the flow graph of nodes instantiated by an application. A timestamp might either be generated by a node taking the current system time (e.g. the time when a video frame was captured), taken from the multimedia data stream (e.g. the timestamps of an MPEG stream), or generated by a node with a constant rate (e.g. for generating audio data with a constant sampling rate). So called *stream timers* help setting timestamps for these different cases (class StreamTimer).

A stream timer either operates in mode REAL_TIME or CONST_RATE. When using the first option, the global clock is queried when setting the timestamp of a given buffer; when using the second option, set timestamps are increased according to a specified interval. This latter mode can be used if the interval between consecutive buffers is known.

### Generic Synchronized Nodes and Controllers

For source or sink nodes that need to access synchronization facilities, generic base classes are provided (class GenericSyncSourceNode or class Generic-SyncSinkNode). The main goal for the design and development of these classes was to transparently provide synchronization facilities for the developers of plug-in nodes. The following sections will show how this was achieved.

These nodes delegate synchronization decisions to a *controller* (namely class Controller and subclasses). The way in which this decision is made for each buffer depends on the specific controller and settings used and will be described below within the context of the presentation of the different implemented synchronization protocols.

The controllers therefore realize different ways of intra-stream synchronization. As intra-stream synchronization has potentially to be performed for every buffer, controller objects resides within the corresponding node (i.e. within the same address space), so no network traffic is involved in this step.

While different classes for controllers exist, the main goal for their design was to provide a complete set of functionality to realize various synchronization protocols.

### Synchronizers

If multiple data streams within different nodes are to be processed synchronously, the corresponding controller objects are connected to a *synchronizer* that realizes inter-stream synchronization by implementing a specific synchronization protocol. A synchronizer also offers an interface that allows an application to modify the operation of the corresponding flow graph, e.g. for pausing data processing.

Notice that the different controller objects might be running on different hosts or in different address spaces as the synchronizer. In order to minimize network traffic, the controller objects take on an important role as they are the only objects that are in the same address space as the corresponding node. Therefore, they should not only realize intra-stream synchronization but also – within certain limits – inter-stream synchronization.

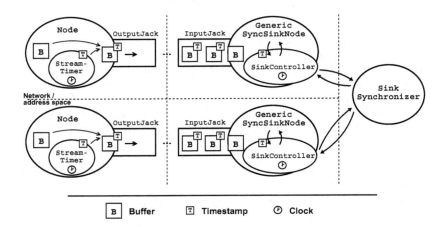

Figure 7.16: Distributed synchronization at sink nodes. Timestamps are set by inter-mediate nodes, such as decoders, with the help of stream timers. Synchronized sink nodes delegate the handling of timestamps to locally running controllers that realize intra-stream synchronization. These controllers are connected to a synchronizer that implements a specific synchronization protocol using the facilities provided by con-trollers. In order to reduce communication needed for performing synchronization in distributed flow graphs, controllers also help realizing inter-stream synchroniza-tion [DL03].

### 7.8.2 Sink Synchronization

The goal for the sink synchronization is to provide synchronized playback – or render-ing – for distributed audio or video sinks. A typical example for such a setup is shown in Figure 7.16, where the two controllers of two sinks are connected to a synchronizer. For simplicity, only two sink nodes are shown; the approach described in the follow-ing will also work for a larger number of sinks. Such a setup can be used to achieve lip-synchronization when rendering an audio and a video stream.

The timestamps of buffers that are processed were generated by intermediate nodes of the flow graph, e.g. with the help of stream timers. A typical setup would include two decoders – one for audio, one for video – that produce buffers with a constant rate. Other setups might only include a single media stream that is rendered synchronously on two distributed systems, e.g. a single audio stream.

#### Adjusting Latencies

As mentioned above, the goal for a concrete synchronization protocol is to minimize communication by employing the facilities provided by controllers to realize certain aspects of inter-stream synchronization. But how can a controller decide when exactly to present a buffer in comparison to another stream of buffers? The main idea is that the different controllers running within different sink nodes should present their buffers as if they had the same *latency* with respect to processing in the flow graph. Figure 7.17

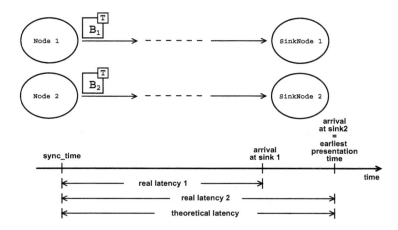

Figure 7.17: After a timestamp is set, a buffer needs a certain time for reaching a sink node. This time – or real latency – can be expressed as difference between the arrival time and the time set within the timestamp. Two buffers with corresponding time-stamps need different times for reaching sink nodes – real latency 1 and real latency 2. The earliest possible presentation time is the maximum of the measured real latencies – the theoretical latency [Did02].

shows that one can imagine the latency as the time it takes for a buffer to stream from the node where its timestamp was set (*sync_time*) to the sink node where the buffer will be presented (*presentation time*). This can be expressed as

$$latency := presentation\ time - sync\_time$$

This can also be expressed the other way round: If a latency is given, the controller tries to present all buffers to the time *sync_time* + *latency*. This given latency is called *the-oretical latency*.

During runtime, a controller computes the latency for each incoming buffer – the *real latency*. If this latency exceeds a certain value depending on the theoretical latency, the buffer is too old:

$$real\_latency > theo\_latency + max\_skew$$

Depending on the set policy, such a buffer might be declared as invalid and can be dropped. According to the tolerable skews between different media discussed in Section 2.2.5, for lip-synchronization of audio and video, offsets of up to 80 msec can be allowed. If the real latency is smaller than the theoretical latency, the presentation of the buffer will be delayed.

Together, the aim of the intra-stream synchronization is to keep the latency constant for the buffers of the stream. A constant latency means that the temporal distance between two buffers is equal to the difference of their corresponding sync_time, and so they are presented with the intended "velocity". In contrast, the goal of the inter-stream synchronization is that the latencies for the different streams are equal. The easiest way to accomplish this is to set the theoretical latencies of all controllers to the maximum of the latencies of all streams: streams with small latencies are delayed until their latencies have reached the value of the "slower" ones. To achieve this, every controllers sends its computed real latency for the first buffer to arrive to the synchronizer. This value is taken as a first estimate of the overall latency. The synchronizer then computes the theoretical latency as the maximum of all latencies and sets this value as the theoretical latency for all connected controllers.

During runtime, all controllers also compute the average value of the latencies of incoming buffers, where the number of buffers to consider may be varied by the synchronizer or the application, a typical value would be for every 25 video buffers or 50 audio buffers – or other values that roughly correspond to an interval of one second can be chosen. Only the computed average latency is sent from the controller to the synchronizer. To further reduce needed communication, values are only sent if they exceed or fall below a certain threshold. Typical values for this threshold are again specific for certain media streams. For synchronizing audio and video, values between 20 msec and 40 msec seem to be reasonable.

The synchronizer then again computes a theoretical latency for all connected controllers and sets this value. Notice that with this architecture, network traffic is reduced to a few messages per second with only a few bytes per message during the initialization of the protocol. If the measured real latencies are constant, no communication is performed after this setup phase.

### Unbuffered and Buffered Controllers

Depending on the used underlying technology for rendering buffers within sink nodes, two different cases need to be distinguished. First, the used technology allows data to be rendered *as fast as possible* and without additional buffering. We found this to be the case for all sink nodes for outputting video, e.g. using the X window system or graphics standards such as OpenGL. In such cases, the real latency can be calculated as

$$real\_latency := current\_time - sync\_time$$

with *current_time* being the time of the global clock.

Second, an inherent (and wanted) buffering takes place prior to data being rendered. This is often the case when handling audio data that is typically buffered inside the corresponding drivers or the hardware devices themselves to compensate for jittering. The additional delay introduced by this process needs to be taken into account since it can be much larger than tolerable skews between different media stream. For example, typical default settings add an delay of 100 msec and more. In such case, the real latency can be calculated as

$$real\_latency := current\_time + output\_delay - sync\_time$$

The additional output delay is specific for a plug-in node and must be determined manually, e.g. by querying the current setting of the underlying used driver. The synchronization architecture of NMM provides classes for controllers for both of these two cases – the `USinkController` or `BSinkController` for unbuffered or buffered media rendering, respectively.

### Master/Slave Approach

The protocol described so far is extended to use a master/slave approach that helps to further reduce communication needed. Since interruptions or dropped buffers of audio streams are much more disturbing than for video streams, the controller of the first audio stream is chosen as master; all other controllers act as slaves that have to adjust their playback speed to the master. To realize this, the synchronizer propagates the latency of the master as theoretical latency to all slaves; only if the controller of a slave detects that its real latency has increased by a multiple of the allowed values (e.g. due to long-term changed networking conditions), it will report this to the synchronizer and the synchronizer will use this value as new desired latency – and therefore also interrupt the master stream once.

Notice that this synchronization protocol also compensates for the drift between the internal clock of a sound board (that controls audio playback) and the system clock (that controls video playback). This drift also needs to be taken into account for locally operating synchronization. We have found this drift to be in the range of one second for 30 minutes of video. While video frames can easily be dropped or delayed, when using more than one audio sink, the controllers of these slave sink nodes have to adjust their playback speed, e.g. by dropping or doubling audio samples. Although these operations are currently not implemented, they can be added easily to our framework.

This protocol is implemented within a synchronizer that can handle several audio and video sinks and allows to dynamically add and remove streams – the `class MultiAudioVideoSinkSynchronizer`. This synchronizer is used for all applications that are described in Part IV of this thesis.

### Preparing and Presenting Buffers

To further ensure timely presentation of multimedia data, the presentation step as implemented in the generic synchronized sink node is divided into several parts. The following shows a simplified version of the processBuffer-method of `GenericSync-SinkNode`.

```
// get the timestamp of the buffer
ts = in_buffer->getTimestamp();
if( !controller->isBufferValid(ts) ) {
  // if the buffer is too old, release it
  in_buffer -> release();
  return 0;
}
else {
  // otherwise, prepare for presentation
  prepareBuffer(in_buffer);
  // wait until the time has come ...
  controller->waitToPresent(ts);
  // ... and finally present it!
  return presentBuffer(in_buffer);
}
```

If the buffers arrives in time, the node first performs any necessary processing on the data within the method `prepareBuffer`. Then the controller will wait until the

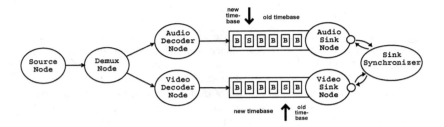

Figure 7.18: The event syncReset (shown as "S" within the figure) is sent instream to mark discontinuities of timestamps of consecutive buffers, e.g. after a seeking operation is performed [Did02]. Nodes handle this event by resetting all parameters related to synchronization. In addition, sink nodes block until all other sinks connected to the same synchronizer have handled the event.

timestamp becomes valid, and finally the data will be presented by calling present-Buffer. This division is extremely useful for nodes that, for example, present video data and perform double buffering. Within prepareBuffer, the incoming buffer will be copied to a frame buffer; in presentBuffer this frame buffer will be swapped with the current frame buffer. This strategy is implemented in all NMM nodes for outputting video, e.g. the XDisplayNode and the GLDisplayNode [Did02]. Sink nodes for rendering audio typically only implement presentBuffer. Correspondingly, plug-in nodes that derive from class GenericSyncSinkNode therefore need to implement at least the method presentBuffer; the method process-Buffer should not be reimplemented.

**Resetting Synchronization**

Since the theoretical latency is only updated from time to time, discontinuities of the values of timestamps impose a problem. Let us consider the case where a seeking operation is performed on a source node reading a media file. Depending on the direction of this operation – e.g. either backward or forward – the values of timestamps of following buffers are either too small – and therefore the buffers are discarded – or too big – and therefore buffers are delayed too long. This is due to the fact that the theoretical latency used is not yet updated.

For handling situations where the timestamps of consecutive buffers have no relationship, the event syncReset of interface ISyncReset can be inserted instream. For our example, this event is to be sent in downstream direction by the node that initially performed the seeking operation prior to sending new buffers. This event is then to be handled by all nodes involved in the synchronization process, i.e. intermediate nodes and sink nodes. In particular, this should result in resetting all synchronization parameters. For synchronized sink nodes, the outcome of this operation forces the sending of newly calculated values of real latencies to the connected synchronizer.

In cases where two or more sink nodes are synchronized, each node needs to receive a syncReset event. However, typically these events will not be received at the

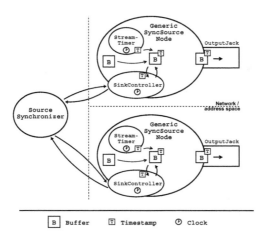

Figure 7.19: Distributed synchronization at source nodes. Timestamps are set at source nodes with the help of stream timers. Handling of buffers and timestamps is delegated to controllers. These controllers are connected to a synchronizer that implements a specific synchronization protocol using the facilities provided by controllers.

same time at all sink nodes. Figure 7.18 shows such a scenario. The event shown as "S" emitted by the source node within a newly created composite event is automatically forwarded to all connected outputs of the demultiplexer node and then enqueued within input jacks of sink nodes (compare Section 7.7.3). Our current implementation for handling the event `syncReset` within these sink nodes blocks further processing until all other nodes connected to the synchronizer have also received and handled the event. This guarantees that no buffers are lost and further data processing of all sink nodes will continue at the same time.

### 7.8.3 Source Synchronization

A concrete synchronization protocol for capturing audio and video using possibly distributed source nodes that employs the elements of the synchronization architecture is presented in the following. Figure 7.19 shows a typical setup for this case. A source synchronizer is connected to two controllers running within two source nodes; one source captures an audio stream, the other the corresponding video stream. The main challenge for this setup is that the corresponding timing elements of the audio and video sink represent different time bases – their internal clocks *drift* compared to the global clock. The drift of a clock $C(t)$ is defined as

$$\frac{C(t + \Delta t) - C(t)}{\Delta t} - 1$$

where $\Delta t$ is a time interval measured by the global clock. Typically, a drift can be observed if different hardware specific clocks are used, e.g. the quartz of a sound or video board. Then, the data generated within one second of time measured on

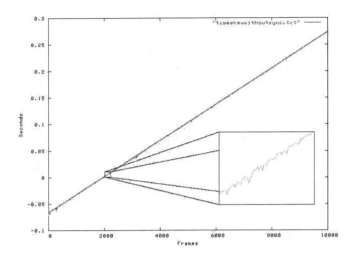

Figure 7.20: The increasing skew between the clock of a video board capturing 25 frames per second (fps) and a sound board capturing audio with 44100 Hz. In this example, more than 25 fps are generated for 44100 audio samples [San03]. Notice that while the long-term drift is relatively constant, the short term drift between the two clocks has different value and sign.

the global clock typically does not correspond to one second of captured media. For example, a sound board might provide more (or less) samples than the intended number samples for one second measured on the global clock; a video board generates more (or less) frames per seconds than specified. Furthermore, the timing elements for different hardware devices provide different drifts when compared to the global time base.

Figure 7.20 shows the increasing skew between corresponding media samples of a sound board capturing audio with 44100 Hz and a board for capturing video with 25 frames per second (fps). Also notice the varying drift between the two internal clocks. While the long term drift is relatively constant, short-term values show varying numbers and sign. In this example, too many video frames are generated and one hour of captured audio results in approximately one hour and three seconds of video. Different possibilities exist to remove this skew. Since modifications of audio streams are easily noticed by humans, the preferred solution is to drop video frames. Another option would be to store the framerate of the video stream as measured with the clock of the sound board. For our example, this would result in a framerate that is slightly higher than 25 fps. However, often a constant framerate is required, e.g. when storing video using container file formats such as AVI.

The goal for the source synchronization protocol is to remove the timing differences that result from the different clocks used by source nodes. This is needed to establish correct timing relations between media. In general, a master/slave approach is used, where the timing information of a single source node (master) is used to correct the timing values of all other source nodes (slaves). Typically an audio source is chosen as master.

The overall approach then works as follows. Each controller calculates the drift $drift_{own}$ of its local clock compared to the global clock. The *local time* corresponds to the number of generated data. For an audio source, the local time is

$$\frac{numberofbytescaptured}{samplerate * numberofchannels * bytespersample}$$

For a video source, the local time is calculated as

$$\frac{numberofbytescaptured}{framespersecond * bytesperframe}$$

Only the drift of the master $drift_{master}$ is forwarded to the synchronizer. This is done whenever the computed value changes, e.g. if no drift was available so far or its value changed more than a certain amount since the last measurement.

The synchronizer propagates $drift_{master}$ to all connected controllers of slaves nodes. Each slave can then uses its own drift and the drift of the master to calculate the drift between slave and master $drift_{overall}$, i.e. the clock of the master is chosen as new global time base. This time base can then be used to adapt the outgoing data rate. For example, video frames can be dropped, if $drift_{overall}$ is positive, or doubled if negative.

Similar to GenericSyncSinkNode, the class GenericSyncSourceNode provides all facilities needed for source synchronization. In particular, the method processBuffer handles the dropping or doubling of buffers for all slave nodes that produce video buffers. To develop a specific plug-in, only the method produceBuffer needs to be implemented.

Figure 7.21 shows the result of the application of the described synchronization protocol. Whenever the skew between video and audio exceeds the presentation time of a single video frame (e.g. 40 msec for 25 fps), a video frame is dropped. For the example shown, this results in a single dropped video frame for approximately every 32 seconds. Contrariwise, in setups where the skew falls below the presentation time of a single video frame, the current frame is doubled.

### Discussion

Notice that the adaptation to the master clock instead of the global clock allows to avoid the need to modify the master audio stream captured. However, if more than a single audio source is used, modification of audio data needs to be used. Then, another solution would be to simply adapt all streams to the global clock.

Also notice that the sink synchronization described in the preceding section could also use the approach used for source synchronization. Then, the drift between the internal clock of the master (i.e. the clock of the audio board) and the global clock needs to be computed and propagated. However, the usage of latencies for sink synchronization is certainly easier and more intuitive. Furthermore, this shows the general applicability of our synchronization architecture that allows different protocols to be implemented. Contrariwise, source synchronization needs to include the the various computed drifts into its operation. This is mainly due to the fact that capturing of video frames is also influenced by an additional hardware clock (i.e. the clock of the video board) and cannot be manually controlled like the rendering of video frames.

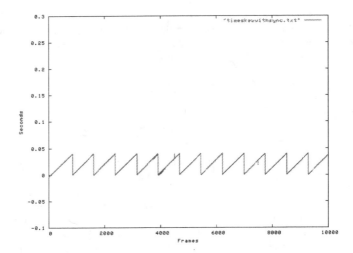

Figure 7.21: The increasing skew between the clock of the video board and the clock of the audio board is decreased by dropping a video frame whenever the skew exceeds the presentation time for a single video frame of 40 msec for 25 fps [San03] (compare Figure 7.20).

### 7.8.4   Remarks on Global Clocks

As discussed above, we use the Network Time Protocol (NTP) to establish a unique time base throughout the network. We found that this protocol allows to synchronize the clocks of various systems, such as commodity PCs and PDAs, within our LAN and WLAN up to some milliseconds accuracy. This is certainly sufficient for realizing lip-synchronization of distributed audio/video rendering.

For strongly-coupled audio tracks of a stereo signal, offsets of only 11 to 20 $\mu$s were identified to be sufficient to recognize spatial distribution [Ste00]. However, for the *same* audio stream being rendered on different distributed systems simultaneously, we found the synchronization achieved with our approach to be sufficient for many application scenarios, e.g. the rendering of audio on different distributed systems. This is in accordance with the results given in [Tru99] and [Lab] that state that for the same audio signal only offsets greater than 30 msec to 50 msec result in a perceivable echo. In Part IV of this thesis, several applications that successfully employ the provided synchronization facilities are demonstrated.

However, the lack of a global clock is known to be one of the typical characteristics of a distributed system [CDK01]. Still, we found that even totally unsynchronized clocks can be synchronized very efficiently using NTP by forcing one system (the slave) to synchronize to another system (the master). In a Linux environment, this can be achieved by stopping the NTP daemon and calling $ntpdate < master >$ one or two times [Loh04c]. After the NTP daemon is restarted again, the clock of the slave instantly synchronizes to the clock of the master.

In addition, NTP also allows to query the offset between distributed systems. This offset can also be taken into account when the resynchronization of clocks is not available. To summarize: Distributed synchronization requires a global clock. NTP provides a well tested and stable solution for establishing such a global time base.

## 7.9 Developing Plug-ins

As a summary of the concepts described in this chapter, we will briefly explain the steps for developing a plug-in for NMM using the generic base classes presented in the previous sections.

Developing plug-in nodes for NMM consists of following steps [Loh03a].

- *Specification.* In this step, the intended functionality needs to be specified without considering a possible realization in terms of base classes or supported interfaces.

- *Defining the granularity and selecting base classes.* A decision has to be made into how many nodes the specified functionality should be split. At the same time, the corresponding base classes have to be chosen out of the set of available generic nodes. In order to be able to extensively reuse specific plug-ins in different application scenarios, nodes should represent very fine-grained processing units. Therefore, it is advisable to develop as many separate plug-in nodes as possible.

- *Providing implementations for state transitions and specifying formats.* In the simplest case, this step only involves to register the generally supported input and output formats within the doInit-method (static property), and the specific combinations of input and output formats for the currently set input formats within the doInitOutput-method (working property). Furthermore, a corresponding computation configuration might need to be specified. Specific plug-ins could also require to implement additional functionality within the remaining do-methods.

- *Defining and implementing interfaces to be supported.* For providing plug-in specific interfaces, definitions in NMM IDL need to be created. In order to provide a generic access to similar plug-ins, the set of already available interfaces should be checked first. The implementations of interfaces are typically very specific for different plug-ins.

- *Providing and implementation for the processBuffer-method.* While the process-Buffer-method provides a generic processing model, again, the implementation is very specific for different plug-ins. Furthermore, the interaction between implemented interface methods and the processBuffer-method has to be realized in this step. For synchronized nodes, the methods described in Section 7.8.2 and Section 7.8.3 need to be implemented.

- *Registering the plug-in using the NMM registry service.* The registry service of NMM administrates all plug-ins available for a particular host and provides access to remote registries. Each plug-in needs to register with this service. This step will be discussed in the scope of Chapter 9.

More then 80 different plug-ins were developed using the generic base classes provided [NMM04b, Loh03b]. These components were mostly developed by students doing an advanced practical or diploma thesis or by students working as student research assistants. Some of the plug-ins were developed by students of the Multimedia course at the Saarland University in the winter term 2001 [Com02] or the summer term 2003 [Com03]. In this case, the students were able to develop even complex plug-ins after a two hour introduction to NMM.

While most of the plug-ins employ existing device drivers, libraries, or other locally operating multimedia architectures to realize their specific core functionality, some plug-ins were also developed newly. Furthermore, prototypical implementations of plug-ins that use the facilities provided by the Java Media Framework (JMF) were also developed [LRS02]. Together, this proves the applicability of the developed framework.

## 7.10   Summary

Based on the facilities described in Chapter 6, a concrete multimedia middleware was presented. This architecture uses the common abstraction of a distributed flow graph for modeling multimedia tasks. In particular, following topics were discussed: nodes as processing elements, jacks as connecting elements, multimedia data formats as meta-data, the setup and representation of flow graphs, efficient memory management for handling high-bandwidth streams, a generic processing model for flow graphs, and a generic architecture for realizing different synchronization protocols for distributed multimedia.

Due to the underlying framework, a network-integrated solution is provided. Furthermore, the generic design of the architecture allows to support arbitrary interaction patterns. Together, from our experience and the feedback given by several external developers, the realized approach has proven its applicability and completeness. However, parts of the architecture could still be improved. Especially the setup of queueing parameters could be guided by higher-level middleware services and should be adapted during run-time. The developed architecture already provides the openness and reflection needed to realize such extensions.

# Chapter 8

# Summary for Network-Integrated Multimedia Middleware

In this chapter, the performance of the current implementation of the developed architecture is evaluated. This concludes the presentation of the base layer of the Network-Integrated Multimedia Middleware (NMM). Correspondingly, a final summary is provided and the achieved results are discussed. Finally, ongoing and future work is briefly described.

## 8.1 Performance Evaluation

In the following, the performance of out-of-band and instream interaction including parallel bindings is evaluated. For all measurements presented in this thesis, a detailed description of the used systems and networks can be found in Appendix A.

### 8.1.1 Out-of-Band Interaction

For evaluating the performance of out-of-band interaction, we first measured the times needed for a `dynamic_cast` followed by a virtual method call performed on a C++ object for different systems. This reflects the typical usage of interfaces within C++ and clearly indicates a lower bound.

In contrast, the time needed for processing the complete stack for a method call on an NMM interface is evaluated. First, this is done for an NMM object instantiated within the local address space, i.e. using a local transport strategy. In order to be able to compare the measured results with other middleware solutions, such as CORBA, we chose different combinations of in and out parameters, either holding the minimum

| System | Time in $\mu$sec per Call |
|:------:|:-------------------------:|
| PC1    | 0.063                     |
| Laptop | 0.195                     |
| PDA    | 1.175                     |

Table 8.1: Times needed for a `dynamic_cast` followed by a virtual method call performed in C++.

| System | Time in $\mu$sec per Call | | | | |
|--------|------------|------|------|------|------|
|        | Invocation | 0 kByte | | 50 kByte | |
|        |            | in | out | in | out |
| PC1    | **5.428**  | **5.828**  | **5.839**  | **5.858**  | **5.862**  |
| Laptop | **16.184** | **18.033** | **18.047** | **18.040** | **18.031** |
| PDA    | **464.405** | **489.423** | **489.497** | **489.456** | **489.439** |

Table 8.2: Times needed for local method calls on NMM interfaces including the complete stack of the NMM communication framework. Since a local optimization is used and the NMM object is instantiated within the address space of the application, this stack only includes a local binding.

| Setup | | | Time in $\mu$sec per Call | | | | |
|-------|-------|---------|------------|------|------|------|------|
| Client System | Server System | Network | Invocation | 0 kByte | | 50 kByte | |
|       |       |         |            | in | out | in | out |
| PC1    | PC1    | -     | **85**   | **99**   | **98**   | **240**    | **312**    |
| PC1    | PC2    | LAN   | **176**  | **193**  | **189**  | **4703**   | **4725**   |
| Laptop | Laptop | -     | **204**  | **243**  | **241**  | **909**    | **1331**   |
| Laptop | PC2    | LAN   | **245**  | **272**  | **266**  | **4806**   | **5000**   |
| Laptop | PC2    | WLAN  | **2301** | **2372** | **2383** | **86322**  | **73948**  |
| PDA    | PDA    | -     | **3775** | **4481** | **4444** | **9056**   | **12174**  |
| PDA    | PC2    | LAN   | **2301** | **2495** | **2485** | **43418**  | **53987**  |
| PDA    | PC2    | WLAN  | **4744** | **4894** | **4757** | **472957** | **450466** |

Table 8.3: Times needed for remote method calls on NMM interfaces including the complete stack of the NMM communication framework. The proxy object is located on the client system, the NMM object on the server system. If no network is specified, communication is performed between different address spaces of the same system.

data size of 0 kBytes or a maximum of 50 kBytes. In addition, method invocations without parameters and return values are measured.

As can be seen in Table 8.2, these times are significantly higher than those needed for a simple C++ virtual method call. However, method calls on NMM interfaces provide a completely different service model. In particular, a unified full-featured messaging system using the concept of the Proxy design pattern is provided that offers reflection, dynamic registration of event dispatching methods, listener notification, state-driven event dispatching, uniform handling of out-of-band and instream interaction, and dynamic reconfiguration of communication channels.

The same measurements as shown in Table 8.2 are performed for a remotely running instance with different configurations of used systems and networks. In particular, we evaluated the performance of different mobile systems, e.g. a laptop or PDA, in combination with a stationary system. Table 8.3 summarizes the results. In all cases, TCP strategies together with magic number value streams are configured for realizing the network binding, either using LAN or WLAN. If no network is specified, communication is performed between different address spaces of the same system to evaluate the performance of NMM without the presence of a physical network.

| Setup | | | | Time in $\mu$sec per Call | | | |
|---|---|---|---|---|---|---|---|
| Client System | Server System | Network | NetStream | 0 kByte | | 50 kByte | |
| | | | | in | out | in | out |
| PC1 | PC2 | LAN | Buffered | 193 | 189 | 4703 | 4725 |
| PC1 | PC2 | LAN | Unbuffered | 931 | 823 | 5308 | 5312 |

Table 8.4: Times needed for remote method calls on NMM interfaces from the client to the server system for buffered and unbuffered networking streams (compare Table 8.3).

The results clearly show the benefits of the local optimizations provided by NMM: If an NMM object, for example an NMM node, is instantiated within the local address space, the binding process automatically establishes a local binding. Some CORBA implementations allow to remove the overhead of serialization and transmission of requests and replies via a "loopback" communication device. While such collocation optimizations provide similar improvements in performance [SWV99], the registry service of NMM presented in Chapter 9 also allows for automatically instantiating NMM nodes that are requested to run on the local host within the address space of the process that initiated the request.

Compared to measurements made for different CORBA implementations according to Open CORBA Benchmarking (OCB) [Dis], the current implementation of NMM already provides competitive results. For example, the average response time for an invocation of all measurements available using similar setups as PC1 or laptop is 207 $\mu$sec – for CORBA client side and server side running on the same system but in different address spaces. For example, for TAO 1.4 running on a 4x2175 MHz 80x86 Linux system, 121 $\mu$sec are reported for the invocation benchmark and 418 $\mu$sec for 50 kBytes of in parameters – compared to 85 and 240 $\mu$sec measured for NMM running on PC1, a single 3000 MHz system.

Notice that the measurements provided by OCB were mostly made using highly optimized commercial CORBA implementations. In contrast to CORBA, NMM provides an open serialization framework that allows for integrating arbitrary data types, state-driven event dispatching, uniform handling of different interaction paradigms and reconfigurable communication channels.

In [KAVP03], the performance of CORBA implementations running on PDAs and commodity PCs connected via WLAN is evaluated. In particular, the same PDA as used for our measurements is being employed. Again, NMM shows competitive results. For example, the response times for an invocation between the PDA an a PC using WLAN are reported to be 8914 $\mu$sec respectively 5698 $\mu$sec for two different CORBA implementations (Table 11 in [KAVP03]). Using a more powerful system on the server side, NMM only requires 4744 $\mu$sec. Since these runtimes are bounded by the computational resources available for the PDA, the measured values can directly be compared. While NMM is faster when transmitting small in or our parameters, further optimizations need to be done for handling large parameters – especially when using WLAN as can be seen from the runtimes for the PDA and the laptop. However, even the current non-optimized implementation of NMM provides competitive performance.

Finally, for remotely running instances, the influence of the used networking stream

| System | Throughput in NMM buffers/sec |
|--------|-------------------------------|
| PC1    | **71078**                     |
| Laptop | **30823**                     |
| PDA    | **2846**                      |

Table 8.5: Throughput of a locally running flow graph with a source node being connected to a sink node.

| Setup | | | Bandwidth in MBytes/sec |
|----------|----------|---------|-------------------------|
| System 1 | System 2 | Network | |
| PC1      | PC2      | LAN     | **11.20** |
| Laptop   | PC2      | LAN     | **11.20** |
| Laptop   | PC2      | WLAN    | **0.75**  |
| PDA      | PC2      | LAN     | **1.04**  |
| PDA      | PC2      | WLAN    | **0.59**  |

Table 8.6: Maximum bandwidth in MBytes/sec as measured using the tool `iperf` [NLA] with data packets of 2048 bytes.

is measured, in particular the difference between a buffered stream using an internal buffer of 2048 bytes at the sending side and an unbuffered stream (compare Section 6.1.4). As can be seen in Table 8.4, for method calls where corresponding events only carry little data, the buffered networking stream provides a much better performance since it reduces the number of low-level function calls. Furthermore, this demonstrates one of main advantages of an open binding approach, namely the possibility to manually or automatically configure bindings for better performance. For example, the size of the internal buffer can be optimized. In addition, the overall performance of the system can be improved by realizing new implementations for different parts of the communication framework of NMM, such as networking streams. This also allows to tailor the overall system to a specific configuration.

### 8.1.2   Instream Interaction

The other important aspect of NMM is its performance of instream interaction. Table 8.5 shows the throughput in NMM buffers per second that can be achieved for a locally running flow graph with two nodes being connected, a source node and a sink node. In order to measure the true performance, the source node only request NMM buffers of size 2048 bytes using its buffer manager; the sink node releases received buffers.

For all following benchmarks, this simple flow graph is distributed to run on two different systems. The instream communication channel is set up automatically to use the default configuration, namely a single pair of TCP strategies using magic number value streams and networking streams. For evaluating the performance of such a distributed flow graph, we first measured the maximum bandwidth that can be achieved using the different configurations of interest. Table 8.6 summarizes the obtained values.

Figure 8.1 shows the influence of the used networking stream. More precisely,

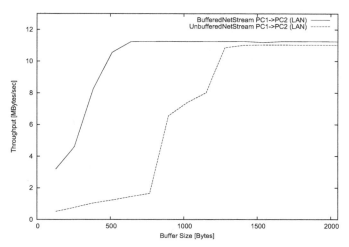

Figure 8.1: Throughput of instream bindings for different sizes of NMM buffers using a buffered or unbuffered networking stream.

the difference between a buffered and an unbuffered networking stream is shown for various sizes of NMM buffers. For the buffered stream, the size of its internal buffer is chosen to hold the complete header of an NMM buffer when being serialized with the magic number value stream. This allows for transmitting a single NMM buffer using only a few low-level system calls. Especially for streams of NMM buffers containing only small amount of data, this greatly helps to improve the performance. For larger amounts of data, the two streams show similar throughput.

Figure 8.2 and Figure 8.3 show the performance achieved for different configurations using the buffered networking stream. Figure 8.2 demonstrates the influence of available computational resources. When using the laptop connected via LAN, the maximum possible throughput is only achieved for NMM buffers of 2048 bytes data size. However, even for relatively small NMM buffers, sufficient throughput is provided for typical data rates of multimedia streams. For WLAN, the laptop already provides maximum performance for the smallest NMM buffers used.

Using the PDA in combination with a stationary PC connected via LAN, the maximum available bandwidth is achieved for NMM buffers of 10 kBytes; using WLAN, NMM buffers of 5 kBytes are sufficient to saturate the network connection (see Figure 8.3).

Together, the performance achieved for locally running or distributed flow graphs is absolutely sufficient, even for high data rates. This is even more true when comparing the performance of NMM to other approaches that extend the facilities provided by object-based middleware solutions with services need for multimedia communication, e.g. by using the CORBA event service [CLD01]. Still, extensions that provide better performance, such as the CORBA A/V Streaming Service [MSS99], can be integrated by providing additional transport strategies (compare Section 4.2.3).

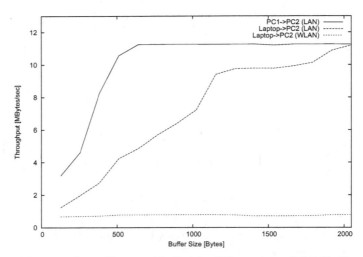

Figure 8.2: Throughput of instream bindings for different sizes of NMM buffers using PCs and a laptop connected via LAN or WLAN.

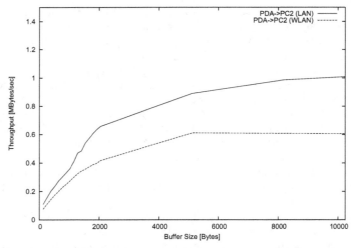

Figure 8.3: Throughput of instream bindings for different sizes of NMM buffers using a PDAs and a PC connected via LAN or WLAN.

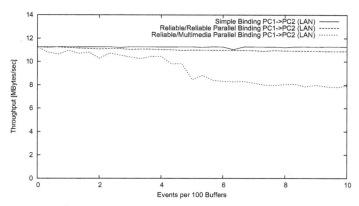

Figure 8.4: Throughput of parallel bindings using different synchronization strategies compared with a simple TCP binding.

To summarize: With NMM, for all configurations, all available networking bandwidth can be consumed when using typical sizes of NMM buffers. In addition, more multimedia data can be transmitted than the used systems can probably process due to limited computational power.

### 8.1.3 Parallel Binding

For evaluating the performance of a parallel binding, three different configurations for realizing instream interaction in downstream direction were measured.

- Benchmark *Simple Binding* uses a single TCP transport strategy to transmit both NMM buffers and composite events.

- Benchmark *Reliable/Reliable Parallel Binding* uses two different TCP transport strategies for sending NMM buffers respectively composite events together with the synchronization algorithm for handling two reliable sub-bindings as presented in Section 6.5.5.

- Benchmark *Reliable/Multimedia Parallel Binding* also uses two TCP transport strategies but the synchronization algorithm for handling one reliable and one multimedia sub-binding is employed. NMM composite events are sent through the "reliable" sub-binding and NMM buffers are sent through the "multimedia" sub-binding. Since both TCP strategies provide reliable data transmission, all messages are guaranteed to be received. In particular, simulating a multimedia sub-binding using TCP allows for comparing the overhead of the used synchronization strategy in a deterministic way.

The message stream to be sent consists of NMM buffers of a constant size of 2048 bytes and composite events. To determine the influence of the parallel binding, a varying number of composite events per 100 NMM buffers is used and the average throughput is measured. The results are presented in Figure 8.4. As can be seen, the synchronization algorithm for the case *Reliable/Reliable Parallel Binding* only adds a small overhead. For the setup *Reliable/Multimedia Parallel Binding*, the throughput also achieves comparable values until more than four events per 100 NMM buffers are sent. Even for 10 events per 100 NMM buffers, the throughput is still sufficient for typical bandwidths of multimedia data streams (compare Section 2.2.2).

## 8.2   Conclusions and Future Work

The presented performance evaluation of the current implementation of the Network-Integrated Multimedia Middleware (NMM) demonstrated the feasibility of the architectural decisions described in the previous chapters. In particular, despite the openness and extensibility, the simple yet unified design of the chosen approach offers competitive performance – even when being compared to highly optimized commercial middleware solutions. While such solutions mainly focus on request/reply interaction, NMM also offers efficient instream interaction, also when using parallel bindings. Together, the developed architecture provides a complete base layer for multimedia middleware. All requirements imposed by the architectural decisions presented in Chapter 5 have been fulfilled.

The following chapters will demonstrate advanced middleware services built on top of this layer. Then, demanding application scenarios that were realized using NMM are described. This will further prove the applicability of the chosen approach.

While possible directions for future work have already been discussed throughout the presentation, these developments can either be seen as logical extensions of the current architecture or to be completely orthogonal to the topics covered in the scope of this thesis. On the one hand, further extensions aim at integrating additional serialization and transport strategies, e.g. for adding support for additional standards or for realizing techniques like forward error correction (FEC), interleaving or traffic shaping (compare Section 2.3.1). While instantiated transport strategies are currently exclusively used for a single binding, the shared usage of communication facilities can also be integrated into the framework. With a growing number of transport strategies additional mechanisms for automatically configuring communication channels might be needed.

On the other hand, the NMM architecture provides the openness and reflective capabilities that allow to develop sophisticated quality of service (QoS) adaptation and reconfiguration techniques. For example, the synchronization framework can provide feedback needed for adapting internal queue sizes and buffers of running processing elements and their connecting communication channels. An integrated QoS management scheme for scheduling processing elements and networking components can further improve the real-time capabilities of the architecture – even when being used in an environment that only provides best-effort services. All these enhancements can either be realized as part of the middleware itself or as additional service.

# Part III

# Middleware Services

# Chapter 9

# Registry Service

As discussed in Section 4.2.5, the task of the registry service as part of a multimedia middleware solution is to administrate the facilities provided by plug-ins. In particular, such a service allows for the discovery, registration, search, instantiation, and reservation of processing elements on local and remote systems. Therefore, a registry offers fundamental services for realizing distributed multimedia applications.

In this chapter, the registry service of NMM is presented [LRS02, Rep03a, LRS03b, Rep04]. First, the basic requirements for this service are motivated – especially in regard to the inherent heterogeneity of the underlying infrastructure – and an overview of the developed architecture is given. Then, related work is reviewed. This is followed by a detailed presentation of the most important aspects of the developed architecture, namely the facilities for representing plug-ins and flow graphs, the discovery and registration of plug-ins, the base classes and their functionality. The mechanisms for querying the registry, and the components involved in processing a query. Several concrete examples are given to demonstrate the programming model offered by the registry service. In this context, the performance of the service will also be evaluated. Then, an approach for managing quality of service parameters within the registry service of NMM is briefly introduced. Finally, conclusions are drawn and possible directions for future work are discussed.

## 9.1 Introduction

A registry service for network-integrated multimedia has to fulfill several requirements. A basic facility of any registry is to register and discover locally available hardware devices and software components, e.g. by dynamically loading libraries of available plug-ins. Particularly for hardware devices that are only present a certain number of times, the precise number of devices needs to be determined. Therefore, developers of plug-ins need an easy way for specifying this value and the corresponding configurations for each device. This is in contrast to software components that typically allow for an unlimited number of instances to run on a single system; only the quality of service (QoS) requirements restrict the number of simultaneously operating plug-ins.

Due to the heterogeneity of available device technologies, a registry service needs to support the integration of various approaches. Especially, the different capabilities

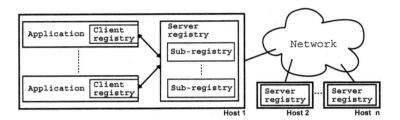

Figure 9.1: The registry service of NMM uses a combination of a client/server architecture and a peer-to-peer architecture. All locally available plug-ins of a single
system are administrated by a registry that acts as server for a number of clients, e.g.
the applications running on the same host. Applications use a client registry to communicate with the server registry. In order to integrate various existing technologies,
different specialized sub-registries exist within the server registry. Requests for distributed plug-ins are dynamically forwarded to remote systems, where they are processed
by the corresponding registry server.

of present technologies need to be taken into account. For example, some technologies
provide features like hot-plugging or allow a single device to be connected to more
than one host at a time (compare Section 2.2.2). In order to handle these requirements,
we use a hierarchical approach, where the main registry service includes a number of
specialized sub-registries that handle capabilities specific for a certain technology.

All attributes of a discovered plug-in need to be stored within the registry service.
For querying plug-ins from this service, suitable facilities have to be provided. Especially all attributes of a certain plug-in node – or subsets thereof – need to be available
for queries. While the manual request for a single instance of a certain plug-in needs
to be supported, higher-level services for setting up complex flow graphs also need to
be provided.

Since several applications run concurrently on a single system, a registry needs to
globally administrate all locally available plug-ins. To this end, the registry service can
be seen as server and the applications as clients that compete for available resources.
Therefore, access control mechanisms and failure handling need to be provided (e.g.
for situations in which an application crashes and does not release reserved components).

Since multimedia middleware allows for the setup of distributed flow graphs, a registry service needs to support the querying and instantiation of plug-ins throughout the
network. Due to the mobility of devices and users in typical application scenarios, the
overall system consists of loosely coupled and changing organizations of participating
hosts. Therefore, a peer-to-peer approach is preferable over a centralized approach
(compare Section 5.1). In particular, while globally administrating all plug-ins for a
single host is certainly required, providing a central administration for all resources
within the network would certainly limit the scalability of the approach. Furthermore,
due the dynamics of the overall system, a constant update of the global state would be
required.

Together, this results in a hybrid approach [LRS02, Rep03a, LRS03b, Rep04]. Figure 9.1 shows the participating entities. A centralized client/server architecture is used to administrate all plug-ins available for a single system. An application uses a *client registry* that resides within its address space to access the *server registry* running on the same system. A server registry allows for integrating different specialized *sub-registries*. For managing distributed resources, a peer-to-peer approach is applied that forwards queries to other systems within the network. To allow each application to use its own list of distributed registries, this step is performed by the client registry. Since locally running and remote server registries run in different address spaces as applications, the distributed object system and the underlying communication facilities as described in Chapter 6 are employed.

One goal for the development of NMM was to be able to provide a purely locally operating multimedia architecture (e.g. for the GNU/Linux operating system) that does not incur the constant overhead of a complete middleware stack, e.g. for inter-process communication between applications and instantiated plug-ins. Since there is only a single registry service running on each system, the developed architecture should allow to reserve plug-ins with this central component, but to perform the instantiation within the address space of the application itself.

## 9.2  Related Work

As already discussed in Section 2.2.2, Section 4.2.5, and Section 4.3.2, various standards for device technology (e.g. IEEE 1394 [139] or USB [AD01]) and device administration and discovery (e.g. UPnP [Uni], HAVi [Hom], or Jini [Jin]) exist that are currently present within typical environments.

While different competing standards share a number of attributes, also distinguishing features – e.g. in the way in which interaction with the provided service model is performed – have to be taken into account. Therefore, ongoing work in the research community aims at integrating these different architectures into a common meta-architecture [FDC01, NT02]. In general, these approaches provide components specific to a particular technology combined with components that perform the mapping between these technologies and the universal interfaces offered. However, this is particular demanding when considering the possible incompatible semantics of interaction within the different approaches. To this end, the integration of a new technology always requires for the manual creation of mappings.

As described in the previous section, we chose a similar approach that integrates available technologies using specialized sub-registries. Furthermore, NMM follows the approach of providing functionality specific for a particular technologies by corresponding plug-ins that are uniformly accessible via generic interfaces (compare Chapter 7). Also, our extension of such an integrating architecture towards a peer-to-peer approach provides further advantages – especially for loosely coupled systems and dynamic environments. Finally, the possibility for automatically instantiating locally operating plug-ins within the same address space of the application – and not within the address space of the registry – offers a performance optimization not addressed by other integrating approaches.

We are not handling initial discovery of systems. In particular, available server registries on remote hosts currently need to be added manually. While protocols liks SLP [GPVD99] can be used for this step, we argue that for typical application scenario the current context, e.g. the location of users and devices, needs to be taken into account during this step – a property that available standards do not provide and that is therefore being researched [FDC01]. Also, for searching within such a peer-to-peer network, simple and fixed strategies are used within the registry service of NMM. However, our architecture can be used to as a test bed for more sophisticated approaches, e.g. [SSJH03] or [HCZ+02]. Section 9.6 will discuss possible directions for future work.

## 9.3  Architectural Elements and Functionality

In this section, the architecture of the registry service will be presented in more detail. Examples for the programming model provided by this service will be given in Section 9.4.

### 9.3.1  Representing Plug-ins and Flow Graphs

The concepts used for describing entities administrated within the registry service are also used for querying entities from this service. For specifying a single plug-in, a *node description* is used; a complete distributed flow graph is stored within a *graph description*.

#### Object Descriptions and Node Descriptions

A *node description* precisely defines all attributes of a certain plug-in node. While the registry service of NMM is currently focussed on administrating plug-in nodes, a future extension might allow for arbitrary objects to be handled. Therefore, an *object description* (class `ObjectDescription`) provides all attributes that are available for arbitrary entities in general. These attributes include:

- *Object name.* This name can be used to specify the type of an entity.

- *Functional specification.* The list of supported interfaces specifies the available functionality. This information is automatically available due to the inheritance from implementation classes (compare Section 6.4).

- *Location.* Holds the location of an entity, e.g. the host – and additionally the port of the corresponding server registry – an entity should be requested from (or an entity is running on). The location of a node can also be set to "disabled" for further evaluation (see below).

- *Additional specification.* To allow for further extensions, the base class already provides the possibility to add additional specifications in the form of a key and a value; both stored as strings.

A node description (class `NodeDescription`) extends this concept by including all further attributes specific for a plug-in:

- *Node name.* This entry holds the type of a node, mostly its class name. However, object name and node name can be different.

- *Node type.* The value of this attribute corresponds to the specific type of the node, such as source, filter, converter, demultiplexer, multiplexer, multiplexer/demultiplexer, or sink (compare Section 7.2.1).

- *Format specification.* This includes all aspects of the supported data formats, such as supported input or output formats, combinations of input and output formats (I/O partners), or complete input and output properties (compare Section 7.4).

- *Sharing attribute.* This attribute allows for specifying whether a node offers shared access to its functionality. This option will be discussed in detail in Chapter 11.

Additionally, a node description stores lists of events – the *configuration events* – that are used to configure a particular instance of a plug-in. More precisely, a list is available for each possible state of a node (see Section 7.2.2). These lists allow to store specific configurations for later retrieval.

### Subset Relation

Particularly interesting for a registry service is the option of testing one object description for being a *subset* of another object description. More precisely, an object description $o^q$ is subset of an object description $o^r$ if following criteria are satisfied.

- If the object name of $o^q$ is specified, it has to be identical with the object name of $o^r$.

- All interfaces provided by $o^q$ have to be available for $o^r$.

- If the evaluation of the location is not disabled, the location of $o^q$ has to be the same as the location of $o^r$.

We denote this relation with $o^q \subseteq o^r$. Possible additional specifications of object descriptions are currently not evaluated.

This subset relation is extended for node descriptions. Since complete node descriptions are stored within the registry, this allows for querying all nodes that fulfill a certain subset of required capabilities. A node description $n^q$ is subset of a node description $n^r$ – denoted as $n^q \subseteq n^r$ –, if following criteria are satisfied.

- The corresponding object descriptions have to be subsets, $o^q \subseteq o^r$.

- If the node name of $n^q$ is specified, it has to be identical with the node name of $n^r$.

- If the node type of $n^q$ is specified, it has to be the same as the node type of $n^r$.

- A format $f^q$ provides a subset of another format $f^r$ if it is *included* in the other format (compare Section 7.4.4). We denote this relation with $f^q \subseteq f^r$. This definition can be extended for properties: If all formats of a property $p^q$ are included in the set of formats of $p^r$, $p^q$ is a subset of $p^r$, denoted as $p^q \subseteq p^r$.

The sharing attribute of a node description is not evaluated in this step. Its usage is described in detail in the scope of Chapter 11. Furthermore, the configuration events are also not considered.

**Graph Descriptions**

A *graph description* (`class GraphDescription`) stores the complete configuration of a distributed flow graph. The properties of a graph description include:

- *Specification of nodes and their connections.* This specification consists of the nodes given as node descriptions, their connected input and output jacks, and the used connection formats of a distributed flow graph.

- *Communication channel specification.* These settings include configurations of used communication channels, such as the used transport strategies or specific parameters thereof.

- *Synchronization.* Finally, synchronizers are specified within a graph description as object descriptions. This allows to choose between different synchronization protocols (compare Section 7.8).

Again, such a configuration can be used for requesting a flow graph from the registry service – and then only a subset of available attributes needs to be specified. For example, the connection formats can be left out and will then be negotiated during the connection setup (compare 7.5.1). In such cases, the graph description will then be updated to reflect the current setup. Furthermore, requests specified as graph descriptions are also stored within the registry service as so called *sessions* – a running flow graph administrated by the registry. Chapter 11 will present a service that allows to jointly use parts of an active flow graph within different applications in order to realize collaborative scenarios.

Besides being used for requesting the processing elements of a distributed flow graph, a graph description also allows to *realize* such a flow graph. This includes the complete setup and configuration of connecting edges and synchronizers. To this end, graph descriptions provide a convenient method for application developers to create complex distributed flow graphs. Since a graph description and all its internal attributes can be serialized, these representations can further be stored or transmitted to other hosts within the network.

A subset relation for graph descriptions, which is similar to the relation given for object descriptions and node descriptions, is not defined. However, a more advanced approach to compare two flow graphs is discussed in the scope of Chapter 11.

### 9.3.2 Discovery and Registration of Plug-ins

For discovering locally available plug-ins, we follow the common approach of dynamically loading *plug-in libraries* that hold one or more NMM nodes. In general, upon loading such a library, nodes are created and brought to state `INITIALIZED`. In this state, all generally available combinations of input and output formats are available – the static properties (compare Section 7.2.2). Since all other attributes of a plug-in are also available at that point, e.g. the implemented interfaces, a node description can be generated. This node description is then stored together with a generated identifier and a reference to the corresponding plug-in library. When querying the server registry using a node description (or subset thereof), libraries of plug-ins that "match" the request are loaded again (see below).

However, as discussed above, for plug-ins that need additional configurations before being initialized, or for plug-ins that represent hardware devices that are only available a certain number of times, additional settings need to be done prior to reaching the state INITIALIZED. For example, a single system might contain more than one internal device for outputting audio, e.g. two or more PCI boards. While all these devices can be handled by a single NMM plug-in, the precise number of devices and the capabilities of each device need to be determined for storing within the registry. Furthermore, the concrete steps for achieving this configuration need to be saved in order to be able to instantiate a particular instance of a plug-in again. As described in Section 9.3.1, a list of configuration events can be stored within a node description for this reason.

For our example, the developer of the audio plug-in needs to provide the implementation for determining this information. A concrete realization of this step for the GNU/Linux operating system sets the audio device to "/dev/dsp" calling the method setDevice of the corresponding interface IAudioDevice implemented by the plug-in. Then, the node is initialized by calling init of interface INode. If this succeeds, the corresponding node description can be stored, and the next audio device "/dev/dsp1" is tested. This process is continued until the setting of an audio device failed.

Internally, NMM events are used to handle method calls. These events can be logged and stored, e.g. by registering a listener for all events to occur. Therefore, generated node descriptions allow to include corresponding events for called methods and their corresponding parameters (for example, the event IAudioDevice::setDevice("/dev/dsp"). Again, the unified messaging system of NMM as presented in Section 6.2 greatly helps to realize the registration of plug-ins and reduces the amount of source code to be written by developers. For common cases, such as testing a number of devices, we also provide generic utility classes.

**Static versus Dynamic Registration**

The discovery and registration of plug-ins is a process that is performed *statically* during the initial setup of the registry service. During the initial setup, the server registry performs the above described procedure for all available plug-ins[1].

However, as described in Section 2.2.2, several standards for device technology allow to add (and remove) devices during runtime, e.g. hot-plugging for IEEE 1394 [139]. Therefore, the registration process also needs to be triggered *dynamically*. For supporting such features within the NMM registry service, plug-in libraries need to be loaded again to determine newly connected devices and their attributes. We propose to add additional processes (or daemons) that watch for dynamically added devices and then

---

[1]This procedure is performed automatically whenever a newly installed NMM system is started for the first time. Additionally, this process can be triggered manually by calling './serverregistry -s' (compare Section 9.4).

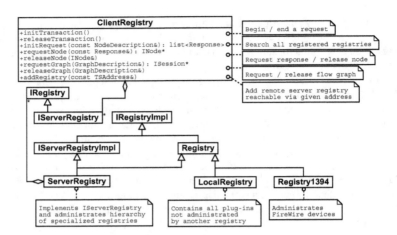

Figure 9.2: A client registry provides a basic interface for searching nodes and requesting possible results. In addition, complete flow graphs can be requested. Per default, the locally running server registry is accessible; further remote registry servers can be added on demand (interface `IServerRegistry`). A server registry administrates a hierarchy of specialized registries (interface `IRegistry`).

trigger the loading of the corresponding plug-in library. This allows to completely abstract from specific device technologies. Another option is to include this functionality into specific sub-registries running inside the server registry.

### 9.3.3 Base Classes and Functionality

The basic interface of the client registry (class `ClientRegistry`) is shown in Figure 9.2. It allows to indicate the begin and end of a request. This also includes a coarse-grained access control that enables exclusive control of all server registries the client has access to. The search and instantiation of nodes is divided into two steps. First, references to all nodes matching the given node description are provided. In this context, *matching* means that the given node description is a subset of a complete description stored within the server registry. Second, out of the list of *response objects*, a node can be requested and is then instantiated. Such a response consists of an identifier for a registry and a list of identifiers of matching objects (i.e. nodes). When requesting a complete flow graph using a graph description, the client registry requests the first possible response and the first possible object thereof for each node.

A client registry is always connected to a locally running server registry (class `ServerRegistry` accessible via interface `IServerRegistry`). Additional remote server registries can be added by specifying their addresses. Our current implementation uses a well-known port for this initial connection setup.

The server registry internally holds a number of specialized registries organized in a hierarchical structure. These registries are all accessed via the interface `IRegistry`. While the `Registry1394` administrates FireWire devices connected to the sys-

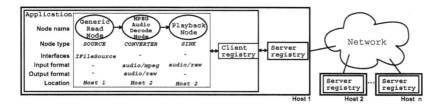

Figure 9.3: A graph description consisting of three connected node descriptions is used to request a complete flow graph. For each node to be created, only a subset of the corresponding complete node description is specified. In this example, the source node is requested from the local host (Host 1); decoder and sink node are requested from a remote host (Host 2).

tem [Rep01], the `LocalRegistry` provides information about all other available plug-ins that are not managed by specialized registries. For integrating other technologies that require specific handling, further specialized registries need to be provided. The interfaces offered by these registry classes are similar to the interface of the client registry. However, as a client registry is meant to reside within the address space of an application, no IDL interfaces are used in this case.

### 9.3.4 Processing of Queries

When the application queries its client registry using a node description, the request is forwarded to the corresponding server registry. More precisely, the location of a node description determines which server registry is to be queried. Per default, the location is set to the local host. If another location is given, the client registries will contact the corresponding remote server registry. If the remote server registry was not already added before by calling `addRegistry`, this will be done on demand.

Figure 9.3 shows how a graph description of a distributed flow graph is used to request a complete flow graph. The source node is queried from the server registry running on the local host; the decoder and sink node from a server registry of a remote host. Also notice that only subsets of complete node descriptions are given.

A server registry processes a request by forwarding it to all internal registries. Each of these registries tests if the given node description is a subset of one of the descriptions of nodes it administrates. Since typically less than 100 different plug-ins are registered for a single server registry, a linear search provides sufficient performance. For each successful test, the response object for this request is extended.

A further option is to disable the evaluation of the location of node descriptions. This can be done by calling `disableLocation` of class `ObjectDescription`. If the location was disabled, the client registry will forward a request to all known server registries. This allows for searching nodes within the currently known part of the network. While this strategy only offers basic support for such queries, more advanced search algorithms suitable for such peer-to-peer approaches can be included. Section 9.6 will discuss future work in this area.

### 9.3.5   Reservation and Instantiation

The reservation and instantiation of nodes is strictly separated. This allows to instantiate nodes that were requested from the local server registry within the address space of the application – and not within the address space of the server registry. Therefore, the most efficient transport strategies can be used for out-of-band interaction with all locally running parts of a flow graph (compare Chapter 6).

In addition, this separation also allows to take the properties of specialized subregistries into account. While the reservation of nodes is done within specialized sub-registries, the instantiation of nodes is performed by *node factories*. Again, for supporting different technologies, corresponding factories can be provided. A call of `requestNode` is handled as follows. First, the registry tests if the response object refers to the registry itself or another registry. In the latter case, the request is tried to be forwarded to the specified registry. The specific registry reserves the node, and creates a `factory ticket` that allows to create a single instance of the node. This ticket also stores an identifier for a node and the configuration events needed for properly setting up the particular instance of the plug-in. For locally instantiating a node from a factory ticket, the corresponding plug-in library is then loaded within the address space of the application. In this step, the identifiers generated for nodes are not regenerated but taken from the information provided by the ticket. This is needed to maintain a global state for all clients of the server registry. In cases where a node is to be instantiated on a remote host, only the needed plug-in library is loaded dynamically by the corresponding server registry. Finally, the requested node is created and configured, and access to its basic interface `INode` is provided.

In order to provide a simple mechanism for handling failures, instantiated and reserved nodes are only *leased*. Applications need to extend such a lease from time to time. This allows a registry to automatically free resources in cases where an application failed to release requested entities.

## 9.4   Results and Applications

The registry service of NMM is used within all applications described in Part IV of this thesis. The registry server of NMM is realized as separate application called *server-registry* [Rep03a, Rep04]. This applications needs to be running in order to establish the client/server infrastructure. Furthermore, this application acts as participating actor within the peer-to-peer network of systems running NMM. A well-known port is used to enable the initial access to remote systems. However, in order to ease application development and testing, the server registry does not need to be started necessarily. In these cases, a server registry is automatically created within the address space of the application; no central administration is available then.

The registry service needs to be set up once ('./serverregistry -s'). In this step, all node descriptions of available nodes of plug-in libraries are determined and corresponding information is written to a file specific for the host and the version of NMM. If this step is not done manually, it will be performed automatically whenever an application is started for the first time after the installation of the NMM system.

### 9.4.1 Programming Model

For application developers to access the registry service, following lines of source code need to be included [Loh04a]:

```
NMMApplication* app =
    ProxyApplication::getApplication(argc, argv);
ClientRegistry& registry = app->getRegistry();
```

The first line creates the central application object for the application. This step will first try to contact the server registry of the system. If this fails, a local instance is created instead. The second line requests the client registry.

The following shows a typical example for requesting a single node specified via its name from the registry service.

```
NodeDescription source_nd("GenericReadNode");

registry.initTransaction();

list<Response> source_response = registry.initRequest(
    source_nd);
if(source_response.empty()) {
  throw Exception("Requested_node_is_not_available");
}
INode* source =
    registry.requestNode(source_response.front());

registry.releaseTransaction();
```

Notice that since the location was not set for the node description, an instance of the plug-in will be created within the address space of the application.

A more complex node description is shown below. In this example, a converter node is specified to be instantiated on a remote host. Furthermore, it is required that the node allows to convert MPEG audio to uncompressed audio. Other often used options include to add a number of supported interfaces to a node description.

```
NodeDescription decoder_nd;
decoder_nd.setLocation("host1");
decoder_nd.setNodeType(INode::CONVERTER);

Format decoder_in_format("audio/mpeg");
decoder_nd.addInputFormat(decoder_in_format);

Format decoder_out_format("audio/raw");
decoder_nd.addOutputFormat(decoder_out_format);
```

A last example shows how to use a graph description to request a simple flow graph consisting of three nodes: A source node for reading data from a file, a converter for decoding MPEG audio, and a sink node for outputting uncompressed audio. In a further step, the flow graph is realized, i.e. all specified edges are connected and all nodes are activated. Finally, the flow graph is started.

```
NodeDescription source_nd("GenericReadNode");
NodeDescription decoder_nd("MPEGAudioDecodeNode");
NodeDescription sink_nd("PlaybackNode");
```

| Setup | | | | Setup Time | | |
|---|---|---|---|---|---|---|
| Local System | Remote System | Network | Local Optimization | Request | Realization | Sum |
| PC1 | PC2 | LAN | disabled | **0.885** | **3.695** | **4.580** |
| PC1 | PC2 | LAN | enabled | **0.675** | **2.492** | **3.167** |
| Laptop | PC2 | LAN | disabled | **1.536** | **9.064** | **10.600** |
| Laptop | PC2 | LAN | enabled | **1.348** | **5.150** | **6.498** |
| Laptop | PC2 | WLAN | disabled | **2.068** | **13.547** | **15.615** |
| Laptop | PC2 | WLAN | enabled | **1.590** | **10.065** | **11.655** |

Table 9.1: Measured runtimes in seconds for requesting and realizing a distributed flow graph consisting of 50 processing elements with the local optimization being disabled or enabled. A detailed description of the used systems PC1, PC2, and laptop can be found in Appendix A.

```
decoder_nd.setLocation("host1");
sink_nd.setLocation("host1");

graph.addEdges(&source_nd,
               &decoder_nd,
               &sink_nd);

registry.requestGraph(graph);
graph.realizeGraph();
graph.startGraph();
```

### 9.4.2   Performance

As presented above, the registry service of NMM provides an optimization that allows to automatically allocate locally running NMM nodes within the address space of applications instead of the address space of the corresponding registry running on the local host. Only the reservation of nodes is performed within the registry service.

For evaluating the benefits of this optimization and the performance of the registry service in general, a distributed flow graph with 50 processing elements is created using a graph description; starting from a source, 48 elements are added in a row, before a sink node is added. The source and every other element is chosen to run on the local host, all other elements are specified to run on a remote hosts. This means that for every connection between two elements a network binding is created during the realization of the flow graph. In order to avoid delays due to data analysis needed during this step, processing elements are used that simply generate or forward buffers.

Table 9.1 summarizes the measured times needed for requesting and connecting processing elements either with or without employing the local optimization. The two systems PC1 and PC2 are connected using LAN, the laptop is either connected using LAN or WLAN; more details on the used systems can be found in Appendix A. While the general performance of the registry service is sufficient for setting up even large flow graphs, the local optimization allows to further reduce the needed setup time. In addition, the results demonstrate the influence of the available processing power and the used networking technology. Further results showing the setup times for smaller "typical" flow graphs are provided within the following chapters.

## 9.5 Quality of Service Management

As the handling of multimedia potentially requires high networking bandwidth and extensive processing power, a multimedia middleware needs to consider the resources that are required for a particular task and the resources that are available within the overall infrastructure. This is especially demanding for distributed multimedia due to the fact that the information about resource requirements are dependent on the particular task running on particularly chosen systems. Furthermore, the overall resource availability is also distributed and undergoes a constant change.

The underlying infrastructure as focussed on in this thesis does not provide strict quality of service (QoS) guarantees (compare Section 2.2.6). As discussed in Section 2.3 techniques like buffering, prefetching, traffic shaping, or forward error correction can be used to provide a better degree of predictable QoS. Consequently, such mechanisms are already integrated into the NMM architecture or can be integrated easily: Buffering and prefetching is automatically provided by the runtime behavior of NMM flow graphs. Traffic shaping and forward error correction schemes can be integrated by providing specific transport or serialization strategies, respectively (see Section 6.1 and Section 6.5).

The possibilities of NMM together with the registry service provide all facilities for setting up distributed flow graphs. This allows to access remote devices and to distribute workload within the network. However, these possibilities add another level of complexity. While in the best case, a distributed flow graph allows to realize a certain task more efficiently, e.g. in terms of overall delays or processing time, an application can easily create a malformed distributed flow graph. In the worst case, an application might choose to instantiate NMM nodes for performing compute intensive tasks on hosts that do not provide sufficient resources for real-time processing. Furthermore, network data transfer between NMM nodes might be chosen to take place at the "wrong" edges, e.g. for uncompressed instead of compressed streams or using slow network connections.

Therefore, even without strict QoS provision of the underlying infrastructure, QoS management is needed. Together, we aim at following benefits [LXN02].

- Support for instantiation of efficient distributed flow graphs. This allows to distribute NMM nodes in a more "optimal" way according to application needs and prevents from setting up flow graphs that violate inherent constraints in terms of resource requirements like overall networking bandwidth or computational resources.

- Support for guided adaptation. While end-to-end QoS cannot be guaranteed, we focus on providing support for adaptation. Knowledge about resource requirements significantly help to guide this process.

- Support for developing adaptation schemes. Finally, the understanding of dependencies between different resource requirements will help to improve possible adaptation schemes.

Notice that adaptation is especially important since NMM flow graphs potentially compete for resources with other external applications running on the operating system platform. These other processes cannot be controlled by the NMM architecture.

Since the support for QoS management within NMM is still under development, it is not discussed in detail in the scope of this thesis. Instead, the taken approach will be described briefly in the following [Bec03], mainly because the advanced middleware services to be presented in the next chapters can benefit from such facilities.

The QoS management service of NMM provides QoS monitoring and probing, QoS specification using multimedia formats, facilities for determining the QoS requirements of previously untested configurations, and admission control and resource reservation within the middleware layer (compare Section 2.2.6).

During the runtime of a distributed flow graph, QoS monitoring can be enabled. In particular, the consumed computational resources and the ingoing and outgoing data rates can be measured for each node, either as average or as maximum values. Since resources are shared between different tasks, measurements are performed using an unloaded overall system in order to obtain precise and meaningful values. For each node, these measurements are then stored together with its complete configuration. Such a configuration consists of the chosen input and output formats and the computation configuration (compare Section 7.4). In addition, the host the node is running on and the type of application is saved, i.e. either real-time or off-line mode as explained in Section 2.1.3.

In order to determine the resource requirements for a certain node using a particular configuration, previously obtained and stored QoS measurements can be accessed. If the given configuration is not available within the set of measurements, *similar* probes are searched and the resource requirements are estimated. In the simplest case, three probes – the query and two stored probes – are similar, if they only differ in a single parameter value given as a number, e.g. the framerate of a video format; the given names hosts and the types of application have to be identical. Then, the estimated resource requirements can be computed by linear interpolation. For parameter values given as strings, this option is not available. Also, if no such two similar probes can be found, more advanced search and interpolation techniques must be applied.

Upon instantiating a node, the required resources can be reserved. Since the underlying infrastructure does not provide strict QoS reservation, this step only updates information stored within the middleware layer. In particular, the currently measured available CPU resources are decreased by the CPU resources required for the node. Networking bandwidth between two hosts is periodically measured with tools, such as iperf [NLA], and updated accordingly. Notice that the reservation of network bandwidth is highly inaccurate since bandwidth is only reserved between two endpoints of the network, e.g. the two participating hosts; all intermediate network elements and all other endpoints are not taken into account. However, as discussed before, strict QoS reservation is not available for the infrastructures we are investigating (compare Section 2.2.6). Still, such coarse grained mechanisms still allow to further guide the setup of distributed flow graphs.

## 9.6 Conclusions and Future Work

In this chapter, the registry service of NMM was presented. This service employs a hybrid approach. Since several applications concurrently request resources from a single system, all locally available plug-ins are administrated by a server registry. For handling features specific for a particular available device technology, specialized sub-registries are available within a single server registry. Client registries allow applications to interact with the server registry running on the same system. For accessing distributed resources, a peer-to-peer approach is used that allows each client registry to dynamically forward request to server registries running on remote systems. Together, this architecture allows to take the dynamics of typical application scenarios into account and provides a test bed for employing advanced search strategies within organizations of loosely coupled systems.

Furthermore, we showed that the NMM messaging system greatly simplifies the registration process of plug-ins. Also, the developed registry service allows to remove the constant overhead of a complete middleware stack for all locally running parts of a flow graph by separating the reservation and instantiation of plug-in nodes. Finally, several examples that demonstrate the programming model provided by the NMM registry showed its applicability and performance. In addition, ongoing work extending the registry service towards better quality of service management was discussed in order to explain the benefits that such facilities provide for the advanced middleware services that are to be presented in the following chapters.

For future work, we would like to further integrate and combine the concept of composite nodes described in Section 7.5.2 and the concept of graph descriptions described in this chapter. For example, a graph description can be used to create a composite node with certain features. Additionally, the integration of further device technologies seems to be worthwhile – especially under the premise of identifying possible needed extensions of our current architecture and implementation. Finally, the realization of advanced peer-to-peer search strategies provides a further direction for future work. Especially strategies that take the current context, such as the locations of users and devices, into account seem to be interesting [FDC01, Mat03]. Such approaches would allow to restrict the search for a plug-in that performs media input or output to the current location of the user. Such a facility would be a suitable extension for the service presented in Chapter 12 that allows to seamlessly hand over media processing and rendering between different systems.

# Chapter 10

# Automatic Creation of Flow Graphs and Format Negotiation

The multimedia middleware as presented so far already provides many facilities for efficiently developing applications that employ distributed flow graphs for realizing multimedia processing. However, the difficulties of setting up a distributed flow graph increase with the complexity of the task to be performed. In particular, many low-level details need to be handled, such as the choice of matching data formats, the inclusion of needed converters to adapt or decode media streams, or how certain devices are to be configured to provide an appealing user experience.

In this chapter, we present different approaches of how middleware services can provide support in setting up distributed flow graphs. In particular, the challenges for such services will be analyzed. Then, related work will be reviewed. This is followed by the description of an algorithm for automatically setting up a flow graph for playing back media received from a single source [LS05]. This first algorithm is then extended in different ways. A more general approach is presented next that tries to maximize the overall "quality" of the formats used within the flow graph [LSW01, Wam01]. Finally, conclusions are drawn, the limitations of both these approaches are discussed, and ongoing and future work in this area is presented.

## 10.1 Introduction

The creation and configuration of flow graphs includes different steps. First, the general structure of the graph that fulfills the imposed task needs be determined. While this structure is often specific for a particular task, different generic instances can be determined. For example, for rendering audio/visual media provided by a single source, data typically needs to be decoded first. In addition, demultiplexing of audio and video might be needed. This brings up the second step during the creation of flow graphs, namely the choice of "matching" processing elements. In this context, matching refers to the fact that a processing elements fulfills a certain sub-task, e.g. by transforming data streams from one format to another. However, in general, there might be several elements that provide the same functionality by offering similar combinations of input and output formats. Furthermore, a certain sub-task within a flow graph can typically be realized by using different combinations of plug-in components. Then, different elements require specific amounts of processing or networking resources to fulfill a task or they provide a different "quality" of operation, e.g. by using different algorithms or formats. Therefore, a third step for creating flow graphs is the configuration of multimedia data formats. More precisely, for connecting two elements, the connection format has to be fully specified (compare Section 7.4).

From this description, one can conclude that the complexity of the creation of flow graphs grows with the complexity of the task to be performed. Together, many low-level details are involved, e.g. the choice of matching processing elements and connection formats. This becomes increasingly complex in distributed environments, where new devices and formats can become available at any time and must be taken into account when deciding how to set up a flow graph of distributed multimedia components. New formats from components at the edges of a flow graph, such as data sources (e.g. cameras) and sinks (e.g. displays), can often be handled by including suitable elements for converting formats to other formats already supported. New processing elements that will be used as internal nodes in a flow graph are more challenging as they can have more impact on the optimal data processing. For instance, optimally using a newly added hardware device that allows for efficiently converting formats might require rerouting of data across the network to the element instead of using local software transcoding.

Due to this complexity, multimedia middleware should provide services for setting up complex flow graphs. At best, this would allow for an application (or an user of the system) to only specify what task should be performed, e.g. playback of media, using a particular source of data. Ideally, an application could optionally add further constraints. For the example of media playback, this could be done by specifying a set of particular devices that should be employed for fulfilling the task, e.g. a display and audio system for rendering media. A more advanced approach could even allow to only specify the current location of the user of the system – or, to determine this location automatically. The middleware service would then automatically request nearby devices for media output; all internal nodes of the flow graph could be instantiated on different systems.

## 10.2   Challenges and Requirements

The problem of *automatic application setup* for distributed flow graphs can be defined as follows [LSW01]: *Given a high-level description of an intended task plus additional constraints, try to find a valid and fully configured distributed flow graph that meets the given constraints and provides the highest possible "quality". If more than one solution is found, prefer a cost optimal solution.*

To this end, automatic application setup is an optimization problem. While the provision of a service for true automatic application setup is certainly a desirable goal, several challenges have to be considered when deciding how to realize such a solution.

### 10.2.1   Task specification

Appropriate means for specifying a task need to be provided. In particular, such a specification needs to provide a high level of abstraction. We propose the concept of

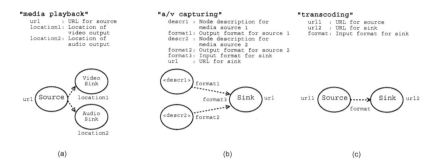

Figure 10.1: A user graph provides an abstract representation of an intended task. For different tasks, generic user graphs can be defined that can be identified by a name. These graphs only represent the general structure and are independent of converters, demultiplexers, multiplexers, or connecting formats. However, additional constraints, such as locations or desired formats, can be specified for each task.

a *user graph*, which defines an abstract flow graph where only the key components, their connections, and additional constraints are defined. More precisely, components are specified as node descriptions (see Section 9.3.1); constraints are given by the properties of the node descriptions and the formats for connecting them.

While graph descriptions as introduced in Section 9.3.1 are used to request distributed flow graphs by defining a precise structure, a user graph is independent of a possible physical realization. In particular, a user graph is incomplete in several ways: Node descriptions only have to define the key features. Connecting edges can be chosen independently of possible connections between nodes in terms of matching formats. To this end, the structure of the graph itself does not need to include converters – to some extent, also demultiplexers and multiplexers can be left out. Only sources, filters, and sinks need to be specified because these components represent the intended functionality. As described in Section 7.2.1, filter plug-ins do not change the format of the data stream. They provide a certain additional functionality. Therefore, such plug-ins always have to be specified to be included.

A user graph can be obtained in several ways. First of all, the application – or even a user – can manually create such a graph. A further possibility is the provision of generic instances. This would allow to access specific predefined user graphs that are described by a textual description. For example, the task "media playback" could be represented by a user graph as shown in Figure 10.1(a), which only requires a URL to be given, e.g. a file. Optionally, the location of devices for media output can be defined, which are then mapped to the sink nodes within the user graph. Likewise, user graphs for tasks like capturing live media ("a/v capturing") or transcoding of files ("transcoding") could be predefined and stored within a repository. In this context, "transcoding" is the conversion of the format of media; an operation typically performed to change single format parameters, such as the resolution of a video stream, or for reencoding compressed media with a different codec. For capturing, only two input devices for audio and video have to be specified by the application or user. Optionally, formats can be provided (see Figure 10.1(b)). For transcoding, an input file and an output file has to be given; desired formats for the output file can be attached to the connecting edge between source and sink (see Figure 10.1(c)). Notice that in general, a single user graph might result in the instantiation of different flow graphs. However, a provided user graph should allow for the non-ambiguous creation of the resulting flow graph.

### 10.2.2    Valid and Fully Configured Flow Graphs

A *valid* distributed flow graph as stated in the above definition of automatic application setup includes following points. First, its processing elements have to be available on the chosen hosts. However, especially when creating distributed flow graphs, one cannot assume the availability of a certain plug-in on all participating hosts. Secondly, all connections as defined by the structure of the graph have to be matching, i.e. a connection format has to exist for each edge. Thirdly, the quality of service (QoS) requirements for all processing elements have to be in accordance with the resource availability as given by the QoS service described in Section 9.5.

For a *fully configured* flow graph, all connection formats have also to be determined precisely. This is especially demanding for cases where ranges and wildcards still exist after a flow graph was found to be valid. Then, values for these parameters have to be determined and propagated within the graph.

To this end, determining a valid and fully configured flow graph can be regarded as a search for paths that connect the elements given by a particular user graph. The constraints expressed within this user graph and the QoS requirements of processing elements further restrict the search space.

### 10.2.3    Quality Model for Flow Graphs

From the problem statement provided above, the notion of "quality" needs to be further defined. While the quality of a single format – and therefore also the quality of a connection format of two nodes – is defined according to the weighting function as described in Section 7.4.3, this approach needs to be extended to flow graphs. We propose to define the *quality of a flow graph* as the minimum quality of the connection formats of all its edges [LSW01]. The intuition behind this definition comes from the fact that the minimum quality along a path of connected processing elements reflects the total quality of the path: Quality can easily be decreased but never be improved. Correspondingly, the minimum quality of all paths within a flow graph represents its total quality.

Figure 10.2 depicts this idea for audio sampling rates; similar observations can be made for other formats or parameters thereof. In this example, two possible paths exist for connecting a source to a sink. Assuming that the value of the sampling rate mainly determines the quality of connection formats, the quality values of all connections can be derived from the sampling rate. The path shown in (a) only needs two additional processing elements; the path shown in (b) needs three. Therefore, the path shown in (a) might be more efficient and could provide lower latency. However, although both paths end with a quality of 1.0, the path shown in (b) provides better total quality, since its *quality bottleneck* offers a value of 0.5 compared to 0.25 at the bottleneck of the

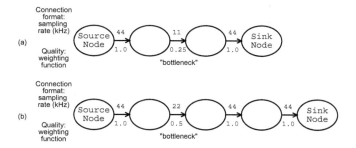

Figure 10.2: The quality of a flow graph is defined as the minimum quality of the connection formats of all its edges. As an example, two possible flow graphs for connecting a source to a sink are shown in (a) and (b). Intuitively, quality can be decreased (e.g. by downsampling the audio stream), but never be improved by (e.g. by upsampling). Therefore, the flow graph in (b) provides better quality since its quality bottleneck offers a quality of 0.5 (for 22 kHz) compared to 0.25 (for 11 kHz) in (a).

path in (a). Intuitively, this means that a downsampled audio stream can never reach its original quality again.

### 10.2.4 Quality versus Costs

For the scope of this thesis, costs are mainly computational resources and network bandwidth (compare Section 9.5). Obviously, there is a trade-off between quality and costs. This trade-off has not only to be considered in cases where additional processing elements can be used to reach a higher quality, but also when a higher valued format is used for a single processing element. This is due to the fact that a better quality typically implies higher values of parameters, which implies higher resource utilization in terms of processing power and networking bandwidth (compare Section 7.4.3).

Notice that the definition of the quality of a flow graph prevents us from using processing elements that try to artificially increase the quality. For example, the quality of a flow graph is never increased by including converters that upsample multimedia data. Contrariwise, when only optimizing for costs, processing elements that decrease the quality – and correspondingly decrease costs – would always be included. Therefore, we argue that approaches for automatic application setup should be quality-driven and regard costs only as additional constraint, e.g. when comparing two possible solutions that provide equal quality or to check whether a solution gives a valid flow graph as defined above.

Furthermore, there might also be a trade-off between quality and latency within the flow graph. If latency values are also known, they should be used as additional constraints and not as optimization criterion. This is in correspondence with users' expectations for a multimedia system. For example, if a flow graph provides a total latency that is suitable for interactive applications, users will typically prefer a better quality over a lower latency.

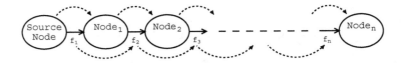

Figure 10.3: Automatic application setup as global problem. Due to the restrictions in terms of supported input and output formats, each chosen node or connection format within a flow graph potentially has influence on all other nodes and formats.

## 10.2.5    Global Approach versus Distributed Dynamic State

Automatic application setup is a global problem. Due to the number of inputs and outputs and the specific combination of possible input and output formats, each node within a flow graph influences all other nodes that are to be included. Furthermore, each chosen connection format potentially has influence on all other formats within a flow graph. Figure 10.3 shows these aspects. The chosen source restricts the set of nodes that are possible to be connected in downstream direction; the chosen output format – and all parameter values thereof – recursively restricts the possible formats for all following connections. Similar observations can be made for any other node or format within the flow graph – in upstream or downstream direction. In addition, for multiplexer and demultiplexer plug-ins, each chosen format for an input or output typically limits the possibilities for all other incoming or outgoing formats.

From the above description, it can be concluded that automatic application setup is a discrete optimization problem, which can be expressed as linear programming problem. In general, linear programming is the problem of minimizing a linear cost function subject to a number of linear equality and inequality constraints [BT97]. The minimization of a cost function can also be expressed as the minimization of the value that the minimum quality within a flow graph is smaller than the maximum possible value, i.e. the value of 1.0. Since the choice for a particular configuration of a flow graph includes decision variables, automatic application setup (AAS) is a mixed zero-one integer programming problem. Since AAS needs to take the computation resources into account, it is intuitively clear that AAS is at least as "hard" as the knapsack problem [Sch95].

However, a proof for this statement is not given within the scope of this thesis, since the consideration of AAS as a global problem is not feasible due to the distributed and dynamic state of the overall system. In particular, the constraints for AAS would need to include all possible configurations of nodes of all possibly involved distributed hosts. Again, one cannot assume the availability of a certain plug-in on all hosts. Contrariwise, the same plug-in might require varying amounts of resources when instantiated on different hosts. Since NMM chooses a peer-to-peer approach whenever possible to take the heterogeneity and the loose coupling of system components into account, acquiring such a global view would require to query all involved distributed hosts – a process which might be too time consuming. Furthermore, since the state of the individual hosts of the overall system dynamically changes, this would require to "lock" the whole system during the setup of a single application.

Another property of processing elements further forbids to consider automatic application setup as global problem: Some elements need to process multimedia data in order to determine their supported output formats. Correspondingly, resource requirements also depend on this step. However, for providing multimedia data for a processing element, all preceding upstream elements already have to be setup and connected properly. Therefore, the creation of flow graphs should be regarded as an iterative search process. While some parts of the graph can be negotiated without streaming data between elements, other parts need access to data. Unfortunately, the partial setup of flow graphs required for providing data also complicates the application of backtracking during the search for a valid flow graph.

### 10.2.6 Setup Time versus User Satisfaction

From the above description one can conclude that due to the complexity of the problem, the optimized setup of a single application can be very time consuming. However, the response time (or setup delay) is another important characteristics of a system, which is especially noticed by human users. Therefore, it is often more desirable to provide a feasible solution, which might only be an approximation of the optimal solution, within a predefined amount of time.

To this end, it would be worthwhile to realize automatic application setup as *any-time algorithm*. For this class of algorithms, the output quality improves gradually over time [DB88]. A first feasible solutions is already available instantly (or after a short period of time); whenever the algorithm is interrupted later on, a solution is provided that provides at least the same output quality. Often, such approaches are controlled by a meta-level decision procedure, which decides when the algorithm should be stopped [RN95].

### 10.2.7 Discussion

From the above discussion it becomes clear that approaches for automatic application setup that try to achieve a global optimum are not applicable. This is mainly due to the complexity of the problem but also because of the distributed state of the overall system and the dynamic characteristics of processing elements. Therefore, we argue that best-first greedy algorithms should be applied that iteratively combine solutions of sub-problems found by the application of suitable heuristics; only some parts of the problem should be solved by following a global optimization criterion.

## 10.3 Related Work

Different protocols and algorithms have been developed for automatically setting up distributed multimedia applications. In [XN02], a solution for finding optimal paths in media service networks is described. A modified Dijkstra algorithm is used in order to find the "best" path with respect to a generic evaluation function, which expresses the "risk" in respect to the ratio "requirements-to-availability" of resources. While the approach includes resource monitoring for host processing capacity and network bandwidth, it operates on predefined service paths that are restricted to serial configurations. Incomplete and general graph based configurations are not supported. A further aspect that is discussed in Section 10.2 but not considered by the approach is

the dynamic characteristics of elements along the service paths, i.e. resource requirements of elements are assumed to be known in advance.

In [BBE⁺00], an architecture for multimedia home entertainment based on IEEE
1394 is described. The concept of an Activity Graph is used to specify a certain functionality such as watching TV. This representation will be mapped to physical units
and network connections by a service called Graph Mapper. In this step, other services are contacted in order to check for available devices. Devices are then chosen
according to criteria like location. Further details on this process are not provided.
The approach does not seem to include the ability to complement incomplete specifications. However, the abstraction of using an Activity Graph that is independent of a
physical realization proves to be useful for describing application needs and is similar
to the concept of user graphs in our system.

The conceptual framework described in [PSG00] allows to use a mobile device
as a unique communication and access interface for other devices in the surrounding.
The central component is the Smart Gateway Server, which maintains a database of all
devices together with their capabilities as well as the available services like streaming
media delivery. This information is updated with every request. Furthermore, it is the
task of the server to select the most appropriate device and to perform media adaption
if no suitable device was found. This step is basically performed by a lookup in a
database and is therefore also restricted to static configurations.

The Automatic Path Creation (APC) service described in [MK00] follows an approach similar to ours. Starting from a logical path with a single source and sink, a
search algorithm tries to determine a sequence of additional operators (such as converters) that allow to connect source and sink [MSK01]. The search uses a shortest
path algorithm that is guided by a single criterion, e.g. quality. As a result, a non-
exhaustive list of possible operator sequences is returned. This list is sorted according
to the used optimization criterion. In a second step, such a sequence of operators is
physically created within a distributed system. The operator placement strategy uses
greedy heuristics such as preferring to instantiate many operators on a single unloaded
host. During runtime, the system allows to perform adaptation. To this end, the system
can force to setup another physical path or to consider another sequence of operators.

While especially the iterative process of path creation seems to be promising, the
search algorithms for logical paths is restricted to a single source and sink. Furthermore, the implementation of the approach seems to restrict all operators along a path
to have only a single input and output [Mao]. A possible matching between two operators is only performed according to their specific input and output type; more complex
properties such as multimedia data formats seem not to be supported. Also, the search
for possible operator sequences and the mapping to physical configurations seems to
be independent. However, we argue that one cannot assume all possible operators to
be available on all hosts. Finally, the output properties of operators are not considered
to be dynamic but also assumed to be predefined; therefore, the approach does not
require to route data to operators during the search.

Some of the locally running multimedia architectures described in Section 2.5 provide possibilities to create a fully configured and valid flow graph from an incomplete
description. DirectShow provides a central abstraction for interacting with a flow graph
called filter graph manager [Pes03]. For using such a manager, a flow graph can be
created manually or an URL can be specified. In this latter case, a flow graph for

playing back a particular media source is set up automatically using a method called Intelligent Connect [Micb]. First, a source filter is chosen according to the given URL. This is done by checking the protocol, the file extension, or a set of specific bytes in the stream. Then, all output pins of the source filter are being connected. In this step, the algorithm first tries to connect to input pins that are already present in the graph, then, if this fails, a new filter is requested from the registry. This assures that filters that are already present in the graph are preferred and new filters are only created if really needed. For choosing a particular filter, all filters are sorted according to their specific *merit* value. Filters with a merit value of MERIT_DO_NOT_USE or smaller – or filters that belong to a category with such a merit value – are not considered.

The depth of this search algorithm is limited to five [Ger]; backtracking is used to follow other possible solutions. If no solution could be found at all, the solution that renders the highest proportion of output pins with the fewest filters is returned.

Additionally, DirectShow provides specialized graph building tools for tasks like DVD playback, or capturing of audio or video. A concept similar to the user graph described in Section 10.2.1 is not provided. Furthermore, for a lot of filters and filter categories, DirectShow has specified merit values smaller than MERIT_DO_NOT_USE, which will not allow to use these filters for Intelligent Connect [Mica]. Also, the merit value only depends on the filter in general and not different input or output formats provided by a filter. Finally, the solution found by the algorithm has no total value as there is no optimization criterion that guides the search.

The Java Media Framework also offers a format negotiation, e.g. when creating a Player from a Data Source (see Section 2.5). Unfortunately, there is no detailed description on this procedure available. However, from personal correspondence via email and the source code of the JMF that is released under Sun's SCSL program [Sunc], one can conclude that a mechanism similar to Intelligent Connect is used. Several optimizations are used, e.g. branches in the search tree that represent combinations that were already found in previous iterations are cut. Again, the search depth is limited to four.

For GStreamer, even less documentation exists: the only documentation is the source code and the mailing-list [GSt]. From these sources, one can conclude that a simple search algorithm is used. Furthermore, no optimization is performed and the approach seems to be restricted to certain configuration, e.g. splitting and merging operations are not supported.

Together, the approaches of DirectShow, JMF, and GStreamer are inherently restricted to create locally operating flow graphs. Therefore, the problem of distributed state is not present. Concepts similar to user graphs are not provided. Instead, all graph building is restricted to certain cases of flow graphs. As mentioned above, QoS requirements are not included into the used algorithms. Furthermore, the problem of dynamically specified properties of processing elements seems also not to be considered. However, despite the fact that only a subset of the problem of automatic application setup as discussed in Section 10.2 is approached, no global optimization for criteria like quality is performed.

## 10.4    Building Flow Graphs

Within the scope of this chapter, a graph building algorithm will be presented [LS05]. Since this algorithm is very restricted in its generic form in the sense that only a subset of the challenges for automatic application setup are considered, following sections will extend the approach to allow for including further features.

### 10.4.1    Defining Sources and Sinks

For defining resources to be used as source or sink of data within a flow graph, so called *graph URLs (Uniform Resource Locators)* are provided [RL04]. A graph URL is then used to request a matching source respectively sink plug-in that can handle a particular kind of resource. Such a plug-in is then used as source or sink within the graph building process, respectively. The specification of graph URLs is similar to URLs as known from the World Wide Web, i.e. a graph URL consists of a protocol, a host, a path for this host, and protocol specific parts such as additional parameters as key-value pairs. Unlike URLs commonly known, graph URLs are also used to specify contents to be accessed from audio CDs or video DVDs. For example, the graph URL "audiocd:///dev/cdrom?track=4" specifies track number four of an audio CD that is accessible via the device "/dev/cdrom" of the local host. The graph URL "dvd://host1/dev/cdrom?title=1&chapter=4&angle=1" allows access to the specified title, chapter, and angle of a DVD that is inserted into the DVD drive of the given host "host1". Further graph URLs are used to access files or hardware devices like different TV boards or cameras.

To request a node that corresponds to a graph URL an iterative process is used that adds as much detail as possible to an empty node description. In order to allow for an easy extension with additional protocols, this process is performed by *graph URL objects* that are specific for a particular protocol. Such an URL object then handles the different steps of the determination of a precise node description by implementing several methods according to the design pattern Template Method [GHJV94]. The following describes the case for graph URLs for source nodes; graph URLs for sink nodes are treated similarly.

- The node name of the node description is tried to be set. Therefore, the protocol of the graph URL is examined first; then, the file extension of the specified resource is considered (if available). If a node name is specified, the node description can be used to query a node. This is due to the fact that node names are unique.

- If the previous step does provide a node name, an output format that needs to be supported is determined. Again, first the protocol is considered, then a possibly available file extension. If still no format can be identified, the content of the resource specified by the graph URL is examined to match certain patterns.

- A number of NMM interfaces that need to be supported by a matching plug-in node can be added to the node description. Again, the provision of interface identifiers greatly helps to specify the set of applicable plug-ins. For example, a source node for reading DVDs typically implements interfaces specific for this functionality.

## 10.4.2  Building Flow Graphs for Media Playback

Using the graph URLs described in the preceding section and the interaction mechanisms for formats discussed in Section 7.4, a first algorithm for building flow graphs for media playback can be derived. Figure 10.4(a) shows the user graph for generic media playback that can be handled by the algorithm. In contrast to Figure 10.1(a), no location for the audio or video sink can be specified but additional jack tags for audio and video (see below).

The algorithm works as follows. First, the complete node descriptions of possible sink nodes for rendering audio or video are queried from the registry by using the node descriptions as given by the user graph. Notice that the node descriptions specified by the user graph may only be subsets of complete specifications. However, complete specifications are needed to access all supported formats of sink nodes during the graph building algorithm.

Then, a node description for the source node is generated from the given graph URL as described above. Notice that arbitrary URLs can be specified, e.g. for files but also for accessing audio CDs, video DVDs, or hardware devices like TV boards or cameras. Since the response of the registry for this node description might include several possible nodes, a node that supports the exact and complete output format as specified by the node description is preferred over a node that only includes the given format. Otherwise, a node that allows to handle all kinds of formats is chosen, i.e. a node that supports the special format called wildcard format given by a type and subtype of "*/*" (compare Section 7.4.4). For example, NMM provides a node called `GenericReadNode` that allows to read all kinds of data from files. However, for the case of playing back an MPEG file, the node called `MPEGReadNode` is chosen since its output property includes the exact format as given by the node description (see Figure 10.4(b)).

In the next step, the source node is configured. This step is also done by the specific graph URL object. First, all methods to be called in the `CONSTRUCTED` state are called using parameters included in the URL, e.g. a track of an audio CD. For our example, the graph URL object for handling files sets the input file name via the interface `IFileHandler`. Then, the same process is performed for state `INITIALIZED` and state `OUTPUT_INITIALIZED`.

The main loop of the graph building algorithm is started then. Within this loop, the algorithm first tries to match the default output format of the current upstream node (the "left" node) with the input property of one of the sink nodes (the "right" nodes) as given by the node descriptions queried from the registry. Notice that only the node descriptions of possible sink nodes are used in this step; nodes are not yet instantiated. This avoid the instantiation of sink nodes that might not be needed to complete the construction of the flow graph. For the first iteration of the loop, the upstream node is given by the source node. If this test is successful, the corresponding sink node is instantiated and both nodes are connected. If no more upstream nodes are available, the algorithm will terminate. For example, when a graph URL that refers to a audio file in WAV format is given, the algorithm will find a `WavReadNode` as source that

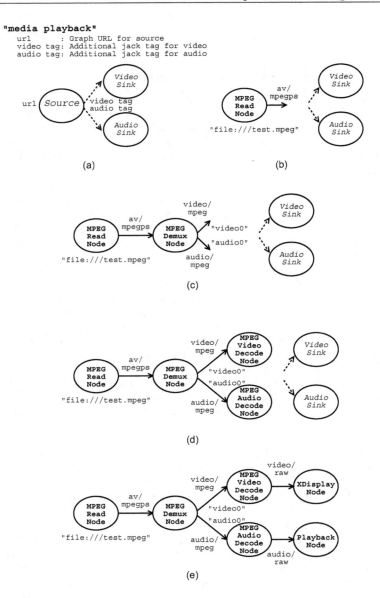

Figure 10.4: Demonstration of a graph building algorithm for media playback. Starting from a user graph shown in (a), first, a matching source node is determined according to the given graph URL (b). Then, additional converters or demultiplexers are inserted in steps (c) and (d) as long as unconnected upstream nodes cannot be linked to possible sink nodes. In (e), the formats of the decoding plug-ins match the formats of possible sink nodes and the corresponding nodes are instantiated and connected.

can be directly connected to an audio sink of type `PlaybackNode`.

However, if no connection is possible, the algorithm will try to find a matching downstream node. In this step, the default output format of the current upstream node is used to create a new request in form of a node description that holds this format as input format. First, the registry is queried for converter nodes. Out of the list of all matching plug-ins returned, a converter that supports the exact format as given by the default output format of the current upstream node is preferred over a converter that only includes this format within its input properties. Since converter nodes that support all kinds of input formats by providing a wildcard format are not reasonable, they are not tested. According to this ranking, the best matching downstream converter node is then connected to the current upstream node. If no such node was found, the algorithm tries to insert a demultiplexer using the same approach. This is the case for our example as shown in Figure 10.4(c), where the node `MPEGDemuxNode` is connected.

The algorithm then continues the main loop by first testing all upstream nodes to be connected to possible sink nodes. Again, if this cannot be completed successfully, additional converters or demultiplexers are tried to be inserted. As can be seen from the demultiplexer in Figure 10.4(c), the algorithm further needs to process several possible outputs per node. However, since an MPEG stream might contain several streams for one output media (e.g. different audio streams in MPEG or AC3 format) and additional streams (e.g an SPU stream for subtitles), the algorithm needs further guidance. Therefore, the user graph shown in Figure 10.4(a) also provides jack tags for connecting the source to the sink nodes. These jacks tags are used to match available jack tags. The jack tag "default" is always chosen first. However, a demultiplexer typically exports different jack tags. By specifying jack tag "audio0", the first audio track will be chosen, which might be either the first MPEG audio stream named "mpeg_audio0" or the first AC3 audio stream "ac_audio0". Correspondingly, a jack tag "video0" is given in the user graph. Notice that this mechanism only works for plug-ins that define their jack tags according to this convention.

Figures 10.4(d) and (e) show the further steps of the algorithm. In (d), the two decoding plug-ins are connected to the demultiplexer. In this case, the algorithm operates in a breadth-first manner, i.e. all outputs of demultiplexers are connected first. In (e), the sink nodes are instantiated and connected because the outgoing formats of the decoding nodes are found to be matching. Notice that for all these steps, multimedia data needs to be streamed and examined by newly connected processing elements in order to determine the precise output format.

If wanted, the sink nodes within the resulting flow graph can be connected to a suitable synchronizer (see Section 7.8).

**Discussion**

The general approach for the algorithm described above is similar to the Intelligent Connect procedure of DirectShow described in Section 10.3. While the algorithm already provides support for playing back all kinds of media from a single source, it is restricted to this specific task and the corresponding user graph. Only the usage of jack tags within a user graph allows for further influencing the resulting flow graph. Furthermore, the algorithm lacks support for distributed flow graphs, the consideration

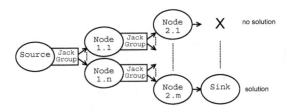

Figure 10.5: The concept of parallel branched search. All possible sub-graphs are constructed in parallel and data is streamed in order to find a path from source to sink. Jack groups directly support the forwarding of a single stream to multiple receivers.

of resource requirements for processing elements, and the global optimization of the resulting quality.

However, the example shown in Figure 10.4 demonstrates the difficulties for achieving these goals by showing the dynamic nature of graph building: In order to determine the overall structure of the graph, the required internal plug-ins, and their connection formats, the algorithm has to operate step-by-step. This is due to the fact that precisely defined output formats are first available after nodes where connected and some data was analyzed – but this is the information needed to determine how to proceed.

### 10.4.3   Backtracking versus Parallel Branched Search

In addition to the limitations discussed above, the algorithm only chooses elements according to local decisions. As a consequence, a decision in early stages of the graph building process might lead to unresolvable conflicts in terms of non-matching formats lateron. In order to extend the algorithm to be complete (i.e. to find a solution when one exists [RN95]), *backtracking* can be performed. More precisely, the algorithm needs to discard already established paths within a flow graph, which do not provide a solution, and construct new paths for cases where more than one option exists, e.g. because more than a single node was returned when querying the registry or more than a single output format was available.

While different strategies for performing such a complete search exist – for example, breadth-first or depth-first approaches for traversing the search space – the integration of backtracking requires the ability to access data again that was already streamed within parts of the constructed flow graph. For live media, this requires to cache data within nodes during the construction of the flow graph. This is an option similar to the functionality provided by the analyze-phase described in Section 7.7.5.

However, as a further approach, *parallel branched search* can be used, where all possible sub-graphs are constructed and data is streamed through all these sub-graphs in parallel. In the end, one solution is chosen, and all other solutions are discarded. Figure 10.5 illustrates this concept. This idea is directly supported by the concept of jack groups described in Section 7.3.2. While the parallel instantiation of sub-graphs certainly requires additional resources, the approach is especially interesting for the construction of distributed flow graphs, because it also allows to forward data to identical sub-graph located on different hosts. Then, the further graph building process can be performed on several hosts in parallel and a final solution can be picked according to QoS measurements.

For both approaches – backtracking and parallel branched search – the corresponding algorithms need to be further extended to detect possible loops during the graph building process. When creating chains with more than one processing element, the danger of including an element that reverts a previously performed operation is given. For example, a required decoding operation can be canceled by a following encoding step. An approach for further guiding the graph building process is discussed in Section 10.5.

### 10.4.4 Adding Local Quality Decisions to Graph Building

As described in Section 7.5.1, when connecting two nodes, a connection format that provides "best quality" according to the weighting model of formats is chosen. While this approach is also applied when establishing the link between two processing elements during the graph building algorithm described above, a quality-driven choice of the next downstream element can also be used to improve the results of the algorithm: Whenever more than one possible option for continuing the graph building process is available – i.e. if more than one processing elements is matching –, the element that provides the best ranked connection format is chosen. For example, if two or more decoding plug-ins are available for each of the steps shown in Figure 10.4(d), the element that provides a "better" connection format when being connected to the demultiplexer is chosen.

This decision can also be extended by providing a look-ahead strategy that examines possible output formats of all processing elements, which are possibly to be inserted next, *before* creating the actual connection. However, since elements are not connected, only possible output formats can be tested. This also allows to quickly find a processing element that potentially allows to be directly connected to an available sink node.

Notice that all these decisions are only made locally; the overall quality of the flow graph as defined in Section 10.2.3 is not optimized. This corresponds to a best-first-search. Section 10.5 will demonstrate how this restriction can be removed at least partially.

### 10.4.5 Support for Distributed Flow Graphs

The algorithm for building flow graphs as presented so far does not consider the host of the given graph URL and the location attributes of node descriptions of sink nodes. A further extension includes these parameters into the user graph. The corresponding processing elements within the resulting flow graph are then requested on the specified hosts. However, where should intermediate elements be located?

For the case of building flow graphs for distributed media playback, following heuristics can be used: Whenever the upstream part of the currently built graph is located on another host as the possible downstream part *and* the total estimated outgoing bandwidth of the next processing element to be inserted is much bigger than its total incoming bandwidth, try to instantiate this processing element at the location of the downstream part; otherwise at the location of the upstream part.

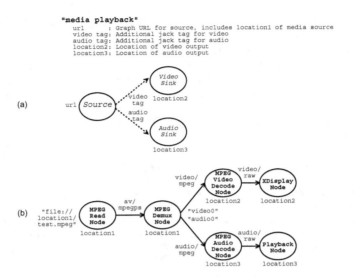

Figure 10.6: Demonstration of a graph building algorithm for distributed media play-back (compare Figure 10.4). Starting from a user graph that allows to specify different locations for the included node descriptions (a), a distributed flow graph is created (b). For sub-graphs of a flow graph that are to be distributed, a heuristics is applied that splits up the different parts of the graph at connections that require lower bandwidth than following connections.

The intuition behind this idea is that decoding elements typically decompress data, i.e. the total incoming bandwidth is much smaller than the total outgoing bandwidth. In this context, the term "much" refers to typical compression ratios for multimedia as presented in Section 2.2.3. A decoding element should be located on the same host as further processing elements such as sink nodes. In general, the heuristics helps to reduce the needed networking bandwidth by collocating processing elements that are connected with a link that requires higher bandwidth, and distributing sub-graphs where connecting links require lower bandwidth.

Notice that the information for applying the heuristics can be queried from the QoS service described in Section 9.5. As the precise output format is needed for requesting the needed bandwidth, possible processing elements need to be instantiated, connected, and data might need to be processed to determine the current output format. Therefore, backtracking or parallel branched search needs to be applied as discussed in Section 10.4.3. However, a further possibility is to query the QoS service for the general relationship of total incoming and outgoing bandwidth of a certain processing element, e.g. by accessing all stored measurements. If the incoming bandwidth is typically much smaller than the outgoing bandwidth, the heuristics can also be applied without the instantiating processing elements.

Figure 10.6 shows the application of the described heuristics for the example first

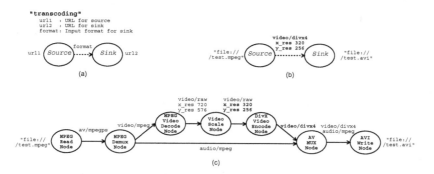

Figure 10.7: Demonstration of a graph building algorithm for transcoding as special case for handling the constraints as given by the user graph. The user graph for transcoding shown in (a) allows an format to be defined. In (b), this format is specified. The graph building algorithm iteratively tries to fulfill the constraints given by the format. The resulting flow graph achieves this by including a node for scaling the video stream and a node for encoding to the given format.

shown in Figure 10.4. For the source node and the two sink nodes, different locations can be specified. The resulting flow graph is split into three parts; the demultiplexer is collocated with the source node, decoding elements are collocated with connected sink nodes. Notice that if location1 != location2 and location2 == location3, the demultiplexer would also be instantiated on the same host as the source node and two networking connections between location1 and location2 respectively location3 would be created. This is in contrast to typical streaming application, where the demultiplexer would be located on host location2 respectively location3. However, the total bandwidth for these connection is the same – or even less, since some streams of the multiplexed MPEG stream might be discarded by the demultiplexer – as for a possible connection between the source node and the demultiplexer.

### 10.4.6 Extending Graph Building for Arbitrary Tasks

So far, we only considered the graph building algorithm for the case of media playback and the corresponding user graph as shown in Figure 10.4(a). However, other user graphs like the ones shown in Figure 10.4(b) and (c) should be supported as well. In the following, we will describe an approach for an algorithm.

Let us consider the user graph for media transcoding shown in Figure 10.7(a) where an input file and an output file (or graph URL) has to be provided and intended formats for the media output are to be attached to the connecting edge between source and sink. Notice that an arbitrary (sub-)format is allowed, e.g. from a simple audio format, where only the sampling rate is specified to a complex recursive format with fully specified audio and video format. Furthermore, the specified format could also be a mixture of different formats, e.g. a combination of parameters found in compressed and uncompressed video formats. This is the case for the instance of the user graph shown in Figure 10.7(b). To this end, the flow graph for transcoding is very demanding to construct because the user graph only contains a minimum specification, which might require a large number of intermediate nodes to be inserted.

The general structure of the algorithm is similar to the algorithm described in Section 10.4.2. During an initial step, a source node is instantiated according to the node description generated by the given graph URL (compare Section 10.4.1). The source node is configured; in particular the state OUTPUT_INITIALIZED is reached, which allows to query the precise specification of the current output format. From the graph URL provided for the sink node, complete node descriptions for possible sink nodes are derived.

Then, the main loop of the algorithm – again – tries to connect the current upstream node (i.e. the source node) with the current downstream node (i.e. the sink node). This step will only succeed if a matching connection format is found. However, this is only the case when the initial media format is equal to the intended output format – a case in which no transcoding at all needs to be done. If a connection is not yet possible, intermediate downstream nodes that offer best matching input formats are queried from the registry and inserted into the flow graph as already described in Section 10.4.2. For our example, only a demultiplexer is found and therefore inserted.

In contrast to the previously described algorithm, the graph building procedure now tries to match the connection format as given by the user graph with the supported formats of nodes that are candidates for inserting them into the flow graph. In this step, complete formats are tested first, but also single parameters of the given format of the user graph are checked. Furthermore, a look-ahead is performed: for nodes that are candidates to be inserted, the supported output formats are queried and tested for possible intersections. Together, the algorithm iteratively tries to fulfill all constraints as given by the user graph.

Figure 10.7c) shows the result of this process for our example. For fulfilling the constraints as given by the video format defined within the user graph, a decoding node is inserted that can be connected to the video output of the MPEG demultiplexer and provides an output format that includes the parameters "x resolution" and "y resolution". The intended values of these parameters are not yet matched: the original video stream provides a different resolution. Therefore, a next step of the algorithm inserts a node that allows to scale the video stream. This property of the node can be concluded from the fact that its working output property provides arbitrary resolutions specified as wildcard parameters. Then, the video is encoded to "video/divx4" by inserting a corresponding converter. This node is inserted due to the look-ahead of one step that shows that the last unfulfilled constraint, namely the format of "video/divx4", can be fulfilled.

Notice that these two nodes are not necessarily found by the algorithm in the first place and inserted in the described order. Instead, backtracking or parallel branched search needs to be performed (compare Section 10.4.3). Then, the first solution to be found is used as resulting flow graph.

For the audio stream, the situation is quite different. Here, no format was specified within the user graph. Therefore, no additional nodes need to be inserted. Therefore, the algorithm is able to select a matching multiplexer that allows to handle both format of upstream nodes (i.e. the audio and video format) and can be connected to a possible sink node as defined by the graph URL (see Figure 10.7c)).

**Discussion**

The algorithm outlined above shows the general principle of fulfilling constraints as given by a user graph while building a flow graph step by step. It can be derived that similar user graphs can be handled successfully by the algorithm as well. However, especially for more complex user graphs – for example, if several filters are additionally inserted along a path – the algorithm potentially needs to perform a large number of backtracking steps or the concept of parallel branched search presented in Section 10.4.3 must be used. As both these approaches are expensive to apply, the following section will provide an algorithm that tries to operates on unconnected flow graphs as long as possible.

## 10.5    Quality-Driven Format Negotiation

The algorithms discussed in the preceding section use a best-first approach to create a valid flow graph from a given user graph. From our experience, many user graphs can be handled successfully that way since often only a single processing element exists that can be used in a certain step of the graph building process – or a number of elements with identical input and output properties is available –, which allows to make a local decisions based on the provided quality of available formats.

Still, in some situations, additional converters need to be included to allow elements with incompatible formats to be connected. In these cases, the above described algorithms operate uninformed. Techniques like backtracking or parallel branched search as discussed above can be applied to examine the search space. However, especially when choosing parameter values in cases where ranges or wildcards are available, these approaches still operate uniformed in the sense that possible values are only chosen according to a greedy strategy.

To further guide the search – and to reduce the number of backtracking steps or parallel branches – an additional observation can be taken into account. Especially for elements that perform format conversion only on single parameters and not on types or subtypes of formats, the currently supported output formats can be determined solely from the set input format without the need of processing incoming data. In such cases, nodes do not need to be connected in order to proceed with graph building. Notice that this property can be determined easily by trying to initialize the output of an unconnected node (state OUTPUT_INITIALIZED, see Section 7.2.2). If successful, no data needs to be accessed. Typical examples for such nodes are plug-ins for converting the colorspace of video streams, or plug-ins for changing sampling rates of audio or video data.

For the sub-parts of the graph building algorithm where such properties hold, a global optimization of the quality of the resulting flow graph can be realized. To this end, also the setting of parameter values for ranges and wildcards is guided according to this criteria. However, whenever a node is inserted that requires to access data to proceed, this node must be used as an "anchor" within the flow graph: up to this point the graph has to be connected and fully configured in order to proceed. Together, this results in an iterative approach. Whenever a sub-part of an algorithm can be handled by a global optimization, we will call this *quality driven format negotiation* or *format negotiation* [LSW01, Wam01]; whenever a best-first approach must be applied, we

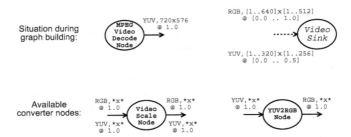

Figure 10.8: Situations during the graph building procedure might occur that allow for a quality-driven format negotiation. In this example, the output format of the MPEGVideoDecodeNode is not compatible with the available input formats of possible sink nodes. However, different combinations of intermediate converter nodes allow for connecting the decoder with the sink. All these converter nodes are able to specify the supported output format from a given input format without accessing multimedia data. The quality values of all formats are given by the @-value.

refer to *graph building*. Intuitively, format negotiation corresponds to extending the look-ahead of one step, which is already performed by the graph building algorithms presented so far, to a larger number of steps.

### 10.5.1 Overview and Motivating Example

Quality-driven format negotiation is performed in several steps. Starting from a user graph, a *negotiation graph* is generated. The user graph is typically not the graph initially provided, but a sub-graph that is generated whenever the graph building algorithm cannot proceed by using a look-ahead of one step. Using the negotiation graph a modified algorithm for solving the single-source-shortest-path (SSSP) problem is applied. Solutions which provide the same quality, are ranked according to their costs. The following sections describe the format negotiation in detail.

As a motivating example, let us consider the situation shown in Figure 10.8. Due to incompatible formats, the output of the video decoder cannot directly be connected to the input of a possible display node; supported video resolutions and colorspaces do not allow to create an intersection format (compare Section 7.4.4). Such situations might occur during the graph building process described in the preceding section. However, by adding a chain of nodes that converts incompatible formats, this conflict can be resolved. For simplicity, only the converters relevant for our example are shown in Figure 10.8; a node that allows to scale video streams (either within RGB or YUV colorspace), and a node that allows to convert from YUV to RGB colorspace. While it might be obvious that three different combinations of converters result in different valid and reasonable flow graphs, it is not clear which combination thereof provides the best quality – or, even the best quality with lower costs when compared to another equally ranked solution.

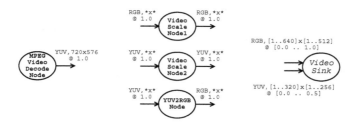

Figure 10.9: The construction of the negotiation graph requires converter nodes to be split according to I/O-partners. For the node called VideoScaleNode first shown in Figure 10.8, this results in the two entities VideoScaleNode1 for RGB colorspace and VideoScaleNode2 for YUV colorspace. The sink node provides separate inputs for different supported input formats. The quality values of all formats are given by the @-value.

### 10.5.2  Construction of the Negotiation Graph

The negotiation graph is constructed in three steps. First, converter nodes are split according to their supported combinations of input and output formats. This is needed to bind a path within the negotiation graph to specific formats – and to propagate decisions for specific formats along the path. In particular, converter nodes are split for each combination of I/O-partners (compare Section 7.4.2). Furthermore, as the format definition allows for sets of values, splitting is also performed for all combinations of entries in the set of supported parameter values of corresponding input and output formats. Ranges and wildcards are treated as single entry. The same operations are performed for provided computation configurations of processing elements (compare Section 7.2).

Figure 10.9 shows the result of this process for the two converter nodes available in our example as first introduced in Figure 10.8. The node for scaling video streams is split per I/O-partner, namely for RGB and YUV colorspace. For source and sink nodes, no splitting is performed but additional edges are provided, e.g. for different supported input formats.

The second step in the construction of the negotiation graph then sets up possible paths between the nodes as given in the user graph. In particular, an exhaustive search is performed by using a depth-first search. During this step, connection formats are created by intersecting input and output formats; available output formats are requested from the working output properties in state OUTPUT_INITIALIZED. As discussed above, *no* connections are created and no data is streamed between the specific nodes. Therefore, this process is restricted to converter nodes that can be brought to state OUTPUT_INITIALIZED without accessing multimedia data provided by their predecessors.

The construction of the negotiation graph also needs to handle possible loops. For example, a converter for encoding uncompressed video could be inserted followed by a corresponding decoder that is again followed by the corresponding encoder, etc. These situations can be determined by checking all predecessors along the current path.

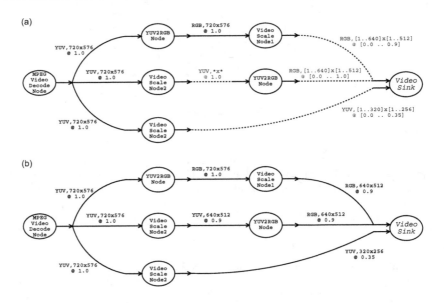

Figure 10.10: The construction of the negotiation graph. In (a), some results of an exhaustive search for possible paths from source to sink are shown. During the creation of these paths, not all connection formats and corresponding quality values are already fully specified. Therefore, in a further step, parameter values of ranges and wildcards are set globally as shown in (b). Corresponding quality values (@-values) of formats are computed from the intersection of input and output formats. Notice that the two paths that end with RGB colorspace provide the same overall quality of 0.9.

Figure 10.10(a) shows the result of this step. Several different paths were found for connecting the source to the sink node within the negotiation graph. For simplicity, we only show the three reasonable paths. Paths that include additional unneeded nodes, e.g. scalers, are not included. While these paths are also handled by all further steps of the approach, resulting solutions are automatically discarded due to higher costs as described below. For all edges of the negotiation graph, the connection formats are evaluated together with the corresponding quality as described in Section 7.4.4. For example, the quality of the edge connecting the VideoScaleNode1 and the VideoSinkNode is determined to be in the range of 0.0 to 0.9.

However, not for all edges a fully specified format – and a corresponding quality value – is already available: ranges and wildcards are still present and need to be resolved during a further step. For example, the connection format of the edge between the scaler VideoScaleNode2 and the colorspace converter YUV2RGBNode provides wildcards parameters for the video resolution since the scaler allows for arbitrary output resolutions and the colorspace converter supports arbitrary input resolutions. Such edges are shown as dotted lines in Figure 10.10(a).

To resolve ranges and wildcards, precise parameter values are set along all paths.

Starting from sink nodes, where the parameter values that provide the highest quality value are chosen, values are propagated towards source nodes. For cases where for-warded values do not match the available values, this process is inverted and newly chosen values are forwarded towards sink nodes. This process must be continued until no more changes are made – or more sophisticated protocols can be applied [RDF97]. Notice that as already discussed above, such propagations are only possible for nodes where parameters within input and output formats correspond to each other.

For our example, this results in a negotiation graph as shown in Figure 10.10(b). The quality values for the video formats with smaller resolutions are determined from the intersection of input and output formats. Furthermore, it can be observed that the two paths that end with an RGB video stream provide the same overall quality, i.e. the maximum minimum quality along the path is 0.9 for both possibilities (compare Section 10.2.3).

### 10.5.3   Quality-Driven Search

Although for our example, it seems to be straight-forward to determine the path or paths that provide the best possible overall quality, this is not true in general. As dis-cussed above, the negotiation graphs sketched in Figure 10.10(a) and (b) do not show all paths available. Paths within the negotiation graph do not need to be necessarily "straight" in the sense the all internal nodes only provide a single outgoing edge. On the contrary, starting from source nodes, different paths might share several nodes until a first branching point. Therefore, we chose to apply a modified algorithm for solving the single-source-shortest-path (SSSP) problem to determine the path that provides the best overall quality.

#### Single-Source-Shortest-Paths and Solutions

For directed graphs that provide a cost value at connecting edges, solving the SSSP problem refers to finding the path from source to sink that implies the lowest total costs, if such a path exists; the total costs are the sum of all costs along the path [CLR97].

The Dijkstra algorithm can be used to efficiently solve SSSP problems where no negative costs are associated with edges. This algorithm works as follows. First, for all nodes $v$ in the graph, two values are initialized. The variable $d(v)$ holds an approximation of the true lowest total costs. The variable $p(v)$ is used to store the predecessor of node $v$ along the corresponding path. In the beginning, these values are set as follows:

```
Initialize()
{
  d(source) = 0;
  p(source) = undefined;
  for(all other nodes v) {
    d(v) = infinite;
    p(v) = undefined;
  }
}
```

After the termination of the algorithm, the value of $d(sink)$ is equal to the lowest total costs (or infinite if no path from source to sink exists); the value of $p(sink)$ can be used to recursively construct the corresponding graph.

The algorithm "relaxes" all outgoing edges of the node $v$ that currently provides the lowest $d(v)$; each node and each edge is only handled once:

```
Dijkstra()
{
  Initialize();
  while(some node was not yet handled) {
    choose unhandled v with minimum d(v) and mark v as handled
      ;
    for(all outgoing edges from current v to w) {
      Relax(v,w);
    }
  }
}

Relax(v,w)
{
  if(d(w) > (d(v)+costs(v,w))) {
    d(w) = d(v) + costs(v,w);
    p(w) = v;
  }
}
```

Intuitively, the algorithm iteratively extends the sub-graph that was already processed. In each step, the node that lies along the path with lowest costs is chosen and all nodes that are reachable via its outgoing edges are updated with the lowest possible costs to reach these nodes. Using a Fibonacci heap for realizing the priority queue needed for selecting the node with minimum $d(v)$, the runtime of the algorithm is $\mathcal{O}(n \log n + m)$ with $n$ denoting the number of nodes and $m$ the number of edges in the graph. A proof for the correctness and runtime of the algorithm can be found in [CLR97].

### Solving the Bottleneck-Problem

Instead of finding the path with the lowest costs, we are interested in the path that provides the best quality. According to the definition of the quality of a flow graph provided in Section 10.2.3, this refers to maximizing the minimum quality along the path – the *bottleneck*. This can be achieved by modifying the Dijkstra algorithm described in the preceding section. First, the values for $d(v)$ are initialized so that they reflect an approximation of the quality for reaching node $v$. The source node gets maximum quality assigned, all other nodes are set to the lowest quality level:

```
Initialize()
{
  d(source) = 1.0;
  p(source) = undefined;
  for(all other nodes v) {
    d(v) = 0;
    p(v) = undefined;
  }
}
```

Then, the relaxation is changed to increase the quality of nodes – and therefore the quality of paths – only if both the preceding node and the current incoming edge provide better quality. Then, the smaller of these two values is taken:

```
Relax(v,w)
{
  if(min(d(v), costs(v,w)) > d(w)) {
    d(w) = min(d(v), costs(v,w));
    p(w) = v;
  }
}
```

Correspondingly, the main loop of the algorithm needs to choose the node $v$ that provides maximum $d(v)$ instead of minimum $d(v)$ for each iteration. A proof of the correctness of this variation of the Dijkstra algorithm can be found in [Way01].

### Ranking Solutions according to Quality and Costs

In order to find a solution that provides the best overall quality *and* the lowest costs for all equally ranked solutions, the modified Dijkstra algorithm needs to be applied several times. After a first solution is found, the last edge along the corresponding path can be removed and the algorithm can be started again. If a second solution is found that provides a lower quality, the first solution is taken. However, if the second solution provides the same quality as the first solution, costs (e.g. computational costs) can be evaluated according to the requirements given by the QoS service described in Section 9.5. This process can be repeated until a final solution is determined.

### 10.5.4   Discussion

From a theoretical point of view, it can be seen that the overall runtime of the proposed quality-driven format negotiation is bounded by the runtime needed for constructing the negotiation graph. In particular, the time for the exhaustive search required is $\mathcal{O}(b^d)$, with $b$ being the branching factor and $d$ being the maximum depth within the search tree [RN95]. In our case, $b$ is the maximum number of matching nodes to connect and $d$ is the longest possible path from source to sink.

From a practical point of view especially the dynamic loading of libraries that contain nodes to be inserted into the negotiation graph results in large runtimes. However, since we focussed on finding the "best" possible solution, an exhaustive search – and therefore the possible consideration of many different nodes – is needed. Finally, it can be observed that many user graphs that are of practical relevance can be handled by only considering moderate sized negotiation graphs. Then, the measured runtime of the algorithmic aspects of the approach are typically in the range of several 100 milliseconds for typical hardware setups.

## 10.6   Results and Applications

Several parts of the above presented services and corresponding algorithms are already fully integrated into NMM. In particular, the graph building algorithm for distributed media playback is employed in various applications. This service allows to specify a

| Setup | | | | | Setup Time | |
|---|---|---|---|---|---|---|
| No. | Application | Source | Audio | Video | Network | Manual | Automatic |
| 1 | PC1 | PC1 | PC1 | PC1 | - | **0.533** | 0.577 |
| 2 | Laptop | Laptop | Laptop | Laptop | - | **1.400** | 1.554 |
| 3 | Laptop | Laptop | PC1 | PC2 | LAN | **1.268** | 1.397 |
| 4 | Laptop | PC3 | PC1 | PC2 | LAN | **1.501** | 1.525 |
| 5 | Laptop | Laptop | PC1 | PC2 | WLAN | **2.827** | 4.736 |
| 6 | Laptop | PC3 | PC1 | PC2 | WLAN | **3.103** | 3.548 |
| 7 | PDA | PC3 | PC1 | PC2 | LAN | **$\sim 30$** | $\sim 38$ |
| 8 | PDA | PC3 | PC1 | PC2 | WLAN | **$\sim 30$** | $\sim 38$ |

Table 10.1: Measured runtimes in seconds for the manual or automatic creation of a flow graph for the playback of multiplexed MPEG audio/video files. A detailed description of the used systems PC1, PC2, PC3, laptop, and PDA can be found in Appendix A.

graph URL that refers to a remote media source. In addition, node descriptions for an audio and a video sink can be specified – again, with the option of choosing remote hosts as locations. Upon successfully generating a distributed flow graph, a composite node is generated that allows to uniformly handle the functionality provided by the created flow graph (compare Section 7.5.2).

The tool `clic` described in Chapter 13 and the networked multimedia home entertainment center presented in Chapter 15 use this service to ease the setup of distributed flow graphs and to realize uniform media handling. In addition, a playback engine for one of the most popular audio players for KDE [KDE], called amaroK [ama], was developed in the scope of the NMM project [NMMd, vF04]. While amaroK provides several engines for audio playback based on other multimedia frameworks, the developed NMM engine transparently supports audio/video playback. Future developments will provide a graphical user interface for configuring remote audio and video sinks.

For evaluating the performance of the described middleware service, the setup times for the common task of MPEG audio/video playback are measured. The used MPEG file is taken from a DVD and provides high bitrates for the audio and video streams. The media source and the sink nodes for audio and video rendering are allowed to be located on different remote hosts than the application (compare Figure 10.4 and Figure 10.6). Table 10.1 shows the results for different setups; the used systems are described in detail in Appendix A. The times needed for the manual creation of flow graphs are compared to the times of the graph building algorithm. When using the PDA for running the application, a remote data source must be used since the tested MPEG file cannot be stored on the PDA itself. In setup number 7 and number 8, the scarce computational resources of the PDA mainly influence the measured times.

The setup times needed for the automatic creation of flow graphs are only significantly higher in the cases where WLAN is used instead of LAN, i.e. in setups number 5, 6, and 8. This is due to the fact that the graph building algorithm requires more interaction with distributed entities, such as the registry service. Especially setup number 6, the setup using the laptop system as source of data, requires much more time since the phase in which data is analyzed within processing elements requires a lot of network traffic using the WLAN, in particular between the source and demultiplexer located on the laptop and the decoding nodes for audio and video located on PC1 and PC2, respectively. This process is described in detail in Section 7.7.5. In contrast, in setup number 6, the nodes are running on PCs connected via LAN.

Also notice that the measured times for setting up a *distributed* flow graph in setup number 3 are smaller than the times needed for setting up a locally running flow graph in setup number 2. This is because the analysis of data streams is partly performed on the systems PC1 and PC2 that provide more computational resources than the laptop.

## 10.7  Conclusions and Future Work

In this chapter, we have motivated and analyzed the problem of automatic application setup for multimedia middleware. In particular, we have proposed the concept of user graphs as high-level concept for specifying multimedia tasks. Furthermore, we introduced a definition for the quality of flow graphs. According to this definition, automatic application setup can be described as creating a distributed flow graph from a given user graph. While this flow graph should provide the best possible quality, it needs to meet additional constraints. Especially, the flow graph should be created in accordance with the current resource availability within the overall system.

However, as this goal is very challenging due to the distributed and dynamic state of the overall system, we only considered several sub-problems of automatic application setup. First, we showed how distributed flow graphs for tasks like media playback and transcoding can be automatically created using a straight-forward and greedy approach that does not consider the overall quality of the solution. Instead, only local decisions are made and heuristics are applied to distribute the processing elements of the resulting flow graph. Other constraints, such as resource availability, are not considered.

In order to further guide the graph building process, we proposed a quality-driven format negotiation for creating certain parts of the overall flow graph. Such a negotiation step requires that all converters to be inserted need to be able to determine the supported output formats solely from the given input format and without the need to access multimedia data. For such case, a negotiation graph is created and a modified version of the Dijkstra algorithm can be applied to find an solution that provides the best possible quality. For equally ranked solutions, the flow graph that requires the least computational costs is chosen.

Compared with the initial goals for automatic application setup, the proposed algorithms only partly solve the imposed requirements. However, as argued in Section 10.2, this problem remains challenging due to the distributed and dynamic state of the overall system, which forbids to apply techniques that try to find globally optimized solutions. In particular, a large number of processing elements needs to access data in order to determine the precise output format. Since this output format is needed to continue the graph building process, all preceding nodes need to be connected and configured. Therefore, it is impossible to globally define the problem without instantiating certain parts of the flow graph. Furthermore, due the different nature of possible tasks, a generally applicable algorithm might not be possible to be developed.

Nevertheless, several directions for further research can be identified. First of all, the algorithms described so far already imply the application of a layered overall approach. Starting from a given user graph, an algorithm that best matches the given task could be selected. For example, for user graphs with audio and video output, different constraints, optimization criteria, and heuristics should be applied than for off-line applications that do not present media to the user.

We already pointed out an iterative approach that allows to combine best-first greedy search and quality-driven format negotiation. The idea of using "anchors" within the graph building procedure seems to be promising. These anchor points define sub-goals that need to be achieved, e.g. because corresponding processing elements need to access data to specify their supported output formats. Then, different solutions for different sub-goals can be combined; for example, by adding additional processing elements.

A completely different approach would try to first find possible flow graphs *without* connecting elements or streaming data at all. While these *virtual flow graphs* form a superset of flow graphs that are possible to realize, a second step could try to instantiate these. This would also allow to apply techniques like bidirectional search, i.e. to search in both direction – from sources to sinks and vice versa. Together, such an approach offers the possibility for applying sophisticated planning techniques [RN95]. An interesting idea could also be to store resulting plans consisting of virtual flow graphs for later application. However, the instantiation of flow graphs then still requires to solve at least some of the problems already described above.

Finally, for all possible approaches discussed so far, the integration of constraints given by available resources and the adaptation to varying resource availability remains an open problem for automatic application setup. While specific solutions already exist in this area, e.g. for optimally distributing predefined and fixed flow graphs [OvR01], or for adapting streams by applying predefined scaling strategies [WKC+97], additional challenges need to be considered for integrating these solutions into a common approach.

# Chapter 11

# Session Sharing

Due to the increased number and ubiquity of stationary and mobile devices that provide multimedia and networking capabilities, new and exciting application scenarios for distributed multimedia can be envisioned. As discussed in Section 4.4.4, particularly interesting is collaborative multimedia access, where a number of users simultaneously enjoys the same or similar content – possibly at different locations using different devices. A consistent middleware layer allows for realizing such advances application scenarios by providing a specific middleware service.

In this chapter, we describe the needed middleware support for such scenarios. In particular, the developed approach – called session sharing [LRS03b] – allows to automatically share parts of an active distributed flow graph within further flow graphs to be created by other applications. We will first introduce some application scenarios, where such a service can be used to realize synchronized and distributed media playback on various devices. Then, related work will be reviewed. For realizing such a service, two aspects need to be examined first: The parts of a flow graph that are allowed to be shared need to be identified and the different criteria for overlapping sub-graphs of two flow graphs need to be formalized. Based on these definitions, an algorithm that identifies overlapping parts of different flow graphs is described and evaluated. The setup of such shared configurations is discussed. Then, different applications that employ the facilities provided by the session sharing service are presented. Finally, conclusions are drawn and possible extensions of out current approach are outlined.

## 11.1  Introduction

Mobile systems, such as portable web pads, personal digital assistants (PDAs), and even mobile phones, already offer reasonable multimedia capabilities. Remaining differences are mainly due to the limited processing power and missing I/O devices. These limitations can be overcome by augmenting mobile systems with the capabilities from commonly available desktop systems. These stationary systems can for instance provide access to sources of multimedia data (e.g. TV receivers or DVD drives), perform audio/video rendering (e.g. via a large screen and a high-fidelity audio system), or they can be used to perform compute intensive tasks (e.g. media transcoding).

All these application scenarios can be realized using the facilities of the multimedia middleware presented so far. Especially the registry service of NMM allows to

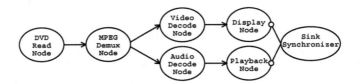

Figure 11.1: A flow graph for DVD playback. The audio/video stream is read by
the DVDReadNode, demultiplexed by using the MPEGDemuxNode, audio is decoded
and played out via the AudioDecodeNode and the PlaybackNode; video is decoded and rendered via the VideoDecodeNode and the DisplayNode. The controllers of both sink nodes are connected to a SinkSynchronizer that realizes an
inter-stream synchronization protocol.

request remote processing elements from stationary systems. These elements can then
be integrated into the flow graph of an application running on a mobile system.

While some application scenarios for collaborative multimedia access were already presented in Section 4.4.4, we will further analyze the requirements for realizing
such setups. A first example motivates our core concept, namely *session sharing*. In
this scenario, the user starts watching a DVD at a stationary system. The audio/video
stream is read, demultiplexed, decoded, and synchronously rendered using an appropriate flow graph of multimedia processing elements, which is shown in Figure 11.1.
This flow graph was requested from the registry service by using a corresponding graph
description (compare Chapter 9).

Starting from this setup, several different application scenarios for collaborative
multimedia access are possible:

- The user that initiated the DVD playback simultaneously wants to watch the
  DVD using a second device as audio/video output – for instance a mobile system.

- Another user wants to join watching the DVD on a different system, maybe at a
  different location.

- Another situation might arise if two users want to watch a DVD on the same
  screen while listening to different audio tracks (e.g. different languages) with a
  mobile device. Such a situation is shown in Figure 11.2.

In any case, beside the initially started application, all further applications will at least
need access to the data stream provided by the DVD. A first idea might therefore be,
to create a separate flow graph (i.e. a copy of the flow graph shown in Figure 11.1)
that employs an additional instance of the source node for reading the DVD. However,
in setups where only a single DVD in a single DVD drive exists, such an operation is
not possible due to several reasons. First of all, the operation system might not allow
to access the same device within several processes at a time. Then, the registry might
not provide a second instance for a single device. Even if the shared access to devices
is allowed, the second instance of the source node will start streaming data from the
beginning of the DVD and not from the position within the data stream that the source

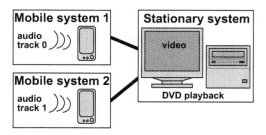

Figure 11.2: An example for collaborative multimedia access. A DVD is inserted into the DVD drive of a stationary system; the corresponding video stream is rendered at the large screen of this system. Users can access audio streams by using mobile systems. Each user is allowed to listen to a different audio track using earphones connected to a PDA, e.g. for a accessing a different language.

node of the initial flow graph is currently processing. Collaborative multimedia access is only available if the complete state of the two source nodes can be forced to be identical at all times – a requirement that is complicated to fulfill. In any case, the redundant instantiation of nodes wastes resources.

Therefore, an optimal solution for realizing such application scenarios is to provide shared access to the same instances of the initially created flow graph. For realizing such a service, we introduce the concept of a *session*: a session is an abstraction for a flow graph of already reserved and connected nodes, and includes used synchronizers. Sessions are stored within the registry service. Nodes of the flow graph of a session — and implicitly edges connecting nodes — can be marked as *sharable* to be reused by other applications within their flow graphs as *shared sessions*.

This situation is shown in Figure 11.3. A session is available for the initially created flow graph. A second application uses a graph description as a *query* to request a flow graph from the registry service. In this first example, for simplicity, only a single running session is considered and only the source node for reading the DVD is then shared between the running flow graph and the query. Therefore, a jack group is used to access the same data stream within both flow graphs. As described in Section 7.3.2, jack groups allow to create a copy of the current output jack; data is then forwarded to all jacks. While jack groups are always used for the outputs of a node, they are only depicted if more than a single output jack is connected.

In order to realize synchronized playback for all connected flow graphs, the corresponding sink nodes need to be linked to a single suitable synchronizer object that handles inter-stream synchronization (compare Section 7.8.2).

The shared access to a single instance of a node from different applications also allows to further enhance collaboration between the participating users. In particular, all connected applications are offered full control via the interfaces exported by the shared node. For our example, this results in all users being able to control the playback of the DVD, e.g. by selecting a different chapter. While such a form of collaboration is certainly interesting, other application scenarios might require restricting control of shared nodes to certain interfaces.

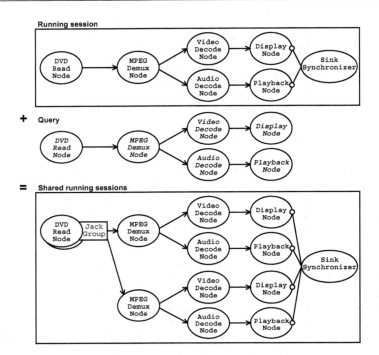

Figure 11.3: An example for session sharing. A running flow graph and its synchro-nizer is stored as session. The graph description of the query of a second application is mapped to this running flow graph. For simplicity, only the source node is shared in this example. A jack group that allows to duplicate the data stream generated by the source node is used to connect both flow graphs. All sink nodes are linked to the sink synchronizer in order to provide inter-stream synchronization. Notice that both flow graphs are distributed, i.e. all nodes are allowed to run on different systems.

Sharing of nodes is not only necessary in cases where only a single device exists to perform a certain operation, but also allows for sharing computational resources among tasks. In particular, shared access to processing elements is not necessarily restricted to source nodes. Especially interesting in this context is the fact that the introduction of mobile systems typically requires the data streams to be adapted to the available capabilities such as processing resources. For example, typical mobile systems are not able to decode audio and video streams of a DVD in real-time. In addition, embedded displays provide smaller video resolutions. Finally, only a restricted number of plug-ins is available for such systems. Therefore, such an adaptation process needs to include transcoding of the original data streams to other formats.

However, for performing such a transcoding operation, media streams need to be decoded first. Since this step is also needed for performing media playback on the stationary system, a larger part of the initial flow graph can be reused – e.g. the demultiplexer and the audio/video decoders shown in Figure 11.3. Furthermore, additionally added mobile systems can be allowed to reuse the newly created parts of the flow graph that provide transcoded media streams. This allows to further reduce processing requirements. Section 11.6 will provide more details on such complex setups.

Together, the session sharing service for collaborative media playback results in following service model: Users are allowed to initiate multimedia playback on any system. As multimedia applications are modeled as distributed flow graphs, other users may then be allowed to share as much as possible of this initially created flow graph. This provides following benefits:

- The problem of multiple access to a single multimedia device is eliminated by providing joint access.

- Processing requirements are reduces when several applications share common tasks.

- Playback is synchronized across all participating devices in these scenarios.

- Controlling of shared nodes is provided for all applications and users.

The next section will review related work; the following sections will then provide more details on the realized session sharing service of NMM [LRS03b].

## 11.2 Related Work

Group communication services such as one-to-many data delivery require efficiency mainly in terms of overall used network bandwith. For approaches where several clients access the same stream provided by a server, IP multicast provides the possiblity to share network bandwitdh at the routing layer [Mat03]. Several solutions for streaming media have been proposed that employ IP multicast, often including the overlayed multicast backbone of Mbone [AMZ95, Nat96, Elk96].

However, due to different technical and marketing reasons, multicast routing is typically not widely available [ESRM03]. Therefore, *application level multicast* (ALM) services have been proposed recently [Mat03, ESRM03, LHLB00]. As application layer protocols, these approaches consider the network to be a "black box" and establish a virtual topology by forming overlay networks. Recent work focuses on the goal of incorporating the common functions of different ALM approaches into a framework [MNMA03]

While ALM typically provides efficient routing for multi-party communication, e.g. by aggregation of streaming data connections, the session sharing service as described above considers a different problem, namely the task of finding and establishing an "optimal" overlap of different flow graphs. Unlike ALM, which typically considers a single source of data and multiple sinks that receive the same (or filtered) data, sharing of flow graphs requires to take the overall structure of the flow graph and its processing elements into account. The edges of such a flow graph do not necessarily represent network connections. However, if an overlap was found, shared edges between different flow graphs that employ network connections could benefit from using IP multicast or application level multicast networking. This idea will be discussed later in this chapter.

Applications for Computer Supported Cooperative Work (CSCW) such as shared white-boards [vSCP96] or design tools [Rot00] typically provide shared access to distributed information together with replication. However, besides the common data structures, which simply needs to be shared completely by all participants, no other parts of the current application need to be shared in such setups.

A system that shares similar goals with our approach is described in [KW02]. The solution uses a proxy architecture together with standard streaming servers and clients for collaborative media streaming. Consequently, only weakly synchronized processes are provided, e.g. for operations such as pausing media playback. Sharing of flow graphs is not available.

While the idea of sharing flow graphs was introduced in [BBE$^+$00], this concept was not examined further; in particular no algorithms were proposed. Together, one can observe that different solutions for "traditional" client/server multimedia streaming that include some form of "collaboration" and different underlying protocols for group communication were proposed so far. However, algorithms for automatically sharing multimedia data flow graphs, synchronization between these shared flow graphs, and the application scenarios that can be realized with such a service were not considered so far.

## 11.3  Administration of Shared Flow Graphs

For realizing a service for sharing sessions, facilities for specifying which parts of a flow graph can be shared need to be provided. In addition, shared flow graphs need to be stored for later retrieval.

### 11.3.1  Shared Nodes and Edges

For specifying which nodes and edges of a flow graph are allowed to be shared, applications need to explicitly set a *sharing policy* for each processing element. This is done for each node description of a graph description (compare Section 9.3.1).

The sharing policy includes the following modes to control application demands:

- **Exclusive:** request a node for exclusive use; if no such node is available exclusively, the query will fail, even if the node exists as a shared node.

- **Shared:** explicitly request a shared node; if no such node is available for shared access, the query will fail, even if the node is available for exclusive access.

- **Exclusive or shared:** try exclusive first; if this fails, try shared.

- **Shared or exclusive:** try shared first; if this fails, try exclusive.

- **Exclusive, then shared:** try exclusive; if successful, share the node.

- **Exclusive, then shared; or shared:** try exclusive; if successful share the node. If the request was not successful, try shared.

- **Shared or exclusive, then shared:** try shared; if request was not successful, try exclusive; if successful, share the node.

The decision of including *or* and *then* statements into the sharing policies was made to ease application development: Only a single attribute has to be set for specifying the intended sharing policies. Per default, the sharing policy is set to *exclusive or shared*. How to set the sharing policy strongly depends on the requirements of an application. Section 11.6 will provide some examples.

When processing a query in the form of a graph description, first, all preferred settings are chosen (i.e. the "left hand" parts of the or-statements). If the overall request could not be handled successfully, other settings are made (i.e. the "right hand" parts of the or-statements) and the request is handled again. If this again fails, applications need to manually adjust sharing policies.

While the sharing policies for nodes have to be set explicitly, edges within running flow graphs are implicitly specified to be shared or not. If both nodes of a connecting edge allow sharing, the corresponding edge is also allowed to be shared within other flow graphs.

### 11.3.2 Storage and Retrieval

Upon successfully creating a flow graph from a graph description, a session is created within the registry service that also stores the sharing policies for all instantiated nodes within node descriptions. Furthermore, instantiated synchronizer objects are administrated. A session is *sharable*, if at least one of its node descriptions allows sharing. A node description *allows sharing*, if the corresponding node was not requested exclusively, or the node was requested exclusively, but is shared now, i.e. "then shared" was specified within the sharing policy. If a node $n$ allows sharing, we denote this as $s(n) = true$.

For storing sessions within the registry service, we chose a peer-to-peer approach. This decision was – again – motivated by the fact that maintaining a single global repository of running sessions is inappropriate for dynamic distributed infrastructures. Therefore, each session is currently only stored within a single server registry (compare Chapter 9). Most often, this is the server registry of the host the application that requested the flow graph is running on. Another option especially interesting for mobile systems, which requested a large number of processing elements from a stationary systems, is to store the session within the server registry of a stationary system, e.g. the server registry from the host from which the most nodes were requested. Since mobile systems, such as PDAs, typically provide scarce computational resources, this allows to run the session sharing algorithm on more powerful systems (see Section 11.5).

Our current implementation requires that for retrieving a running session, the host that administrates the session has to be queried. As discussed in Section 9.6, the extension of the registry service to include advanced peer-to-peer search strategies in general will also allow to retrieve running sessions in ad-hoc organizations of distributed systems. Section 11.7 will further discuss this topic.

## 11.4 Definition of Overlapped Flow Graphs

If an application sends a graph description $Q$ as query to the registry service, the main idea for the session sharing service is to find overlapping sub-graphs of the current

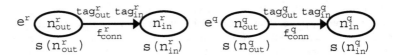

Figure 11.4: An edge $e^r$ of a running flow graph $R$ and an edge $e^q$ of a query $Q$. For both edges, sharing policies, node descriptions, jack tags, and connection formats are shown (see text).

query $Q$ and some already running session $R$. For computing the overlap between two graphs, individual tests for edges $e^q$ of graph description $Q$ and edges $e^r$ of the running session $R$ are performed.

An edge $e^q$ in a graph description marks the connection from node description $n_{out}^q$ to $n_{in}^q$ (see Figure 11.4). Sharing policies are given by $s(n_{out}^q)$ and $s(n_{in}^q)$. Since nodes can have several inputs or outputs, the intended connection has to be further specified by $tag_{out}^q$ and $tag_{in}^q$ for the wanted output and input jack, respectively. In addition, a connection format $f_{conn}^q$ can be associated with an edge. Corresponding definitions exist for $e^r$.

### 11.4.1   Complete Overlap

The edge $e^q$ from node description $n_{out}^q$ to $n_{in}^q$ *completely* overlaps edge $e^r$ from $n_{out}^r$ to $n_{in}^r$, if all of the following criteria hold (tests 1 to 4):

1. The **sharing policy** allows sharing for all node descriptions: $s(n_{out}^q) = s(n_{out}^r) = true$ and $s(n_{in}^q) = s(n_{in}^r) = true$.

2. The **node descriptions** of $e^q$, namely $n_{out}^q$ and $n_{in}^q$, are subsets of $n_{out}^r$ and $n_{in}^r$, respectively (compare Section 9.3.1): $n_{out}^q \subseteq n_{out}^r$ and $n_{in}^q \subseteq n_{in}^r$.

3. Since nodes can have several outputs or inputs, the **tags** specifying outputs and inputs are equal: $tag_{out}^q = tag_{out}^r$ and $tag_{in}^q = tag_{in}^r$. If $tag_{out}^q$ or $tag_{in}^q$ were not specified, the jack tag "default" is chosen.

4. If the **connection format** $f_{conn}^q$ of $e^q$ is specified, it has to be a included in $f_{conn}^r$ (compare Section 7.4.4): $f_{conn}^q \subseteq f_{conn}^r$.

This case is termed *complete overlap*. Test 2 furthermore involves several other tests that were already described in Section 9.3.1. All these tests are only performed if the corresponding information has been specified for node descriptions $n_{out}^q$ or $n_{in}^q$; otherwise a test is assumed to be fulfilled. Notice that particularly the locations set in node descriptions have to be match if specified.

At best, a completely overlapped edge of $R$ can be reused when creating the flow graph for $Q$; no additional resources need to be requested, no setup time is needed. Figure 11.5 illustrates a complete overlap for edges $e^q$ and $e^r$. However, some cases exist, in which such an overlap exists but cannot be used. These cases will be discussed in Section 11.5.

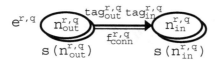

Figure 11.5: Complete overlap of edges $e^q$ and $e^r$ (compare Figure 11.4). Sharing policies, node descriptions, jack tags, and connection formats allow to reuse the edge $e^r$ of a running flow graph $R$ when creating edge $e^q$ of query $Q$.

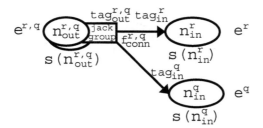

Figure 11.6: Partial copy overlap of edges $e^q$ and $e^r$ (compare Figure 11.4). Sharing policies, node descriptions, jack tags, and connection formats only allow to reuse the *outgoing* parts of edge $e^r$ of a running flow graph $R$ when creating edge $e^q$ of query $Q$. For node description $n_{in}^q$, a node needs to be instantiated. For connecting this node, an additional output jack is created and inserted into the outgoing jack group.

### 11.4.2 Partial Copy Overlap

The edge $e^q$ *partly* overlaps $e^r$, if test 4 is satisfied and tests 1 to 3 are satisfied only for *outgoing* elements, namely $s(n_{out}^q)$, $n_{out}^q$ and $tag_{out}^q$:

1. The **sharing policy** allows sharing for node descriptions: $s(n_{out}^q) = s(n_{out}^r) = true$.

2. The outgoing **node descriptions** of $e^q$, namely $n_{out}^q$, is a subset of $n_{out}^r$: $n_{out}^q \subseteq n_{out}^r$.

3. Since nodes can have several outputs, the **tags** specifying outputs are equal: $tag_{out}^q = tag_{out}^r$. If $tag_{out}^q$ was not specified, the jack tag "default" is chosen.

4. If the **connection format** $f_{conn}^q$ of $e^q$ is specified, it has to be a included in $f_{conn}^r$: $f_{conn}^q \subseteq f_{conn}^r$.

This case is termed *copy overlap*. As can be seen in Figure 11.6, when realizing this case, a copy of the corresponding output jack and an additional connection to the node instantiated for node description $n_{in}^q$ is created. Both jacks are inserted into a jack group. Such a jack group then forwards the data stream to all internal output jacks. Although, jack groups are used for each available output – even if only one output jack is present –, we only depict them if two or more jacks are used (compare Section 7.3.2).

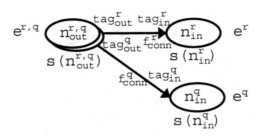

Figure 11.7: Partial output overlap of edges $e^q$ and $e^r$ (compare Figure 11.4). Sharing policies, node descriptions, jack tags, and connection formats only allow to reuse the *outgoing* parts of edge $e^r$ of a running flow graph $R$ when creating edge $e^q$ of query $Q$. For node description $n_{in}^q$, a node needs to be instantiated. This node is connected to a previously unconnected output $tag_{out}^q$ of the node representing $n_{out}^q$ and $n_{out}^r$, respectively.

An example for a partial copy overlap is a session with a shared node for reading from a DVD (DVDReadNode) connected to a shared node for demultiplexing (MPEGDemuxNode) both running on host A. This edge is only partly overlapped by another edge connecting a DVDReadNode on host A to an MPEGDemuxNode on host B because this demultiplexer node should be located on another host. Figure 11.3 shows such a setup.

### 11.4.3   Partial Output Overlap

Another case, in which the edge $e^q$ only *partly* overlaps $e^r$, exists: If tests 1 and 2 for a complete overlap are satisfied – again, only for outgoing elements, namely $s(n_{out}^q)$ and $n_{out}^q$ –, and $tag_{out}^q$ is a valid tag that corresponds to an output jack that is not yet connected.

1. The **sharing policy** allows sharing for node descriptions: $s(n_{out}^q) = s(n_{out}^r) = true$.

2. The outgoing **node descriptions** of $e^q$, namely $n_{out}^q$, is a subset of $n_{out}^r$: $n_{out}^q \subseteq n_{out}^r$.

3. The **tag** that specifies the output $tag_{out}^q$ has to be available for $n_{out}^q$ and $n_{out}^r$, and the corresponding output jack of the node for $n_{out}^r$ is not yet connected.

4. If the **connection format** $f_{conn}^q$ of $e^q$ is specified, it has to be a included in the set of valid formats for output $tag_{out}^q$ of the node for $n_{out}^r$.

This case is termed *output overlap*. Figure 11.7 illustrates this case. An example for this would be a node within a session with one or more unconnected outputs, e.g. an MPEGDemuxNode that provides additional unconnected outputs for all available audio tracks of a stream. In this case, such an unconnected output can be used without any further restrictions within another session. Only a node for node description $n_{in}^q$ needs to be instantiated.

## 11.5   Session Sharing Procedure

First, an overview of the developed approach for session sharing will be given. Then, the individual steps of this procedure will be described in more detail.

### 11.5.1   Overview

The session sharing service performs several independent steps. First, if an application sends a graph description $Q$ to the registry service that includes node descriptions $n$ with a sharing policy that allows sharing (i.e. $s(n) = true$ for some node description $n$), all registered sessions $R_1, \ldots, R_n$ that allow to share resources are tested for sub-graphs that can be overlapped with the flow graph to be created for $Q$. Such an overlapping sub-graph is denoted with $O$.

Since the "value" of an overlapping sub-graph can be specific for an application, during this first step, all possible overlaps for all $R_i$ and $Q$ are computed. In a second step, all found overlaps are valued. This allows different value functions to be applied. For example, the most obvious value function prefers overlapping sub-graphs that provide a large number of shared nodes and edges. Another optimization criterion can be to reduce the number of additionally networking connections needed when creating the flow graph for $Q$.

Furthermore, since the main algorithm for finding overlapping sub-graphs is independent of a specific optimization criterion, a very clear and simple structure can be used. Finally, the valuation of possible solutions also allows to identify invalid overlaps.

As final step, the setup of shared flow graphs is performed. This includes the creation of new processing elements for $Q$ but also the connection of these elements with shared elements provided by the chosen $R_i$. Also, the synchronization for all sink nodes is established in this final step.

### 11.5.2   Finding Overlapping Graphs

The computation of an overlap between two graphs is divided into individual tests for edges $e^q$ of graph description $Q$ and edges $e^r$ of the currently processed running session $R$. For each test, the possible overlap types – namely complete overlap, partial copy overlap, and partial output overlap – are checked (compare Section 11.4).

The session mapping procedure then works as follows. For each running session $R$, all nodes $r_1, \ldots, r_m$ with no incoming edges are identified. These nodes represent the sources of data for a session. Also for the query $Q$, all nodes $q_1, \ldots, q_n$ with no incoming edges are identified. Intuitively, an overlapping between $R$ and $Q$ only makes sense, if at least one partial overlap between an edge leaving some $r_i$ and an edge leaving some $q_j$ can be found. Otherwise, the two different sessions would try to share internal nodes for different sources of data.

Starting from such an initial overlap, the algorithm tries to "expand" overlapping sub-graphs. More precisely, for each $r_i$ and each $q_j$ the algorithm tries to find an overlap by comparing all outgoing edges of $r_i$ with all outgoing edges of $q_j$. The test for a partial copy overlap is performed first since it is a subset of a complete overlap. If the test was successful, the test for a complete overlap is carried out. In any case,

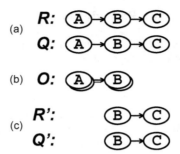

Figure 11.8: One step of the recursive algorithm for finding overlapping sub-graphs. A complete overlap was identified for the first edge of the running session $R$ and the query $Q$ shown in (a). The generated overlap graph $O$ is depicted in (b). For a complete overlap, the shared edge is removed. In (c), the resulting representations $R'$ and $Q'$ for the next step of the recursion are shown.

the test for an partial output overlap is performed in the end. For each successful test, a recursion of a depth-first search is started with sub-graphs $R'$ and $Q'$ of the original graphs $R$ and $Q$, respectively. Furthermore, an overlap graph $O$ is stored for later evaluation.

**Complete Overlaps**

For a complete overlap, the remaining sub-graphs $Q'$ and $R'$ no longer contain the completely overlapped edge. This situation is shown in Figure 11.8. In Figure 11.8(a), the running flow graph $R$ and the query $Q$ are shown. For simplicity, only the node names are provided; all other attributes are not shown. Sharing policies are assumed to allow sharing for all nodes. Therefore, a complete overlap is found within the first iteration of the algorithm and an overlap graph $O$ is created (see Figure 11.8(b)). This graph contains references to the corresponding node description of $R$ and $Q$, and the shared edge in $R$.

In Figure 11.8(c), the generated representations for $R'$ and $Q'$ are shown with the completely overlapped edge removed. These representations are used in the next recursion step. Also, the overlap graph $O$ is passed as argument and tried to be extended. Obviously, in this example, the second and final recursion step will find another complete overlap of the edges between B and C. Therefore, depending on the used value function, the "best" solution could be to completely reuse the running session of $R$ when realizing query $Q$.

**Partial Copy Overlaps and Partial Output Overlaps**

When identifying a partial copy or output overlap, the complete sub-graph starting from the current $q_j$ is removed from $Q$. Intuitively, this reduction of the search space is legal because starting from this point, the graph $Q$ and $R$ continue to "grow" in different directions. Figure 11.9 shows such a situation for a partial copy overlap. Again,

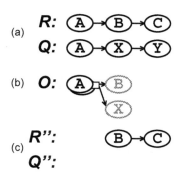

Figure 11.9: One step of the recursive algorithm for finding overlapping sub-graphs. A partial copy overlap was identified for the first edge of the running session $R$ and the query $Q$ shown in (a). The generated overlap graph $O$ including a jack group is depicted in (b). For a partial copy overlap, the complete sub graph of the corresponding edge is removed from $Q$; the shared edge is removed from $R$. In (c), the resulting representations $R''$ and $Q''$ for the next step of the recursion are shown.

in Figure 11.9(a), the running flow graph $R$ and the query $Q$ are shown. However, in this case, the node description for X forbids for a complete overlap to be created in the first iteration. For example, the node description of X is not a subset of the node description of A in the running session. Therefore, a partial copy overlap is found and the corresponding overlap graph $O$ is created (see Figure 11.9(b)). If this solution is finally chosen, a jack group will be used as described in Section 11.4.2.

In Figure 11.9(c), $R''$ and $Q''$ are shown. More precisely, $Q''$ is an empty graph description since the edge from node description A to node description X and the complete following sub-graph were removed. For a partial output overlap, the same process is applied.

**Invalid Overlap Graphs**

Even if a complete overlap exists, the tests for partial overlaps are performed and a recursion is started if they succeeded. On the one hand, computing all possible overlaps allows to apply different value functions. On the other hand, a complete overlap might lead to a "dead end" in the search later on, which results in an invalid solution. This is the case, if no overlap exists for the next edges within the subgraph of $Q$ used in the next step of the recursion.

Figure 11.10 shows such a situation. In Figure 11.10(a), the running flow graph $R$ and the query $Q$ are shown. In this example, connection formats are included, namely X, Y, and Z. Figures 11.10(b.1) and 11.10(b.2) show the result of the first iteration: $O_1$ is the overlap graph for a complete overlap (compare Figure 11.8); $O_2$ is the overlap graph for a partial copy overlap (compare Figure 11.9).

Figures 11.10(c.1) and 11.10(c.2) show the resulting representations for $R'$ and $Q'$, and $R''$ and $Q''$, respectively, to be used in the next recursion steps of the algorithm.

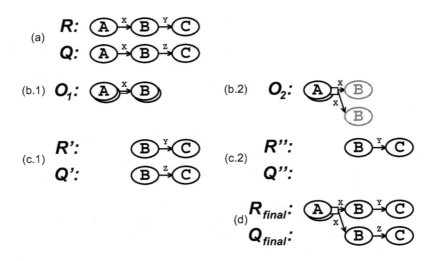

Figure 11.10: An example for an invalid overlap graph. The running session $R$ and the query $Q$ shown in (a) include connection formats. The results of the first step of the recursion for a complete overlap are presented in (b.1) and (c.1) (compare Figure 11.8); the corresponding information for a partial copy overlap is given in (b.2) and (c.2) (compare Figure 11.9). Since format Z is not included in format Y, no further overlap can be found for $R'$ and $Q'$; no connection for node descriptions B and C is possible. Therefore, the corresponding overlap graph $O_1$ is invalid. The only possible solution is shown in (d).

However, since format Z is not included in format Y, no further overlap can be found for $R'$ and $Q'$ shown in Figure 11.10(c.1). Thus, there is no possibility to connect nodes B and C with format Z specified by $Q$ (and $Q'$) : Even if a new instance for C would be created, the output format Z is not available since the shared node B requires format Y. This situation is a "dead end". The previously found complete overlap has "no value" and the corresponding overlap graph $O_1$ is invalid. The only possible solution in this example therefore uses the partial copy overlap and results in a setup shown in Figure 11.10(d).

As can be seen from the above example, the identification of invalid solutions requires to perform a look-ahead and further processing of solutions during the search. Since these operations are difficult to realize within the recursive algorithm, we chose to eliminate invalid solutions during the valuation of solutions. This step is described in more detail in Section 11.5.3.

**Summary and Implementation Issues**

To summarize, the approach used for finding overlapping sub-graphs, Figure 11.11 outlines the structure of the developed recursive algorithm. This algorithm is started using the current running session $R$, the query $Q$, an empty overlap graph $O$, and an empty list of results as parameters.

For simplicity, various details of the current implementation of the algorithm are not shown. For example, since jack tags are unique for a particular node – or its corresponding node description –, at most a single combination of outgoing edges can match. This allows to break the innermost for-loop whenever such a match was found. Furthermore, only for the first recursion step, all combinations or the sources of $R$ and $Q$ have to be tested. In further recursion steps, the predecessors of the currently considered source nodes of $R$ and $Q$ also have to correspond to each other. Intuitively, this means that the search has to "stay" on the previously chosen path.

Finally, since the algorithm performs an exhaustive search at *all* recursion levels, a single solution can be enumerated several times. To avoid further processing in such cases, the list of resulting overlap graphs can be queried before starting a new recursion step. While an exhaustive search is required to allow for a clear separation between the search algorithm and the valuation – i.e. all possible solutions are provided for the chosen value function –, this optimization greatly helps to improve runtime by "cutting" large parts of the search space.

As a further optimization, depending on the used value function, not all possible overlaps are of interest but only those with the largest number of overlapping nodes and edges. If this is the case, the exhaustive algorithm can be modified to operate "greedy". This works as follows. The first step of the recursion is performed as usual, namely all combinations of source nodes of $R$ and $Q$ are tested to find all possible entry points for a further search. Then, the search space is limited by reducing the first for-loop of the algorithm to only consider the first possible source of $Q$ – all other sources of $Q$ will then be considered in further recursion steps. Notice that while this variation of the algorithm will also find the overlap with the maximum number of nodes and edges, not all solutions with less overlapping elements are enumerated in cases when more than a single source is available for $Q$ within a recursion step.

### 11.5.3   Valuation of Solutions

As mentioned above, all different overlaps for $Q$ and the currently considered running session $R_i$ are computed. Furthermore, this step is done for all $R_i$'s of the sharable running sessions $R_1, \ldots, R_n$ administrated by the registry service. Therefore, all computed overlap graphs are finally evaluated, and the "best" solution according to some optimization criterion is chosen. We are currently using a very simple approach that maximizes the number of shared nodes and edges. More precisely, for each complete overlap, the overall value of the current overlap graph is increased by two; for a partial overlap this value in increased by one.

More advanced value functions can include the evaluation of measured quality of service (QoS) requirements needed for nodes and edges that need to be additionally created. Then, an overlap that requires the least additional resources can be chosen. Yet other value functions can prefer overlap graphs that provide a large number of nodes running on a particular host. Such a criterion avoids adding networking connections between connected nodes and is useful in cases where node descriptions of the query do not contain any locations. Then, nodes running on arbitrary hosts will be considered.

As already discussed, the valuation of solutions includes the identification of in-

```
shareSubGraphs(GraphDescription R,
               GraphDescription Q,
               GraphDescription O,
               list<GraphDescription> Results)
{
  Sourced_Q = nodes with no incoming edges in Q;
  Sources_R = nodes with no incoming edges in R;
  for(each node q of Sources_Q) {
    for(each node r of Sources_R) {
      for(each outgoing edge e_q of q) {
        for(each outgoing edge e_r of r) {
          if(copy_overlap(e_r, e_q)) {
            O = create_copy_overlap_graph(O, e_r, e_q);
            Results = Results + O;
            R'' = remove_edge(R, e_r);
            Q'' = remove_sub_graph(Q, e_q);
            shareSubGraphs(R'', Q'', O, Results);
            if(complete_overlap(e_r, e_q)) {
              O = create_complete_overlap_graph(O, e_r, e_q);
              Results = Results + O;
              R' = remove_edge(R, e_r);
              Q' = remove_edge(Q, e_q);
              shareSubGraphs(R', Q', O, Results);
            }
          }
          if(output_overlap(e_r, e_q)) {
            O = create_output_overlap_graph(O, e_r, e_q);
            Results = Results + O;
            R'' = remove_edge(R, e_r);
            Q'' = remove_sub_graph(Q, e_q);
            shareSubGraphs(R'', Q'', O, Results);
          }
        }
      }
    }
  }
}
```

Figure 11.11: Outline of the recursive algorithm for finding overlapping sub-graphs. Several implementation details are not shown but discussed in the text.

valid solutions. There are several cases that have to be considered to determine whether a solution is valid or not. First, a complete overlap only makes sense, if for all following edges, some overlap was found. For example, for a demultiplexer that has a complete overlap at its incoming edge, all outgoing edges need to provide some sort of overlap – otherwise, the complete overlap led to a "dead end" as discussed above. For multiplexers to be shared, all incoming edges of the query need to be available as complete overlaps.

### 11.5.4 Setup of Shared Flow Graphs

The final setup of a session with shared nodes is straight-forward. Both nodes of a completely overlapped edge are referenced in the new session – no additional elements are instantiated. For a partial copy overlap, the output jack is duplicated within the corresponding jack group and then connected to a newly instantiated node. When handling a partial output overlap, the previously unconnected output is connected to a further node to be created. Nodes that cannot be shared at all are requested and connected as usual.

Due to the state machine of NMM nodes presented in Section 7.2.2, when connecting two nodes, the upstream node (i.e. the "left" node) has to be in state OUTPUT_-INITIALIZED and the downstream node (i.e. the "right" node") has to be in state INITIALIZED. This is also true when connecting newly created nodes to a running session. Therefore, there is the possibility that an interruption of media processing and presentation occurs during this step of the session sharing procedure. However, since the dynamic setup of additional connections of a *running* node in state STARTED would require to guard the passing of *each* message with an additional lock, we deliberately did not choose this option to avoid the corresponding decrease in throughput. Chapter 12 will present a further middleware service that allows for the seamless reconfiguration of active flow graphs.

If a suitable synchronizer is already provided by the running session, the controller objects of all synchronized sink nodes are linked to that instance. For realizing inter-stream synchronization, timestamps generated within all connected flow graphs need to refer to the same global time base. Most often, this is the inherent time base of the shared media stream. For example, the shared flow graphs presented in Section 11.6 all refer to the time base of the used MPEG streams. In other cases, such a global time base needs to be established explicitly, e.g. by resetting synchronization parameters. This can be achieved by inserted a syncReset event instream for all partial overlaps. For example, for newly added jacks within a jack groups, this event can be created automatically. In Chapter 12, this topic will be further discussed.

When a running session with shared nodes is destroyed, reference counting avoids deleting shared objects such as nodes or synchronizers.

### 11.5.5 Discussion

As can be seen from Figure 11.11, an exhaustive depth-first search is performed. As discussed before, such an exhaustive search is needed in order to provide all possible solutions for the value function to be applied. For finding the "best" solution, a complete search is therefore required.

In general, the runtime of a depth-first search is $\mathcal{O}(b^m)$ with b being the branching factor and m being the maximum depth of the search tree [RN95]. In our case, the branching factor is given by the four for-loops. More precisely, this factor is determined by the maximum numbers of sources of $R$ and $Q$ (namely $|Sources_{max}^R|$ and $|Sources_{max}^Q|$), and the maximum numbers of outgoing edges of these sources (namely $|E_{max}^r|$ and $|E_{max}^q|$). Since at least a single edge of $Q$ is removed for every recursion, the depth of the search is limited by maximum of the total numbers of edges of $Q$ (namely $|E^Q|$). This results in a runtime of

$$\mathcal{O}((|Sources_{max}^R| * |Sources_{max}^Q| * |E_{max}^r| * |E_{max}^q|)^{|E^Q|}).$$

Furthermore, this runtime needs to be spent for every running session to be considered. Other steps, such as the valuation of flow graphs, are typically linear in the number of edges of overlap graphs.

While the upper bound of the runtime does not seem very promising, the effective measured runtime – and therefore also the number of iterations – is indeed very low, which results in a applicable solution. Several reasons can be identified. First, typical flow graphs only have a very limited number of sources and a small number of overall edges and nodes. For example, the most complex practical relevant flow graphs we have developed employ less than 20 nodes and 20 edges – overlaps contain even less elements.

Second, the number of recursion steps is restricted due to the strict criteria that need to be fulfilled for one of the three different types of overlaps to be applied – the large number of attributes that need to "match" limits the number of found overlaps. In particular, jack tags are unique and need to match, which results in only a single combination of edges to be tested for overlaps. Furthermore, for partial overlaps, complete sub-graphs are removed for the next step of the recursion. Finally, the optimized implementation of the algorithm described above further reduces the number of recursions. Together, this results in a branch-and-cut algorithm with a large number of "cuts" within the search space [BT97].

Even for complex scenarios, the runtime of the complete procedure – i.e. from the point in time where the query is received by the registry to the point in time where all results for a single running session are valued – is below 400 msec. Considering the setup times for distributed flow graphs, we argue that such time values are tolerable – even when multiple running sessions need to be considered. The following section will provide further measurements for several application scenarios.

## 11.6   Results and Applications

The session sharing service described above is fully integrated into the registry service of NMM. Based on these two services, we have realized various application scenarios. All scenarios can be seen as examples for distributed multimedia home entertainment, where a number of users employs various stationary and mobile systems in combination.

In general, a stationary system provides sufficient computational resources to perform a number of typical tasks, such as media playback and transcoding, simultaneously. Furthermore, such a system provides high-quality media output, e.g. via a

| Application Scenario | Step | System PC1 | System PC3 |
|---|---|---|---|
| 100 Negative Tests | Search | 17 | 29 |
| | Valuation | - | - |
| | **Sum** | **17** | **29** |
| Different/Identical DVD Audio Track | Search | 2 | 6 |
| | Valuation | 1 | 1 |
| | **Sum** | **3** | **7** |
| Shared TV | Search | 18 | 45 |
| | Valuation | 1 | 1 |
| | **Sum** | **19** | **46** |
| Additional System Shared TV | Search | 147 | 371 |
| | Valuation | 2 | 3 |
| | **Sum** | **149** | **374** |

Table 11.1: Measured runtimes in milliseconds of the session sharing algorithm itself for two different systems. A detailed description of the used systems PC1 and PC3 can be found in Appendix A.

high-fidelity audio system and a large screen, and offers access to a number of sources of media, e.g. media files are stored on internal hard disks, DVDs or audio CDs are read via internal drives, or PCI boards receive analog or digital TV. We use commodity multimedia PCs running the GNU/Linux operating system for such stationary systems.

Two different types of mobile systems are employed. First, commodity laptop computers are used – again running under GNU/Linux. Compared to stationary PCs, these systems provide less computational resources; no direct access to sources of data, like TV boards or DVD drives might be available. Second, personal digital assistants (PDAs) are employed. We are currently using the model Compaq iPAQ H3870 running under GNU/Linux [End03]. These systems are especially interesting due to their inherent resource restrictions. In particular, only relatively little computational power is available. Memory capacity is also limited. Furthermore, output capabilities are restricted, especially the screen size. Finally, no direct access to special sources of data is available. However, since mobile and stationary systems all provide networking capabilities, e.g. for LAN or WLAN, each system can access and combine the features of all devices available throughout the network using the facilities of NMM.

For the different examples to be described in the following, we first measured the runtimes of the session sharing algorithm itself using two different systems. The results are shown in Table 11.1. More details of the used systems can be found in Appendix A. As discussed in the previous section, the runtimes of the session sharing procedure are measured from the point in time where the query was received by the registry service to the point in time where all results are valued and the "best" result according to above described value function is determined. For all provided examples, we are regarding the exhaustive optimized algorithm as described in the preceding sections; the times for the "greedy" algorithm are obviously smaller. While the measured times increase with the numbers of overlapped edges, they are below 400 msec even for PC3. The measured times show that nearly all of the time is spent within the recursive algorithm for finding overlapping sub-graphs; only very little time is spent during the valuation

| Application Scenario | Session 1 | Setup Time | Session 2 | Network | Setup Time |
|---|---|---|---|---|---|
| Different/Identical DVD Audio Track | PC1 | **2.615** | PC2 | LAN | **0.403** |
| | | | Laptop | LAN | **1.236** |
| | | | Laptop | WLAN | **1.840** |
| | | | PDA | LAN | **approx. 10** |
| | | | PDA | WLAN | **approx. 10** |
| Shared TV | PC1 | **0.748** | PC2 | LAN | **1.455** |
| | | | Laptop | LAN | **2.759** |
| | | | Laptop | WLAN | **4.943** |
| | | | PDA | LAN | **approx. 19** |
| | | | PDA | WLAN | **approx. 20** |
| Application Scenario | Session 2 | Setup Time | Session 3 | Network | Setup Time |
| Additional System Shared TV (Session 1 on PC1) | PC 2 | **1.455** | Laptop | LAN | **3.197** |
| | | | Laptop | WLAN | **4.587** |
| | | | PDA | LAN | **approx. 14** |
| | | | PDA | WLAN | **approx. 15** |

Table 11.2: Measured runtimes in seconds for the complete setup of initially created sessions (session 1) and further sessions (session 2 and session 3). A detailed description of the used systems PC1, PC2, laptop, and PDA can be found in Appendix A.

of solutions. This allows for adding more complex value functions without influencing the overall runtime too much.

We also measured the times needed for testing additional running sessions that do not match the query at all, i.e. no overlapping sub-graphs are found. Testing 100 non-matching sessions takes 17 msec for system PC1 and 29 msec for systems PC3 (see Table 11.1). Both times are negligible.

In addition, we also measured the complete duration of the session sharing procedure for different setups, i.e. the period of time starting with the request of a shared distributed flow graph to the point in time where sessions run as shared sessions. The results are shown in Table 11.2 as *session 2* and *session 3*. In order to evaluate the measured times, we also provide the setup times for the corresponding initially created session, *session 1*. For all setups, this session is chosen to operate completely on system PC1. Therefore, its graph description is stored within the registry of this system. Correspondingly, the session sharing algorithm also runs on this system. Three different systems are used when creating a new request for *session 2*, namely system PC2, laptop, and PDA. For the systems laptop and PDA, either LAN or WLAN is employed. Furthermore, PC1, PC2, and one of the two mobile systems is used for sessions 1, 2, and 3, respectively, as described below.

### 11.6.1 Shared DVD Playback

The application scenario presented in Section 11.1 allows for shared access of the data stream provided by a single DVD. The application controlled by a first user started

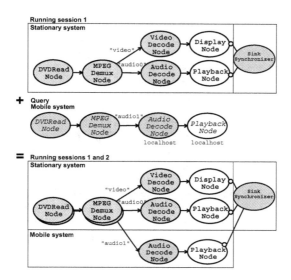

Figure 11.12: Shared DVD access. The running session 1 and the query for a different audio track (i.e. "audio1" instead of "audio0") are mapped to a shared sub-graph that uses a complete overlap and a partial output overlap. While running session 1 operates on a stationary system, running session 2 performs decoding and playback of the audio data on a mobile system. The controllers of all sink nodes are connected to a single sink synchronizer to realize distributed inter-stream synchronization.

DVD playback at a stationary system using the flow graph shown in Figure 11.12 as running session 1. Nodes that allow for shared access are shaded dark. In this example, the application chose to share the nodes required for reading and decoding; sink nodes for rendering audio and video are not shared. This is a typical specification, since applications (and users) will generally allow the sharing of internal processing elements but prefer to have exclusive access to output devices.

Notice that by using the facilities of NMM and its registry service, all processing elements of the running session 1 shown in Figure 11.12 are allowed to operate on different remote hosts. In particular, the source node for reading DVDs can be located on another system than the application.

### Mobile Access to Different Audio Tracks

In order to access a particular audio track, e.g. for a specific language, of the DVD being used in the running session, a second user can start another application on a mobile system that will use a query such as the one shown in Figure 11.12. Here, the mode "exclusive or shared" is set for all node descriptions, except the one for audio playback. Furthermore, to perform decoding and playback on the mobile system, the corresponding node descriptions are specified to run on the local host. In this first example, audio track "audio1" is chosen instead of "audio0".

Figure 11.12 shows the result of the session sharing procedure as running sessions 1 and 2. The DVDReadNode and the MPEGDemuxNode and the connecting edge are shared for the second session (i.e. *complete overlap*), whereas an additional edge was created to connect the second audio output of the MPEGDemuxNode to the newly instantiated nodes AudioDecodeNode and PlaybackNode that are running on the local host (i.e. *partial output overlap* to previously unconnected edge). With this setup, a different audio stream will be rendered on the mobile system.

The sink synchronizer provided by the initial session is used to provide synchronized playback for the complete distributed flow graph. The audio sink of the running session is chosen as master; the video sink of the first running session and the second audio sink of the second session act as slaves (compare Section 7.8.2). If the first few buffers for the second audio sink arrive too late to be presented synchronously with the master sink, they will be discarded. The system running the second session will then need sufficient processing power to "catch up" with the running session 1. However, if multimedia data buffers are enqueued within input jacks of nodes of the running session 1, media presentation within the new sub-graph of the running session 2 will typically have to be delayed.

Using the value function described in Section 11.5.3, the total value of the best solution consisting of a complete overlap and a partial output overlap is three. Table 11.1 and Table 11.2 show the runtimes for this setup. Notice that the time for initially accessing a DVD greatly influences the setup time for session 1. Furthermore, for systems that provide sufficient resources, such as the laptop, the setup time for session 2 increases when using WLAN instead of LAN. Compared to other systems, the PDA requires significantly higher setup times due to its inherent resource restrictions. Therefore, no difference between LAN and WLAN can be determined.

**Mobile Access to Identical Audio Tracks**

The query in Figure 11.12 requests a different audio track than the one used within the running session 1. A situation, in which the application running on the mobile system requests the same audio track, is shown in Figure 11.13. Again, this results in a complete overlap for the edge connecting the DVDReadNode and the MPEGDemuxNode. In this case, however, a partial copy overlap is present for the edge connecting the "audio0" output of the MPEGDemuxNode and the remote AudioDecodeNode running on the mobile system.

Using the value function described in Section 11.5.3, the total value of the best solution consisting of a complete overlap and a partial copy overlap is three. Table 11.1 and Table 11.2 show the runtimes for this setup.

Notice that for both provided examples, an additional MPEGDemuxNode will be instantiated if for some reason, no complete overlap between the DVDReadNode and the MPEGDemuxNode is possible, e.g. because the demultiplexer does not allow sharing.

### 11.6.2 Shared TV Access

Another application scenario realized using the session sharing service allows to watch TV on a stationary system and a mobile system simultaneously. Particularly interesting

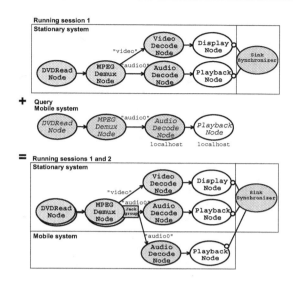

Figure 11.13: Shared DVD access. The running session 1 and the query for the same audio track (i.e. "audio0") are mapped to a shared sub-graph that uses a complete overlap and a partial copy overlap. As for the situation shown in Figure 11.12, the running session 1 operates on a stationary system; running session 2 performs decoding and playback of the audio data on a mobile system. The controllers of all sink nodes are connected to a single sink synchronizer to realize distributed inter-stream synchronization.

is how the adaptation of media streams needed for the mobile system can be included (compare Section 2.3.2).

Figure 11.14 illustrates the setup for this application scenario. The running session 1 started on the stationary system allows to share all nodes except the `PlaybackNode` and the `DisplayNode`. For receiving TV, the `DVBReadNode` is used that provides access to a DVB stream received via satellite; the corresponding MPEG stream is demultiplexed with the `MPEGDemuxNode` (see Section 2.2.3). Again, by using NMM, all nodes of this running session can transparently operate on different distributed systems. For example, the node for receiving DVB is not necessarily located on the stationary system itself.

The query used by the application running on the mobile system uses a complex graph description for adapting media streams to the available processing power and output capabilities. In particular, audio and video are transcoded. Audio is decoded, downsampled to 22050 Hz mono audio using the `AudioConverterNode`, and encoded to MPEG audio again. For video, even more operations are performed. First, the framerate of decoded video is reduced to adapt to the computational resources available at the mobile system. Since the received video stream is provided as half-frames, video is *deinterlaced* using the `VideoDeinterlaceNode` to obtain a single frame from two half-frames [Poy96]. This step is not performed for the stationary system,

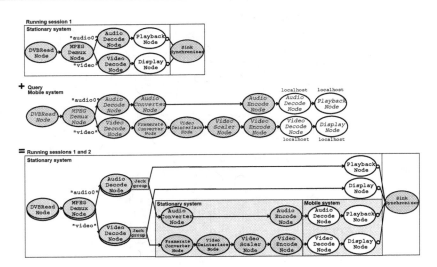

Figure 11.14: Shared TV access. Digital TV is accessed at a stationary system within the running session 1. The query of the mobile system for adapted media streams can reuse four nodes, namely DVBReadNode, MPEGDemuxNode, AudioDecodeNode, and VideoDecodeNode running on the stationary system. Additional requested nodes for media transcoding are instantiated on the stationary system; only decoding and rendering of adapted streams is performed on the mobile system using corresponding nodes. The controllers of all sink nodes are connected to a single sink synchronizer to realize distributed inter-stream synchronization.

since we assume that this system is connected to a TV set that allows to handle interlaced video. In order to further reduce the computational resource required for processing video on the mobile system, the resolution of the video is then downscaled using the VideoScalerNode. This step is also useful, since the mobile system only provides a restricted video resolution of 320 by 240 pixels[1]. Finally, video is reencoded, but this time a codec available for the mobile system is used, e.g. MPEG4. The transcoded audio and video streams are specified to be decoded and rendered on the mobile system using the corresponding nodes. Therefore, only for these node descriptions the locations are set to "localhost".

The result of the session sharing service finds three complete overlaps, namely for the connection between the DVBReadNode and MPEGDemuxNode, and the connection between this demultiplexer and the nodes AudioDecodeNode and VideoDecodeNode running on the stationary system. The outputs of these decoding nodes are then duplicated within jack groups for realizing partial copy overlaps between the flow graph of the running session 1 and the query. All further nodes specified within

---

[1]Notice that the usage of a node for downscaling might avoid the need for a node for deinterlacing. For example, by dropping a half-frame, the video resolution is automatically halved in vertical direction. However, if the original video resolution and the desired video resolution for the PDA are not known in advance, both operations need to be performed.

the query are instantiated and set up. Especially interesting is the fact that the session sharing service allocates all nodes needed for transcoding on the stationary system. This is done since no location was specified for these nodes and the session itself is running on the stationary system. This step could be further optimized by guiding the instantiation of nodes needed for transcoding by evaluating their quality of service (QoS) requirements together with resource availability within the network.

On the mobile system, only the nodes for decoding and rendering audio and video streams are created. The controller objects of sink nodes are then connected to the sink synchronizer of the running session 1 as additional slaves (compare Section 7.8.2). While there is currently still a short interruption during the setup of this complex distributed flow graph (see Section 11.5.4), playback stays synchronized on all participating systems of the running session 1 and 2 later on. In particular, only a few video multimedia buffers are discarded; instead, latencies are updated due to the interruption.

Notice that the application running on the mobile system will both use remote and local nodes within its flow graph, where remote nodes are partly taken from another session. With the current implementation, the iPAQ is able to display up to 15 frames per second with a resolution of 320x240 and 22 kHz mono audio. The overall bitrate transferred to the mobile system is around 500 kbps. While these values are currently determined manually, a future extension of the NMM system will include the dynamic adaptation of these settings.

Using the value function described in Section 11.5.3, the total value of the best solution consisting of three complete overlaps and two partial copy overlaps is eight. Table 11.1 and Table 11.2 show the runtimes for this setup. Again, the provided computational resources of the system used for session 2 and the used network influence the setup times.

### Additional Mobile Systems

A particular advantageous property of the session sharing service is that all created sessions can be shared – initially created sessions but also sessions that were created later and that already use shared resources. For the above described application scenario, this allows further mobile systems to be added without requiring additional resources needed for media adaptation.

This situation is shown in Figure 11.15. The running sessions 1 and 2, which are also shown in Figure 11.14, can be used to satisfy an additional query of a second mobile system. The parts of the graph description of this query needed for media transcoding can be mapped completely to the running session 2; only additional nodes for the decoding and rendering of audio and video streams on the mobile system need to be instantiated for session 3. All three systems are synchronized by using a single synchronizer.

Notice that all three systems are also offered full control of shared nodes, e.g. for changing the TV channel. Future extensions could restrict control to only provide access to some specific interfaces. Also notice that the session for a mobile system can be started first and an application running on the stationary system can join later on. In this case, however, the location for all nodes to not run on the mobile system need to be specified.

Using the value function described in Section 11.5.3, the total value of the best

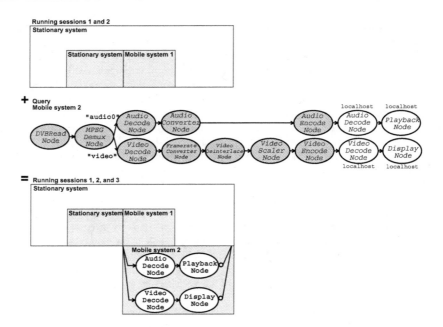

Figure 11.15: Shared TV access for several mobile systems. Digital TV is accessed at a stationary system and a first mobile system within the running session 1 and 2 (compare Figure 11.14). The query of a second mobile system for adapted media streams can reuse the complete flow graph needed for receiving TV and transcoding media streams that is already employed by the running session 2 of the first mobile system. All three systems are synchronized by a single sink synchronizer.

solution consisting of nine complete overlaps and two partial copy overlaps is 20. Table 11.1 and Table 11.2 show the runtimes for this setup. In particular, session 1 is running on PC1 and session 2 on PC2; then, session 3 is added and running on an additional mobile system, e.g. the laptop or the PDA. Notice that while the session sharing procedure adds a certain delay due to the needed runtime of the algorithm, the overall resource consumption of the application is reduced since a large part of the requested flow graph is reused.

Notice that the setup time for session 3 running on the laptop with LAN is higher than that for session 2 running on the laptop. This can be explained as follows. Since the system running session 1, namely PC1, is already highly loaded because it also runs the flow graph needed for transcoding media for session 2, the overall setup time for session 3 is limited by the computational resources of PC1. When using WLAN for the laptop, the additional delay during connection setup is the limiting factor; therefore, the setup time for session 3 is smaller than that for session 2 in this case. For the PDA, setup times are again much higher. However, in this case, session 3 can also be set up faster than session 2 since the resources of the PDA are the limiting factor.

## 11.7 Conclusions and Future Work

In this chapter, session sharing as middleware service for distributed multimedia applications was presented. This service enables collaborative applications, where a number of users accesses the same or similar content using different mobile or stationary systems. Running distributed flow graphs are stored within the registry service as so called sessions. Parts of such flow graphs can be shared within other applications. Based on different criteria for overlapping edges of flow graphs, an algorithm for mapping new requests to already running sessions was presented. Application-specific value functions can be applied to overlapping graphs. Together, the session sharing service eliminates the problem of multiple access to a single multimedia device and reduces the processing requirements when different applications share common tasks. Synchronized distributed rendering and shared control of processing elements further enhances collaboration.

Several application scenarios have demonstrated the benefits and the performance of this service. Further examples will be described in the scope of Chapter 13 and Chapter 15. In Chapter 13, an application for setting up distributed flow graphs from a textual description is presented that allows to directly use the facilities of the session sharing service. In Chapter 15, a networked multimedia home entertainment center is described that uses the session sharing service, e.g. for realizing shared access to a single TV device for a digital video recorder and an application for watching TV.

Several directions for future work were already sketched. Since a session is only stored within the server registry of a single host, advertisement and directed search for running sessions within peer-to-peer networks could be a first extension. This topic is also discussed in Section 9.6.

Also, the criteria for overlaps can be enhanced. First, meta-data such as the played media file or the watched TV channel can also be included. Second, tests for "matching" capabilities of connecting communication channels between two nodes can be performed. Particularly interesting in this context is the support for multicast networking for partial copy overlaps. For example, instead of using two unicast network connections for realizing a partial copy overlap, multicast can be used. This allows to automatically reuse a single networking connection for several connected flow graphs. Such an extension requires to dynamically change network settings from unicast to multicast when first creating such an overlapped connection.

The currently used value function is quite simple. Additional value functions should be created and evaluated. For example, previously measured quality of service (QoS) requirements for different nodes can be used to further guide the process of finding suitable overlapping sub-graphs. Such measurements can also be applied to automatically determine needed adaptations for shared sessions. Furthermore, dynamic adaptations, e.g. for mobile systems accessing streams from DVDs or TV boards, can be included.

The process of setting up shared sessions currently needs to interrupt running sessions in order to connect partial overlapped edges. To avoid large delays, additional care must be taken. The following chapter will present a service for seamless reconfiguration that internally employs the session sharing service.

Finally, for realizing collaborative application scenarios, users need a suitable way for selecting queries and for specifying the set of running sessions to be tested for overlapping sub-graphs. While queries are often fixed for a single task (e.g. "watch TV") and can then be selected manually (e.g. by selecting "TV" from a menu), users might also want to join specific activities performed by other nearby users. For such cases, suitable interaction mechanisms and user interfaces need to be provided. In Section 15.6.2, a first approach for selecting and joining activities within a multimedia home entertainment scenario is described.

# Chapter 12

# Seamless Reconfiguration

Dynamics can be seen as one of the main characteristics of distributed multimedia systems. This is especially due to the ubiquity of stationary and mobile devices on the one hand, and the mobility of users and devices on the other hand. As discussed in Section 4.4.2, in such computing environments, middleware needs to allow multimedia processing to be flexibly distributed across different devices that are currently available in a network while supporting dynamic migration between devices as users move or requirements change.

In this chapter, we present a service that provides dynamic reconfigurations of flow graphs [LRS03a]. In particular, we concentrate on the ability to perform a synchronized, seamless, and continuous handover of entire parts of an active distributed media flow graph. This is demonstrated using a mobile media player that can instantly hand over its audio rendering to nearby stationary systems that have richer I/O capabilities. We will first introduce this application scenario in more detail. In the following, related work is reviewed. The realized service will be described in detail then. The abstractions for specifying intended reconfigurations are discussed. We will show how the session sharing service presented in the preceding chapter can be used to identify and set up additional required processing elements. Then, a protocol for seamless handover of media processing and its implementation based on the generic synchronization architecture of NMM is presented. Different strategies and optimizations are discussed before presenting results and applications of the developed service.

## 12.1 Introduction

Today, there is a strong trend towards mobile and ubiquitous computing. On the one hand, mobile computing devices like personal digital assistants (PDAs), cellular phones, or small audio players enjoy great popularity. Yet, the inherent constraints on size and weight significantly limit the fidelity of multimedia rendering on the devices themselves. On the other hand, we are ever surrounded by a constantly growing number of networked media devices, like video recorders, set-top-boxes, TVs, hi-fi systems, or multimedia PCs. These devices offer high-quality input and output capabilities often together with enough computing power and programmability to perform a variety of multimedia operations. To offer rich multimedia access to mobile users, the Network-Integrated Multimedia Middleware (NMM) as presented so far allows to

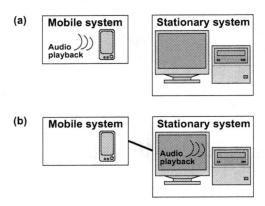

Figure 12.1: Session handover for audio playback. In (a), an application running on the mobile system performs media output on the device itself, e.g. through its internal speakers or earphones. In (b), media output is performed on a nearby stationary system because this systems provides richer I/O capabilities. The application running on the mobile system is given full control of the media output on the stationary system, e.g. for changing the volume.

transparently access remote I/O devices, e.g. in the environment of the user, and to integrate these devices into multimedia processing.

As already discussed in Section 4.4.3, especially interesting are applications that allow to seamlessly employ nearby devices for media rendering. Let us consider, a media playback application running on a PDA playing audio data through its internal speakers or earphones. When the user enters an environment that offers devices with richer I/O capabilities (e.g. the audio system in the living room, car, or office), output should be handed over to these more capable devices. This procedure should be performed with as little delay as possible. In addition, the handover should be *seamless* and *continuous*: no audio data should be lost or duplicated, media playback should be synchronized at all times, and finally media output is performed at the exact same position within the stream using a new device. All these features that are especially important for the playback of music – but also when listening to streamed content, such as a news report received via the Internet. Finally, after the completion of a handover, the application is offered full control again, e.g. for adjusting the volume of the media output. Figure 12.1 shows such an scenario. In (a), audio output is performed locally on a mobile system (e.g. a PDA); in (b), the hi-fi audio system connected to a nearby stationary system (e.g. a PC) is used.

We use the term *session handover* for such a procedure to distinguish it from the term *handoff* that usually describes the functionality of changing network connections. During such a handover, parts of the currently active flow graph for media processing are migrated to another system while the multimedia processing stays synchronized and continuous.

This application scenario is just one example for the need to dynamically adapt an active multimedia flow graph to a changing environment. Other scenarios would be the adaptation to changes in quality of service (QoS) levels by changing compression algorithms or by delegating parts of the media processing to other hosts. This sort of adaption becomes particularly important in a mobile environment where the environment is constantly changing.

Dynamic adaptation of active flow graphs in distributed media processing imposes a number of issues for a general multimedia middleware. In the scope of this chapter, we focus on middleware support for dynamic adaptation of an active flow graph in form of a session handover [LRS03a]. Several requirements have to be addressed for realizing such a service. Abstractions need to be provided for specifying the parts of an active flow graph that need to be reconfigured. Such a specification must be mapped to the active flow graph and required additional processing elements need to be created. For realizing this step, the session sharing service presented in Chapter 11 is used. The middleware must be able to set up alternative routes and synchronize the respective media streams across the network. Finally, seamless handover between these alternatives with little delay and no discontinuities in media processing and presentation needs to be provided. In order to implement this feature, a specialized synchronizer was developed that realizes a handover protocol based on the facilities provided by the generic synchronization architecture described in Section 7.8.

## 12.2   Related Work

Different solutions for mobility support have been proposed for lower layers of the ISO-OSI layering model, like Mobile IP [Per02, Joh95] for the network layer, or TCP Migrate [SB00] for the transport layer (compare Section 2.2.4). These approaches provide mobility transparency for applications but require changes in the existing infrastructures. However, we argue that such functionality is best provided at the middleware layer where it can operate on top of different lower layer protocols.

Different approaches for location-aware multimedia services and multimedia access for mobile users exist. Some solutions concentrate on using mobile devices as unique communication and access interface for other stationary devices in the environment and do not allow migration during runtime [PSG00].

Various sophisticated handoff protocols have been proposed. A proxy architecture for streaming multimedia data with support for handoffs is described in [MSK01]. During handoff, the data streams is temporarily interrupted; caching, prefetching, and retransmission is used to minimize this interruption. In [KG01] a procedure for dynamic handoff of multimedia streams is described that tries to minimize the number of frames that have to be discarded by using a circular buffer. The focus for the work presented in [RSSK02] is the integration of transcoding servers for MPEG into the handoff scheme. While these solutions offer interesting approaches, they do not provide seamless and synchronized handover as defined above but rather try to minimize handoff delays.

As a generalization of a vertical handoff, the ability to move application sessions across different devices is described in [LGGB02]. Other approaches that also allow to access audio and video on nearby stationary devices are presented in [BBE$^+$00] for IEEE 1394 networks and as an OSGi compatible solution in [EB02]. A solution for "follow-you-and-me video" is described in [NT02]. Multimedia service delivery with dynamic handoffs to mobile or stationary devices is also presented [CNX04]. In [RHC02b, RHC$^+$02a], an application framework for so called active environments is proposed that can map running applications between different environments depending on the users position. Similar approaches are presented in [SG02] and [JFW02].

The usage of standard protocols like the Session Initiation Protocol (SIP) [RSC$^+$02] to support mobility is examined in [WS99], but without the aspect of synchronized playback and continuous handoff. The approach described in [KIK$^+$03] uses SIP to realize transfer of streaming services among mobile and stationary systems but only aims at restarting transferred services at the same position within the stream where is was stopped during handoff.

Together, the main disadvantage of these approaches is the lack of synchronized playback during handoff. Furthermore, as some of these approaches use off-the-shelf media players, they are restricted to perform a handoff at one particular position within the overall configuration of processing elements [LGGB02, EB02, CNX04, KIK$^+$03].

The idea of using two simultaneous processing chains for seamless handoff is introduced in [CS02] in the context of media transcoding. This approach provides zero-loss behavior but cannot ensure timely playback during handoff. While the general idea of using simultaneous processing chains is similar to our taken approach, we allow to set up these chains dynamically on different hosts.

Although the main ideas behind all these approaches come very close to our goals, our solution allows the migration of arbitrary sub-parts of an application while ensuring synchronized and continuous playback during the session handoff. According to the above definition we use the term handover for such a procedure. Furthermore, our approach provides suitable abstractions to be used within applications to specify the changes within a flow graph. This new configuration is then mapped automatically to the active flow graph by using the session sharing service described in Chapter 11.

## 12.3 Seamless Handover Procedure

We will first give an overview of the chosen approach. Then, all steps of the seamless reconfiguration procedure are presented in detail.

### 12.3.1 Master-Slave Approach

While Figure 12.1 illustrates our basic application scenario, the underlying used configuration of processing elements is shown in Figure 12.2. The user wants to playback media files stored on a mobile system. If no other system is nearby, the presentation of the media data is performed on the mobile system. In our case, this would be the decoding and playback of encoded audio files. The flow graph for this example consists of three nodes, all running locally in the beginning, but all accessed via proxies and interfaces as described in Part II of this thesis. The ReadfileNode reads the encoded file from the internal memory or a memory card, the AudioDecodeNode decodes the data (e.g. MPEG-audio or Ogg/Vorbis), and the PlaybackNode performs the audio output using the integrated speakers of the mobile system. Notice that the source node can also be transparently located on a remote host, which then allows

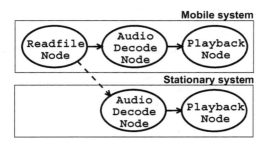

Figure 12.2: Flow graphs for session handover of audio playback. The initially created flow graph for audio playback running on the mobile system – the master graph – is reconfigured to perform media decoding and rendering on a stationary system, e.g. the system nearby the user of the mobile system. The reconfigured sub-graph is called slave graph.

to access files from the file system of that host.

If a stationary system with richer I/O capabilities is nearby, the playback session can be handed over from the mobile system to the stationary system. As discussed in Section 4.4.2, the technology to be used to sense the current location of the user, the used mobile system, and nearby stationary systems is beyond the scope of this thesis – the selection of locations and systems is currently done manually. If the user moves on, the session might get handed over back from the stationary system to the mobile system or from one stationary system to another.

As there are different application scenarios where such a dynamic adaptation of an active flow graph is needed, the basic idea is always the same:

- The new and adapted configuration of the active flow graph is mapped to this running flow graph; additionally needed processing elements are identified and instantiated.

- We configure and start the new parts of the current flow graph while keeping the original media processing running continuously until both are synchronous. The currently active flow graph is called *master graph*; the newly created sub-graph is called *slave graph*.

- Once master and slave graph operate synchronously, processing is switched to the newly created sub-graph and the previously used processing elements of the master graph that are no longer needed are disconnected and released.

Due to the fact that at some time during this procedure, new data connections will be established and other data connections are to be torn down, there is no guarantee that the playback will stay continuous and synchronized. Therefore, the main idea for providing this feature is to setup the slave graph as soon as possible and additionally start streaming data through the slave graph while still streaming data through the master graph. Presentation of multimedia data (e.g. playback of audio) will be done within the master graph only until the slave graph can present data synchronized with the master

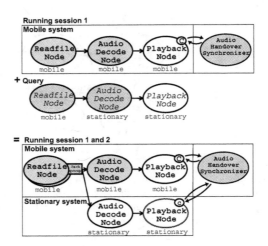

Figure 12.3: The session sharing service described in Chapter 11 maps the reconfig-ured flow graph (slave) specified by the query to the active flow graph of the running session 1 (master). Overlapping sub-graphs are automatically identified and addition-ally needed processing elements are set up and connected. In this example, a partial copy overlap is found for the source node. The nodes for decoding and playback of audio data of the running session 1 cannot be shared since the query specifies these nodes to operate on another host (i.e. "stationary" instead of "mobile"). All sink nodes are connected to the synchronizer of the session.

graph. Then, the presentation within the master graph is stopped and synchronously started within the slave graph.

This synchronized handover might also include the migration of nodes to remote hosts. For our example, this results in the creation of new nodes for decoding and audio output on the stationary system (see Figure 12.2. The decoding can also be performed on the mobile device after a handover to a stationary system is completed. In this case, the required network bandwidth is higher due to the transport of uncompressed audio over the network but the required processing resources on the stationary system are lower. Our approach for synchronized continuous session handover as described below will work with both approaches since it is independent of the distribution of nodes, the usage of media types, or the application of certain network protocols.

While the process described above shows the basic idea of the developed recon-figuration procedure, several issues are not addressed, such as the specification of the intended reconfiguration, the mapping of newly created reconfigured elements to the already running flow graph, and – most importantly – the seamless and synchronized handover of the media processing. The developed approaches are presented in detail in the following.

### 12.3.2 Specification and Setup of the Slave Graph

As described above, in the first step, the reconfigured instance of the currently active flow graph needs to be provided and mapped to the active flow graph. The session sharing service described in Chapter 11 already provides all facilities needed for this step, namely the automatic creation of the slave graph.

All an application has to do, is to create a query in form of a graph description that is first of all a copy of the currently running flow graph. Then, in this copy, all parameters can be reconfigured as wanted: in our example, the node for decoding audio and the sink node are configured to no longer run on the mobile system but on the stationary system (see Figure 12.3). Also, additional nodes can be inserted, or specific configurations of nodes such as used connection formats can be changed.

The query is then forced to be mapped to the active flow graph by specifying the corresponding running session – in form of the NMM interface of type `ISession`. The session sharing service automatically maps the query to the specified running session; additional nodes are created and connected. For our example, the `Readfile-Node` is found to be shared (as it runs on the specified host "mobile"), and the `Audio-DecodeNode` and the `PlaybackNode` are instantiated on the stationary system as set in the query (see Figure 12.3). The output jack of the `ReadfileNode` is duplicated within its jack group and connected to the remote `AudioDecodeNode` (partial copy overlap, see Section 11.4.2). All sink nodes within these shared flow graphs are connected to the synchronizer provided. A special synchronizer, the `AudioHandoverSynchronizer`, described below realizes the handover protocol. The controller of the current master graph is depicted with a `C`; the controller of the slave graph with a `c`.

Together, seen from an application, this abstraction reduces the reconfiguration of active distributed flow graphs to the same interaction mechanisms needed for creating initial instances using the facilities of the registry service.

### 12.3.3 Establishing a Global Time Base

As already discussed in Section 11.5.4, when setting up shared sessions, a single synchronizer can be used. For realizing synchronized processing within all flow graphs of such shared session, a common global time base needs to be established. This means that for corresponding buffers generated within different sub-graphs, corresponding timestamps need to be set. In the easiest case, this time base is given by the inherent timing information of the used data streams, e.g. the timestamps given by an MPEG stream.

However, as can be seen in Figure 12.3, for the running sessions 1 and 2, the only shared node is the source node for reading data from files. A typical implementation of such a component will simply read blocks of data from a file – no timing information is added to the stream. Therefore, the only type of node within our example that sets timestamps for media buffers is the decoder. The establishment of a global time base for the two decoders of the two different sub-graphs is complicated by the fact that typically no inherent timing information is given for compressed audio formats, such as MP3 or Ogg/Vorbis. Therefore, starting from a zero-timestamp, such decoders set the timestamps of outgoing buffers according to the total number of decoded samples.

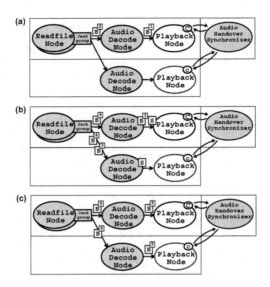

Figure 12.4: Synchronizing media processing within the master and slave graph. The controller of the master is marked with C; the controller of the slave graph with c. While data buffers (marked as B, timestamps as numbers) are flowing in the master graph, remote nodes are setup as shown in (a). In (b), instream events for resetting the synchronization are emitted from the jack group (S for syncReset) before any buffers are sent to the slave graph. Data is flowing in both flow graphs simultaneously in (c).

This process is eased by the use of a matching stream timer object as described in Section 7.8.

In order to establish a global time base between the two decoders running on different hosts, the process of setting timestamps has to be reset once data is streaming through the master and the slave graph simultaneously. To achieve this, the functionality of the jack group is extended to send a syncReset event instream to all its internal output jacks, once a new jack is added dynamically. This event is then handled by nodes of all connected sub-graphs.

This process is shown in Figure 12.4. For illustration purposes, timestamps are also indicated as numbers for buffers B leaving the source node. Furthermore, for simplicity, for a single buffer received by a decoder, a single buffer is generated – an assumption which is typically not fulfilled for decoding compressed media (compare Section 7.7). In Figure 12.4(a), timestamped data buffers are only flowing in the master graph and playback is therefore only performed on the mobile system. The slave graph is already set up on the stationary system as described above. Both controllers are connected to the audio handover synchronizer; the controller of the current master graph is depicted with a C; the controller of the slave graph with a c.

Once the additional connection to the slave graph is set up, the jack group sends an instream event `syncReset` to both of its connected outputs *before* sending any multimedia data to its second output. This instream event will flow downstream as shown in Figure 12.4(b). When reaching a decoder, the generation of timestamps will be restarted to begin from the zero-timestamp again. Within a sink node, this event will force to reset the controller objects that will in turn inform the connected synchronizer object. Notice that due to the fact that the event `syncReset` is sent to all output jacks of the jack group, these operations are performed for the master and the slave graph. Therefore, starting from this moment, the same multimedia data with the same timestamps will arrive at both sink nodes although with different latencies, as the slave graph is running on a remote system.

As described in the scope of Section 7.8, due to the `syncReset` event, the controller objects will send their average latencies to the synchronizer. Since the controller of the sink in the slave graph has so far only received a single data buffer, it will take this latency. The synchronizer will then send the controller of the slave graph the latency as measured in the master graph. The playback within the master graph is not interrupted during handover and therefore the slave graph has to "catch up" with the master graph.

Depending on the used networking technology and protocol and due to the fact that the pipeline of the slave graph has to be filled first (including the delay of the algorithms for decoding multimedia data), the first data buffers might arrive too late at the sink in the slave graph. Therefore, the controller of the slave graph will discard these buffers. This behavior was set by the audio handover synchronizer. Protocols like RTP can further ensure timely delivery of multimedia data over a network, e.g. by dropping buffers *before* they are forwarded to the decoder, but in general our approach is independent of such services. In other cases, there might be sufficient data enqueued within the master graph. Then, the slave graph can instantly catch up.

The next step in the handover procedure can be performed as soon as data in the slave graph arrives "in time" at its sink node. Since the slave graph will discard data that arrives too late, this will always be the case, if the time it takes for one buffer to stream through the complete slave graph is smaller than the time the same buffer will be presented (in our case: the raw audio data will be played back in the master graph). If this is *not* the case, the delay of the slave graph is *always* too large to ensure timely playback, which – in our case – would mean that the processing power provided for the slave graph is not sufficient for timely decoding and playback of the encoded audio data. Of course, such a precondition should be fulfilled.

### 12.3.4 Synchronized Handover

As soon as the first data buffer arrives in time within the slave graph, it could be played back synchronously with the sink node of the master graph (see Figure 12.4(c)). Depending on the behavior specified by the application there are two possibilities: The audio streams in both graphs – the master and slave graph – can be played back *simultaneously* from now on. This is basically the same behavior as used for session sharing in general.

The second possibility is to perform a *complete handover*: the audio playback would then stop within the master graph and start within the slave graph at the same time. To realize a complete handover, the sink node in the slave graph is configured to

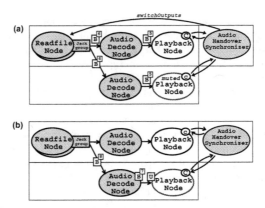

Figure 12.5: Complete Handover using strategy *instream*. In (a), the controller c of the slave graph has caught up with the controller C of the master graph. Therefore, the synchronizer notifies all nodes for which a partial copy overlap was created during the session sharing procedure. As a result of this notification, an instream event U (for "unmute") is sent downstream to the previously muted slave graph. Simultaneously, no more data is sent downstream from the jack group to the master graph. In (b), this event has reached the sink node of the slave graph and media playback is seamlessly stopped in the master – since no more data is received – and started in the slave. The controller of the slave graph is chosen as new master for the distributed synchronization.

not start playback as soon as the first data buffer arrives in time – it is *muted*. Instead, its controller simply sends the measured latency to the synchronizer. The synchronizer in turn concludes that the slave graph has "caught up" playback by comparing this latency with the latency measured in the master graph.

**Instream Strategy for Complete Handover**

Using the *instream strategy* for complete handover, the synchronizer will then notify all nodes for which a partial copy overlap was found during the session sharing procedure. These nodes can be requested from the graph description of the query. For our example, this is only a single node, namely the source node. As can be seen in Figure 12.5(a), the notification is done by calling method switchOutputs of interface ISwitch implemented by GenericNode (compare Section 7.7). Such a notified node then triggers all its jack groups that dynamically created an additional output during the setup of the slave graph. Such a jack group will then insert an instream event unmute into the outgoing data stream to the slave graph. This event is shown as U in Figure 12.5(b). From this moment, the jack group will also stop sending data to its first output, namely the output that is connected to the master graph. This is due to the fact, the the playback within the master graph will be stopped anyway, so no more multimedia data needs to be processed.

Upon receiving the unmute-event, the sink node in the slave graph will start play-

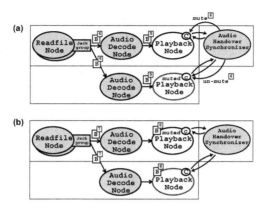

Figure 12.6: Complete Handover using strategy *out-of-band*. In (a), the controller c of the slave graph has caught up with the controller C of the master graph. Therefore, the synchronizer notifies the controller of the master graph to "mute" playback and the controller of the slave graph to "un-mute". For both these operations to be performed simultaneously, an additional timestamp is given starting from which this changed configuration should take place. This timestamp is estimated from the maximum delay needed for a method call between synchronizer and connected controllers. In (b), media playback is seamlessly stopped in the master and started in the slave because the corresponding buffer is processed. The controller of the slave graph is chosen as new master for the distributed synchronization.

back with the *first* data buffer that was *not* sent to the master graph. Due to the fact that master and slave graph are already running synchronously at that time, this handover is seamless – audio playback starts at the slave when it stops at the master. Section 12.4 will provide some measured results. The application can be registered as listener for the unmute-event event to occur at the sink node and can then destroy the master graph.

**Out-of-band Strategy for Complete Handover**

Another realization of this last step – called *out-of-band strategy* – lets the synchronizer directly "un-mute" playback in the slave graph respectively "mute" playback in the master graph. This is done by estimating the maximum delay it takes to send a message to the two corresponding controllers. Due to the global clock, this value can be estimated by half the time a method call from synchronizer to the controller takes. The method calls setBuffersInvalidTimed(true) for "mute" and setBuffers-InvalidTimed(false) for "un-mute" invoked on the corresponding controller objects additionally hold a timestamp that refers to the execution time of the respective commands (see Figure 12.6(a)). This timestamp is evaluated for the timestamp of every buffer passed to the controller of the specific sink node. For example, buffers that arrive "later" at the sink of the master than the given timestamp are simply discarded.

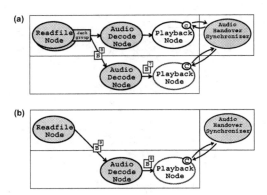

Figure 12.7: Destruction of the (former) master graph (compare Figure 12.5). The corresponding controller is unlinked from the synchronizer. Nodes that are no longer needed are destroyed.

The application can simply wait until this timestamp has passed and then destroy the master graph.

An additional property of this second approach for performing a complete handover is that it allows to specify an interval in which both master and slave graph perform media playback simultaneously before the master graph is muted. This can be achieved by sending a large timestamp, e.g. a timestamp that lies several seconds "in the future", to the master graph.

We found both approaches to be similarly efficient. While the first method takes additional time for the instream event unmute to be passed from source to sink, the time estimated for a single method call currently also includes an additional interval for security reasons.

Also notice that at the end of this step of the handover process, the controller of the slave graph is chosen as new master for the distributed synchronization. This is depicted with a C in Figure 12.5 and Figure 12.6.

### 12.3.5 Destruction of the Master Graph

As a final step during the handover procedure, the master graph is destroyed. First, the controller of its sink node is unlinked from the synchronizer, then the complete graph is released. As described in Section 11.5.4, for all nodes a reference counter is decreased. Nodes with a reference counter of zero are destroyed. These steps are already provided by the session sharing service and the registry service.

For our example, the destruction of the master graph is shown in Figure 12.7 for the complete handover presented in Figure 12.5. Finally, the slave graph is chosen as new master graph.

### 12.3.6 Extensions and Optimizations

The main drawback of the handover procedure as described so far is that there is still the possibility that during the setup of the slave graph the media processing in the master graph is interrupted. This is because of two different reasons. First, shared nodes within the master graph need to be interrupted when connecting them to the nodes of the slave graph. In our example, the source node needs to be brought to state OUTPUT_INITIALIZED when connecting it to the remote decoder, which is in state INITIALIZED (compare Section 7.2.2). Only after this connection is made, the source node can be restarted again. The pausing of media processing during the setup of partially overlapped connection cannot be removed. However, as all other nodes in the master graph are in state STARTED and therefore keep processing data, this step will only lead to interruptions in media playback when sufficient data is not enqueued in the master graph to compensate for this delay. For the special case of handover of audio playback, we found this operation to be implemented sufficiently efficient even when only little data is enqueued within the master graph, i.e. even when using queue sizes of one and very small buffer sizes for reading data from the current file (see Section 12.4.2).

The second reason for an interruption during the creation of the slave graph is weightier. Due to the self-regulation of downstream traffic via blocking message queues, media processing of a single node – and therefore also the generation of outgoing buffers – is only triggered, when the queues of *all* connected nodes are not blocked. This process is further described in Section 7.7. For our example, this means that the source node will only generate further outgoing data buffers, if the incoming queue of the decoder in the master graph *and* the incoming queue of the corresponding decoder in the slave graph are not blocked.

However, since flow graphs are recursively connected from "left" to "right" (i.e. from upstream direction to downstream direction), the initial setup of the complete slave graph might take too long, and therefore, the source node might be not generate enough buffers for the master graph to be filled. This results in an interruption of audio output in the master graph. Although this situation does not occur for simple flow graphs as used in our example, different approaches can be used to avoid this problem in general.

#### Realization of Handover Slave Graphs

For the specific reconfiguration of a handover, it can be observed that the slave graph is a "copy" of the master graph. This means that the overall structure of master and slave graph are identical in terms of used nodes and connection formats; only the locations of nodes are different. In such cases, all non-shared parts of the slave graph can be setup and connected in advance by using the information given by the master graph. In particular, nodes in this sub-part of the slave graph can be forced to be connected using the formats given by the master graph. Since this operation bypasses the usual initialization of the output jacks and output formats of nodes, a specific method needs to be used, namely getUninitializedOutputJack of interface INode.

In a second step, all connections between shared nodes of the master graph and the already configured parts of the slave graph are set up. This step only involves the inherent interruptions of shared nodes of the master graph as discussed above. Together, this strategy is realized in the method `realizeHandoverGraph` of class `Graph-Description` and can be called instead of method `realizeGraph`. For accessing the connection formats of the master graph, this method additionally requires the graph description of the master graph as argument.

### Realization of Arbitrary Slave Graphs

For realizing arbitrary slave graphs, a solution for avoiding the interruption of the processing of shared nodes in the master graph is to temporarily increase the incoming queue sizes of newly created nodes of the slave graph that are to be connected to the master graph. In our example, this strategy would increase the incoming queue size of the remote decoder.

However, for efficiently realizing this strategy, several issues have to be addressed. First, since the slave graph will have to catch up with the master graph, it will have to process (e.g. decode) all buffered messages. Therefore, an optimized implementation of this approach will drop selected enqueued messages, i.e. all messages that *will* receive too late at the sink node of the slave graph since the setup process took too long. To realize this step, the synchronizer can use the first measured latency of the slave graph $l_s$, which includes the setup time, and the current latency of the master graph $l_m$ to determine the offset between master and slave. Since the first timestamp received in the master respectively slave graph after the connection setup will be the zero-timestamp due to the previously sent `syncReset` event, the slave graph then is allowed to skip all buffers with timestamp $t < l_s - l_m$. Using an instream event sent *upstream* from the sink of the slave graph to the jack groups of partial overlapped nodes, buffers that are "too old" can be flushed before being processed by the synchronization mechanisms.

A second issue that needs to be addressed is which queues should be temporarily increased and to what extend this should be done. For example, by increasing the queue size of a *remote* processing element, all messages are first sent over a network connection – even those message that are later discarded as described above. By using an outgoing queue within the jack group, this can be avoided. Furthermore, for more complex flow graphs the location of queueing elements should be guided by the amount of "time per byte" they provide. This means that queues holding compressed data allow to enqueue the same amount of "time" using less memory. Finally, the overall size of an incoming queue can be restricted to the maximum number of iterations needed for analyzing the corresponding output formats as described in Section 7.7.5. While a decoder might require tens of buffers for this step, a simple converter can determine its output format from a single buffer. However, the limitation of incoming queue sizes requires to use a non-blocking queueing strategy such as `MODE_KEEP_OLDEST` (compare Section 7.3.1) and the flushing of all queues in downstream direction before a continuous stream of data can be received again.

### 12.3.7  Discussion

The service for seamless reconfiguration as presented so far does not provide migration transparency for processing element (compare Section 3.2.3 and Section 4.4.2). More precisely, in the end of a complete handover process, all interfaces of all non-shard processing elements of the master graph become invalid since the corresponding node objects were destroyed. However, as will be shown in the following section, since the reconfiguration process is using graph descriptions as abstractions, the graph description of the slave graph can be used as "new" master graph that provides full access to all used processing elements.

Furthermore, as a future extension, migration transparency for NMM objects can be realized easily by updating the used communication channel between proxy object and NMM object. This will allow to add an higher-level service on top of the current facilities.

## 12.4  Results and Applications

In this section, we will first provide more details on the programming model provided by the service for seamless and synchronized reconfiguration. In particular, the source code of a concrete application is presented – an audio player for MP3 files that allows to hand over parts of a running flow graph to remote devices. This application directly realizes the scenario described throughout this chapter and will demonstrate the provided abstractions and benefits of the developed service. Then, the performance of the handover process will be evaluated using different configurations.

### 12.4.1  Programming Model

As described above, for an application developer, seamless reconfiguration is reduced to creating a master graph and a reconfigured slave graph.

#### Master Graph

As a first step, the master graph is created. This step uses the facilities of the registry service. The nodes for reading and decoding data are set to be requested exclusively and shared then (compare Section 11.3). The synchronizer object to be used is specified as `AudioHandoverSynchronizer`. Then, the graph is requested and a reference to the corresponding session is saved for later usage. Finally, the file to be read is specified using the corresponding interface of the source node, and the master graph is set up and started:

```
// create master graph description
GraphDescription* master = new GraphDescription();

NodeDescription readfile_master("GenericReadNode");
NodeDescription mp3dec_master("MPEGAudioDecodeNode");
NodeDescription audioplay_master("PlaybackNode");

readfile_master.setSharingType(NodeDescription::
   EXCLUSIVE_THEN_SHARED);
mp3dec_master.setSharingType(NodeDescription::
   EXCLUSIVE_THEN_SHARED);

master->addEdges(&readfile_master, &mp3dec_master,
```

```
  &audioplay_master);

// specify object description of synchronizer
master->setSinkSynchronizerDescription(ObjectDescription(
  "AudioHandoverSynchronizer"));

// request master graph description from registry
ISession_var master_session(registry.requestGraph(*master));

// set file to be read using corresponding interface
INode* readfile_node = master->getINode(readfile_master);
IFileHandler_var filehandler(readfile_node->getParentObject()
  ->getCheckedInterface<IFileHandler>());
filehandler->setFilename(filename);

// setup master graph
master->connectSinkSynchronizer();
master->realizeGraph();
master->activateGraph();
master->startGraph();
```

**Slave Graph and Seamless Handover**

For realizing a handover, first, the graph description for the slave graph is created. For this example, the source node of the master graph should be reused. Therefore, its sharing policy needs to be specified as SHARED (compare Section 11.3). Furthermore, the reconfiguration sets the location of the decoder and sink node to a remote host. As mentioned before, other reconfigurations, such as including additional nodes, are also possible.

```
// create slave graph description
GraphDescription slave = new GraphDescription();
NodeDescription readfile_slave("GenericReadNode");
NodeDescription mp3dec_slave("MPEGAudioDecodeNode");
NodeDescription audioplay_slave("PlaybackNode");

readfile_slave.setSharingType(NodeDescription::SHARED);
mp3dec_slave.setSharingType(NodeDescription::
  EXCLUSIVE_THEN_SHARED);

// decoder and sink node should run on a remote host
mp3dec_slave.setLocation(remote_host);
audioplay_slave.setLocation(remote_host);

slave->addEdges(&readfile_slave, &mp3dec_slave,
  &audioplay_slave);
```

For guiding the session sharing service, the graph description is set to be mapped to the running session of the master graph. The slave graph is requested from the registry service. Since the sharing policy of the source node was set to SHARED and an additional running session was specified, the session sharing service is automatically queried in this step.

```
// use the session of the master in session sharing service
slave->setISession(*(master->getISession()));

// request slave graph
ISession_var slave_session(registry.requestGraph2(*slave));

// END OF STEP ''Request'' (see below)
```

Then, all partial overlapped nodes are requested and added to the handover synchronizer. This is only needed, if the complete handover strategy *instream* is used (see Section 12.3.4).

```
// get list of nodes that now have an additional shared
// connection (e.g. a new jack within a jack group)
list<INode*> switch_nodes =
  slave->getPartialOverlappedNodes();
for(list<INode*>::iterator i = switch_nodes.begin();
    i != switch_nodes.end(); ++i) {
  ISwitch_var switcher(switch_nodes.front()->getParentObject()
     ->getCheckedInterface<ISwitch>());
  sync->addSwitch(switcher.get());
}
```

Finally, the slave graph is set up and started – the handover process is performed.

```
// setup synchronization for slave graph
slave->connectSinkSynchronizer();
slave->realizeGraph();
slave->activateGraph();
slave->startGraph();
// END OF STEP ''Connect'' (see below)
```

As described in Section 12.3.4, when using the strategy *instream*, the termination of the handover process can be determined by registering as listener for the "un-mute" event. Then, the master graph is disconnected from the synchronizer and released, and the slave graph is set as new master.

```
// remove master from synchronizer
master->disconnectSinkSynchronizer();
registry.releaseGraph(*master);

// make slave the new master
delete master;
master = slave;
```

### Discussion

As can be seen from the above provided source code, many steps of the handover process could still be "hidden" inside higher-level components. In particular, the determination of partial overlapped nodes, the setup of the slave graph, and the final change of the reference to the master graph could be integrated into such a component. Such a higher-level service could also provide migration transparency for processing elements as discussed in Section 12.3.7. However, the above shown example clearly demonstrates the general programming model of the developed service.

| System 1 | PC1 | Laptop | Laptop | PDA | PDA |
| System 2 | PC2 | PC2 | PC2 | PC2 | PC2 |
| Network | LAN | LAN | WLAN | LAN | WLAN |
|---|---|---|---|---|---|
| Request | 0.050 | 0.094 | 0.191 | 1.829 | 1.917 |
| Connect | 0.178 | 0.269 | 0.759 | 4.777 | 4.958 |
| Synch'ed | 0.002 | 0.003 | 0.087 | 0.191 | 0.326 |
| **Sum 1** | **0.230** | **0.366** | **1.037** | **6.797** | **7.201** |
| Complete | 0.050 | 0.052 | 0.052 | 1.515 | 1.588 |
| **Sum 2** | **0.280** | **0.418** | **1.089** | **8.312** | **8.789** |
| Request | 0.039 | 0.133 | 0.154 | 1.469 | 1.515 |
| Connect | 0.104 | 0.277 | 0.287 | 1.696 | 1.706 |
| Synch'ed | 0.002 | 0.003 | 0.028 | 0.074 | 0.083 |
| **Sum 1** | **0.145** | **0.413** | **0.469** | **3.239** | **3.304** |
| Complete | 0.005 | 0.005 | 0.013 | 0.232 | 0.300 |
| **Sum 2** | **0.150** | **0.418** | **0.482** | **3.471** | **3.604** |

Table 12.1: Measured times in seconds for a complete handover from system 1 to system 2 and back for the five different configurations described. The application is running on the system 1; a registry server on system 2.

## 12.4.2  Performance

The synchronized continuous handover procedure is implemented as part of the NMM architecture. Five different setups are evaluated in the following. In all cases, the application is running on *system 1* and a registry server is started on *system 2* (see Section 9.4). Two complete handover processes are measured, first from system 1 to system 2, then back to system 1. For being able to evaluate the performance of the handover procedure itself, we use the TCP protocol for establishing instream bindings in all cases.

Table 12.1 summarizes our measurements for five different scenarios. A detailed specification of the systems used can be found in Appendix A. For all entries, we computed average values for a large number of tries. "Request" measures the time for requesting the slave graph using the session sharing service within the registry service. The entry "Connect" refers to the setup of the slave graph, i.e. the second connection of the jack group of the source node is created. Notice that the steps "Request" and "Connect" are also labelled in the above provided source code. The entry "Synch'ed" means, that the first buffer arrived in time at the sink node of the slave graph. From that moment, playback can be performed simultaneously and synchronized for both sub-graphs. The next row shows the sum of the former two rows. The entry "Complete" refers to the additional time until the end of a complete handover, where the audio sink in the master graph is muted and playback is only performed in the slave graph. The last row sums the total time elapsed until this moment. The following lines show the same measurements for a complete handover from system 2 back to system 1. In general, these values are smaller, since newly created nodes are instantiated and connected locally.

The differences in timing between the setups using the PDA and all other setups

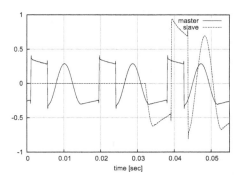

Figure 12.8: Recordings of the audio outputs of master and slave system, respectively. Depending on the synchronization of the clocks of the two systems involved, the offset during the handover process between master graph and slave graph is in the range one to two milliseconds. For demonstrating this, a concatenation of a sine and a rectangle curve is used and the recorded output of the master system is amplified; no complete handover is performed.

are due to the fact that the PDA offers much less resources than a PC, e.g. CPU power and memory bandwidth. For systems that provide sufficient computational resources, the usage of WLAN results in an increase of measured times since establishing new connection incurs higher latencies in wireless networks.

Together, even with our current non-optimized implementation, we think that the results are quite promising; especially, since this handover procedure is realized as high-level interaction within a multimedia middleware solution. Finally, we argue that these delays are much more tolerable since the media playback stays continuous and synchronized all the time. While setups using a PDA certainly require to use fine-tuned parameters, e.g. for queue sizes of NMM processing elements and networking buffers of transport strategies, all other setups work similarly efficient for arbitrary configurations.

For measuring a possible offset between the two audio streams during handover, we recorded the audio output of the two systems involved: from both systems, we recorded the same stereo channel as the left respectively the right channel of the stereo input of a third system. Figure 12.8 shows this recording for the simultaneous handover (case 1 in Section 12.3.4) in the moment when playback starts at the slave system. We chose a concatenation of a sine and a rectangle curve and amplified the output of the slave system for illustration purposes. We found that the offset between the two streams typically is in the range of one to two milliseconds – if clocks are synchronized sufficiently by NTP (compare Section 7.8). We argue that considering the acoustic velocity, this offset is not noticeable to human listeners when performing a *complete* handover, i.e. when audio output is stopped at the master system and started at the slave system.

## 12.5   Conclusions and Future Work

In this chapter, a service that allows for the seamless and synchronized reconfiguration of active distributed flow graphs was presented. We focussed on the handover of audio presentation as one of the most synchronization sensitive parts of media processing. The presented approach, however, is generally applicable to a larger variety of dynamic changes of active flow graphs. As a middleware service, the approach is independent of chosen media formats or networking technologies. In particular it can also be used to implement the vertical handoff procedures required for switching between different network technologies or input streams.

In general, the developed service uses a master-slave approach. While the original flow graph – the master graph – keeps running, a second reconfigured instance – the slave graph – is set up and started in parallel. Therefore, for specifying reconfigurations, the same abstractions as for creating initial instances can be used. The session sharing service identifies common parts of master and slave graph – only additionally needed processing elements are requested and set up. Once a global time base is established for the flow graphs operating in parallel, a handover protocol realizes the synchronous change of configurations. Media rendering stays continuous and is not interrupted.

The demonstrated programming model of the service and the evaluation of its performance have shown that even such a high-level service can be provided efficiently. In the scope of Chapter 15, an application is described that uses this service to realize location-dependent audio playback for users of mobile systems.

In Section 3.2.3, the support for transparency was identified as one of the key requirements for distributed systems. While network transparency or migration transparency, are well-understood in the area of distributed systems, the service presented in this chapter can be seen as one step towards *reconfiguration transparency* – the seamless provision of a service in dynamic, heterogeneous, and distributed environments. In order to seamlessly provide a certain service, middleware needs to provide high-level abstractions combined with automatic mechanisms that guide the reconfiguration process.

In general, reconfiguration can be required for several reasons. Location-dependent media playback is only one example. Other scenarios include changes in resource availability – for example, additional application requests need to be evenly distributed to existing computational resources, or, network bandwidth needs to be shared among a growing number of users.

When handling multimedia, seamless service provision especially requires continuous media processing during the reconfiguration phase. Therefore, the approach presented in this chapter can be seen as an essential facility for future work. In particular, the extension of the handover procedure for combined audio/video rendering should be easy to realize. It is also interesting to extend the controller-synchronizer approach to a hierarchy of synchronizers where each level of synchronizers is responsible for only certain aspects and operates within the constraints imposed by higher-level synchronizers.

The reconfigurations available so far are restricted to certain structures of flow graphs supported by the session sharing service. However, arbitrary reconfigurations, such as the change of internal parts or the sources of a flow graph, should also be possible. Different algorithms for finding overlapping sub-graphs need to be developed for these cases.

Finally, the automatic creation of distributed flow graphs and the quality-driven format negotiation presented in Chapter 10 can be used to further ease the specification of alternative configurations. Especially interesting in this context is the usage of quality of service (QoS) measurements for guiding the process of the initial setup of a flow graph and its later reconfiguration.

# Part IV

# Applications

# Chapter 13

# Clic – Command Line Interaction and Configuration

The development of distributed multimedia applications is greatly simplified by the facilities provided by NMM. In order to further ease the testing and setup of distributed application scenarios, we additionally developed a tool called *clic* (command line interaction and configuration) [RL04]. This tools allows to create and configure a distributed flow graph from a textual description.

In the following, the features provided by clic will be described. Then, a case study for using clic for setting up a video wall is presented that will demonstrate most of the available features. This will show that even complex scenarios that require advanced services, such as the session sharing service of NMM, can be realized efficiently using clic. Finally, we will draw conclusions and discuss some possible extensions of the developed tool.

## 13.1   Overview

For specifying the distributed flow graph to be set up by clic, two possibilities exist. First, for automatically setting up a distributed flow graph from a given URL, the graph URL objects presented in Section 10.4.1 can be used by providing the corresponding string including additional parameters available for the given URL. Then, clic uses the facilities of the graph building service that automatically creates and configures a distributed flow graph for rendering the audio and video streams provided by the specified source of data. This step is discussed in detail in the scope of Chapter 10.

Second, more complex setups can be created manually by providing a textual description that corresponds to a graph description as presented in Section 9.3.1. Such a description is provided in a *.gd* file. The syntax of .gd files is presented exemplarily in the following section; more information can be found in [RL04]. A provided file is parsed and a corresponding graph description object is generated; then the specified flow graph is requested, configured, and started.

One of the great benefits of clic is that is allows to define nearly all aspects of a distributed flow graph with a simple syntax that is consistent with the commands and interfaces to be used when developing with NMM. In particular, following features are available:

- Complex distributed flow graphs using several demultiplexing nodes and a single multiplexing node can be specified. Nodes and connecting jacks are defined by strings, i.e. for the node name and the jack tag.

- Connection formats can be precisely defined for all connecting edges.

- Distributed flow graphs can be specified by providing locations for used nodes.

- Distributed inter-stream synchronization can be automatically set up.

- The session sharing service can be used by defining the sharing policy for nodes.

- For each node in the flow graph, methods of NMM interfaces can be specified to be executed in a certain state of the corresponding node.

- Finally, communication channels can be configured, e.g. by selecting transport strategies for out-of-band and instream bindings.

Together, the available features allow to precisely set up the intended configuration of the distributed flow graph. In addition, the session sharing service can be used, which allows to easily create shared application setups by running clic using different .gd files.

The facilities provided by the unified messaging system of NMM greatly eased to implement support for many of these features. For example, a method to be called for a node is given by a string within the .gd file. By requesting an event prototype for dispatching the specified method, additional given parameters can be converted in a type-safe manner. While this step is currently restricted to basic data types, complex data types can also be supported, e.g. by providing specific input value streams that allow to handle string representations of types such as lists.

## 13.2   Case Study – Video Wall

This section describes how to set up a video wall based on commodity PC technology using NMM [Loh04b]. In particular, this demonstrates how the creation of complex distributed multimedia scenarios can be eased by using the clic.

A video wall consists of several video screens, such as TVs, CRT monitors, or LCDs, that are placed on top of each other or side by side. Each of the available screens only shows the section of a video frame that corresponds to its position within the array of screens. Therefore, a video frame – or each frame of a video stream – to be rendered is split into different sections. This allows to use the overall screen size of all available display devices to create a large screen.

Figure 13.1 shows the setup of a video wall consisting of three systems[1]. Two systems, the "clients", offer a single video output each that is connected to a screen. The video stream is provided by a third system that also performs the audio output.

Together, a video wall is a complex distributed multimedia application that requires inter-stream synchronization. More precisely, all parts of a video frame have to be rendered synchronously on all used client systems. Furthermore, lip-synchronization between audio and video needs to be provided.

---

[1]A video showing such a video wall is available online at http://www.networkmultimedia.org/Gallery/

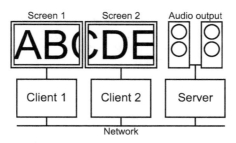

Figure 13.1: A video wall consisting of three systems. Two clients are used to render the sections of a video stream. A cropped section for a particular client corresponds to the position of its connected screen. A server provides the video stream and performs audio output via connected speakers. Inter-stream synchronization needs to be provided for all media rendering.

Instead of using an application running on the server and another specific application running on *each* client system, using NMM only a single main application is needed – the tool clic together with a corresponding graph description file. Therefore, the following discussion also demonstrates the benefits of using distributed flow graphs that transparently provide fine-grained access to distributed resources.

### 13.2.1  Two-Screen Video Wall

The following shows the file dist_video_wall.gd to be used for the above described video wall consisting of three systems.

```
DVDReadNode
$ select(1, 1, 1) OUTPUT_INITIALIZED
! MPEGDemuxNode
{
  { ["ac3_audio0"]  ! AC3DecodeNode
                    ! PlaybackNode
  }
  { ["mpeg_video0"] ! MPEGVideoDecodeNode
                    # setLocation("client1")
                    ! VideoCropNode
                    # setLocation("client1")
                    $ setCrop(0,0,384,288) INITIALIZED
                    ! XDisplayNode
                    # setLocation("client1")
                    $ setFullscreen(1) ACTIVATED
  }
  { ["mpeg_video0"] ! MPEGVideoDecodeNode
                    # setLocation("client2")
                    ! VideoCropNode
```

```
                              # setLocation("client2")
                              $ setCrop(384,0,384,288) INITIALIZED
                            ! XDisplayNode
                              # setLocation("client2")
                              $ setFullscreen(1) ACTIVATED
    }
}
```

As can be seen from this example, a very simple and intuitive syntax is used. Connections between nodes are denoted with a " ! "; different branches within a flow graph are enclosed in "{" and "}". For configuring the descriptions of nodes to be requested, a "#" followed by the property to be set is used; for methods to be called on implemented interfaces during runtime, a "$" followed by the method and the state of the node, in which the method is to be executed, has to be written. For specifying settings that correspond to the edges between nodes, a "@" is used. This allows to define connection formats or transport strategies. While these options are not used in the following, examples can be found in [RL04].

Since the NMM serverregistry is running as a daemon on the server and the clients, these systems together provide a peer-to-peer NMM network. When using clic together with the above graph description file, following command needs to be executed on system "server" in order start the video wall:

```
server> ./clic dist_video_wall.gd
```

The general idea of this setup is to provide the compressed video stream of a DVD to all connected clients, namely "client1" and "client2". Each client decodes the stream. Every decoded video frame is then "cropped" to the configured size. More precisely, data is read from a DVD inserted locally into the DVD drive of system "server". The "select" method allows to choose the title, chapter, and angle of the DVD. The stream read from the DVD is demultiplexed. The first AC3 audio stream "ac3_audio0" is decoded and played out on the local system. The first MPEG video stream "mpeg_video0" is decoded, cropped, and rendered on both client systems. On the first client, only the left part of the video stream is shown, namely a region of 384 pixels width and 288 pixels height starting from (0,0). On the second client system, the adjacent region is shown starting from (384,0). For both clients, video output is performed in fullscreen mode.

### 13.2.2   Two-Screen Video Wall with Overview on Third Screen

The above presented graph description can be used as starting point for further configurations. For example, the cropped sections of the video stream can be changed. The locations of all nodes of the branch of the flow graph that decodes and renders the audio stream can be modified. In addition, you can employ a different source node, e.g. for reading an audio/video file. Using clic, different configurations can be tested within seconds.

For rendering the *complete* video stream on a third screen, e.g. the screen attached to the server, the above provided graph description file needs to be extended slightly. An additional branch for decoding and displaying the video on the local system is added:

```
DVDReadNode
$ select(1, 1, 1) OUTPUT_INITIALIZED
! MPEGDemuxNode
{

  . . .

  { ["mpeg_video0"] ! MPEGVideoDecodeNode
                    ! XDisplayNode
                      $ setFullscreen(1) ACTIVATED
  }

  . . .

}
```

### 13.2.3   Dynamically Adding Systems

Instead of statically configuring a video wall, clic also allows to dynamically add systems by using the facilities provided by the session sharing service that allows to reuse parts of a running distributed flow graph within different applications (compare Chapter 11). Media processing and rendering is automatically synchronized for all participating flow graphs.

To enable session sharing, the sharing policy of requested nodes has to be changed. In the following example, dist_video_wall_shared.gd, the source node and the demultiplexer are chosen to be requested exclusively and are shared then; the remaining nodes are requested and configured exactly like shown above in dist_video_wall.gd.

```
DVDReadNode
# setSharingType(EXCLUSIVE_THEN_SHARED)
$ select(1, 1, 1) OUTPUT_INITIALIZED
! MPEGDemuxNode
# setSharingType(EXCLUSIVE_THEN_SHARED)
{
  . . .
}
```

Clic is started as usual using this the following command on system "server":

```
server> ./clic dist_video_wall_shared.gd
```

An additional client systems "client3" can be added (and removed) dynamically by using following graph description called dist_video_wall_shared2.gd:

```
DVDReadNode
# setSharingType(SHARED)
! MPEGDemuxNode
# setSharingType(SHARED)
{
  { ["mpeg_video0"] ! MPEGVideoDecodeNode
                    # setLocation("client3")
```

```
                              ! VideoCropNode
                                # setLocation("client3")
                                $ setCrop(192,0,384,288) INITIALIZED
                              ! XDisplayNode
                                # setLocation("client3")
                                $ setFullscreen(1) ACTIVATED
      }
   }
```

A second instance of clic is started:

```
server> ./clic dist_video_wall_shared2.gd
```

In this example, an additional video output is opened for the screen connected to "client3" that shows a different cropped section of the video in fullscreen mode, e.g. a region that overlaps the regions of "client1" and "client2". The session sharing service automatically shares the source node for reading the DVD and the MPEG demultiplexer since these nodes were explicitly requested as shared instances. Notice that the second instance of clic can be stopped at any time and restarted again, e.g. for quickly testing different cropping parameters. To this end, the session sharing service of NMM greatly helps to set up such complex scenarios.

### 13.2.4   Discussion

Together, the facilities provided by clic demonstrate the advantages of NMM – especially when compared to "traditional" client/server streaming approaches. Instead of using a single distributed flow graph that transparently allows to access, control, and combine remote resources, client/server setups need to start a client application on each system connected to a display. Each client application needs to be configured manually to the data format provided by the server and the section of the video stream to be cropped. Once started, the server application has no control over the clients. If the complete setup needs to be restarted, each client needs to be stopped and started again. This is especially circumstantial if a large number of screens and connected clients is used. Since there is no interaction between clients and server besides the streaming data connection from the server to the clients, no inter-stream synchronization is provided – a feature that is absolutely required for a video wall.

## 13.3   Conclusions and Future Work

The tool clic developed on top of NMM provides an easy way to test and configure distributed flow graphs given as textual descriptions. Since many facilities provided by NMM can directly be access when using clic, even complex applications, such as the above described video wall, can be realized quickly. To this end, the distributed inter-stream synchronization and the session sharing service can be used. In addition, the graph building service for media playback applications is directly accessible when using clic.

While the current version of clic only offers simple interaction mechanisms for running flow graphs, such as pausing of media processing, for future versions, we would like to add a fully interactive programming environment that offers the possibility to control all nodes by sending textual commands to the messaging system of NMM. Such an environment can even allow to create flow graphs step-by-step. Furthermore, the development of a graphical user interface on top of clic is planned that allows to interactively create and configure distributed flow graphs.

# Chapter 14

# Recording and Playback of Presentations

The goal of the project Virtual Courseroom Environment (VCORE) [VCO] is the development of a system for recording and broadcasting all aspects of a presentation, such as a talk or lecture. This includes an audio and video stream of the speaker but also the used additional material like slides and written text or annotations. Within this project, NMM is used as underlying multimedia architecture. In a first step, an application for recording presentations including audio, video, and slides was implemented [San03]. From these three sources of data, a compact representation in SMIL format is generated [W3Cb]. While available media players can be used for playing back such a representation, an application developed on top of NMM was developed in order to demonstrate how certain subsets of SMIL can be handled.

In the following, we will first briefly describe the hardware setup of the recording system. Then, the recording application and the playback application will be presented, Finally, conclusions are drawn and future work is discussed.

## 14.1 Hardware Setup

Figure 14.1 gives an overview of a typical hardware setup when using the VCORE system. The speaker connects a laptop computer to a beamer as usual for showing the presentation, e.g. by using a program like Microsoft's Powerpoint running under a Windows operating system. In addition, the laptop is connected to the same LAN network as the recording system. This system is a commodity PC running GNU/Linux. The network connection is needed to capture the slides shown by the speaker via the virtual network computing (VNC) protocol [Reac].

Since the provided audio quality is vital for the acceptance of the system, a professional wireless speech transmission set is used for recording the speech of the speaker via a small pluggable microphone and a mobile sender. The corresponding receiving unit is directly connected to the audio input of the sound board of the recording system.

A video stream of the presentation, e.g. a video of the speaker, is generated from an analog camera connected to a TV board or video capture board of the recording system.

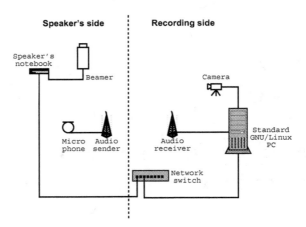

Figure 14.1: Hardware setup of the VCORE system. The speaker's laptop is connected to a beamer and the network. The audio and video streams, and the presented slides are recorded by the a system based on commodity PC technology (Figure according to [San03]).

## 14.2   Recording Application

For capturing the complete desktop shown at the speaker's laptop, e.g. the slides presented, the VNC protocol is used. Therefore, a VNC server needs to be installed at the laptop. Such a server is available for a large number of operation systems. By using VNC, the speaker is therefore allowed to use an arbitrary application for giving a presentation.

The complete NMM flow graph of the application running on the recording system is shown in Figure 14.2. For receiving updates of the speaker's desktop via VNC, the VNCSourceNode is used [San03, GP04]. For example, this node generates a single image stored within an NMM buffer whenever the speaker changed the slide being displayed.

In addition, nodes for capturing audio and video are included into the flow graph. The two constant-rate streams for audio and video, respectively, and variable-rate stream of captured images via VNC is synchronized via a source synchronizer, provided by class MasterSlaveSourceSynchronizer, that realizes a synchronization protocol similar to the one described in Section 7.8.3.

For storing the high-bandwidth audio and video streams, both are compressed using the AudioEncodeNode and VideoEncodeNode, respectively. In particular, we used MP3 audio and MPEG4 video codecs since the corresponding plug-ins are provided by NMM. Furthermore, the stream of video frames can be deinterlaced prior to compression to obtain single frames out of the the stream of two corresponding half-frames typically provided by a board for capturing video from an analog camera. The compressed audio and video streams are multiplexed using the AVMuxNode and then stored within an AVI file, a file format supported by many media players, using

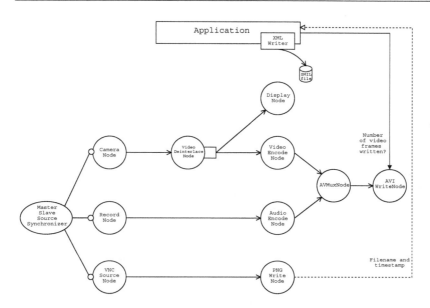

Figure 14.2: The NMM flow graph for the recording application. Audio and video is recorded, compressed, multiplexed, and then written to a file; captured slides are received via VNC and written to separate files. A SMIL file representing the complete presentation is generated within the application (Figure according to [San03]).

the `AVIWriteNode`.

An additional display node, the `DisplayNode`, can be added to the flow graph to control the image captured by the connected camera. This node can be added by using a jack group (compare Section 7.3.2).

The sink node `PNGWriteNode` generates an image in PNG format for every frame received from the `VNCSourceNode`. In addition, this sink node is configured to use the timestamps of frames as filenames. For generating a SMIL representation of the complete recorded presentation, the application itself is registered for receiving every filename and timestamp used. Furthermore, the total number of video frames written by the `AVIWriteNode` is queried in the end of the recording. This number allows to determine the total time of the presentation, a value needed for generating the SMIL file.

While SMIL allows very complex presentations to be described in terms of temporal and spatial relationships, only a small subset is needed in our case. A simple layout of the video stream and the captured slides is chosen, i.e. the video stream and captured slides are chosen to be side by side. This results in following SMIL header:

```
<head>
 <layout>
  <root-layout width="1024" height="480"
       background-color="white" />
```

```
<region id="video" left="0" top="0"
    width="384" height="288" />
<region id="slide" left="384" top="0"
    width="640" height="480" />
</layout>
</head>
```

For representing the correct temporal relationship of the recorded media, namely the audio/video stream stored in the AVI file and the captured slides, the parallel element of SMIL is used together with the sequence element. This results in following body:

```
<par>
 <video src="Data/cg20030428a.avi" region="video"/>
 <seq>
  <img src="Data/0000.0.png" region="slide"
      dur="9.7s"/>
  [...]
  <img src="Data/3073.2.png" region="slide"
      dur="26.4s"/>
 </seq>
</par>
```

The durations for presenting the slides is determined from their timestamps; only the duration of the last slide is calculated by subtracting the timestamp of the last slide from the total duration of the presentation.

## 14.3  Playback Application

The SMIL file presented in the preceding section can be played back using media players such as the RealPlayer [Reaa][1]. Figure 14.3 shows the provided layout; slides being shown on the right side are updated according to the position within the audio/video stream.

An NMM flow graph for the playback of the used subset of SMIL is shown in Figure 14.4. From the given SMIL file, the filename of the AVI audio/video file and the filenames of the PNG files storing the slides are determined and used to configure the corresponding source nodes. The timestamps of the NMM buffers holding the slides can be set according to the corresponding filenames. Another possibility is to use the durations of slides stored in the SMIL file. In any case, the sub-graph for decoding the audio/video file and the sub-graph for presenting the slides are both connected to a single sink synchronizer that provides inter-stream synchronization (see Section 7.8.2).

Notice that while in the flow graph shown, two separate sink nodes for rendering video and slides are used, an additional multiplexer can be included that allows to convert the two decoded streams to a single stream with the video frames on the left side and the slides on the right side. However, in this case, the source node for reading the slides has to generate NMM buffers according to the intended time of presentation.

---

[1]Since all tested available media players for GNU/Linux do not support seeking operations within SMIL files properly if an AVI file is included, recorded audio/video streams were often converted to a RealMedia (RM) file in a post-processing step.

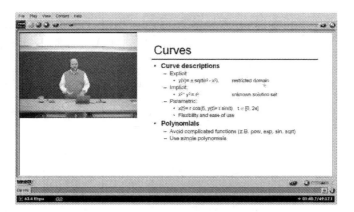

Figure 14.3: The RealMedia player presents the SMIL file generated by the VCORE recording application. Slides being shown on the right side are updated according to the position within the audio/video stream. (Figure according to [San03]).

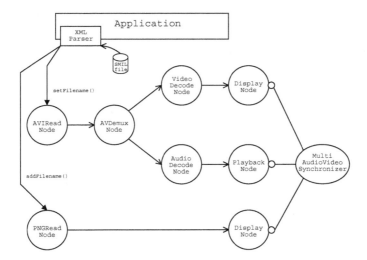

Figure 14.4: The NMM flow graph for the playback application. The audio/video file and the slides are decoded and presented by using a corresponding sub-graph. A single sink synchronizer provides inter-stream synchronization.(Figure according to [San03]).

## 14.4   Conclusions and Future Work

In this chapter, applications for the recording and playback of presentations based on NMM were presented. Especially, the recording system was already successfully used for capturing more than 80 lectures of three complete courses given at Saarland University [VCO].

While several other solutions for recording talks and lectures exit, e.g. [Abo99], [MSW03], or [Row01], the VCORE system as described in this chapter can only be seen as starting point for future development and research. Therefore, the presentation in this chapter focussed on how the NMM architecture supports the development of recording applications in general. To this end, recently introduced advanced features of the system, such as support for annotations on top of presented slides [GP04], clearly demonstrate the applicability of NMM. Furthermore, for future extension, the VCORE system can make full use of the networking facilities of NMM. For example, this allows to transparently use and control distributed devices, such as a camera connected to a remote system, within the recording application. Current development also aims at providing a distributed streaming server [Pet05]. This server will automatically use distributed resources for performing media adaptation needed in order to support the streaming to various clients, such as laptop computers or PDAs using wired or wireless networking technology.

# Chapter 15

# Networked and Mobile Multimedia Home Entertainment

With the availability of cheap, small, quiet, and powerful multimedia PCs on the one hand, and mobile multimedia devices like personal digital assistants (PDAs) on the other hand, it is now possible to create an open and extensible platform for multimedia home entertainment. In this chapter, we describe the design of an application framework. This framework is used to create a networked home entertainment system that provides a uniform user interface to a variety of entertainment options [BCE+02, LS02, LS03, Kle03, End03, Loh03c, LRS05][1].

We will first introduce the developed system. Then, related work is reviewed. The underlying hardware platform will be described in more detail. In the following, the architecture of the application framework is presented together with the realized functionality. Finally, the more advanced features of the system are discussed. These features extensively use the facilities provided by the middleware services of NMM.

## 15.1 Introduction

In almost every household several systems can be found that provide multimedia home entertainment. While traditional systems like radio or TV are still widely used, there is a clear trend towards media convergence, where most of the home entertainment options will be based on digital media existing in various formats. However, even today, typical newly developed home entertainment appliances only provide a restricted and fixed set of features. Advanced application scenarios that include some sort of networking have only recently been introduced.

On the other hand, commodity PC technology allows to provide all necessary multimedia services by using I/O devices, such as DVD drives, PCI boards for receiving TV, or boards for outputting audio and video. Therefore, together with the official start of the NMM project in 2001, we also started to develop an "all-in-one" solution for a home entertainment center based on a GNU/Linux PC. This solution is called *Multimedia-Box* and can be seen as a replacement and extension for traditional devices like CD or DVD players, video recorders, etc. The overall system offers a

---

[1]Videos, photos, and screenshots are available online at http://www.networkmultimedia.org/Gallery/

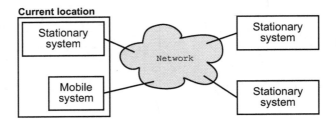

Figure 15.1: Scenario for networked multimedia home entertainment using stationary
and mobile systems. Stationary systems use commodity PC technology; mobile systems are typically laptop computers or programmable PDAs that provide multimedia
capabilities. The Multimedia-Box application framework is running on all systems.
Fully equipped stationary systems can be connected to a TV set in the living room and
provide an "all-in-one" solution for watching TV, DVD, etc. For all connected systems, the underlying NMM framework allows to access remote multimedia devices or
to distribute compute intensive task. Multimedia entertainment options can be enjoyed
on several systems simultaneously and synchronously. Mobile systems can hand over
media playback between different systems.

unified and simple user interface suited for being displayed on TVs or smaller screens
of mobile devices. When being used in the living-room, the system can be controlled
completely with a remote control. Due the integration of different functionality within
a single system, advanced features like unique access to all available media types or
the simultaneous access to different entertainment options, i.e. application-level multi-
tasking, can be realized.

The Multimedia-Box application is realized completely on top of NMM. To this
end, the stepwise development of the application greatly helped to identify requirements that needed to be fulfilled by the underlying middleware. In addition, the
Multimedia-Box offered a perfect test-bed for newly developed plug-ins as well as
for additional features of the NMM core architecture or advanced middleware services. Being a complex "real-world" application, the system also allows to prove the
applicability of the developed middleware and shows its efficiency.

While the idea of providing an all-in-one solution is also followed by a lot of
commercially available systems, the underlying NMM architecture allows to realize
new and advanced application scenarios. For example, remote devices like special
hardware (e.g. a board for receiving digital TV) can be transparently used and the time
consuming tasks (e.g. video transcoding of recorded TV shows) can be distributed to
remote systems. Furthermore, by using the facilities of the session sharing service of
NMM, activities like watching TV can be simultaneously and synchronously enjoyed
by several users using different systems available throughout the household.

With the emergence of fully programmable mobile multimedia devices like PDAs,
the initial Multimedia-Box application was extended to allow for a seamless integration of these systems. In particular, the session sharing service and the service for
seamless reconfiguration are used to realize rich and location-aware multimedia ac-

cess for mobile users. Users can initiate playback on mobile devices, or transparently hand off playback sessions to stationary systems in order to access their computational resources and rich I/O capabilities. In such case, also the user interface of the mobile device is replicated on the particular stationary system. Figure 15.1 shows this overall scenario, where a number of stationary and mobile systems work cooperatively within a household.

Another disadvantage of other available multimedia home entertainment systems is their fixed set of features and monolithic application design that does not allow for future extensions. To avoid this drawback, the Multimedia-Box application is thoroughly designed as a flexible application and user interface framework for creating all kinds of multimedia home entertainment systems. The core framework is extensible through application-level plug-ins that support different entertainment options, such as watching TV or recording TV. A general but very thin user interface layer describes the appearance and the interaction mechanisms. The application and the user interface are configured through XML configuration files, which allows to modify the provided set of functionalities and the overall appearance at the user interface. To this end, the framework allows to quickly configure and tailor the application to the resources available for different systems, e.g. by only including the features available for a particular system.

## 15.2 Related Work

Today's home entertainment appliances are usually based on a closed hardware and software design and do not provide the extensibility and flexibility needed for realizing networked multimedia home entertainment scenarios. Only recently, simple and restricted systems were made available for sale that allow to stream media content stored on the hard disk of a PC to a set-top box connected to the TV in the living room [Han04]. While these systems work within LAN or WLAN networks, current streaming clients only support a restricted and fixed set of media formats. Furthermore, the capabilities of these devices cannot be extended. For example, data transfer is only supported in one direction needed for streaming media playback.

While current streaming clients are based on closed proprietary hardware and software design, other recently introduced approaches aim at providing a single integrated solution for the living-room based on commodity PC technology [SZ04a]. These software solutions are often bundled with appealing looking PCs and can be controlled with a remote control or wireless keyboard. The most prominent representative of the commercially available software solutions is the Microsoft Windows XP Media Center Edition (MCE) [Micf]. Since MCE is based on the multimedia facilities provided by the underlying operating system – in particular Microsoft's DirectShow (see Section 2.5.1) –, in theory, it provides an extensible solution that allows to add new codecs or entertainment options in an integrated manner. This is in contrast to other Windows based programs that often only try to present a consistent user interface on top of other monolithic third-party products, such as software for DVD or MP3 playback. Due to the fixed functionality of these external applications, possible extensions are only available by integrating further applications – no fine-grained cooperation or configuration of the media processing parts of applications is available.

Several competing solutions from the Open Source community offer a similar set of features and have reached a maturity comparable to commercial systems. Examples for such solutions are vdr [Vida], Freevo [Freb], and MythTV [Myt]. The most mature solution is certainly the Linux video disk recorder (vdr) [SZ04b]. Initially developed for watching and recording TV received via DVB, newer versions of vdr offer a variety of other entertainment options. However, since these options are often realized by monolithic external applications, the same restrictions as discussed above for Windows-based solutions apply.

The main drawback of all these solutions is that the underlying architectures do not allow for true networked multimedia home entertainment – if an extensive multimedia architecture is used at all. Mostly the functionality provided is restricted to operate locally on a single system. If the networking capabilities provided by the employed hardware are used, only restricted and fixed client/server streaming approaches are realized.

Solutions being developed in the research community only consider specific tasks within multimedia home entertainment, such as middleware support or handoff of media streams, and have already been discussed in the corresponding chapters of this thesis. Yet other approaches focus on topics that are not covered in the scope of this work, such as context-awareness [Dey00, CNM01], intuitive interaction [KHS01], or social interaction, e.g. via chatting [AAB01].

An important standard in the area of interactive TV is the Multimedia Home Platform (MHP) that specifies an interface between interactive digital applications and the terminals they run on [Mul, Wor01]. As MHP aims at enhancing the basic TV functionality with interactive content and only defines the required interfaces, applications are needed as well as a middleware layer, like the OpenTV SDK [Ope00].

As discussed in the previous section, the initial goal for the development of the Multimedia-Box was to have a test-bed for NMM. However, since our overall home entertainment system developed beyond our initial plans, it can be used for demonstrating the new and advanced application scenarios made possible by the facilities provided by NMM. Finally, the locally running Multimedia-Box application also provides an alternative for other Open Source approaches [Zot04].

## 15.3   Hardware Setup

Figure 15.2 shows the available input and output capabilities of the stationary and mobile systems used. Each device is typically represented by one or more NMM plug-in nodes.

### 15.3.1   Stationary Systems

The stationary systems are based completely on commodity PC technology. To this end, all available I/O devices are mostly optional and different configurations are valid. For example, a single stationary system that acts a host for performing compute intensive tasks only needs to provide a network device and a hard disk. In addition, such a system can also include one or more boards for receiving TV. By using corresponding NMM plug-ins, both, analog and digital TV can be provided. One can also imagine

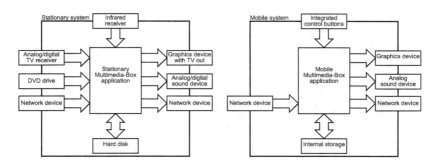

Figure 15.2: Hardware setup for stationary and mobile systems. Stationary systems are based on commodity PC technology and allow different configurations of I/O devices to be used for the Multimedia-Box application. Mobile systems provide fewer and fixed I/O capabilities that can be transparently extended by employing resources of remote stationary systems accessed via NMM.

that this system acts as Internet router for a household, e.g. for accessing the WWW but also for receiving Internet radio or querying media databases. Together, such systems can be seen as "servers" typically located in the basement of a house.

Contrariwise, another stationary system can only provide a networking device and an audio device, e.g. for listening to music. If the operating system is loaded via the network – e.g. from a server –, this system does not even need an internal hard disk. For systems that are configured like this, the term "client" can be used. Notice that the terms "client" and "server" are only used to describe hardware configurations; the underlying NMM architecture operates in a peer-to-peer mode, i.e. all systems are allowed to access remote resources provided by all other systems. A typical place for such a client within a household is the kitchen, where only audio output is needed. The control of such lean systems can be performed by using another device, e.g. a PDA that acts as "remote control" by transparently accessing the remote resources provided by the stationary system via NMM. Alternatively, direct control with a commodity remote control and an included infrared receiver is possible.

Inbetween these two extremes, the configurability of PC technology allows to provide various other systems – for example, a stationary Multimedia-Box for the living-room that is fully equipped as shown in Figure 15.2 and connected to a hi-fi system and TV. Figure 15.3 shows different prototypes we have set up. Further details on the chosen hardware can be found in [BCE+02], [Kle03], and [NMMc]. Finally, a commodity PC in the study room can also be integrated into the overall scenario, e.g. for providing computational resources on the one hand, but also for accessing TV received by remote devices on the other hand.

### Discussion

Due to the provided configurability and programmability, stationary systems based on PC technology offer an interesting possibility for quickly prototyping networked mul-

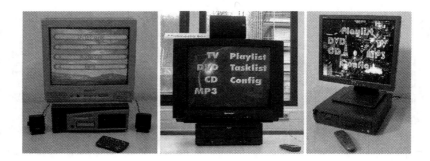

Figure 15.3: Three different prototypes for a stationary Multimedia-Box system from the years 2002 [BCE⁺02], 2003 [Kle03], and 2004 [NMMc] showing a possible main menu of the application.

timedia home entertainment scenarios. However, from our experience, there are still several factors that limit the applicability of commodity PC technology for typical scenarios in the living-room. First of all, special care must be taken to reduce the noise emission of systems. Second, the underlying operating system must be hidden as far as possible from users, e.g. by reducing boot and wake-up times. Finally, the quality of video signals provided by the TV out of graphics adapters needs further improvement. In particular, support for facilities like the MLdc API of OpenML discussed in Section 2.5.1 are required. Such extensions allow to guarantee the intended framerate of video rendering within certain limits and therefore reduce the jittering of the rendering process.

### 15.3.2    Mobile Systems

A large variety of mobile systems exists. We chose the PDA Compaq iPAQ H3870 with a 206 MHz StrongARM SA-1110 RISC processor, 32 MByte Flash-ROM, and 64 MByte RAM (see Figure 15.4). This choice was made for several reasons. First, this devices allows to replace the originally installed Windows system with the GNU/Linux operating system needed for NMM [End03]. Second, the iPAQ provides decent multimedia capabilities, e.g. stereo audio output and a 320x240 pixel display that offers 65536 colors. Third, by using an additional expansion "jacket", commodity PCMCIA cards can be used, e.g. for 100 Mbps LAN and 11 Mbps WLAN networking.

We found that only little effort was needed to provide full NMM support for this platform [End03]. In particular, we only needed to provide a specific sink node suited for the video device of the iPAQ. In addition, some optimized assembler routines for commonly used algorithms such as alpha-blending or color space conversions were implemented.

Compared to stationary systems, the I/O facilities of typical mobile systems are restricted and fixed as can be seen in Figure 15.2. However, by using the facilities provided by NMM, these limitations can be overcome. While the CPUs used within stationary systems provide much more than sufficient computational resources for performing a large variety of multimedia tasks such as DVD playback or media

Figure 15.4: The iPAQ 3870 using an expansion jacket holding a PCMCIA card for WLAN access [NMMa].

transcoding in parallel, the CPUs of mobile devices and their I/O performance is significantly lower. However, as discussed before, the needed media adaptations for these systems impose especially interesting requirements for a multimedia middleware. Furthermore, the computational and memory resources provided by the iPAQ PDA are by now available for most of the newer mobile phones. Networking technologies like UMTS [UMT, 3rd] – or additionally WLAN for future mobile phones – already provide adequate bandwidth. Only the restricted programmability of these devices limit their availability for networked multimedia home entertainment with NMM.

## 15.4 Application Framework

The goal for the development of the Multimedia-Box application was to create an open and extensible home entertainment system on top of NMM [LS02, LS03, Loh03c]. An important aspect of the design of the application framework was easy configuration and extension. This requires the ability to adapt and extend the structure of the application itself. Therefore, the whole application is built as a plug-in architecture that is assembled using an XML-based configuration language that describes the hierarchical menu structure the user can navigate in and the multimedia entertainment options available at the leaves of this hierarchy, e.g. "actions" such as DVD playback. In addition, the XML-based configuration allows to easily change the look of the application with so called *skins* [Kle02].

### 15.4.1 User Interface

For the user interface of the Multimedia-Box application, we chose to use a very simple approach. The user interface presents a set of hierarchical menus – either shown as intuitive and descriptive icons or simply as text. The structure of the hierarchy is specified in the XML-based configuration file. The user can navigate these menus with a remote control or – for mobile systems – by pressing integrated buttons. Visual

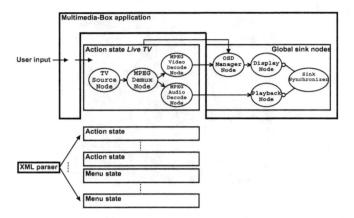

Figure 15.5: The Multimedia-Box application framework. All functionality is separated into menu state objects and action state objects. The application object provides nodes for rendering audio and video, and for presenting on-screen menus overlaid onto the current video frame. These nodes can be accessed by the currently activated state. A sink synchronizer provides inter-stream synchronization for the connected state. An XML parser sets up the complete application from the given XML-based configuration file.

feedback is given via the connected TV or the display of the system. At the leaves of the menu hierarchy are special "actions", such as DVD playback. While each of these actions provides different functionality and therefore presents its own specific user interface, only a small set of commonly used interaction elements are used, such as a list of media files shown in a window-like element. The user interface elements also display feedback on the state of the specific application. For example, for "play" or "pause" the symbols known from commodity multimedia appliances are used.

The realized entertainment options are further described in Section 15.5. Furthermore, Figure 15.8 gives an impression of the visual appearance of the provided user interface.

### 15.4.2 Architectural Elements and Functionality

The overall system architecture of the Multimedia-Box application consists of several interacting parts shown in Figure 15.5:

- The *Multimedia-Box application object* and its sink nodes for rendering audio and video together with a corresponding synchronizer, and a node for performing the overlay of on-screen elements onto the current background. We will refer to this setup as *global sink nodes*.

- A number of *state objects*, either for menus or for actions, such as DVD playback.

- The *XML parser* that reads a given XML file and sets up the complete configuration of the application.

In a first step, the application is automatically set up from the given XML-description: for each menu or action, a *menu state* or an *action state* object is created, respectively. Every menu state object is able to display the correct activated and deactivated items of its menu according to user navigation by updating and evaluating an internal state. The rendering of the graphical representations is performed by a special node provided by the application object as described below. As every menu state object provides the same functionality it is implemented by a single class and instantiated for each entry in the hierarchy of menus. Contrariwise, a specific implementation is provided for each action state object.

Internally, all states are realized as flow graphs of NMM nodes. For example, the background image of a menu state is generated by a simple flow graph that reads and decodes an image from a file specified as background in the used XML configuration. Action states typically provide more complex flow graphs.

During runtime, events are generated according to user input with a remote control or the pressed buttons integrated into the device. These events are forwarded to the currently active state object. More precisely, the corresponding method is called, e.g. up, down, right, left, start, stop, etc. Together with the application object, the state objects implement the State design pattern, which allows an object to change its behavior according to its internal state, i.e. the object acts as if its class changed [GHJV94].

Depending on the received events the active state objects performs an internal state transitions or an external state transition is triggered. For example, when the action state for DVD playback is activated, a "play" event triggers the corresponding method that implements an internal state transition, e.g. by starting the flow graph of NMM nodes. Contrariwise, a "kill" events results in an external state transition. In particular, the current state is terminated an the previously running state is activated again. For example, when the action state for DVD playback is terminated, its predecessor in the hierarchy of menus as specified in the XML configuration is activated again if the action state for DVD playback was reached from that state.

Since the sink nodes for rendering audio and video, and the node for blending on-screen elements onto the current video background are potentially needed by every activated state objects, these nodes are made available for all states by the application object of the Multimedia-Box. As shown in Figure 15.5, these sink nodes are the `PlaybackNode` and the `DisplayNode` for rendering audio and video, respectively. For adding user interface elements to be blended over on the current video background, an additional node `OSDManagerNode` is provided as predecessor of the video sink. In particular, this node provides the functionality of rendering all available user interface elements onto the current video background including alpha-blending [Kle03]. Since this operation eventually needs to be performed for every single frame of a video stream of 25 or more frames per second, all blending operations are implemented by using optimized assembler code.

Since a Multimedia-Box system only provides a single output for audio and video, access to the global sink nodes is controlled by the application framework. When obtaining full access to the global nodes, the currently activated state can be connected to the audio and video output and manipulate the on-screen elements to be displayed by calling methods on the interface provided by the corresponding node. Figure 15.5 shows the action state *Live TV* for watching TV being activated. Its flow graph for decoding digital TV is connected to the both global sink nodes. Additionally, on-screen elements are set by using the facilities of the corresponding node. Notice that the figure only shows the connected nodes; the proxies and interfaces being controlled by the state are not shown for simplicity.

For synchronizing audio and video rendering, the Multimedia-Box application object also provides a sink synchronizer that is initially connected to the controllers of the global sink nodes. However, the currently activated state can also disable inter-stream synchronization as described below.

### 15.4.3  Application-Level Multi-Tasking

Not all state objects need access to the audio *and* the video output. For example, a state that allows to read and transcode the audio/video streams of a DVD, the *DVD Transcoder* does only need to provide user interface elements during its initial start; then it can operate in the background for a larger period of time. Other states only need access to either the audio *or* the video sink. For example, a simple audio playback application realized as state, e.g. an *MP3 Player*, only needs access to the audio sink; on-screen elements are only needed for selecting tracks, etc. Contrariwise, a state for displaying images, e.g. the images obtained from a digital camera, does not need access to the audio sink but requires to be connected to the video sink. Therefore, for every state object, two flags have to be specified, namely *needaudio* and *needvideo*. These flags control the behavior during the external state change of the Multimedia-Box application. These flags can be set in the XML configuration either to "yes" or "no". For example, all menu states set both flags to "no".

Using these two flags the application framework provides *application-level multi-tasking*: Instead of completely terminating a state object, it can also be put to background by pressing the corresponding button, e.g. on the remote control. When a running state is put to background, it needs to clear its on-screen elements. Then, as described above, its predecessor is activated again. If the predecessor does not require a global sink node that is used by the state that is being put to background, the current connections to the global sink nodes can be kept. For example, when deactivating a state that is connected to both sinks (e.g. the *Live TV* state) with a state that does neither need an audio nor a video output (e.g. a menu), the TV state can be kept fully connected and can continue to work in the background.

As another example, let us consider the situation shown in Figure 15.6. A state for playing MP3 files is connected to the audio sink (i.e. the state *MP3 Player*) and a state for viewing images is connected to the video sink simultaneously (i.e. the state *Image Viewer*). Both states are running in the background. Since only a single sink node is connected to each of these states, no inter-stream synchronization is required and therefore disabled. In addition, the user started a state that reads and transcodes the audio/video streams of a DVD (i.e. the state *DVD Transcoder*). This state is running completely in the background. Finally, the user started an additional state *EPG* that provides an electronic program guide (EPG) for browsing within textual descriptions of the broadcasted TV program. This state is currently focussed by the user. Therefore, all control events are forwarded to it and the on-screen elements are set by this state.

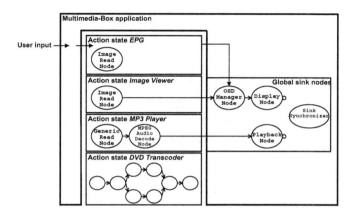

Figure 15.6: Application-level multi-tasking within the Multimedia-Box application framework. State objects that do not require a resource that is used by another activated state can operate concurrently. In this example, the previously started states *ImageViewer*, *MP3 Player*, and *DVD Transcoder* are put to background. Since the states *ImageViewer* and *MP3 Player* only require access to a single sink, they are allowed to operate concurrently; inter-stream synchronization is disabled. An electronic program guide provided by th state *EPG* is currently focussed by the user and therefore provided access to the node for displaying on-screen items – in this case, on top of the image provided by the *ImageViewer*.

Notice that the XML-based configuration allows to restrict the possibility to perform multi-tasking by changing the *needvideo* or *needaudio* flags of states.

For managing all running states, a special action state *Tasklist* is provided that allows to change the user focus to a state running in the background or to terminate a running state. Section 15.6 will demonstrate how this state can also be used to access and share states running on distributed systems.

Notice that when using application-level multi-tasking, the on-screen menus are rendered on top of every video frame generated by the flow graph connected to the video branch of the global sink nodes. For example, when the state *Live TV* is running in the background and the state EPG is currently focussed by the user, the on-screen menu will be rendered onto every single video frame.

To summarize, the chosen design results in an extended State design pattern. The state currently focussed by the user receives all control events and has full access to the on-screen user interface. An arbitrary number of states is allowed to be run in the background. Only a single state is provided access to the audio sink and only a single state is provided access to the video sink. Also, a single state can be connected to both global sinks. If a state that is activated requires access to a sink that is being used by another state, the currently connected state is terminated and all connections to global sink nodes are removed.

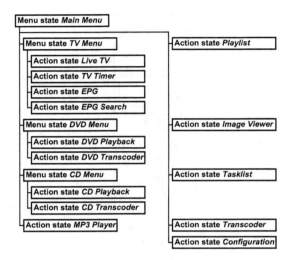

Figure 15.7: A hierarchy of menu states and currently available actions states for the Multimedia-Box.

### 15.4.4   Integrating Entertainment Options

Using the provided application framework, integrating a new entertainment option is straightforward. First, an implementation of a new action state needs to be provided. This state only has to handle the intended interaction types, such as left, right, up, down, play, stop, by implementing the corresponding methods. These methods realize internal state transitions specific for the state. The multimedia functionality provided by the state is to be realized by a flow graph of NMM nodes. For handling external state transitions, do-methods according to the design pattern Template Method are provided by the superclass of all states [GHJV94]. Within these methods, all functionality required for creating, destroying, putting the state to the background, or reactivating the state again need to be implemented.

As a second step, the newly developed state needs to be identified with a unique string. This identifier can then be used to add an additional entry to the XML-base configuration file. Finally, the source code for parsing this particular entry needs to be provided, e.g. for accessing XML elements specific for the new state.

## 15.5   Realized Functionalities

Figure 15.7 shows a hierarchy of menus states and action states. In the following, the functionality provided by each of the currently available action states is described briefly. This overview will focus on the special aspect of *distributed* multimedia home entertainment. Further information can be found in [Loh03c, BCE+02, Kle03, Maa05, Wel04, Wel05, NMM04a].

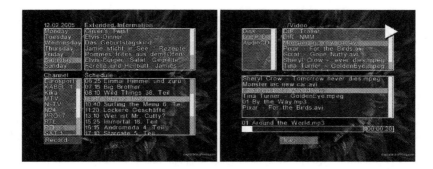

Figure 15.8: The user interface of the Multimedia-Box. On the left, the user interface of the EPG state is shown, which can also be rendered on top of the video stream of the live TV state running in the background. On the right, the user interface of the playlist state is shown; on-screen elements can be hidden upon user interaction. For further screenshots, see [NMMc].

**Live TV.** Allows to watch the current TV program using a distributed source node for receiving analog or digital TV [Kle03, Wel05]. In addition, a feature called time-shifting is available that allows to pause and resume the current live stream received. Since a temporary buffer is used to realize this feature, seek operations within this buffer are also supported. Together, this functionality is provided by a specific plug-in node. Finally, this state also allows to view additional textual information for the currently selected TV channel provided by the electronic program guide (EPG) as described below.

**TV Timer.** Provides the functionality known from commodity video cassette recorders, namely the manual setting of start time, end time, and channel to record [Kle03, Wel05]. The actual recording is provided by a separate state.

**Electronic Program Guide (EPG).** Allows to browse within the program information obtained from different source, e.g. from DVB or specific web services [Wel04, Wel05]. All information is organized according to date, time, and channel. By selecting a specific entry, an entry for the TV timer is automatically created. Figure 15.8 shows the user interface of this state, which can also be rendered on top of the video stream of the live TV state running in the background.

**EPG Search.** Allows to search the available EPG information, e.g. by specifying the name or genre of a TV show [Wel04, Wel05]. Again, by selecting an entry, an entry for the TV timer is automatically generated.

**DVD Playback.** This option provides the functionality known from commodity DVD player appliances, i.e. DVD playback with support for DVD menus [Kle03]. While access to a remote source for DVD playback is currently not supported, this feature can be added easily.

**DVD Transcoding.** For storing the content of a DVD to the hard disk, a state for transcoding audio/video streams available is provided. Various parameters, such as audio/video bitrates, can be chosen interactively before the transcoding process is started. Particularly interesting is the option of using remote hosts for performing the compute intensive decoding and reencoding of the media streams. In this case, only reading and writing of data is performed on the local host.

**CD Playback.** This option allows to playback the tracks of an audio CD [BCE+02]. In addition, to the operations also supported by commodity CD player appliances, the names of artists and tracks of the currently used audio CD are requested from a CDDB web service [frea].

**CD Transcoding.** For storing the transcoded content of an audio CD to the hard disk, this state can be used [BCE+02]. Audio streams read from an audio CD are transcoded to the media format specified in the user settings (see below). In addition, the names of artists and tracks queried via CDDB are used to store transcoded media tracks.

**Transcoder.** As a generalization of the transcoding states for CD and DVD, a generic transcoder is provided [Maa05]. This state allows to transcode an arbitrary number of sources in parallel. Possible flow graphs for handling specific media types are specified in text files holding graph descriptions, the .gd files (see Chapter 13). Within these files, options to be manually set via the graphical on-screen user interface are defined, e.g. possible bitrates or alternative codecs for audio/video streams. For distributing the workload needed for media processing, simple heuristics such as round-robin greedy strategies are used.

**MP3 Player.** This action state was one of the first to be developed [BCE+02]. It allows to playback MP3 files stored within the accessible file system, e.g. the internal hard disk of the system.

**Image Viewer.** This state allows to view images of various formats [Loh03c].

**Playlist.** A generic media browser and player is provided by the playlist state [Kle03]. This state allows to access all media files stored on the accessible file system, e.g. the local hard disk. In addition, sources such as audio CDs can be integrated. Selected items are organized within a playlist. All media formats supported by NMM can be handled. In particular, this state uses the facilities provided by the graph building service described in the scope of Chapter 10. In this case, the global sink nodes of the Multimedia-Box application act as sink nodes for the algorithm. The service provides a composite node that allows to uniformly handle all supported file formats, media types, and codecs. In addition, the generated composite node provides a common interface for operations such as seeking (compare Section 7.5.2). Figure 15.8 shows the user interface of the playlist state.

**Tasklist.** This state allows to reactivate all states that are currently running in the background – or to terminate such a running state. In addition, all states running within the network of Multimedia-Box systems can be joined. This option will be further described in Section 15.6

**Configuration.** For most of the action states presented, user specific configurations are possible. While the possible values for these settings are stored within the XML-base configuration, the actual chosen values are stored within a single text file, the *.mm-boxrc* [BCE⁺02]. During runtime, most of these settings can be changed within the configuration dialog, e.g. the default bitrates for transcoding operations, or the currently used skin.

## 15.6 Sharing of Resources

Within the developed networked home entertainment system, the session sharing service described in Chapter 11 is used for realizing different functionality.

### 15.6.1 Simultaneous Live TV and Recording

As described in Section 15.5, the Multimedia-Box application framework provides a state for watching TV. In addition, the TV timer state, the EPG state, and the EPG search state allow to specify TV broadcastings to be recorded. The actual recording is implemented within a separate action state that is not accessible from the user interface directly. This state employs a flow graph that includes a source node for receiving TV.

In situations where the state for watching TV and the state for recording TV are activated concurrently – for example, when the live TV state is started during the recording of a TV show – the session sharing service allows to easily share the source node to be used in both setups. In particular, if the live TV state is started, it tries to request a source for receiving TV exclusively first. If this fails, the source node is requested as shared component. Then, the changing of channels is disabled within the user interface of this state as long as another state – in our example, the state for recording – is accessing the source node. Instead, a message is displayed to the user stating that a recording is currently performed; the user is only allowed to change the channel again, if this operation is terminated.

Contrariwise, if the state for watching TV is started first, and an recording is activated afterwards, a similar process is performed. If the source node for receiving TV can only be accessed shared by the state that performs the recording, the channel is changed to the one specified within the entry of the TV timer and an additional messages is displayed within the state for watching live TV.

While this feature can also be implemented in other ways, we think that the session sharing service greatly simplified the realization of this step. Furthermore, this service also allows advanced features to be developed easily. For example, if several sources for receiving TV are available within the network, the session sharing service will automatically identify nodes that can be accessed exclusively. This allows to easily develop a networked digital video recorder that employs several available sources for receiving TV.

### 15.6.2 Sharing of Entertainment Options

For allowing for collaborative multimedia home entertainment, the tasklist of the Multimedia-Box does not only provides access to states running on the local host but also to all other running states within the network of connected systems. Figure 15.9 shows the user interface of the tasklist that provides a list of textual descriptions for all available states. Entertainment options running on remote hosts are additionally indicated

Figure 15.9: The user interface of the tasklist state of the Multimedia-Box. States running locally in the background can be reactivated or terminated. States running on distributed systems are labelled with the name of the corresponding host and can be joined by using the facilities of the session sharing service.

with the corresponding name of the host. The list of remotely activated states is generated by querying a given set of systems. Again, as discussed in Section 9.6, a future extension of the registry service that includes advanced peer-to-peer search strategies will allow to dynamically identify running states within the network of connected home entertainment systems.

While locally running states can be reactivated or terminated, states operating on distributed systems can be joined by using the facilities provided by the session sharing service. For example, if the state for watching TV running on a remote system is joined, a local instance of the corresponding state is generated as usual. The only difference is that the source node is requested as shared processing element from the specific remote system. The session sharing will automatically create shared running sessions and set up distributed inter-stream synchronization. If a running state using a shared session is terminated, the other connected state will continue to operate.

If a node providing time-shifting functionality is used as successor of the source node for receiving TV, both nodes can be shared. In this case, time-shifting operations, such as pausing the current live stream, are performed for all shared sessions simultaneously. If this is not wanted, the shared usage of the time-shifting node and the setup of inter-stream synchronization can also be disabled. Then, shared sessions only access the same source node but are provided exclusive control of all time-shifting features.

As discussed in the scope of Chapter 11, full control of all nodes of the shared flow graphs is then granted for all connected states. A future extension of the session sharing service will allow to restrict the set of shared NMM interfaces.

Notice that by using the session sharing service only little modifications to the initial Multimedia-Box application are needed to realize collaborative multimedia home entertainment scenarios. Furthermore, the provided service allows to setup such shared applications for all available entertainment options.

Figure 15.10: Seamless Handover. On the left side: The user interface of the mobile audio player. The entry in the lower left allows to select a host, on which the media decoding and output should be performed. Media processing is then hand over seamlessly to the chosen system. On the right side: Once the handover process is completed, the user interface of the mobile system is also shown at the stationary system. The user interfaces of both systems are updated according to user interaction.

## 15.7 Seamless Integration of Mobile Systems

The Multimedia-Box application framework used for mobile systems with scarce resources is very similar to the full-featured framework discussed so far. The main difference is that a simpler user interface is provided that does not use memory consuming icons for representing a hierarchy of menus and entertainment options. Instead, simpler graphical elements are used, such a list of text lines shown in a window. Since the same NMM node is used for generating on-screen items, the user interfaces provided at mobile and stationary systems provide the same "look".

Using the PDA described in Section 15.3.2, the application scenario described so far can be extended to allow for mobile multimedia home entertainment.

### 15.7.1 Rich and Shared Multimedia Entertainment

By using the facilities provided by NMM, mobile systems can be offered the same rich multimedia entertainment options available for stationary systems – only the used media streams have to be adapted to the resources provided by the mobile system. In particular, full access to options such as watching TV or DVD can be realized. In general, an action state running on a mobile system uses a remote source node together with a complex flow graph of nodes for media transcoding. For example, the setup discussed in Section 11.6.2 can be used to provide TV access on a mobile system. A similar yet more complex distributed flow graph can be used for realizing full-featured DVD playback including support for DVD menus.

The session sharing service of NMM presented in Chapter 11 furthermore allows to jointly access entertainment options using different mobile and stationary systems. This option was already discussed in Section 15.6.

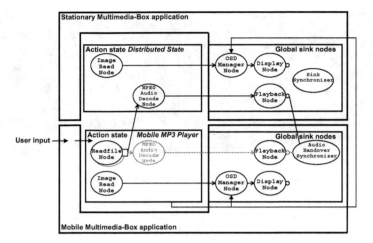

Figure 15.11: Setup for synchronized handover of audio decoding and playback from a mobile to a stationary system. The action state *Distributed State* allows to seamlessly integrate this step into the application framework of the Multimedia-Box. After the handover process is completed, the parts of the figure shown in grey are to be destroyed, i.e. the decoding node running on the mobile system and its connections. The action state running on the mobile system controls both on-screen displays using the provided interfaces and adapts the shown graphical elements to the resolution of the provided display nodes.

### 15.7.2   Mobility Support

For demonstrating the support for mobile users and systems provided by NMM, we especially integrated the service for seamless reconfiguration presented in Chapter 12 into the overall application scenario. In particular, the action state providing an MP3 player for the mobile system offers the extended functionality of handing over the current media playback to a nearby stationary system in order to use the remotely provided high-quality audio output.

The user interface for this setup is shown in Figure 15.10 on the left side. A textual description indicates the currently selected system that performs the audio output. Upon selecting another host out of a list of generally available hosts, e.g. a nearby stationary system, a seamless reconfiguration is performed similar to the one described in Section 12.3, i.e. the audio decoding and output is handed over to the selected host. Furthermore, the user interface initially presented on the mobile system is replicated on the stationary system. Such a situation is shown in Figure 15.10 on the right side.

In order to integrate the handover process seamlessly into the application framework of the Multimedia-Box, a special action state for operating on the remote system is provided. This state offers the same behavior as all other states, i.e. it can be put to background, etc. Together, the handover process results in a setup shown in Figure 15.11. The initially started action state *Mobile MP3 Player* instantiates the action state *Distributed State* on the remote stationary system. Within this state, an MPEGAudioDecodeNode is running. For rendering a background image, both states provide an ImageReadNode that is connected to the locally running sink node DisplayNode via its predecessor, the OSDManagerNode. Also, on-screen elements, such as the lists of available music tracks, are displayed on both systems using the corresponding OSD nodes. Since the resolution of the stationary system might be different, the size of user interface elements can be adapted.

The AudioHandoverSynchronizer realizes the seamless change of media output from the mobile to the stationary system. Since both application frameworks provide global sink nodes, in particular an audio sink node, the service for seamless reconfiguration does not need to create (or destroy) these nodes. Only the parts of the figure shown in grey are to be destroyed in the last step of a complete handover, i.e. the MPEGAudioDecodeNode and its connections to the ReadfileNode and the PlaybackNode.

## 15.8   Conclusions and Future Work

In this chapter, a user interface and application framework for multimedia systems was presented. This framework was demonstrated within a networked home entertainment system that consists of a number of mobile and stationary systems. The configurability of the described approach allows for different system setups to be used. In particular, we developed an "all-in-one" home entertainment system based on commodity PC technology that integrates the functionality usually only provided by combinations of several appliances. The provided extensibility of the application framework offers and easy way to add further entertainment options. To this end, a large number of application-level modules, called states, was developed. Each of these states provides a certain multimedia functionality, such as watching TV, and internally uses the facilities provided by NMM. Therefore, remote multimedia devices can be integrated into local processing and time consuming jobs can be distributed in the network.

In addition, our approach allows for several entertainment options to operate concurrently in a multi-tasking mode. We found that this feature greatly increases the quality of user experience – especially, since it is easily accessible with a remote control. Due to the fact that a Multimedia-Box provides an "all-in-one" multimedia system that offers a single user interface to a large number of entertainment options, application-level multi-tasking seems to be particularly useful.

The advanced middleware service of NMM, namely the session sharing service and the service for seamless reconfiguration, were used to ease the development of additional application scenarios. In particular, the session sharing service allows for locally running states to operate concurrently using the same multimedia device. In addition, users are allowed to share activities initiated by other users at different systems. The service for seamless reconfiguration enables mobility support, e.g. by handing over the audio playback from a mobile to a stationary system. In such cases, the user interface is also replicated among participating systems.

Several states of the Multimedia-Box will be improved in the future, e.g. the transcoding state [Maa05]. Especially the realization of a networked TV system within the application framework will be examined [LRS05, Wel05]. This extension will allow several users to transparently access a number of available media sources for watching or recording TV. Tasks will then be automatically distributed within the network.

Initially developed as test-bed for the emerging NMM architecture, we are now planning to further extend the capabilities of the Multimedia-Box framework itself. To this end, we would like to improve especially the support for collaborative multimedia home entertainment – for example, by automatically adding additional context information to all multimedia applications running within the network. This would allow for a better representation and selection of running multimedia tasks within the tasklist of the application framework. Users should be notified when other users join or leave running activities; in addition, admission control mechanisms need to be provided. Finally, the automatic adaptation of replicated user interfaces presented on different systems would allow to further ease application development.

# Part V

# Final Summary, Conclusions, and Future Work

# Chapter 16

# Final Summary, Conclusions, and Future Work

In this final part of the thesis, the content of all previous chapters will be summarized again. Then, conclusions are drawn and the main contributions achieved are discussed. Finally, possible directions for future work, which were partly already pointed out throughout the presentation, will be summarized.

## 16.1   Summary

In this thesis, the foundations of distributed multimedia systems were described and challenges for multimedia middleware were analyzed (Part I). The design and implementation of the Network-Integrated Multimedia Middleware (NMM) was presented (Part II) and additional fundamental and advanced middleware services were described (Part III). Finally, several real world applications developed on top of NMM were discussed (Part IV).

### Part I: Foundations of Multimedia Middleware

Multimedia systems consist of devices and software components that process high-bandwidth time-sensitive data streams. Commonly available architectures for handling multimedia adopt a PC centric approach, where all processing is restricted to operate on a single host. The network is, at best, used for streaming predefined content from a server to a client.

Middleware as a software layer between distributed systems and applications provides different dimensions of transparency and suitable abstractions that allow for masking out the complexity of the underlying infrastructure. To this end, all aspects of communication is completely hidden and not accessible for upper layers. Available middleware solutions most often only provide support for a single interaction paradigm, such as object-based request-reply interaction; multimedia communication is typically not addressed. Furthermore, such solutions do not provide the openness and reflective capabilities needed for integrating and accessing different available technologies, e.g. for using protocols especially suited for handling time critical data streams.

Based on these observations, the notion of a network-integrated multimedia middleware was derived by discussing the requirements and challenges for such an approach. The abstractions used in locally operating multimedia architectures, namely processing elements and flow graphs, are extended towards distributed flow graphs that provide network transparent control and cooperation. While the former requires a programming model known from object-based middleware, network transparent connections between the processing elements of a distributed flow graph demands support for streaming data interaction. To this end, several extensions for existing middleware solutions and the facilities provided by different protocol frameworks were discussed. Especially open and explicit binding techniques were identified to offer a suitable model for establishing bindings. However, these approaches can only be considered as possible building blocks for an integrating multimedia middleware,

Due to the inherent heterogeneity of today's infrastructures, a multimedia middleware especially needs to provide a high degree of openness and extensibility in order to provide a technology transparent architecture. Furthermore, for a general purpose multimedia middleware, an extensible architecture for realizing different protocols for distributed synchronization is a further requirement.

Additional challenges for multimedia middleware can be characterized by the dynamics and complexity involved in the setup and reconfiguration of distributed multimedia flow graphs. These challenges can be handled by providing additional advanced and new services. Seamless reconfigurations and support for collaborative multimedia applications were identified as particular demanding. In addition, the setup of complex application scenarios requires further guidance when creating flow graphs.

## Part II: Network-Integrated Multimedia Middleware

Based on the identified challenges and additional requirements for multimedia middleware, the architectural decisions of the developed middleware, the Network-Integrated Multimedia Middleware (NMM), were presented in this part of the thesis. Then, the integrating communication framework and the generic multimedia middleware based on this framework were described.

In particular, we decided to focus on an integrating micro-core architecture that provides a relatively small base functionality, basically only for handling messages and single events. This part of the architecture provides support for different interaction paradigms: On the one hand, out-of-band request-reply interaction is modeled according to the Proxy design pattern and includes an object-oriented interface system. In addition, listener notification is made available. On the other hand, one-way instream communication takes place between connected processing elements.

The approach of specifying object-oriented interfaces using an interface definition language (IDL) was taken from traditional approaches. However, this model was extended in different ways. First, it is unified to specify both out-of-band and instream interaction relying on control events. Second, the execution of methods can be restricted or required to certain states – a property particularly useful for defining the state-driven functionality of multimedia processing elements. Finally, for playing an integrating role, the IDL supports to include arbitrary existing data types that can be serialized. Since the interface system internally uses events, it provides the reflective capabilities needed for heterogeneous environments.

Instead of a strong coupling to a certain lower level technology, communication channels realize the interaction between two entities. A communication channel is composed out of several components, namely serialization and transport strategies. In particular, a stack of corresponding serialization and deserialization strategies is configured to be used within the sending and receiving side of transport strategies. For the two different types of interaction, specific communication roles have to be fulfilled. While this concept is similar to channels according to RM-ODP, our architecture provides a more flexible approach that allows for using a single component to fulfill different roles. Again, this choice was made to take the different properties of available communication technologies into account. Furthermore, to enable advanced interaction between connected processing elements, instream interaction consists of both multimedia data buffers and control events. In order to configure and combine different transport mechanisms especially suited for the transmission of one of these two types of messages, parallel bindings were introduced. At the receiving side of such a binding, a synchronization strategy reestablishes the correct ordering of messages.

While communication channels provide a unified abstraction of all kinds of communication, the openness of the architecture offers extensibility and scalable transparency. Extensibility is achieved by several architectural elements. First, the serialization framework allows for the integration of arbitrary data types and therefore eases the usage of available components. Furthermore, by providing specific serialization and networking strategies, previously incompatible technologies can be connected or specialized and optimized strategies can be integrated. To this end, communication between colocated entities can be realized very efficient. Scalable transparency allows to automatically set up communication channels or to manually configure all aspects involved.

The various implemented serialization and transport strategies already cover many different technologies that all provide specific capabilities. This clearly demonstrates the openness and integrating nature of the overall architecture of the communication framework.

The multimedia middleware developed on top of the facilities provided by the communication framework of NMM realizes the concept of a distributed flow graph by "hiding" the streaming data connections between processing elements within the edges of the graph, i.e. within communication channels. Compared to approaches that add additional processing elements for establishing streaming network connections, this choice further enhances the scalable transparency provided.

In general, the part of NMM implementing all aspects concerned with the handling of multimedia uses a very intuitive and simple design that only consists of nodes as processing elements that are connected by jacks. Multimedia formats specify the meta-data of possible connections. The state machine controls the life cycle of nodes, especially for the connection setup between nodes. Memory managers allow for the efficient handling of high-bandwidth streams. The generic processing model supports arbitrary interaction patterns used for instream communication. Together with the provided generic base classes, this greatly helps to integrate existing multimedia functionality. The synchronization architecture of NMM completes the approach by offering a framework that is especially suited for realizing different distributed synchronization algorithms.

An evaluation of different performance characteristics for out-of-band and instream interaction concluded this part of the thesis. Together, we were able to demonstrate that despite its open design, the current implementation offers competitive performance – even when being compared to highly optimized commercial traditional middleware solutions that do only partly provide the features required for multimedia middleware.

## Part III: Middleware Services

In this part of the thesis, four middleware services especially suited for distributed multimedia in heterogeneous and dynamic environments were presented: the registry service, a service for automatically setting up distributed flow graphs from a high-level description, session sharing as service that enables collaborative application scenarios, and a service that allows for the seamless reconfiguration of an active distributed flow graph.

The registry service is the most fundamental service for a multimedia middleware solution and administrates available processing elements throughout the network. To this end, we chose a hybrid approach. All elements available for a single system are administrated by a locally running server registry. A client registry can query local and remote server registries using a peer-to-peer approach. This allows for the efficient handling of loosely coupled systems. Furthermore, a registry server can contain specialized sub-registries for integrating additional technologies for device management.

Requests forwarded to the registry service can either contain subsets of node descriptions or complete graph descriptions. To avoid unnecessary inter-process or network communication, locally requested NMM nodes are instantiated in the address space of the application. We also found that the reflective capabilities of the NMM messaging system greatly helped to realize the initial discovery, registration, and defined recreation of nodes. Finally, the measured runtimes for setting up even large distributed flow graphs demonstrated the applicability of the chosen approach.

An advanced service for the automatic setup of flow graphs was presented. First, the challenges and requirements for such a service were analyzed in detail. In this context, a definition of the quality of a valid and fully configured flow graph was provided that was made according to the quality perceived by users. Furthermore, we found that a general approach for true automatic application setup will remain an open problem.

Therefore, we focussed on two subproblems. First, algorithms for automatically setting up a distributed flow graph for specific tasks, such as media playback, were described. Since in general, the available output formats of a processing element can only be determined after the element has received and analyzed some multimedia data from its predecessors, these algorithms can only operate step by step and can then either use backtracking or parallel branched search to solve the search problem involved in automatic application setup. Therefore, quality-driven decisions during the search can only be made locally. We also showed how a service for managing certain quality of service aspects can be used to guide the distribution process during the automatic setup of flow graphs.

Second, a quality-driven format negotiation was presented that operates on subgraphs that allow to statically determine possible output formats for all processing elements. This algorithm then creates a negotiation graph, in which a modified algorithm for solving the Single-Source-Shortest-Path (SSSP) is used to determine the solution that provides the best quality according to our definition.

While the realized approaches already provide many benefits for application development and the performance achieved is already quite promising, we concluded that the integration of quality of service (QoS) measurements will require to extend the described algorithms.

In the next chapter, session sharing as middleware service for enabling collaborative application scenarios was presented. In such scenarios, the same – or similar – content is presented to different users simultaneously using different devices, possibly at different locations. This service builds upon the idea of sharing parts of running distributed flow graphs within newly created flow graphs. Distributed synchronization and shared control of all shared processing elements then helps to increase the sense of collaboration among users.

The service itself was realized by extending the registry service towards storing complete running flow graphs and additional sharing attributes for every processing element. An algorithm for finding all possible overlaps between a running flow graph and a query was described and augmented by a specific valuation function that determines the "best" overlapping subgraph according to a specific optimization criteria, e.g. by counting overlapped elements and edges.

The reuse of parts of active flow graphs not only helps to establish collaborative application scenarios, it also solves the technical problem of multiple access to a single device and allows to reduce the computational and networking resources by sharing active flow graphs for common tasks.

Finally, several application scenarios were demonstrated that show the applicability and utility of the service together with its performance. This especially showed that this service provides great benefits for integrating mobile devices with restricted resources into the environment.

At last, a further service that allows for the seamless reconfiguration of active distributed flow graph was presented. While we focussed on the synchronization sensitive handover of audio presentations, the developed approach can be extended to provide reconfiguration transparency, an additional dimensions of transparency for multimedia middleware.

This service is built directly on top of the session sharing service and uses a master-slave approach. Parts of the running graph to be reconfigured are created using the session sharing service; overlapping subgraphs are therefore automatically found and only additionally needed processing elements and connections are set up. A specific distributed synchronization protocol was implemented within the synchronization architecture of NMM that handles the seamless handover of the media processing; no audio data is lost or duplicated. Media processing stays continuous and is not interrupted at any time.

Since seamless reconfiguration is realized within the middleware layer it is independent of media codecs or chosen network technologies. To this end, we demonstrated the high-level of abstraction provided by the programming model of the service. In addition, the performance of the current implementation showed that only short delays occur during the reconfiguration process. Also, the minimum offset that can be achieved during the final change of configurations is negligible.

## Part IV: Applications

In this part of the thesis, different applications developed on top of NMM were presented. These applications extensively use the facilities provided by the base architecture of NMM and its additional services.

The tool clic (command line interaction and configuration) allows to set up a distributed flow graph either from a textual description or by using the graph building service. In this step, the registry service of NMM is used and distributed synchronization can be configured automatically. Using the first option, it is also possible to control instantiated processing elements. The messaging service of NMM allows to easily map textual descriptions to events. Furthermore, the session sharing service of NMM can be used.

The developed tool has proven to be extremely useful for quickly setting up distributed flow graphs and for testing the session sharing service. Even complex application scenarios, like the presented video wall, can be configured within minutes.

In the following chapter, first developments made within the project Virtual Courseroom Environment (VCORE) were presented. In this application scenario, NMM is used as framework for developing a system for recording and playback of lectures and presentations, including audio, video, and additional material, such a electronic slides. These applications are of particular interest since they demonstrate extended source and sink synchronization.

For developing a demanding test-bed for the emerging NMM architecture, a networked multimedia home entertainment system was developed. This systems consists of different stationary and mobile systems. A user interface and application framework was presented that allows for extensibility and configurability. In particular, an "all-in-one" solution for a home entertainment center based completely on top of NMM was realized that provides a large variety of entertainment options within a single system and is controllable with a remote control. Especially the large number of implemented application modules and corresponding processing elements shows that NMM is definitely usable, even for such large scale developments. To this end, even the on-screen menus are realized by providing a particular processing elements. Furthermore, applications such as DVD playback including subtitles could be implemented seamlessly within the processing model provided by NMM. For generalized media playback, the graph building service of NMM and composite nodes are used.

The developed framework also allows for application-layer multi-tasking, i.e. the possibility to put active entertainment options to the background and start additional options in parallel. Distributed flow graphs are used for realizing access to remote devices, such as TV receivers, or to distribute time-consuming tasks, such as media transcoding, within the network. The session sharing service furthermore allows for the transparent and simultaneous access of TV receivers, e.g. when watching TV while recording the same channel. In addition, all tasks running within the network of connected systems can be joined using this service.

Finally, mobile devices, such as PDAs and laptop computers, were seamlessly integrated into the scenario. Again, the session sharing service allows for joining activities. Then, required media adaptations can be distributed within the network. In addition, the service for seamless reconfiguration allows for location-aware audio playback by handing over the media decoding and output from a mobile system to a nearby stationary system.

Together, this application scenario shows all facilities provided by the NMM base architecture and its additional services in combination and clearly demonstrates the applicability of NMM for realizing such complex application scenarios.

## 16.2 Conclusions

In this thesis, the Network-Integrated Multimedia Middleware (NMM), its additional services, and applications developed on top of the provided facilities were presented.

We demonstrated that the open micro-core architecture of NMM is especially suited for playing an integrating role in today's heterogeneous environments and allows for considering the network as integral part. We identified multimedia middleware to consist of a relatively small base system plus additional connecting elements. While the basis provides a reflective messaging system and the possibility to realize different interaction paradigms – especially with support for multimedia communication –, proxy objects and communication channels allow for integrating existing lower level technologies. To this end, the approach can be seen as meta-architecture combining various available approaches for establishing communication. Scalable transparency allows to hide the complexity of the overall system but also provides fine grained control and configuration if required. A generic processing model for multimedia offers the means for integrating existing arbitrary multimedia components. Furthermore, the chosen design principles are also applied to all other aspects, namely the synchronization framework and the additionally implemented middleware services.

The base architecture of NMM was extended by several middleware services. The hybrid approach of the registry service combines the client/server and peer-to-peer paradigm and proved to be suitable for loosely coupled systems. Support for existing technologies for device management is realized by specialized sub-registries. Furthermore, additional advanced and new services were proposed, realized, and evaluated. These services show many features and approaches previously not demonstrated. The graph building and format negotiation service provides first practical results for the automatic and quality-driven creation of distributed flow graphs. Session sharing as new middleware service for distributed multimedia allows for collaborative application scenarios by providing shared access to parts of running flow graphs, distributed synchronization, and shared control for applications. At the same time, this service reduces resource requirements for common tasks. Seamless reconfiguration finally provides lossless and synchronized adaptations for active distributed flow graphs together with a high level of abstraction – a service that was not presented before. Together, these services complement the NMM architecture to support the dynamics present in ubiquitous computing scenarios for distributed multimedia. They cover new ideas and provide facilities not available before – and therefore show a further major contribution of this thesis.

Due to the openness of the NMM architecture, its individual building blocks can be exchanged and extended, which allows for tailoring the system. To this end, a purely locally operating multimedia architecture can be derived. Collocation optimizations for the middleware core and the registry service were made available.

The performance evaluations of all parts of NMM, its base architecture and its services, demonstrated that despite the open design approach, the clean, simple and unified design still allows for great efficiency. Especially those performance characteristics that can be directly compared to commercial and highly optimized traditional middleware solutions showed competitive or even better results.

The described applications developed on top of NMM clearly demonstrate its applicability, even for large scale projects. As a result, we were able to present a networked multimedia home entertainment system consisting of stationary and mobile devices, which is completely based on NMM. To our knowledge, the rich set of features of this system is not available elsewhere. Especially the success of this application as test-bed for further research but also as an emerging Open Source project proves the feasibility of our approach. Other described applications showed that NMM is suitable to support all different kinds of multimedia applications.

Besides the many other contributions of this thesis discussed so far, the NMM architecture, its services, and applications demonstrated provide a degree of integration that has not been achieved before – neither in research or commercial projects. We think that especially for multimedia entertainment, our approach provides the largest coverage within a single architecture presented so far – a result of the clear, simple, and unified design of NMM and its integrating approach.

To this end, we would also like to mention that NMM is fully implemented and available as Open Source under the LGPL and GPL for the GNU/Linux operating system. Since all lower level components are abstracted, support for other Unix platforms, or even for other operating systems, should be relatively easy to achieve. To this end, NMM is used for current and future research and developments at Saarland University, but also within other organizations and companies, and the Open Source community in general. From the feedback we receive especially from external developers, we also think that we achieved our goal to provide a standard multimedia middleware, in particular for Open Source developments under GNU/Linux. To our knowledge, NMM is the only fully implemented multimedia middleware made available as Open Source.

## 16.3   Future Work

Although the current implementation of NMM already provides a complete multimedia middleware solution, several directions for future work can be identified. While the topics described in the following were mostly already discussed throughout the presentation, this summary will try to provide a broader context.

### Communication Framework

For the communication framework of NMM, the integration and evaluation of additional serialization and transport strategies together with the development of further synchronization strategies for parallel bindings is an interesting starting point to enhance the current implementation. An important question in this context is whether a certain technology can be used as "black-box" or if further algorithms for resynchronizing parallel streams need to be developed.

Future extensions of the concept of parallel binding aim at supporting additional message streams, e.g. a stream of only partially ordered and unreliable composite events that are sent with a higher density than reliably sent composite events.

## Multimedia Middleware

One of the most interesting aspects for the multimedia architecture of NMM seems to be whether the notion of a global clock needed for distributed synchronization can be improved. Especially for distributed and continuous playback of a single audio stream on different systems, the accuracy and jitter provided by NTP might not be sufficient. By accessing lower layers of a certain technology, e.g. clocks used for isochronous network transmission, an advanced global time can be derived – at least between devices connected via that specific technology. An interesting aspect will be how to integrate and combine the different time bases provided by clocks throughout the network.

## Search Strategies for Peer-to-Peer Networks

As already mentioned before, different services need the possibility to employ efficient search strategies within the dynamic and only loosely coupled hosts participating in an NMM network. For example, the registry service will benefit from identifying systems that provide a certain resource, such as a specific multimedia device or sufficient computational power. Furthermore, running sessions to be joined can then be determined in a more efficient way. While the research community in the area of peer-to-peer networks is currently very active, especially the support of context information within a search request seems to be worthwhile. This, for example, will allow for restricting search algorithms to a certain physical location, e.g. for realizing location-aware services.

## Predictable Quality of Service

Current work towards providing quality of service (QoS) management within NMM was briefly introduced in Section 9.5. The evaluation of such a service – a service that due to the lack of strict QoS support of today's infrastructures only operates within the middleware layer – will be the next step of our work. In particular, the influence of the measured QoS requirements of processing elements will help to increase the quality of many of the algorithms used within the middleware services presented in this thesis. For example, the session sharing service can then identify the "best" overlapping sub-graph according to such measurements. Contrariwise, the evaluation of QoS requirements for automatic application setup will certainly lead to new algorithms that provide a bounded runtime together with the possibility to value solutions. As discussed in Section 10.7, anytime algorithms might be suitable for such tasks.

## Reconfiguration Transparency

In Section 12.5, we identified reconfiguration transparency as additional requirement for multimedia middleware. A first step towards this goal will be to extend the handover synchronization protocol towards an arbitrary number of audio and video streams. Then, reconfigurations within internal parts of a flow graph need to be supported in a seamless manner. In addition, support for fine-grained adaptation and scaling techniques should be provided. Especially the provision of a seamless feedback loop between QoS monitoring, adaptation, and reconfigurations of complete sub-parts of running flow graphs seems to be demanding.

### Security

For a distributed system, security requirements need to be taken into account. To this end, the NMM architecture already provides some mechanisms, e.g. by restricting access to distributed registries with a password or by limiting the access to the file system of the operating system to specified points. However, for large scale installations with multiple users, these facilities need to be extended.

### Applications

Finally, realizing additional and advanced application scenarios on top of NMM can further help to identify new requirements. In particular, support for ubiquitous computing environments, which include really large numbers of sensors connected to networks, will provide a demanding test-bed.

### Support for other Operating Systems

We are currently already working on porting the NMM architecture to other operating systems, in particular to Windows. Since access to all lower-level interfaces of the operating system is encapsulated within generic classes, the base system of NMM should be available for Windows soon. We then plan to integrate available native multimedia APIs, such as DirectShow, into NMM. This will allow for using Windows systems as full-featured NMM systems – or to perform distributed decoding and transcoding of proprietary codecs that are only available for Windows.

### Summary

Since NMM already provides a complete multimedia middleware solution, the presented directions for future work can be either seen as natural extensions of the framework or as orthogonal to the topics covered in the scope of this thesis. In both cases, especially the open design of the NMM architecture provides an ideal basis for further research and development activities.

# Appendix A

# Systems used for Benchmarks

For all presented measurements, the systems described in the following were used running a Linux kernel 2.4.x and NMM compiled using a corresponding gcc 2.95.x compiler with optimization flags set to "-02".

- **PC1** and **PC2** represent current commodity GNU/Linux PCs.

    - Pentium 4, 3 GHz
    - 512 MByte RAM
    - 100 Mbps LAN

- **PC3** represents the current low-end class for commodity GNU/Linux PCs and is used to evaluate the influence of available computational resources for certain algorithms.

    - Pentium III, 866 MHz
    - 512 MByte RAM
    - 100 Mbps LAN

- **Laptop** represents the current low-end class for laptop computers and is also used as a mobile device, for example as a web-tablet.

    - Pentium III, 700 MHz
    - 128 MByte RAM
    - Either 100 Mbps LAN or 11 Mbps WLAN

- **PDA** represents the current low-end class for GNU/Linux personal digital assistants and can also be seen as a representative for upcoming mobile phones including WLAN.

    - Compaq iPAQ H3870 206 MHz StrongARM SA-1110 RISC processor
    - 32 MByte Flash-ROM and 64 MByte RAM with an additional 128 MByte memory card
    - Video resolution of 320x240
    - Either 100 Mbps LAN or 11 Mbps WLAN using commodity PCMCIA cards within expansion "jacket"

# Bibliography

[139]      1394 Trade Association. http://www.1394ta.org/.

[3rd]      3rd Generation Partnership Project (3GPP). http://www.3gpp.org/.

[AAB01]    Jorge Abreu, Pedro Almeida, and Vasco Branco. 2BeOn - Interactive Television Supporting Interpersonal Communication. In *Multimedia 2001 – Proceedings of the Eurographics Workshop*. Springer, 2001.

[Abo99]    Gregory D. Abowd. Classroom 2000: An Experiment with the Instrumentation of a Living Educational Environment. *IBM Systems Journal, Special issue on Pervasive Computing*, 38(4), 1999.

[AD01]     Don Anderson and Dave Dzatko. *Universal Serial Bus System Architecture*. Addison-Wesley Professional, 2nd edition, 2001.

[Adv]      Advanced Linux Sound Architecture (ALSA). http://www.alsa-project.org/.

[ama]      amaroK - the audio player for KDE. http://amarok.kde.org/.

[AMZ95]    Elan Amir, Steve McCanne, and Hui Zhang. An Application Level Video Gateway. In *Proceedings of ACM International Conference on Multimedia*, 1995.

[And01]    Andrei Alexandrescu. *Modern C++ Design – Generic Programming and Design Patterns Applied* . Addison Wesley, 2001.

[AOS+99]   Ken Arnold, Bryan O'Sullivan, Robert W. Scheifler, Jim Waldo, and Ann Wollrath. *The Jini Specification*. Addison-Wesley, 1999.

[App]      Apple. Quicktime. http://developer.apple.com/quicktime/.

[aRt]      aRts – analog realtime synthesizer. http://www.arts-project.org/.

[ATW+90]   David P. Anderson, Shin-Yuan Tzou, Robert Wahbe, Ramesh Govindan, and Martin Andrews. Support for continuous media in the DASH system. In *Proceedings of 10th International Conference on Distributed Computer Systems (ICDCS)*, 1990.

[BBC+98]   Steven Blake, David L. Black, Mark A. Carlson, Elwyn Davies, Zheng Wang, and Walter Weiss. RFC 2475: An Architecture for Differentiated Services. http://www.ietf.org/rfc/rfc2475.txt, 1998.

[BBE⁺00]    Heribert Baldus, Markus Baumeister, Huib Eggenhuissen, Andras Mont-
            vay, and Wim Stut. WWICE – An Architecture for In-Home Digital
            Networks. In *Proceedings of Multimedia Computing and Networking
            (MMCN)*, 2000.

[BBK00]     Andreas Butz, Jörg Baus, and Antonio Krüger. Augmenting Buildings
            with Infrared Information. In *Proceedings of the International Sympo-
            sium on Augmented Reality (ISAR)*, 2000.

[BCCD00]    Gordon Blair, Geoff Coulson, Fabio Costa, and Hector A. Duran. On the
            design of reflective middleware platforms. In *Proceedings of IFIP/ACM
            Middleware 2000 Workshop on Reflective Middleware*, 2000.

[BCE⁺02]    Patrick Becker, Patrick Cernko, Wolfgang Enderlein, Marc Klein, and
            Markus Sand. The Multimedia-Box – Design and Development of a Mul-
            timedia Home Entertainment System for Linux. Advanced practical re-
            port, Computer Graphics Lab, Computer Science Department, Saarland
            University, Germany, October 2002.

[BCK03]     Len Bass, Paul Clements, and Rick Kazman. *Software Architecture in
            Practice*. Addison-Wesley Professional, 2nd edition, 2003.

[BCP03]     Alex Buchmann, Geoff Coulson, and Nikos Parlavantzas. Introduction to
            middleware. *IEEE Distributed Systems Online*,
            http://dsonline.computer.org/middleware/, 2003.

[BCS94]     Robert Braden, David D. Clark, and Scott Shenker. RFC 1633: Integrated
            Services in the Internet Architecture: an Overview.
            http://www.ietf.org/rfc/rfc1633.txt, 1994.

[Bec03]     Patrick Becker. Ressourcenmanagement für verteilte Multimedia-
            Anwendungen. Diploma thesis, Computer Graphics Lab, Computer Sci-
            ence Department, Saarland University, Germany, October 2003.

[BHK⁺02]    Andrew P. Black, Jie Huang, Rainer Koster, Jonathan Walpole, and Cal-
            ton Pu. Infopipes: An abstraction for multimedia streaming. *Multimedia
            Systems*, 8(5), 2002.

[Bir97]     Kenneth P. Birman. *Building Secure and Reliable Network Applications*.
            Prentice Hall, 1997.

[BKW02]     Jörg Baus, Antonio Krüger, and Wolfgang Wahlster. A resource-adaptive
            mobile navigation system. In *Proceedings of IUI2002: International
            Conference on Intelligent User Interfaces 2002*, 2002.

[Blu]       Bluetooth.org – The Official Bluetooth Membership Site.
            http://www.bluetooth.org.

[Blu01]     Bluetooth SIG. Specification of the Bluetooth System, Core, Vol. 1, Ver-
            sion 1.1, 2001.

[BP00]    Paramvir Bahl and Venkata N. Padmanabhan. RF-Based User Location and Tracking System. In *Proceedings of IEEE Infocom*, 2000.

[Bro]     Preston Brown. Desktop Communication Protocol (DCOP). http://developer.kde.org/documentation/library/kdeqt/kde3arch/dcop.html.

[BS98]    Gordon Blair and Jean-Bernard Stefani. *Open Distributed Processing and Mulitimedia*. Addison-Wesley, 1998.

[BSGR03]  Christian Becker, Gregor Schiele, Holger Gubbels, and Kurt Rothermel. BASE – A Micro-broker-based Middleware For Pervasive Computing. In *Proceedings of PerCOM*, 2003.

[BSL00]   Don Box, Aaron Skonnarda, and John F. Lam. *Essential XML*. Addison-Wesley Professional, 2000.

[BT97]    Dimitris Bertsimas and John N. Tsitsiklis. *Introduction to Linear Optimization*. Athena Scientific, 1997.

[BWB+04]  Richard John Boulton, Erik Walthinsen, Steve Baker, Leif Johnson, and Ronald S. Bultje. *GStreamer Plugin Writer's Guide (0.7.4.1)*, 2004.

[BZB+97]  Robert Braden, Lixia Zhang, Steven Berson, Shai Herzog, and Sugih Jamin. RFC 2205: Resource ReSerVation Protocol (RSVP)–Version 1 Functional Specification. http://www.ietf.org/rfc/rfc2205.txt, 1997.

[Car]     Carnegie Mellon Software Engineering Institute. How do you define software architecture? http://www.sei.cmu.edu/architecture/definitions.html.

[CBM02]   Geoff Coulson, Shakun Baichoo, and Oveeyen Moonian. A retrospective on the design of the GOPI middleware platform. *Multimedia Systems*, 8(5), 2002.

[CDK+98]  Linda S. Cline, John Du, Bernie Keany, K. Lakshman, Christian Maciocco, and David M. Putzolu. DirectShow RTP Support for Adaptivity in Networked Multimedia Applications. In *Proceedings of IEEE International Conference on Multimedia Computing and Systems*, 1998.

[CDK01]   George Coulouris, Jean Dollimore, and Tim Kindberg. *Distributed Systems: Concepts and Design*. Addison-Wesley, third edition, 2001.

[CH98]    Rohan Coelho and Maher Hawash. *DirectX, RDX, RSX, and MMX Technology*. Addison-Wesley Professional, 1998.

[CLD01]   Desmond Chambers, Gerard Lyons, and Jim Duggan. Stream Enhancements for the CORBA Event Service. In *Proceedings of ACM International Conference on Multimedia*, 2001.

[CLR97]   Thomas Cormen, Charles Leiserson, and Ronald Rivest. *Introductions to Algorithms*. MIT Press, 1997.

[CM96]    Patricia Creek and Don Moccia. *Digital Media Programming Guide*. Silicon Graphics, 1996.

[CNM01]    George Coulouris, Hani Naguib, and Scott Mitchell. Middleware Support for Context-Aware Multimedia Applications. In *Proceedings of Conference on Distributed Applications and Interoperable Systems (DAIS)*, 2001.

[CNX04]    Yi Cui, Klara Nahrstedt, and Dongyan Xu. Seamless User-level Handoff in Ubiquitous Multimedia Service Delivery. *Multimedia Tools and Applications Journal, Special Issue on Mobile Multimedia and Communications and m-Commerce*, 22, 2004.

[Com02]    Computer Graphics Lab, Saarland University, Germany. Multimedia lecture. http://graphics.cs.uni-sb.de/Courses/ws0102/Multimedia/, winter term 2001/2002.

[Com03]    Computer Graphics Lab, Saarland University, Germany. Multimedia lecture. http://graphics.cs.uni-sb.de/Courses/ss03/Multimedia/, summer term 2003.

[Cou03]    Geoff Coulson. What is Reflective Middleware? *IEEE Distributed Systems Online*, http://dsonline.computer.org/middleware/RMarticle1.htm, 2003.

[CS02]     Darren Carlson and Andreas Schrader. Seamless Media Adaptation with Simultaneous Processing Chains. In *Proceedings of ACM International Conference on Multimedia*, 2002.

[DB88]     Thomas Dean and Mark Boddy. An analysis of time dependent planning. In *Proceedings of the Seventh National Conference on Artificial Intelligence*, 1988.

[Deu02]    Benjamin Deutsch. An Introduction to the Network-Multimedia Software Architecture. Advanced practical report, Computer Graphics Lab, Computer Science Department, Saarland University, Germany, January 2002.

[Dey00]    Anind K. Dey. *Providing Architectural Support for Building Context-Aware Applications*. PhD thesis, College of Computing, Georgia Institute of Technology, 2000.

[DH98a]    Stephen Deering and Robert Hinden. RFC 2460: Internet Protocol, Version 6 (IPv6) Specification. http://www.ietf.org/rfc/rfc2460.txt, 1998.

[DH98b]    David Duke and Ilvan Herman. A Standard for Mulimtedia Middleware. In *Proceedings of ACM International Conference on Multimedia*, 1998.

[Did02]    Stephan Didas. Synchronization in the Network-Integrated Multimedia Middleware (NMM). Advanced practical report, Computer Graphics Lab, Computer Science Department, Saarland University, Germany, October 2002.

[Diga]     Digital Living Network Alliance. http://www.dlna.org/.

[Digb]     Digital Video Broadcasting Project. http://www.dvb.org/.

[Dig04a]    Digital Living Network Alliance. Overview and Vision – White Paper, June 2004.

[Dig04b]    Digital Living Network Alliance. Use Case Scenarios – White Paper, June 2004.

[Dis]       Distributed Systems Research Group, Charles University, Prague. Open CORBA Benchmarking. http://nenya.ms.mff.cuni.cz/~bench/.

[DL03]      Stephan Didas and Marco Lohse. *Synchronization in NMM*. Computer Graphics Lab, Saarland University, Germany, http://www.networkmultimedia.org/Docs/, April 2003.

[EB02]      Heinz-Josef Eikerling and Frank Berger. Design of OSGi Compatible Middleware Components for Mobile Multimedia Applications. In *Protocols and Systems for Interactive Distributed Multimedia Systems, Joint International Workshops on Interactive Distributed Multimedia Systems and Protocols for Multimedia Systems, IDMS/PROMS 2002, Proceedings*, 2002.

[EGPJ02]    Denise J. Ecklund, Vera Goebel, Thomas Plagemann, and Earl F. Ecklund Jr. Dynamic end-to-end QoS management middleware for distributed multimedia systems. *Multimedia Systems*, 8(5), 2002.

[EKPR00]    Frank Eliassen, Tom Kristensen, Thomas Plagemann, and Hans Ole Rafaelsen. MULTE-ORB: Adaptive QoS Aware Binding. In *Proceedings of IFIP/ACM Middleware 2000 Workshop on Reflective Middleware*, 2000.

[Elk96]     Jens Elkner. Mbone - Tools und Applikationen. http://www.linofee.org/~jel/Mbone/paper2.html, 1996.

[End03]     Wolfgang Enderlein. Einsatz der Netzwerk-Integrierten Multimedia Middleware auf mobilen Geräten. Diploma thesis, Computer Graphics Lab, Computer Science Department, Saarland University, Germany, November 2003.

[Eso]       EsounD - The Enlightened Sound Daemon. http://www.tux.org/~ricdude/EsounD.html.

[ESRM03]    Ayman El-Sayed, Vincent Roca, and Laurent Mathy. A survey of Proposals for an Alternative Group Communication Service. *IEEE Network magazine, Special issue on "Multicasting: An Enabling Technology"*, January/February 2003.

[Fat02]     Hassan M. Fattah. The Other Bill. *Economist*, September 19th, 2002. http://www.hassanfattah.com/article2466.htm.

[FBC⁺98]    Tom Fitzpatrick, Gordon Blair, Geoff Coulson, Nigel Davies, and Philippe Robin. Supporting Adaptive Multimedia Applications through Open Bindings. In *Proceedings of the 4th International Conference on Configurable Distributed Systems (ICCDS '98)*, 1998.

[FDC01]     Adrian Friday, Nigel Davies, and Elaine Catterall. Supporting Service
            Discovery, Querying and Interaction in Ubiquitous Computing Environ-
            ments. In *Proceedings of MobiDE*, 2001.

[FGB⁺01]    Tom Fitzpatrick, Julian J. Gallop, Gordon S. Blair, Christopher Cooper,
            Geoff Coulson, David A. Duce, and Ian J. Johnson. Design and Appli-
            cation of TOAST: An Adaptive Distributed Multimedia Middleware. In
            *Interactive Distributed Multimedia Systems, 8th International Workshop,
            IDMS 2001, Proceedings*, 2001.

[FGM⁺99]    Roy T. Fielding, Jim Gettys, Jeffrey C. Mogul, Henrik Frystyk, Larry
            Masinter, Paul J. Leach, and Tim Berners-Lee. RFC 2616: Hypertext
            Transfer Protocol-HTTP/1.1. http://www.ietf.org/rfc/rfc2616.txt, 1999.

[Fit99]     Tom Fitzpatrick. *Open Component-Oriented Multimedia Middleware for
            Adaptive Distributed Applications*. PhD thesis, Computing Department
            Lancaster University, 1999.

[frea]      freedb.org. Freedb.org database. http://www.freedb.org/.

[Freb]      Freevo. http://freevo.sourceforge.net/.

[frec]      freshmeat.org. Popularity. http://freshmeat.net/stats/#popularity.

[Gei01]     Kurt Geihs. Middleware Challenges Ahead. *IEEE Computer Magazine*,
            34(6), 2001.

[Ger]       Geraint Davies Consulting Ltd. An overview of the DirectShow filter
            architecture. http://www.gdcl.co.uk/dshow.htm.

[GHJV94]    Erich Gamma, Richard Helm, Ralph Johnson, and John Vlissides. *Design
            Patterns*. Addison-Wesley, 1994.

[GLi]       GLib Reference Manual. http://developer.gnome.org/doc/API/2.0/glib/.

[GP04]      Christian Gerstner and Eric Peters. Aufzeichnung und Wiedergabe von
            Folien mit VNC und SVG für E-Teaching-Anwendungen. Advanced
            practical report, Computer Graphics Lab, Computer Science Department,
            Saarland University, Germany, 2004.

[GPVD99]    Erik Guttmann, Charles Perkins, John Veizades, and Michael Day. RFC
            2608: Service Location Protocol, Version 2.
            http://www.ietf.org/rfc/rfc2608.txt, 1999.

[GS96]      Len Gilman and Richard Schreiber. *Distributed Computing with IBM
            MQSeries*. John Wiley, 1996.

[GS98]      Aniruddha S. Gokhale and Douglas C. Schmidt. Measuring and Optimiz-
            ing CORBA Latency and Scalability Over High-Speed Networks. *IEEE
            Transactions on Computers*, 47(4), 1998.

[GSt]       GStreamer. http://gstreamer.net/.

[GSt04]      GStreamer. Mailing List gstreamer-devel.
             http://gstreamer.freedesktop.org/lists/, April 2004.

[Han04]      Sven Hansen. Stream Team, Fünf Streaming-Clients fürs Wohnzimmer.
             *c't – Magazin für Computertechnik*, 16, 2004.

[HCZ⁺02]     Todd D. Hodes, Steven E. Czerwinski, Ben Y. Zhao, Anthony D. Joseph,
             and Randy H. Katz. An Architecture for Secure Wide-Area Service Dis-
             covery. *Journal on Wireless Networks*, 8(2-3), 2002.

[Hei02]      Heise Newsticker. RealNetworks macht auf Open Source und ärgert Mi-
             crosoft. http://www.heise.de/newsticker/meldung/29311, July 2002.

[Hei04]      Heise Newsticker. RealNetworks gibt Medienplayer für Linux frei.
             http://www.heise.de/newsticker/meldung/49734, August 2004.

[Hew93]      Hewlett-Packard Company and IBM Corporation and SunSoft Inc. Mul-
             timedia System Services Version 1.0, 1993.

[Hom]        Home Audio Video interoperability (HAVi). http://www.havi.org.

[How01]      Steve Howell. OpenML V1.0 Specification. Technical report, Khronos
             Group, 2001.

[HV99]       Michi Henning and Steve Vinoski. *Advanced CORBA Programming with
             C++*. Addison-Wesley, 1999.

[hypa]       hyperdictionary. Definition: Framework.
             http://www.hyperdictionary.com/dictionary/framework.

[hypb]       hyperdictionary. Definition: Multimedia.
             http://www.hyperdictionary.com/dictionary/multimedia.

[hypc]       hyperdictionary. Definition: Stream.
             http://www.hyperdictionary.com/dictionary/stream.

[IEEa]       IEEE. IEEE 802.11, Working Group for Wireless Local Area Networks.
             http://grouper.ieee.org/groups/802/11/main.html.

[IEEb]       IEEE. IEEE 802.15 Working Group for Wireless Personal Area Networks
             (WPANs). http://grouper.ieee.org/groups/802/15/.

[IEEc]       IEEE. IEEE 802.3 CSMA/CD (ETHERNET).
             http://grouper.ieee.org/groups/802/3/.

[ION97]      IONA Technologies and Lucent Technologies and Siemens Nixdorf. Con-
             trol and Management of Audio/Video Streams OMG RFP Submission.
             telecom/98-10-05, 1997.

[ISO]        ISO/IEC. 35.100.01 Open systems interconnection in general, 35.100.05
             Multilayer applications, 35.100.10 Physical layer, 35.100.20 Data link
             layer, 35.100.30 Network layer, 35.100.40 Transport layer, 35.100.50
             Session layer, 35.100.60 Presentation layer, 35.100.70 Application layer.

[ISO98]      ISO/IEC. MPEG-1, official title: 11172-1 to 5: Information technology –
             Coding of moving pictures and associated audio for digital storage media
             at up to about 1,5 Mbit/s – Part 1 to 5, 1993 to 1998.

[ISO04a]     ISO/IEC. MPEG-2, official title: 13818-1 to 11: Information technology
             – Generic coding of moving pictures and associated audio information –
             Part 1 to 11, 1994 to 2004.

[ISO04b]     ISO/IEC. MPEG-4, official title: 14496-1 to 16: Information technology
             – Coding of audio-visual objects – Part 1 to 16, 2000 to 2004.

[ISO98]      ISO/IEC. ISO/IEC 10746-1 to 4, ITU-T Recommendation X.901 to
             X.904, Open Distributed Processing – Reference Model, 1995-98.

[jac]        jack audio connection kit. http://jackit.sourceforge.net/.

[Jas97]      Jason Nieh and Monica S. Lam. The Design, Implementation and Evalu-
             ation of SMART: A Scheduler for Multimedia Applications. In *Proceed-
             ings of the Sixteenth ACM Symposium on Operating Systems Principles*,
             1997.

[JFW02]      Brad Johanson, Armando Fox, and Terry Winograd. The Interactive
             Workspaces Project: Experiences with Ubiquitous Computing Rooms.
             *IEEE Pervasive Computing Magazine*, 1(2), 2002.

[Jin]        Jini. http://www.jini.org/.

[Joh95]      David B. Johnson. Scalable Support for Transparent Mobile Host Inter-
             networking. *Wireless Networks*, 1(3), 1995.

[JRST01]     A. Jungmaier, E.P. Rathgeb, M. Schoop, and M. Tuxen. SCTP – A multi-
             link end-to-end protocol for IP-based networks. *International Journal of
             Electronics and Communications*, 55(1), 2001.

[KAVP03]     Tom Kristensen, Lars Preben S. Arnesen, Eirik Valen, and Thomas Plage-
             mann. Evaluation of Middleware for Distributed Objects on Handheld
             Devices. In *Interactive Multimedia on Next Generation Networks, Pro-
             ceedings of First International Workshop on Multimedia Interactive Pro-
             tocols and Systems, MIPS 2003*, 2003.

[KBH+01]     Rainer Koster, Andrew Black, Jie Huang, Jonathan Walpole, and Calton
             Pu. Thread Transparency in Information Flow Middleware. In *Middle-
             ware 2001, IFIP/ACM International Conference on Distributed Systems
             Platforms Heidelberg, Proceedings*, 2001.

[KDE]        KDE Desktop Environment (KDE). http://www.kde.org.

[KG01]       Roger Karrer and Thomas Gross. Dynamic Handoff of Multimedia
             Streams. In *Proceedings of International Workshop on Network and Op-
             erating Systems Support for Digital Audio and Video (NOSSDAV)*, 2001.

[Khr01a]     Khronos Group. An Overview of the Khronos Group and OpenML, 2001.

[Khr01b]   Khronos Group. OpenML BOF Siggraph 2001.
           http://www.khronos.org/openml/presentations/, 2001.

[KHS01]    Thomas Kirste, Thorsten Herfet, and Michael Schnaider. EMBASSI:
           multimodal assistance for universal access to infotainment and service
           infrastructures. In *Proceedings of the 2001 EC/NSF workshop on Uni-
           versal accessibility of ubiquitous computing*. ACM Press, 2001.

[KIK+03]   Shigeru Kashihara, Katsuyoshi Iida, Hiroyuki Koga, Youki Kadobayashi,
           and Suguru Yamaguchi. Multi-path Transmission Algorithm for End-
           to-End Seamless Handover across Heterogeneous Wireless Access Net-
           works. In *Proceedings of 5th International Workshop Distributed Com-
           puting – IWDC 2003*, 2003.

[Kle02]    Marc Klein. *XML Configurations for the NMM Multimedia-Box*. Com-
           puter Graphics Lab, Saarland University, Germany,
           http://www.networkmultimedia.org/Docs/, June 2002.

[Kle03]    Marc Klein. Design und Entwicklung eines Multimedia Home-
           Entertainment Systems. Diploma thesis, Computer Graphics Lab, Com-
           puter Science Department, Saarland University, Germany, January 2003.

[KLW01]    Charles Krasic, Kang Li, and Jonathan Walpole. The Case for Streaming
           Multimedia with TCP. In *Interactive Distributed Multimedia Systems and
           Telecommunication Services, 7th International Workshop, IDMS 2000,
           Proceedings*, 2001.

[KMC+00]   Eddie Kohler, Robert Morris, Benjie Chen, John Jannotti, and M. Frans
           Kaashoek. The Click modular router. *ACM Transactions on Computer
           Systems*, 18(3), 2000.

[KR01]     James F. Kurose and Keith W. Ross. *Computer Networking: A Top-Down
           Approach Featuring the Internet*. Addison-Wesley, 2001.

[Kur01]    Budi Kurniawan. Program Multimedia with JMF. *JavaWorld*, April 2001.

[KW02]     Verena Kahmann and Lars Wolf. A proxy architecture for collaborative
           media streaming. *Multimedia Systems*, 8(5), 2002.

[Lab]      CT Labs. A Question about Echo Cancellation and VoIP.
           http://www.ct-labs.com/Dr%20C/q44.htm.

[LGGB02]   Jinsong Lin, Glenn Glazer, Richard Guy, and Rajive Bagrodia. Fast Asyn-
           chronous Streaming Handoff. In *Protocols and Systems for Interactive
           Distributed Multimedia Systems, Joint International Workshops on In-
           teractive Distributed Multimedia Systems and Protocols for Multimedia
           Systems, IDMS/PROMS 2002, Proceedings*, 2002.

[LHB99]    Jia-Ru Li, Sungwon Ha, and Vaduvur Bharghavan. HPF: A Transport
           Protocol for Heterogeneous Packet Flows in the Internet. In *Proceedings
           of IEEE Infocom*, 1999.

[LHLB00]   Kang-Won Lee, Sungwon Ha, Jia-Ru Li, and Vaduvur Bharghavan. An application-level multicast architecture for multimedia communications. In *Proceedings of ACM International Conference on Multimedia*, 2000.

[Liv]   Live Networks. LIVE.COM Streaming Media. http://www.live.com/liveMedia/.

[LKW03]   Rainer Lienhart, Igor Kozintsev, and Stefan Wehr. Universal synchronization scheme for distributed audio-video capture on heterogeneous computing platforms. In *Proceedings of ACM International Conference on Multimedia*, 2003.

[LMB92]   John R. Levine, Tony Mason, and Doug Brown. *Lex & Yacc*. O'Reilly, 1992.

[LMS85]   Leslie Lamport and P. M. Melliar-Smith. Synchronizing Clocks in the Presence of Faults. *JACM*, 32(1), 1985.

[Loh03a]   Marco Lohse. *Developing Plug-ins for NMM*. Computer Graphics Lab, Saarland University, Germany, http://www.networkmultimedia.org/Docs/, April 2003.

[Loh03b]   Marco Lohse. *Directory Structure of NMM*. Computer Graphics Lab, Saarland University, Germany, http://www.networkmultimedia.org/Docs/, April 2003.

[Loh03c]   Marco Lohse. Ein Knoten für alle Fälle, NMM – Vernetztes Multimedia Home Entertainment mit Linux. *c't – Magazin für Computertechnik*, 22, 2003.

[Loh03d]   Marco Lohse. *Format Programming for NMM*. Computer Graphics Lab, Saarland University, Germany, http://www.networkmultimedia.org/Docs/, April 2003.

[Loh03e]   Marco Lohse. *NMM Coding Style*. Computer Graphics Lab, Saarland University, Germany, http://www.networkmultimedia.org/Docs/, April 2003.

[Loh03f]   Marco Lohse. *States and State Transitions of NMM Nodes*. Computer Graphics Lab, Saarland University, Germany, http://www.networkmultimedia.org/Docs/, April 2003.

[Loh03g]   Marco Lohse. *The NMM Interface Definition Language*. Computer Graphics Lab, Saarland University, Germany, http://www.networkmultimedia.org/Docs/, April 2003.

[Loh04a]   Marco Lohse. *Hello World! Welcome to NMM Application Development*. Computer Graphics Lab, Saarland University, Germany, http://www.networkmultimedia.org/Docs/, May 2004.

[Loh04b]    Marco Lohse. *Setting up a Video Wall with NMM.* Computer Graphics Lab, Saarland University, Germany, http://www.networkmultimedia.org/Docs/, October 2004.

[Loh04c]    Marco Lohse. *Setting up NTP for NMM.* Computer Graphics Lab, Saarland University, Germany, http://www.networkmultimedia.org/Docs/, October 2004.

[Loh04d]    Marco Lohse. *The Network-Integrated Multimedia Middleware (NMM) : Basic Introduction.* Computer Graphics Lab, Saarland University, Germany, http://www.networkmultimedia.org/Docs/, May 2004.

[LRS02]    Marco Lohse, Michael Repplinger, and Philipp Slusallek. An Open Middleware Architecture for Network-Integrated Multimedia. In *Protocols and Systems for Interactive Distributed Multimedia Systems, Joint International Workshops on Interactive Distributed Multimedia Systems and Protocols for Multimedia Systems, IDMS/PROMS 2002, Proceedings*, Lecture Notes in Computer Science. Springer, 2002.

[LRS03a]    Marco Lohse, Michael Repplinger, and Philipp Slusallek. Dynamic Distributed Multimedia: Seamless Sharing and Reconfiguration of Multimedia Flow Graphs. In *Proceedings of the 2nd International Conference on Mobile and Ubiquitous Multimedia (MUM 2003).* ACM Press, 2003.

[LRS03b]    Marco Lohse, Michael Repplinger, and Philipp Slusallek. Session Sharing as Middleware Service for Distributed Multimedia Applications. In *Interactive Multimedia on Next Generation Networks, Proceedings of First International Workshop on Multimedia Interactive Protocols and Systems, MIPS 2003*, Lecture Notes in Computer Science. Springer, 2003.

[LRS05]    Marco Lohse, Michael Repplinger, and Philipp Slusallek. Dynamic Media Routing in Multi-User Home Entertainment Systems. In *Proceedings of The Eleventh International Conference on Distributed Multimedia Systems (DMS).* Knowledge Systems Institute, 2005.

[LS02]    Marco Lohse and Philipp Slusallek. An Open Platform for Multimedia Entertainment Systems. In *Proceedings of EUROPRIX Scholars Conference at MindTrek Media Week*, 2002.

[LS03]    Marco Lohse and Philipp Slusallek. Middleware Support for Seamless Multimedia Home Entertainment for Mobile Users and Heterogeneous Environments. In *Proceedings of The 7th IASTED International Conference on Internet and Multimedia Systems and Applications (IMSA).* ACTA Press, 2003.

[LS05]    Marco Lohse and Philipp Slusallek. Towards Automatic Setup of Distributed Multimedia Applications. In *Proceedings of The 9th IASTED International Conference on Internet and Multimedia Systems and Applications (IMSA).* ACTA Press, 2005.

[LSW01]   Marco Lohse, Philipp Slusallek, and Patrick Wambach. Extended Format
          Definition and Quality-driven Format Negotiation in Multimedia Sys-
          tems. In *Multimedia 2001 – Proceedings of the Eurographics Workshop*.
          Springer, 2001.

[LXN02]   Baochun Li, Dongyan Xu, and Klara Nahrstedt. An integrated runtime
          QoS-aware middleware framework for distributed multimedia applica-
          tions. *Multimedia Systems*, 8(5), 2002.

[Maa05]   David Maass. Distributed Media Processing for Networked Home En-
          tertainment Applications. Advanced practical report, Computer Graphics
          Lab, Computer Science Department, Saarland University, Germany, Au-
          gust 2005.

[Mao]     Z. Morley Mao. Automatic Path Creation Service – APC.
          http://iceberg.cs.berkeley.edu/release/APC.html.

[Mat03]   Laurent Mathy. Group Communication Routing Services for Multimedia
          in the Internet. Tutorial, International Workshop on Multimedia Interac-
          tive Protocols and Systems (MIPS), 2003.

[McL03]   Michelle McLean. How to design a wireless LAN. *Communications
          News*, September 2003.

[Mica]    Microsoft. DirectShow.
          http://msdn.microsoft.com/library/default.asp?url=/library/en-
          us/directx9_c/directx/htm/directshow.asp.

[Micb]    Microsoft. DirectShow: Intelligent Connect.
          http://msdn.microsoft.com/library/default.asp?url=/library/en-
          us/directx9_c/directx/htm/intelligentconnect.asp.

[Micc]    Microsoft. DirectX. http://www.microsoft.com/windows/directx/.

[Micd]    Microsoft. Distributed Component Object Model (DCOM) – Downloads,
          Specifications, Samples, Papers, and Resources for Microsoft DCOM .
          http://www.microsoft.com/com/tech/DCOM.asp.

[Mice]    Microsoft. Microsoft COM Technologies – Information and Resources
          for the Component Object Model-based technologies.
          http://www.microsoft.com/com/.

[Micf]    Microsoft. Windows XP Media Center Edition Home Page.
          http://www.microsoft.com/windowsxp/mediacenter/default.mspx.

[Mil91]   David L. Mills. Internet Time Synchronization: the Network Time Pro-
          tocol. *IEEE Transactions on Communications*, 39(10), 1991.

[MK00]    Z. Morley Mao and Randy H. Katz. Achieving Service Portability in ICE-
          BERG. In *Proceedings of IEEE GlobeCom 2000, Workshop on Service
          Portability (SerP-2000)*, 2000.

[MK01]     Dave Marples and Peter Kriens. The Open Services Gateway initiative:
           An introductory overview. *IEEE Communications Magazine*, December
           2001.

[MNMA03]   Nodoka Mimura, Kiyohide Nakauchi, Hiroyuki Morikawa, and
           Tomonori Aoyama. RelayCast: A Middleware for Application-level Mul-
           ticast Services. In *In Proceedings of 3rd International Workshop on
           Global and Peer-to-Peer Computing on Large Scale Distributed Systems
           (GP2PC 2003)*, 2003.

[Mpl]      Mplayer. http://www.mplayerhq.hu/.

[MSK01]    Zhuoqing Morley Mao, Hoi-sheung Wilson So, and Byunghoon Kang.
           Network Support for Mobile Multimedia using a Self-adaptive Distribu-
           ted Proxy. In *Proceedings of International Workshop on Network and Op-
           erating Systems Support for Digital Audio and Video (NOSSDAV)*, 2001.

[MSS99]    Sumedh Mungee, Nagarajan Surendran, and Douglas C. Schmidt. The
           Design and Performance of a CORBA Audio/Video Streaming Service.
           In *Thirty-second Annual Hawaii International Conference on System Sci-
           ences*, 1999.

[MSW03]    Christoph Meinel, Volker Schillings, and Vanessa Walser. Overcoming
           Technical Frustrations in Distance Eductaion – TeleTASK. In *Proceed-
           ings of e-Society 2003*, 2003.

[Mul]      Multimedia Home Platform (MHP). http://www.mhp.org.

[Myt]      MythTV. http://www.mythtv.org/.

[Nat96]    National Support Centre London, Revision by Jens Elkner. Guide to Mul-
           timedia conferencing using MBONE tools, 1996.

[NBPF96]   Bradford Nichols, Dick Buttlar, and Jacqueline Proulx Farrell. *Pthreads
           Programming*. O'Reilly, 1996.

[NLA]      NLANR/DAST. Iperf – The TCP/UDP Bandwidth Measurement Tool.
           http://dast.nlanr.net/Projects/Iperf/.

[NMMa]     NMM work group. Mobile Multimedia Access with NMM.
           http://www.networkmultimedia.org/Status/Mobile/index.html.

[NMMb]     NMM work group. Network-Integrated Multimedia Middleware (NMM).
           http://www.networkmultimedia.org/.

[NMMc]     NMM work group. NMM/Multimedia-Box.
           http://www.networkmultimedia.org/Status/MMBox/index.html.

[NMMd]     NMM work group. The NMM Engine for amaroK.
           http://www.networkmultimedia.org/Status/amaroK/.

[NMM04a] NMM work group. *Controlling the NMM Multimedia-Box*. Computer Graphics Lab, Saarland University, Germany, http://www.networkmultimedia.org/Docs/, March 2004.

[NMM04b] NMM work group. *List of available Plug-ins for NMM*. Computer Graphics Lab, Saarland University, Germany, http://www.networkmultimedia.org/Docs/, May 2004.

[NSO04] Silvio Neef, Leon Shiman, and Brian O'Brien. Writing network multimedia applications with MAS. LinuxTag, 2004.

[NT02] Jin Nakazawa and Hideyuki Tokuda. A Pluggable Service-to-Service Communication Mechanism for Home Multimedia Networks. In *Proceedings of ACM International Conference on Multimedia*, 2002.

[NTP] NTP: The Network Time Protocol. http://www.ntp.org/.

[NXWL01] Klara Nahrstedt, Dongyan Xu, Duangdao Wichadakul, and Baochun Li. QoS-Aware Middleware for Ubiquitous and Heterogeneous Environments. *IEEE Communications Magazine*, 39(11), 2001.

[Nyq28] Harry Nyquist. Certain topics in telegraph transmission theory. *Trans. AIEE*, 47, April 1928.

[OB00] Joao Orvalho and Fernando Boavida. Augmented Reliable Multicast CORBA Event Service (ARMS): A QoS-Adaptive Middleware. In *International Workshop on Interactive Distributed Multimedia Systems and Telecommunication Services*, 2000.

[Obja] Object Managment Group. http://www.omg.org.

[Objb] Object Managment Group. Common Object Request Broker Architecture (CORBA). http://www.corba.org/.

[Obj02a] Object Managment Group. *Minimum CORBA Specification – Version 1.0*. OMG, 2002.

[Obj02b] Object Managment Group. *Notification Service Specification – Version 1.0.1*. OMG, 2002.

[Obj04] Object Managment Group. *Common Object Request Broker Architecture: Core Specification – Version 3.0.3*. OMG, 2004.

[OKS+00] Carlos O'Ryan, Fred Kuhns, Douglas C. Schmidt, Ossama Othman, and Jeff Parsons. The design and performance of a pluggable protocols framework for real-time distributed object computing middleware. In *Middleware 2000, IFIP/ACM International Conference on Distributed Systems Platforms, Proceedings*, 2000.

[Opea] Open Graphics Library (OpenGL). http://www.opengl.org/.

[Opeb] Open Media Library (OpenML). http://www.khronos.org/openml/.

[Opec]      Open Services Gateway initiative (OSGi). http://www.osgi.org.

[Ope00]     OpenTV. Multimedia Home Platform (DVB-MHP). Technical White
            Paper, 2000.

[OvR01]     Wei Tsang Ooi and Robbert van Renesse. Distributing Media Transfor-
            mation over Multiple Media Gateways. In *Proceedings of ACM Interna-
            tional Conference on Multimedia*, 2001.

[Per02]     Colin Perkins. RFC 3344: IP Mobility Support for IPv4.
            http://www.ietf.org/rfc/rfc3344.txt, 2002.

[Pes03]     Mark D. Pesce. *Programming Microsoft DirectShow for Digital Video
            and Television*. Microsoft Press, 2003.

[Pet05]     Eric Peters.  Distributed Streaming Server on top of the Network-
            Integrated Multimedia Middleware (NMM) (working title). Diploma the-
            sis, Computer Graphics Lab, Computer Science Department, Saarland
            University, Germany, in preparation, 2005.

[PHH98]     Colin Perkins, Orion Hodson, and Vicky Hardman. A Survey of Packet
            Loss Recovery Techniques for Streaming Audio. *IEEE Network Maga-
            zine*, 12(5), 1998.

[Pla02]     Thomas Plagemann. Middleware + multimedia = multimedia middle-
            ware? *Multimedia Systems*, 8(5), 2002.

[Pos80]     Jonathan Postel. RFC 768: User Datagram Protocol.
            http://www.ietf.org/rfc/rfc768.txt, 1980.

[Pos81a]    Jonathan Postel. RFC 791: Internet Protocol: DARPA Internet Program
            Protocol Specification. http://www.ietf.org/rfc/rfc791.txt, 1981.

[Pos81b]    Jonathan Postel. RFC 793: Transmission Control Protocol.
            http://www.ietf.org/rfc/rfc793.txt, 1981.

[Pos82]     Jonathan Postel. RFC 821: Simple Mail Transfer Protocol.
            http://www.ietf.org/rfc/rfc0821.txt, 1982.

[Poy96]     Charles A. Poynton. *A Technical Introduction to Digital Video*. John
            Wiley & Sons, 1996.

[PR85]      Jonathan Postel and Joyce Reynolds. RFC 959: File Transfer Protocol
            (FTP). http://www.ietf.org/rfc/rfc0959.txt, 1985.

[PSG00]     Thai-Lai Pham, Georg Schneider, and Stuart Goose. A Situated Com-
            puting Framework for Mobile and Ubiquitous Multimedia Access Using
            Small Screen and Composite Devices. In *Proceedings of ACM Interna-
            tional Conference on Multimedia*, 2000.

[Raj98]     Gopalan Suresh Raj. A Detailed Comparison of CORBA, DCOM and
            Java/RMI. http://my.execpc.com/~gopalan/misc/compare.html, 1998.

[RBZ01]     Angela Scheller Reinhard Baier, Christian Gran and Andreas Zisowsky.
            Multimedia middleware for the future home. In *Proceedings of Interna-
            tional Workshop on Multimedia Middleware*, 2001.

[RDF97]     Kurt Rothermel, Gabriel Dermler, and Walter Fiederer. QoS Negotiation
            and Resource Reservation for Distributed Multimedia Applications. In
            *Proceedings of IEEE International Conference on Multimedia Computing
            and Systems*, 1997.

[Reaa]      Real.com. RealPlayer. http://www.real.com/.

[Reab]      RealNetworks. RealNetworks SDKs.
            http://www.realnetworks.com/resources/sdk/index.html.

[Reac]      RealVNC Ltd. About RealVNC. http://www.realvnc.com/index.html.

[Rep01]     Michael Repplinger. L1394-Bibliothek: Entwurf und Implementierung
            einer FireWire Bibliothek unter Linux. Advanced practical report, Com-
            puter Graphics Lab, Computer Science Department, Saarland University,
            Germany, May 2001.

[Rep03a]    Michael Repplinger. Eine Architektur zur Anbindung und Kontrolle
            von im Netz verteilten Multimedia-Geräten. Diploma thesis, Computer
            Graphics Lab, Computer Science Department, Saarland University, Ger-
            many, April 2003.

[Rep03b]    Michael Repplinger. *Object Serialization in NMM*. Computer Graphics
            Lab, Saarland University, Germany,
            http://www.networkmultimedia.org/Docs/, May 2003.

[Rep04]     Michael Repplinger. *Using the NMM Registry*. Computer Graphics Lab,
            Saarland University, Germany,
            http://www.networkmultimedia.org/Docs/, May 2004.

[RH97]      Kurt Rothermel and Tobias Helbig. An Adaptive Protocol for Synchro-
            nizing Media Streams. *ACM/Springer Multimedia Systems*, 5(5), 1997.

[RHC+02a]   Manuel Roman, Christopher K. Hess, Renato Cerqueira, Anand Ran-
            ganathan, Roy H. Campbell, and Klara Nahrstedt. Gaia: A Middleware
            Infrastructure to Enable Active Spaces. *IEEE Pervasive Computing*, 1(4),
            2002.

[RHC02b]    Manuel Roman, Herbert Ho, and Roy H. Campbell. Application mobil-
            ity in active spaces. In *Proceedings of 1st International Conference on
            Mobile and Ubiquitous Multimedia (MUM)*, 2002.

[Ric98]     Richard W. Stevens. *Unix Network Programming: Networking APIs:
            Sockets and XTI*. Prentice Hall, 2nd edition, 1998.

[RKC01]     Manuel Roman, Fabio Kon, and Roy Campbell. Reflective Middleware:
            From Your Desk to Your Hand. *IEEE Distributed Systems Online*, 2(5),
            2001.

[RKTS94]   Ramachandran Ramjee, Jim Kurose, Don Towsley, and Henning
           Schulzrinne. Adaptive Playout Mechanisms for Packetized Audio Ap-
           plications in Wide-Area Networks. In *Proceedings IEEE Infocom*, 1994.

[RL02]     Michael Repplinger and Marco Lohse. *Threads in NMM*. Computer
           Graphics Lab, Saarland University, Germany,
           http://www.networkmultimedia.org/Docs/, June 2002.

[RL04]     Michael Repplinger and Marco Lohse. *Clic - An Application for Setting
           up NMM Multimedia Flow Graphs*. Computer Graphics Lab, Saarland
           University, Germany, http://www.networkmultimedia.org/Docs/, July
           2004.

[RN95]     Stuart J. Russell and Peter Norvig. *Artificial Intelligence - A Modern
           Approach*. Prentice Hall, 1995.

[Rot00]    Jörg Roth. DreamTeam – A Platform for Synchronous Collaborative Ap-
           plications. *AI & Society*, 14(1), 2000.

[Row01]    Lawrence A. Rowe. Streaming Media Middleware is more than Stream-
           ing Media. In *Proceedings of International Workshop on Multimedia
           Middleware*, 2001.

[RSC+02]   Jonathan Rosenberg, Henning Schulzrinne, Gonzalo Camarillo, Alan
           Johnston, Jon Peterson, Robert Sparks, Mark Handley, and Eve Schooler.
           RFC 3261: SIP: Session Initiation Protocol.
           http://www.ietf.org/rfc/rfc3261.txt, 2002.

[RSSK02]   Sumit Roy, Bo Shen, Vijay Sundaram, and Raj Kumar. Application Level
           Hand-off Support for Mobile Media Transcoding Sessions. In *Proceed-
           ings of International Workshop on Network and Operating Systems Sup-
           port for Digital Audio and Video (NOSSDAV)*, 2002.

[RVC01]    Eric C. Rosen, Arun Viswanathan, and Ross Callon. Multiprotocol Label
           Switching Architecture. http://www.ietf.org/rfc/rfc3031.txt, 2001.

[RWLS04]   Michael Repplinger, Florian Winter, Marco Lohse, and Philipp Slusallek.
           Parallel Bindings in Distributed Multimedia Systems (extended version of
           the ICDCS paper). Technical report, Computer Graphics Lab, Computer
           Science Department, Saarland University, November 2004.

[RWLS05]   Michael Repplinger, Florian Winter, Marco Lohse, and Philipp Slusallek.
           Parallel Bindings in Distributed Multimedia Systems. In *Proceedings of
           the 25th IEEE International Conference on Distributed Computing Sys-
           tems Workshops (ICDCS 2005)*. IEEE Computer Society, 2005.

[San03]    Markus Sand. Design and Implementation of a System for Recording
           and Playback of Presentations. Diploma thesis, Computer Graphics Lab,
           Computer Science Department, Saarland University, Germany, July 2003.

[SB00]      Alex C. Snoeren and Hari Balakrishnan. An End-to-End Approach to
            Host Mobility. In *Proceedings of the Sixth Annual ACM/IEEE Interna-
            tional Conference on Mobile Computing and Networking*, 2000.

[SCFJ96]    Henning Schulzrinne, Stephen Casner, Ron Frederick, and Van Jacobson.
            RFC 1889: RTP: A Transport Protocol for Real-Time Applications.
            http://www.ietf.org/rfc/rfc1889.txt, 1996.

[Sch]       Henning Schulzrinne. Real-time Transfer Protocol (RTP): About RTP
            and the Audio-Video Transport Working Group.
            http://www.cs.columbia.edu/~hgs/rtp/.

[Sch95]     Uwe Schöning. *Theoretische Informatik - kurzgefaßt*. Spektrum
            Akademischer Verlag, 1995.

[SCW+99]    Burkhard Stiller, Christina Class, Marcel Waldvogel, Germano Caronni,
            and Daniel Bauer. A flexible middleware for multimedia communication:
            Design, implementation, and experience. *IEEE Journal on Selected Areas
            in Communications*, 17(9), 1999.

[SDEF98]    Jochen Seitz, Nigel Davies, Michael Ebner, and Adrian Friday. A
            CORBA-based Proxy Architecture for Mobile Multimedia Applications.
            In *Proceedings of International Conference on Management of Multime-
            dia Networks and Services (MMNS)*, 1998.

[SG96]      Mary Shaw and David Garlan. *Software Architecture – Perspectives on
            an Emerging Discipline*. Prentice Hall, 1996.

[SG02]      Joao Pedro Sousa and David Garlan. Aura: an Architectural Framework
            for User Mobility in Ubiquitous Computing Environments. In *Software
            Architecture: System Design, Development, and Maintenance (Proceed-
            ings of the 3rd Working IEEE/IFIP Conference on Software Architecture)*,
            2002.

[SGG02]     Stefan Saroiu, P. Krishna Gummadi, and Steven D. Gribble. A Mea-
            surement Study of Peer-to-Peer File Sharing Systems. Proceedings of
            Multimedia. In *Proceedings of Multimedia Computing and Networking
            (MMCN)*, 2002.

[Shi]       Shiman Associates Inc. MAS – MediaApplicationServer.
            http://www.mediaapplicationserver.net/.

[Sim]       Simple DirectMedia Layer. http://www.libsdl.org/.

[SJ02]      John G. Spooner and Sandeep Junnarkar. IBM talks up 'computing on
            demand'. *CNET News.com*, October 30th, 2002.

[SK00]      Douglas C. Schmidt and Fred Kuhns. An Overview of the Real-Time
            CORBA Specification. *IEEE Computer Magazine*, 33(6), 2000.

[SN95]      Ralf Steinmetz and Klara Nahrstedt. *Multimedia: Computing, Communi-
            cations and Applications*. Prentice Hall, 1995.

[SRL98]    Henning Schulzrinne, Anup Rao, and Rob Lanphier. RFC 2326: Real Time Streaming Protocol (RTSP). http://www.ietf.org/rfc/rfc2326.txt, 1998.

[SSJH03]   Vasughi Sundramoorthy, Hans Scholten, Pierre Jansen, and Pieter Hartel. Service Discovery At Home. In *Proceedings of PACRIM*, 2003.

[SSNA95]   Narayanan Shivakumar, Cormac J. Sreenan, B. Narendran, and Prathima Agrawal. The Concord Algorithm for Synchronization of Networked Multimedia Streams. In *Proceedings of International Conference on Multimedia Computing and Systems*, 1995.

[SSR00]    Douglas C. Schmidt, Michael Stal, and Hans Rohnert. *Pattern-Oriented Software Architecture, Vol.2 : Patterns for Concurrent and Networked Objects*. John Wiley and Sons, 2000.

[Sta04]    Michael Stal. Janeva: Zugriff von .Net- auf J2EE- und CORBA-Objekte. *iX*, February 2004.

[Ste00]    Ralf Steinmetz. *Multimedia-Technologie. Grundlagen, Komponenten und Systeme*. Springer, third edition, 2000.

[Str97]    Bjarne Stroustrup. *The C++ Programming Language*. Addision-Wesley, third edition, 1997.

[Suna]     Sun Microsystems. Java 2 Platform, Enterprise Edition (J2EE). http://java.sun.com/j2ee/.

[Sunb]     Sun Microsystems. Java Remote Method Invocation (Java RMI). http://java.sun.com/products/jdk/rmi/.

[Sunc]     Sun Microsystems. Sun Community Source Licensing (SCSL) – Java Media Framework API (JMF). http://wwws.sun.com/software/communitysource/jmf/.

[Sun99]    Sun Microsystems. *Java Media Framework API Guide*, JMF 2.0 FCS edition, November 1999.

[SWV99]    Douglas C. Schmidt, Nanbor Wang, and Steve Vinoski. Collocation Optimizations for CORBA. *C++ Report*, 11(9), 1999.

[SXM+00]   Randall R. Stewart, Qiaobing Xie, Ken Morneault, Chip Sharp, Hanns J. Schwarzbauer, Tom Taylor, Ian Rytina, Malleswar Kalla, Lixia Zhang, and Vern Paxson. SCTP – The Stream Control Transmission Protocol. http://www.ietf.org/rfc/rfc2960.txt, 2000.

[SZ04a]    Georg Schnurer and Volker Zota. Medienkraftpakete, Komplette Media Center PCs fürs Wohnzimmer. *c't – Magazin für Computertechnik*, 18, 2004.

[SZ04b]    Peter Siering and Volker Zota. Der PC als Alleinunterhalter, Freie Medien-PCs: TV, Musik und Filme. *c't – Magazin für Computertechnik*, 8, 2004.

[Tan96]     Andrew S. Tanenbaum. *Computer Networks*. Prentice Hall, 3rd edition, 1996.

[Tay01]     Jim Taylor. *DVD demystified*. McGraw-Hill, 2nd edition, 2001.

[TBW04]     Wim Taymans, Steve Baker, and Andy Wingo. *Application Development Manual (0.7.4.1)*, 2004.

[TH99]      Shreekant Thakkar and Tom Huff. The Internet Streaming SIMD Extensions. *Intel Technology Journal*, 2nd quater, 1999. http://www.intel.com/technology/itj/q21999/articles/art_1.htm.

[Tru99]     Barry Truax. *Handbook for Acoustic Ecology*. Cambridge Street Publishing, second edition, 1999.

[TvS02]     Andrew S. Tanenbaum and Maarten van Steen. *Distributed Systems : Principles and Paradigms*. Prentice Hall, 2002.

[UMT]       UMTS Forum : UMTS Forum Home. http://www.umts-forum.org/.

[Uni]       Universal Plug and Play (UPnP). http://www.upnp.org/.

[VCO]       VCORE work group. Virtual Courseroom Environment (VCORE). http://graphics.cs.uni-sb.de/VCORE/.

[vF04]      Wolfram von Funck. *Building amaroK with NMM Support*. Computer Graphics Lab, Saarland University, Germany, http://www.networkmultimedia.org/Docs/, May 2004.

[Vida]      Video Disk Recorder. http://www.cadsoft.de/vdr/.

[Vidb]      VideoLAN. http://www.videolan.org/.

[Vin98]     Steve Vinoski. New Features for CORBA 3.0. *Communications of the ACM*, 41(10), 1998.

[vSCP96]    Marten van Sinderen, Phil Chimento, and Luis Ferreira Pires. Design of a shared whiteboard component for multimedia conferencing. In *Proceedings of International Workshop on Protocols for Multimedia Systems (PROMS)*, 1996.

[W3Ca]      W3C. Simple Object Access Protocol (SOAP) 1.1. http://www.w3.org/TR/SOAP/.

[W3Cb]      W3C. W3C Recommendation 07 August 2001 : Synchronized Multimedia Integration Language (SMIL 2.0). http://www.w3.org/TR/smil20/.

[W3Cc]      W3C. W3C Synchronized Multimedia Home page. http://www.w3.org/AudioVideo/.

[Wam01]     Patrick Wambach. Formatdefinition und Formatverhandlung von Multimedia-Geräten. Diploma thesis, Computer Graphics Lab, Computer Science Department, Saarland University, Germany, July 2001.

[Way01]     Kevin Wayne. Theory of Algorithms. Technical report, Princeton University, 2001.

[WC97]      Daniel Waddington and Geoff Coulson. A Distributed Multimedia Component Architecture. In *Proceedings of 1st International Enterprise Distributed Object Computing Conference (EDOC '97)*, 1997.

[Wei91]     Mark Weiser. The computer for the 21st century. *Scientific American*, 9 1991.

[Wel04]     Christoph Wellner. *Setting up the EPG of the NMM Multimedia-Box.* Computer Graphics Lab, Saarland University, Germany, http://www.networkmultimedia.org/Docs/, April 2004.

[Wel05]     Christoph Wellner. Networked Multimedia Home-Entertainment with Stationary and Mobile Devices (working title). Diploma thesis, Computer Graphics Lab, Computer Science Department, Saarland University, Germany, in preparation, 2005.

[Wes]       Stefan Westerfeld. Multimedia Communication Protocol (MCOP) documentation. http://www.arts-project.org/doc/mcop-doc/.

[WH98]      Daniel Waddington and David Hutchison. Supporting Multimedia in Distributed Object Environments. Technical report, Distributed Multimedia Research Group, Lancaster University, 1998.

[Wika]      Wikipedia. Bluetooth. http://en.wikipedia.org/wiki/Bluetooth.

[Wikb]      Wikipedia. IEEE 802.11. http://en.wikipedia.org/wiki/IEEE_802.11.

[Wikc]      Wikipedia. IPv4. http://en.wikipedia.org/wiki/IPv4.

[Wikd]      Wikipedia. IPv6. http://en.wikipedia.org/wiki/IPv6.

[Win06]     Florian Winter. Development and Evaluation of Communication Strategies for the Network-Integrated Multimedia Middleware (NMM). Advanced practical report, Computer Graphics Lab, Computer Science Department, Saarland University, Germany, November 2006.

[WKC⁺97]    Jonathan Walpole, Rainer Koster, Shanwei Cen, Crispin Cowan, David Maier, Dylan McNamee, Calton Pu, David Steere, and Liujin Yu. A player for adaptive MPEG video streaming over the internet. In *Proceedings of the 26th Applied Imagery Pattern Recognition Workshop*, 1997.

[Wor01]     Tom Worthington. Internet-TV Convergence with the Multimedia Home Platform. Communications Research Forum, 2001.

[WR04]      John Watkinson and Francis Rumsey. *Digital Interface Handbook.* Focal Press, 3rd edition, 2004.

[Wro97]     John Wroclawski. RFC 2210: The Use of RSVP with IETF Integrated Services. http://www.ietf.org/rfc/rfc2210.txt, 1997.

[WS99]     Elin Wedlund and Henning Schulzrinne. Mobility Support Using SIP. In
           *Proceedings of Second ACM International Workshop on Wireless Mobile
           Multimedia*, 1999.

[Xina]     Xine. http://xinehq.de/.

[Xinb]     Xine Hackersguide: Architecture.
           http://xinehq.de/index.php/hackersguide#AEN463.

[xmm]      xmms – X Multimedia System. http://www.xmms.org/.

[XN02]     Dongyan Xu and Klara Nahrstedt.   Finding Service Paths in a Me-
           dia Service Proxy Network. In *Multimedia Computing and Networking
           (MMCN)*, 2002.

[Yod]      Victor Yodaiken. The RTLinux Manifesto.
           http://www.rtlinux.org/articles/archive/rtmanifesto.pdf.

[Zot04]    Volker Zota. VDR-Alternativen, MythTV, freevo und NMM verwandeln
           Linux in einen Videorecorder und mehr. *c't – Magazin für Computertech-
           nik*, 8, 2004.

www.ingramcontent.com/pod-product-compliance
Lightning Source LLC
LaVergne TN
LVHW062302060326
832902LV00013B/2008

9 783836 449625